TOUGH TRIP
through paradise
1878–1879

TOUGH TRIP
through paradise
1878-1879

by
Andrew Garcia

edited by
Bennett H. Stein

University of Idaho Press
Moscow, Idaho

Idaho Yesterdays is a reprint series developed and published by the Idaho State Historical Society and the University of Idaho Press.

Cover: *Sunset Light, Wind River Range of the Rocky Mountains,* 1861 by Albert Bierstadt (1830–1902). *Courtesy of the New Bedford Free Public Library.*

04 03   5 4 3

Published 2001 by the University of Idaho Press, Moscow, Idaho 83844-1107
Printed in Canada

Library of Congress Cataloging-in-Publication Data
Garcia, Andrew, d. 1943.
   Tough trip through paradise, 1878–1879 / Andrew Garcia; edited by
      Bennett H. Stein.
   p. cm.
   Reprint. Originally published: Boston: Houghton Mifflin, 1967.
   ISBN 0-89301-250-5 (alk. paper)
      1. Montana—Description and travel. 2. Montana—History—19th century. 3. Frontier and pioneer life—Montana. 4. Trapping—Montana—History—19th century. 5. Indians of North America—Montana—History—19th century. 6. Nez Perce Indians—Montana—History—19th century. 7. Nez Perce Indians—Wars, 1877. 8. Garcia, Andrew, d. 1943. 9. Pioneers—Montana—Biography. 10. Adventurers—Montana—Biography. I. Stein, Bennett H. II. Title.
   F731.G3 2000
   978.6'02—dc21   00-048853

This reprint edition was created from the clothbound edition of *Tough Trip Through Paradise, 1878–1879,* which was published in 1967 by Houghton Mifflin, Boston.

This book is especially for Isabel,
the beautiful kid on the Nez Perce Trail
B.H.S.

Contents

Maps

INTRODUCTION

In 1948 I found the manuscript from which this book was written. It was stored in dynamite boxes, packed solid in the heavy waxed paper that powder comes in—several thousand pages of legal-sized paper, both handwritten and typed.

Also in the collection were newspaper clippings showing Andrew Garcia at meetings of the Society of Montana Pioneers through the 1930's. He was pictured with shoulder-length hair and fringed buckskin jacket. Each year he was written up as the most colorful character attending. There were also many letters from other old-timers, telling of their regard for him and exchanging memories and facts about the old days. The Squaw Kid, as he was known, was more than an old codger who had outlived a role. His nine years with Indian wives were an adventure of significance that impelled him to dress the part for the balance of his long life. His tepee days occurred at the very time when the free life of the Plains Indian was on the brink of extinction. He witnessed that extinction, and had a story that no one else could tell.

He was past sixty years old when he began writing. At that time he was a rancher, a guide and outfitter, a dairyman and fruitgrower. Five years after his death I saw his large arbor of Concord grapes, near his log home. The grapevines had climbed to the tops of tall blue spruce trees which he had planted years before. The derelict purple clusters ornamented the bright evergreens like symbols of a devil-may-care kind of life that went wild in the West. In 1966 no trace remains of the grapevines above the gorge of the Clark Fork River. The neighbors who made wine from Garcia's grapes lie in mountain cemeteries.

Let no one feel that this book is a dirge. There is a sad note in the loss of something wild and hearty. There is a curse blasting the atrocities and dishonor that ruined good and courageous people and separated them from their land and ways. But there is also the story of reckless pirates of the prairies, sampling what was left of glorious days when the hills were loaded with meat and fun and plunder: young hard-drinking toughs taking what they could get, making love to half-breed hussies and full-blood Indian royalty—never thinking of tomorrow, except that they had a canny care for dry powder and keeping their scalps intact.

Garcia writes an unvarnished recollection, differing from the usual story of those times. In Chapter Eight he takes time out from a harrowing pursuit to state:

> The novelist always manages to cover up the trail on the Indians or villains who are pursuing the hero with the red-headed maiden in his arms on horseback. I never had such luck. They could always find my trail dead easy and run the hell out of me. It was always a matter of speed with me. We all like to see the hero and fair damsel make their get-away from the villain and for her to live happily with the hero until some nigger in the woodpile coaxes her to fly the coop. I am sorry to have to dispell the beautiful hallucination and tell, in most cases, that is B.S. In the many years that I have lived I have seen more heroes get it in the neck from the villain than were left to go around. If it was not for the strong Arm of the Law and the brave men who enforce it, there would not be a hero left to tell the tale, and the woods would be full of grass widow heroines. Many flourishing jails and penitentiaries will bear me out on this.

There are a number of references to Garcia and his first Indian wife in the works of L.V. McWhorter, historian of the Nez Perce. The fact that Garcia was married to a girl who was wounded in the Battle of the Big Hole, combined with the fact that he served with Sturgis' Boys in Blue out of Fort Ellis, made the author a well-known source of history. His collection contains much correspondence with historians. Here, for example, is an excerpt from a 1941 letter:

Dear Friend McWhorter:...I was pleased to hear that you are at it hammer and tongs and are making headway in your Field History of the Nez Perce embroilment of 1877, and in which you say, it will be no tame affair and that one side of the Story maybe good untill you hear the other fellows side of it.

Never were words more truly spoken, for the hell of it is, in this continual overworked field of over half a century of over croping, still yet they keep acoming. For there is quite a bunch, that in the last two years have had new books published, on this already over-worked subject, namely the Nez Perce War of 1877, the cause that led to it, with all the Historical trimmings thrown in for good measure, that led to their down-fall at the Bear Paws.... With still to be heard from, the unlimited number of aspiring Will Shakespears, who have taken up the much travelled Nez Perce route, on their way to fame.

In fact, without any doubt, the whole writing fra-ternity seems to have gone nutts, on this much mooted subject. With the most of them favoring the Indian, with them not forgetting to heroize and put a seraphic crown on the Sub-Chief Joseph, as the one who done it all from beginning to end. When in real-ity Looking-Glass as war-chief, untill he was killed at the Bear Paws, was the brains of the whole outfit, with White Bird no slouch either. Still yet they are never given any credit by Joseph himself.

During more than twenty years of writing, Garcia made an effort to compare his own recollections with those of others, Indian and white. Yet he was untrained as a historian, and a completely unschooled writer. He wrote to a friend in 1939: "I have been trying to put enough of my ravings together, to send them to you…But as most of this stuff has been written with a hard No.4 lead pencil, over ten years ago…so that it is now badly faded and hard to make out…and among all the plunder I have got it is harder still to find. As not even the devil himself…could put it all together if I should die tomorrow…It will have to go to the grave with me."

Several interested people tried to help him put his work into publishable form. He resisted all offers, fearing that his books would be stripped for the benefit of his would-be helpers, and also fearing that his personal manner of expression would be lost. He allowed McWhorter the use of no more than a few facts. His greatest fear was that his story would be appropriated for the western fiction market. He died in 1943 without having seen any of his work in print.

Garcia's adventure occurred at the very height of change. From 1878, four years saw the mopping up of the buffalo, and the end of the era of the Plains Indian. This story tells of that time in the Musselshell country. There were bands of Blackfeet, Piegans, Pend d'Oreilles, Crows, Crees, and half-breeds—with families, dogs and horses—living on big game and trading for guns and whiskey with whatever white men came their way—drunks, desperadoes, tenderfeet from St. Louis, Mexicans, and one amorous Spaniard from the Rio Grande—Garcia.

At times Garcia called this the melting pot of hell. More often he called it the Squaws' Paradise, for he met the girls more than halfway, and was rewarded with affections that compensated for a diet of bloody buffalo meat.

He had left his home on the Rio Grande as a boy and wandered north, driving cattle. The padres on the border had instilled into him a keen sense of hell, and as he succumbed to the beauties of primitive life, he fairly smelled the brimstone. He continually weighed himself in the balance of good and evil, as he remembered the delights of untrammeled and unspoiled nature. To the end of his days he wondered what it meant. Was he good or was he bad? He knew that after leaving the Indians he was never again so happy. This was the force behind his urge to write. As a homesteader and civilized white man, he felt like a leopard in a cage. Few white men had seen what he had, and none of them were writers.

A 1940 interview tells that Andrew Garcia and his wife Barbara settled in 1909 on the ranch west of Missoula which they occupied for the rest of their lives. In Garcia's words about this period:

I then married a white girl and have by her four sons, with the youngest son going on to twenty-nine years. I have the second oldest and youngest sons at home with me here. I have also the other two sons living at Rivulet. Both of them are Section Foremen and are married and have familys. Still though the oldest son holds a twenty year Foreman's rights, he has been bumpted and cannot hold down a permant section. On account of the way that the Railroads have cut down and lengthened the sections. Railroading is no more like when Mike Dillon used to be Road Master, when they had to coax the Jerrys to stay, in them good old days when a fellow had to be working on the section nine years, before he was allowed to oil the car.

I have a ranch of six hundred and sixty-seven acres, a whole lot of it has gone back to jack-pine and I only cultivate about a hundred and thirty acres, as there is no use in putting in stuff and then not be able to sell it for anything. I used to keep a couple hundred Aberdeen Angus cattle right along and made some money that way, but since cattle and everything else went to hell. As I had to give the others away, I have quit raising them now and have only thirty left. I also used to make good money raising fruit, but that bliz-

zard of 1924 got quite a lot of the trees, while now the
fruit trucks from Yakima put the fruit business on the
bum proper.

Throughout the long nights, by lantern light, on this little mountain ranch, Garcia wrote a story that took place in
a land so vast and varied that it is almost impossible to
comprehend. Photographs and maps are helpful, but even
for one who knows the trails across the ridges of the
Rockies, and has ridden long days through the lush valleys,
and has experienced the sudden opening of the country
when you round the last range to the eastward and view the
endless Plain, it is hard to believe that the Indian hunter was
so familiar with thousands of miles of trail. The Nez Perce
had such a knowledge of the land that they were able to call
General Howard, General Day-after-tomorrow. Howard was
always two days behind in his pursuit, even when the
Indians were a thousand miles from home. Trails to the land
of the buffalo had been used year after year. Indians who
headquartered on the Idaho border had words in their language for each feature of the landscape through the valleys
of Helena, Deer Lodge and Bozeman. The Flathead word for
the Gallatin Valley translates "Valley of Flowers."

The tragedy of abrupt transition from stone age culture
to machine culture in a few years is not reflected in the
sounds of Indian talk or song. Now the trails are overlaid by
hard-surface roads, but the land remains a place of predom-
inant space. From an airplane, Montana still appears almost
empty. Irrigated patches appear diminutive and settlements
few in the great rangelands and forest-sided valleys. Many
times I have heard the sounds of the Western Indians, while
searching for their story in the Bitterroot and Flathead. The
sound of Salish speech has a soft and rustling effect. There
is also the sound of music. I will never forget one winter
night in the hills near the shore of Flathead Lake. The hills
were shimmering in moonlight, and the air had a crisp bite.
From the creek bottom I heard the sound of chanting, ris-

ing and falling like a music of the wind, delicate and pulsing as the changing light on rustling aspen leaves, with a drumming beat that seemed to come from the very heart of the country.

It was during my travels among the Flatheads that I happened to discover the Garcia manuscript. On first reading, I felt that Garcia's story gave a truer feeling of Indian life than anything I had ever read. Years of search have not changed my opinion. Historians tell what happened; scholars describe customs; literary men, who identified themselves with Indians, have told of their life as if the white man were non-existent or a remote predatory villain. Garcia tells a many-faceted story. He was not merely a sympathetic observer. He did not gloss over his own position as an interloper—a white man with good guns, bad whiskey and fake jewelry to trade. Garcia saw himself as an adventurous Spanish kid from the Rio Grande, and he remained a white man, drifting into Indian ways.

This book comprises a number of Garcia's unfinished works. In editing, I have attempted to preserve the author's manner of expression. As he himself said, "It will all have to be retyped, punctuated, and set up for effect in a better way than I can do it." He would go for pages with no other form of punctuation than a comma, and as he grew older he tended to ramble. So I have punctuated, and cut, and re-ordered the material somewhat, but the words are all his. I wish to acknowledge the help of Mrs. Ruth K. Hapgood of Houghton Mifflin Company in the final pruning, trimming and re-shuffling of the manuscript.

In a fragment of a letter, Garcia described his difficulties as a writer:

> In regard to the manuscript that I am working on, will say that I have been at it for five years and there is still considerable yet to be done...I figure it will then approximately contain and be in three volumes, of sixty thousand words per volume. It is slow work as I

have to work every day and write up to eleven every night. In this way I loose the only time from seven in the morning till about ten o'clock a.m. when I am any good and can write better in an hour or so, than I can for all the rest of the day put together. I am trying to do and finish what I ought to have started twenty years ago. For this writing business as you must know by this time, that it is not as easy to pick up as it looks, a whole lot of them never learn it in their whole life, unless this gift is born in you, it is better to leave it alone. With the limited education I have got at first I shure was up against a hard row of stumps, but I have learned a whole lot since then…

Bennett H. Stein
Wilsall, Montana
October 23, 1966

TOUGH TRIP
through paradise
1878–1879

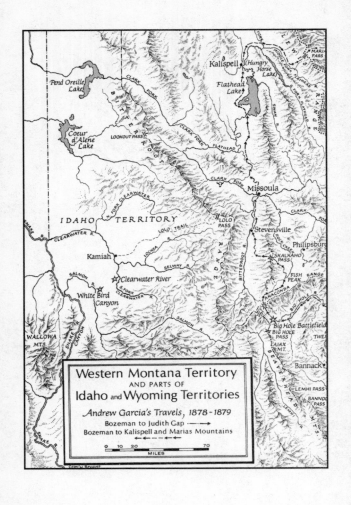

Western Montana Territory
AND PARTS OF
Idaho and Wyoming Territories

Andrew Garcia's Travels, 1878-1879

Bozeman to Judith Gap ⟶
Bozeman to Kalispell and Marias Mountains ⟵⟶

0 10 20   70
MILES

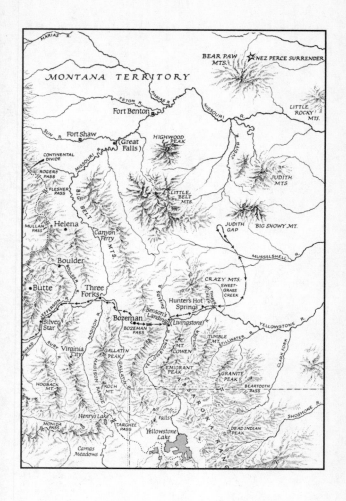

PART ONE
The Trail with Beaver Tom

CHAPTER ONE
Hell-Bent for Musselshell

I worked for Uncle Sam mostly as a herder and sometimes as a packer since I came to Montana in 1876. I followed the Boys in Blue through all of the Yellowstone country and parts of the Musselshell country when they went chasing after some band of Indians that was out plundering or on horse-stealing raids. At the different forts I would see all kinds of trappers and hunters come in; wild and woolly they were, with long hair and buckskin clothes. I was young and I used to look at them with envy and dream of the day when I would be one of them and go roaming over the prairies and hills.

I ought to have known better, for I already had several runs by the Indians. But I was of the age—just coming twenty-three years old—when a fellow thinks that he knows it all, and in reality he doesn't. This is the time in life when a fellow ought to have a guardian—one of the good old-fashioned, short-arm kind that will kick or pound the conceit out of him.

In the early part of the summer of 1878, I met at Fort Ellis a hunter and trapper named Beaver Tom. What his right name was I never knew and I never asked him. He was a middle-aged man and everyone said that he was the best beaver trapper in the Yellowstone country. He was also a good buffalo hunter, but the trouble with him was his love for whiskey. As long as he could get a drink he would hang around. He was known to travel many miles for it. I used to take pity on him and feed him sometimes. He would tell me of the fights and escapes he had with the Indians, and how him and others trapped and hunted in the Powder River and Big Horn country right in among Old Red Cloud's and

Crazy Horse's bands of Sioux, who were thick as flies there. Although the Sioux killed many of the trappers, Beaver Tom had always managed to get the fur and to get away from them. He told how he had trapped and hunted along the Missouri and in the Musselshell country and of his troubles with the Blackfeet and Piegan Indians there. There was no doubt that Beaver Tom did have the experience.

It was not a hard job for him to talk me into quitting my job and going with him on a trapping and trading trip into the Musselshell country. He said that if I would furnish the outfit, he would pay me back in furs for his share. I also could buy blankets and other stuff dear to the Indian's heart and trade this stuff to them for fur and buffalo robes. Because I had to buy the stuff, the profit from trading would be mine. One of us would have to stay and watch camp, but I could hunt and go wolfing near the camp while he would be out tending to the line of traps. Beaver Tom said we would be partners in the trapping and hunting. Someday he would pay me half the cost of grub and other things we needed.

He was down and out, flat broke and he had nothing but a 45-120 Sharps buffalo gun. In taking this generous offer of his I was not very bright, for he had nothing to lose but his time and life, which was useless anyway, while I had to furnish and buy everything and take the risk of getting robbed and set afoot and maybe even killed. The only thing he was furnishing was his experience which became somewhat doubtful if he could get whiskey.

He told me in glowing words how we could profit in the Musselshell country, and that he knew where there were plenty of beaver and all kinds of buffalo and wolf. I had been in there twice with the soldiers and I knew that this was so. I also knew that there were plenty of Indians and that they would gladly rob and steal our horses if they could. Although it was bad enough, there was not as much danger of getting killed as if we went among the Sioux. So I told him I would do it.

In the year and a half I had been in Montana I worked steady as a herder and sometimes as a packer at sixty dollars plus rations. I had saved almost all my wages, and had it in gold and vouchers, something around a thousand dollars. While I was not good, still I was not bad and had one good habit if I did not have many others. I never drank whiskey. Because whiskey and gambling were about all you could spend your money for in those days, and because I had not yet learned to gamble, it was easy for me to keep my money. I was nearly always on the go with the soldiers in places where money was of no use anyway.

The corral boss and boss packer and the Boys in Blue of the 2nd Cavalry were all sorry to see me go. They said that I was a damn fool to leave and go running off through the country with that locoed whiskey soak—and that I'd get killed by Indians, and that a hunter's and trapper's buck was the same as a fisherman's, a wet and hungry gut, and that was all I would get for my money. Anyhow, I quit a good job and a bunch of good friends, who, while a little rough at times, would do anything for me and always gave me more than a square deal.

I went to Bozeman to see Walter Cooper, and I told him what I had done; I asked him to fix me out the best he could. One thousand dollars wasn't much of a stake because everything was very high. He told me, "I like to sell my stuff, but I think that you are foolish and you will be sorry if you go over in Musselshell country with all them kinds of horse-stealing cutthroats and murdering Indians. They will set you afoot and you will be lucky to get away from them with your life." He gave Beaver Tom hell good and plenty for starting me on this.

Bozeman, at that time, was quite a town. Nearly all of the people who lived here had crossed the plains in prairie schooners and were of the good old-fashioned kind. They were always more than willing to lend a helping hand to anyone who was on the square. When people around town heard what I had done, they came to me—Cap Fridley and others, and tried to talk me out of going with Beaver Tom. They gave me good advice, saying that I had a nice little start, and if I had to quit as a herder why not take up a ranch, as there was plenty of good land.

But I was a woolly Texan from Spanish America and did not believe in doing any more work with plow or shovel than I could help. I turned down good, friendly advice that would have made me somebody and a good, respected citizen.

Little did I know that day that I was giving up all hope to be a white man again—that I was leaving the white man and his ways forever, and that I would become inoculated with the wild life of the old-time Indian and be one of them, to live and run with them, wild and free like the wild mustang, and do what few white men can do—that is to gain the respect and confidence of the Indian, and overcome the fear and mistrust that all Indians have—and not without just cause—of the white man. Unscrupulous white men might make me pay dearly for saying that the Indian is one of God's creatures and is entitled to live and have a square deal—something he never received from the white man. It is forty-three years today since I left them and tried again to be a white man. Though I now follow the white man's ways and have a good home, and many will tell you I ought to have no kick coming, still I am a leopard in a cage.

I returned to the Fort to get ready and to round up the twelve cayuses that at different times I was foolish enough to buy. They had been more bother to me than my money. Then I rustled up several condemned *aparejos* and fixed them up. I had a good outfit of ten pack horses and two saddle horses ready, but I had to buy all the traps, ammunition and provisions for eight months. When I got several blankets, tobacco, calico and other articles to trade to the Indians, besides the necessities, I had used up my grubstake, except two hundred and fifty dollars cash. Walter Cooper trusted me for nearly three hundred dollars. It was not yet against the law to sell Indians guns, so I picked up several needle guns (those old fellows that kick like a mule) and sev-

eral hundred rounds of ammunition to fit them. I had a 73-
model Winchester carbine, but I had to buy a buffalo gun.
Like the Chinaman who took the largest sized boot if it was
the same price as the smaller size to get more leather for the
money, I bought a 45-120 caliber Sharps rifle buffalo gun,
which weighed over fifteen pounds and cost seventy-five
dollars, although I could have gotten a lighter 45-90 No. 13
for the same price. Anyway my stock of goods took five pack
horses and the stuff for Beaver Tom and I, five more.

Included was a five-gallon keg of whiskey that Beaver
Tom talked me into getting, saying that it was as necessary
as it was for the sun to rise and shine. "There is nothing that
will warm the cockles of an Indian's heart and gain his
undying friendship like a couple of shots of good old red-
eye whiskey under his belt." I was soon to learn that the
cockles of Beaver Tom's own heart just loved whiskey and if
he had anything to say about it the noble red man would fall
short of his share.

We were set to leave in two days when three men with
light pack horses rode into town. They were hunters and
trappers and, when they found out we were going into the
Musselshell country, they said they were also going in there
to trap and hunt. "What is the matter with all of us going in
there together as it would be safer from the Indians and
besides there is plenty of country for all of us?" We said all
right, but Beaver Tom said, "If they are trappers and hunters
then I am a preacher."

They claimed that they came from that part of Utah near
Green River, Wyoming. The one with the large potato nose
said that his name was George Reynolds and the tall, light-
complexioned fellow said he was called Al Shinnick. The
third one was very dark and said his name was Davis, but
the other two called him Brock, I suppose because of the
smallpox pits on his face. All of them were good, large husky
men and went heavily armed. Beaver Tom was suspicious of
them and said, "If you fellows are trappers and hunters,
where are your traps?"

They said, "There are two more men with us who have gone ahead across the divide to the Yellowstone with the traps and other stuff. They will wait for us somewhere near the mouth of the Shields River. One of them is a Frenchman who has been here before and knows all parts of the country." Anyone could see that the three of them would be bad hombres to run up against or to fool with. They did not bring very much grub, but they bought plenty of ammunition and six five-gallon kegs of whiskey.

At first Beaver Tom was certain that we ought not to trust them as they looked more and more like the road agent class, but when he saw the cargo of whiskey they were getting, he suddenly changes his mind. They gave him a couple of shots of whiskey, and told him there was plenty more where that came from. So he now swears by them and pronounces them number one true-blue trappers and hunters of the first water. Again several people in town warned me and said, "Kid, we are sorry to see you leave with that bunch and, though we don't know them or anything against them, still we don't like their looks." But as I already had bought all this stuff I said I had to go now. Besides, a fool is a fool wherever he is.

Next morning we were going to start. We planned to cross over the divide and go on to the Yellowstone. From there we would follow down the river to the Big Timber. I knew a Piegan trail there that crossed the Sweet Grass near its head and went on into the Musselshell country. I had been over this trail twice with the soldiers when they were chasing Piegan war parties which had been raiding Uncle Sam's slippery friends the Crows. That afternoon I went over to the Fort to bid good-bye to my friends the mule skinners, herders, packers and the corral and wagon bosses, and not forgetting the Boys in Blue of the 2nd Cavalry, that were good and true.

CHAPTER TWO

We Leave in Dubious Company

Early the next morning, several days after the fourth of July, 1878, we got up at daylight. It was not long until we hit the trail and were on our way to the Yellowstone. The three other trappers helped us to pack our stuff, and anyone could see that they were old hands at the packer business. We had ten pack horses with heavy loads; we did not push them much because they were fresh. We took the Bozeman trail and crossed over the divide, but did not make the Yellowstone that day.

We camped about eight miles from the river, but we wouldn't have any trouble making the mouth of the Shields River next day, if everything went right. Beaver Tom got a few drinks already. Those men were good enough fellows and were willing to help us, but I didn't like two of them, George Reynolds and Al Shinnick. They were always whispering to each other and shut up whenever I went near them. Even though Brock Davis was not of an engaging appearance, there was still something about him that I liked. Something seemed to tell me I could trust him, but to watch out for the other two. I said nothing of this to Beaver Tom as they were the ones that gave him the whiskey to drink and he thought that they were O.K.

Next morning, before we started to pack up, the three of them held some kind of a confab which neither Beaver Tom nor myself was invited to join. George Reynolds, after asking us the way to Shields River—the three of them claimed that they were never in this part of the country before— took his rifle and rode off alone.

When we were on the trail, Brock Davis told me, "Reynolds went to locate the other two men that went ahead, so that we will not have any trouble in finding them when we camp tonight."

We had packed up and were started on our way, going by the big bend of the Yellowstone* and on down the river past Benson's Landing. The landing was a tree on the bank of the Yellowstone. This was where the old-timers took the Yellowstone if they went down in small boats as they sometimes did. As we trailed along Brock Davis became friendly, but Shinnick had nothing to say to me and seemed not to want any conversation.

About four o'clock we made Shields River, but found no one there. Brock Davis said, "We will camp here anyway." This was the place La Brie, the one who knew the country, had told them to wait and camp. We unpacked and it was not long before Reynolds and the other two men rode into camp from someplace in the foothills. Both of them were heavily armed. They had only one pack horse with a bundle of blankets and a small camp outfit. I thought, "Surely to God this can't be all the trapping outfit they have got."

One of the newcomers was a young man not more than three or four years older than myself. He had a smiling and jolly face and sunburned cheeks and red hair. He looked out of place with the other man, who was tall and powerful, with the dark, glittering and vicious eyes of a polecat. He did not need to tell anyone that he was a bad one, for hell was written all over his face. He called himself a French Canadian, but if he was not a half-breed, then I never saw one (or else some Injun must have scared his mother). He said his name was Hypolite La Brie and he was the man who knew the country so well.

The younger one with the red hair, who was riding and breaking in a vicious bronco, told me after we all had supper that his name was Henry Redman. He wanted to hear all the news from Bozeman and said no matter how old the news was to tell him anyway, for he was as lonesome as death for someone to talk to after being out so long with La Brie, a silent one.

---

* Where the city of Livingston stands today.

The country was not quite as dangerous as it had been before, but still one had to keep a watch for Indians all night. We turned in, leaving Beaver Tom on guard till he would call the next one. We were all up at daylight. I thought that we would pull out and keep going, but the five of them held another confab by themselves. When I wanted to know when they were going to pack up and pull out, George Reynolds said, "Not today, kid. Why this hurry?" Then Al Shinnick and Henry Redman, who they called Red, saddled up, took their rifles and rode off into the foothills the way that they came from last night. I had asked them several times where their trapping outfit was. They never said anything and met this question now with blank silence.

This was three years after the government had moved the Crow agency to Rosebud Creek on the Stillwater, but some of the old agency was still held and occupied and it was located not far from us across the river on what was the Crow Reservation. Now I knew that something was wrong with this outfit, but what could I do? I wanted Beaver Tom to pull out and leave them and go it alone. He said, "We had better wait a day or so; then if they don't move we will pull out and leave them."

After a while the three men in camp called me over and wanted to know where they could find an Injun camp not too close to the old agency. I knew many of the river Crows stayed in this part of the Yellowstone on account of the Sioux. Here they had troops most of the time to protect them. I said, "How can I tell? An Injun is here today and away tomorrow. Why do you want to find Injuns?"

La Brie says, "Just a friendly visit and maybe swap for a horse or two."

I knew when he said swap that the only thing they had to trade was whiskey and I knew they would go anyway, so I said, "You might find a camp further down the river, but you will have to find a ford to cross over."

CHAPTER THREE
One of the Bunch was on the Square

So now La Brie and Reynolds saddled their horses, took their rifles and rode off down the river, leaving Brock Davis to watch their part of the camp. This man was of a friendly disposition, though rough in some ways. I could see that when it came to a showdown he had the whole bunch afraid of him and I was not sorry to see it so. I had been raised on the Rio Grande and among the Apaches of Arizona. At the time, most of the people belonged to the cutthroat or outlaw class. I suspected that something was wrong with this bunch. I asked Brock Davis what was the reason they did not pull out this morning.

He said, "We think we ought to pick up a few more horses while we got the chance. We will pull out tomorrow morning, only don't be in too much of a hurry. I want to tell you something for your own good. Don't be too scrupulous about what you may see and don't be foolish enough to make La Brie and the others mad at you. In a friendly way keep out of anything they may want you to do and I will see that you have a square deal, for Brock Davis is on the square and your friend."

We hung around camp nearly all day and then about five o'clock La Brie and Reynolds returned leading three horses with them. Instead of turning them loose with the other horses they picketed them to be sure they would not get away. In a little while Shinnick and Red came riding into camp from the foothills down by the river. Although we traveled together, each outfit was separate and cooked for itself. After supper they all went off a little way from camp and held another council of war. When it got dark we rolled in for the night with each one taking his turn watching horses and camp.

We were up at daylight and were ready to pull out when La Brie said to us, "Make camp on the river a mile or so below the Hot Springs," meaning Doc Hunter's Hot Springs. Then, he, Davis, Shinnick and Red all rode off toward the foothills, taking the three horses they had picked up some place the day before. Only Reynolds stayed with us to help drive and trail the outfit along.

We took the trail or road to the Springs where Doc Hunter lived. I had been there before and knew the Hunters pretty well. They had a little girl named Sally who was lame. I think that they had another daughter married in Bozeman.

Now I did not feel any too good, for while I had nothing on the bunch proving they were crooked, I still knew and thought they were. If it was so and anything should turn up or they should commit any deviltry around here, then those people would put me down as one of them because I was traveling along with them. Since we had started from Bozeman we met no one, white man or Injun, on the trail. Before we came to the Springs I asked Reynolds if he wanted to stay a while at the Springs and take a look at them. We could not very well go by without stopping and visiting a while in this country where houses are kind of scarce.

He said, "Sure, that's right, give me a knock-down to your friends." So we rode up and got off, and I introduced Reynolds to Doc Hunter. There happened to be an old-timer there named Brockway; I had met and seen him several times. This was a good thing for me as he had just come from Bozeman two or three days before and had heard about our great trapping expedition to the Musselshell.

He jokingly remarked to Doc Hunter that it was too bad there would be no more buffalo or beaver in the Musselshell country after we got through trapping there. I thought, here is one witness if anything should turn up; for, like all Texans, I knew what most people thought and said behind our backs. Mainly, that it was just as natural for a Texan to take up stage-robbing and horse stealing as it was for a duck to take to water.

Beaver Tom and Reynolds went to look at the Spring where it came bubbling hot out of the ground. Doc Hunter wanted to know who, what and from where was Reynolds. I could only tell him the truth, that he knew as much about him as myself and I thought it best to tell him how we met at Bozeman. I said they were only a bunch of honest trappers, traveling along with us so if we had any trouble with the Indians they would come in handy. When he asked where the other four men were, I manfully lied and said they had crossed over the river and were coming down the other side. Beaver Tom and Reynolds came back and, although the Hunters wanted us to stay longer, we rode away. About one and one-half miles further on we left the trail and went down to the river bottom and camped. We ate then because Reynolds said La Brie had said it would be late before they would get to camp.

It was nearly dark when the four of them rode into camp from the foothills. The funny thing about them was that they were dusty and tired and their horses were all sweat and dust and nearly played out. They were not the same horses they rode away on this morning either. They did not bring back the three head of horses they had got from the Crows at Shields River.

Reynolds was not long in getting them something to eat and I could see that they were not in good humor enough to ask any pointed questions, so I said nothing. I asked Beaver Tom just what he thought, but he was non-commital; all I could get out of him was a hog grunt. They turned in, leaving me to stand guard. Early in the morning we were all ready to pull out when La Brie, who now seemed to be running the outfit, said, "We will camp at the Big Timber tonight, someplace near the mouth where there will be feed for the horses." Then he, Reynolds, Shinnick and Red rode off for the foothills, leaving Brock Davis to drive their outfit along with us. We started and went back on the main road.

It was not long till we came to the Gage ranch, which was called Four Miles because of its distance from Hunter's Hot

Springs. It was also the last house or ranch in this part of the Yellowstone country. From here it was several miles to Old Man Countryman's ranch and trading post at the Stillwater, which was the last ranch on the Yellowstone. I asked Beaver Tom and Brock Davis if they did not want to stop awhile, but for some reason they did not seem to care that they were leaving civilization behind and said "no" and kept on going. I rode up to the door, for I knew these good and kind people and wanted to bid them good-bye. Everyone who had been through this part of the country knew Mother Gage. She was a good, kind and noble woman, who, by this time, was more used to the war whoops of savage Indians than the music of a piano. She came to the door with another lady I did not know and wanted me to get off and stay. The men were out, but would soon come in. Because I had to catch up with the others, I could only say goodbye and soon I caught up with the outfit. As we trailed along I thought that this would be as good a time as any and told Brock Davis what I thought and wanted to know, on the square, if they were not crooked.

In one way he did not deny it and said, "As long as we don't hurt you, what is the difference? If you don't have to do anything crooked, you had better jog along and let sleeping dogs lie. Should the others want you to do anything crooked, remember that I told you to keep out of it and you will have nothing to fear in the end."

I liked this man and had been taught down on the Rio Grande never to ask a man his name, religion or politics, and as long as he left you alone and did not injure you, it was none of your business where he came from or what he did. Even though I believed that I had done right, I now knew it not to be the best, and should have left this bunch when I had the chance. I was soon to find out to my sorrow that crookedness and honesty cannot travel together in the same outfit without mixing. We came to the Big Timber, but camped on the banks of the Yellowstone as this creek was all gravel with no feed for the horses.

We were not in camp long until we heard a wagon cross-
ing the creek. Soon a four-horse covered wagon drove up
with two men on the seat and two others, Old Man
Countryman and Ike Allen, behind on horseback with rifles
riding as a rear guard. The one driving I did not know, but
they said he was Ed Moran, who had come from the Black
Hills country and was stopping at the Countryman place.
They were on their way to Bozeman for a load of supplies.
They already knew Beaver Tom, so I said, "This man is
Brock Davis from Utah." They said they might as well camp
with us for the night as company was scarce; they unhooked
and made a camp. I could see that Brock Davis was not any
too well pleased about them camping with us. Then they
wanted to know what I was doing with all the pack outfit so
I told them about our great trapping and trading trip, taking good care to let them know that while we were traveling
together with Davis and the others, we still had nothing to
do with them except in case of trouble with Indians.

At first they thought I was joking about the Beaver Tom
trading and trapping outfit. When they found it was so they
thought I was foolish and made no bones in telling Beaver
Tom that a man of his experience ought to know better than
for the two of us to take the Musselshell alone. They wanted
to know where the other four men were. I told them they
were scouting around up the creek somewhere. I knew that
Beaver Tom would keep his mouth shut, for the
Countryman outfit had no whiskey to give him while this
outfit did. I could see that Brock Davis sat up when I said
"scouting around." He was uneasy as to what would happen
if the others came into camp unaware of who is here now.
He need not have feared, however, for a man like La Brie was
seldom caught napping. They all soon rode into camp as
innocent as babes and we had a fine time that night around
the campfire. Old Man Countryman and Ike Allen could
sure deliver the goods about the runs and times they had
with the Indians. For once, La Brie was willing to talk and let
us know that he had some experience in that line himself.

I wanted to see a Mexican man named Souce who lived on Deer Creek. He was married to a Crow squaw and had a son named Johnny Souce and a daughter named Helen. She later married a man named Fox, whom the Crows killed. Old Man Countryman told me that Souce was camped at Sweet Grass and so was Enis, a Mexican half-breed. Enis lived up on the Boulder with a Crow squaw and had a son and two girls. They were all there with the Iron Bull outfit and some other Crows holding a powwow on account of the Piegans who were still making raids on them. The Piegans had, a few days before, run many of the Crow horses off besides killing some Crows. They were now waiting for the Crow bucks that went chasing after the Piegans to return. I could see that La Brie and company were taking in all this information and did not seem to be sorry about it.

I said, "I will go to Sweet Grass tomorrow, as those people are my friends and I would like to see them if the rest would wait a couple of days."

La Brie said in a friendly way, "Sure, take all the time you want and go and see your friends."

CHAPTER FOUR
A Full House of Squaw Cooks

In the morning the Countryman outfit pulled out for Bozeman and Old Man Countryman said to me, "See here, kid, I want to tell you something about the Indian. Whenever he wants anything and makes you great promises to pay you in the future, don't be foolish and let him have it that way. If you don't get the cash first, then it is never with the Indian."

I caught my horse and was ready to start for Sweet Grass when La Brie said, "I intend to move the camp about three miles up the Big Timber. This place is too close to the trail and there is no feed here for the horses. You can go, and we will help Beaver Tom pack up and drive the pack horses there."

I rode off and went down to the Sweet Grass and there were twenty-eight lodges of Crows, besides some squaw men. I was having a good time with the Souce outfit and others and everything was going fine. Along toward evening Johnny Souce staggered in yelling, drunk as a lord. We went out of the lodge and I could see that there were several bucks and squaws who had been to the Alcohol Springs and now didn't care whether school kept or not. I found that the dispensers of the booze were my friends La Brie and George Reynolds, who had been above camp nearly all afternoon, trading whiskey to any Injun that wanted it at the rate of one horse for a quart bottle. They were not taking any mares either, and having no competition, they were doing a land office business.

Two brothers, Mexican Joe and Pete, came into the camp that night. They had married Piegan squaws. Some of the white men claimed that they were only stool pigeons for the Piegans and located the horses for the Piegans to raid, but of course I did not know. They came from the Musselshell and I tried to find out all I could. They wanted me to go in with them, as they were friends of the Piegans. But I was already traveling with a bunch I thought was thieving horses, and I didn't want to go in with another bunch many claimed was the pure thing.

I stayed in the Crow camp two days, but the second day none of the whiskey bunch came up to camp peddling booze. I was glad and thought that this would be the end. But alas, I ought to have known that men of La Brie's and Reynolds's abilities believed in advertising, and would not let a good thing slip by. When I was riding into the camp they had moved three or four miles up on the Big Timber to a nice secluded spot and, while still some distance away, I could hear a carnival going on in our camp. It did not need any calliope to call attention to the fact. It was my astonishment when I rode into camp to see that all this barbaric hilarity came from several half-drunk Crow bucks and more than a dozen copper-colored maidens.

With all kinds of ki-yi's they encouraged the senior member of the Beaver Tom Trapping and Trading Company, Tom, who was now branching out and was drunk as a fiddler's bitch. He had a young Crow squaw of magnificent girth and beauty. She looked like a large sack of flour with a string tied in the middle. This Amazonian prairie Juno went under the poetical and soul-stirring nom de plume of Leather Belly, because of the large leather belt she wore around her ample waist. The belt was five inches wide and had about three pounds of big-headed brass tacks driven and clinched all over it. Both of them were trying to dance together some kind of a grizzly-bear tango. The orchestra was a drunken Crow buck using the dishpan of the La Brie outfit for a drum, accompanied by the squaw chorus of "a-heap a good." That and whiskey were the only English words they knew.

Sitting down in the La Brie part of the camp was Al Shinnick with a sardonic grin on his face. He was the bartender, chief cook and bottle washer in this man's town, and over among our stuff sat Brock Davis with a bad look on his face. I had been away three days and now expected the worst; Crows could skin any band of gypsies when it came to picking up or swiping anything. I got off my horse. I knew Beaver Tom was too drunk to give a damn for anything and still keep it up with his divinity.

I went over to Brock Davis and he said, "I am sorry for all this, kid." He claimed he had had nothing to do with getting "this whiskey soak of a partner of yours drunk and you know well enough he needs no coaxing. But I have seen that your stuff is all right. I have slept and stayed with it since you left."

I had to tell him that I was thankful. Then I said, "I suppose you heard Old Man Countryman tell me that there is more than a troop of the 2nd Cavalry staying around near the agency now. There is not much Indian fighting for them and they are wishing for something to do. As soon as the agent hears of this he will sic them on you fellows and they will run you all down. I know them, but I don't want them to find me traveling with your outfit, for I think you are up to something. You don't want them to find the horses with you."

He said, "It is a go. Tomorrow we hit the trail and get out of here when the going is good, or there is going to be trouble and in big letters, too." He then got up and went over to Al Shinnick and they had some kind of a talk. I went to the pack to see if Beaver Tom had broken into our five-gallon keg, but everything was all right and just as Brock Davis said. I was more than glad that we would pull out in the morning, and thought I had done a bright thing in talking to Brock Davis.

It was not long till the other three of the La Brie bunch came into camp and some more bucks and squaws with them. This was certainly a gala day for them, as it was not every day they could get all the whiskey they wanted, even if it cost them a horse to get a bottle. By now Beaver Tom was dead to the world and was snoring his jag off at the foot of a tree, and the La Brie outfit was cooking its supper with a full house of squaw cooks on their bill of fare tonight. As long as one was willing to put up the grub, an Indian would stay.

After they had eaten, La Brie came over to our side of the camp and said to me, "We will pull out in the morning so don't feel gloomy. Just hug a squaw for luck. They smell a little smoky at first, but you will soon get used to it. Don't feel sore at those people having a good time tonight; we want to trade for a horse or so more to use for trapping."

I said, "Funny trappers you are, who use whiskey for bait and carry no traps with you."

More bucks and squaws arrived and, from the look of things, there must have been some more horse trading, for instead of getting more sober they got drunker. The Crow squaws were the best looking Indian women that I had ever seen. Those squaws were fine looking and most of them were strictly up to date. They were firm believers in women's rights, free love, companionate marriage, fishing trip affinities, and they did not go back on a chunk of Uncle Sam's pork or the mighty Iron Dollar. Those flapper squaws were no fools and knew the value of their jewels. With whoops and yells they kept up their antics.

I was thinking about the opinion of some good people in Bozeman, who, whenever I went into town from the Fort, used to coax me to go to church. When I said I had no Bible, as it was not popular with the soldiers, mule skinners and packers, people they called Philistines, a nice little girl gave me a small Bible. If they could see the way things are going on tonight, I am afraid that all the preachers in Bozeman could not convince them that this is an old-style camp meeting and that those whooping bucks and squaws have got religion.

A half-breed, who was known all through the country as a bad one, rode into camp and with him was a bad Injun. They and the La Brie outfit held a long confab together. Then they picketed their horses and stayed all night. Well along in the night the drunken jamboree, like everything else, came to an end. The bucks and squaws rolled up in their blankets and now silence reigned supreme in camp.

We were up early, and the bucks and squaws wanted to keep the party up, and said they had plenty of horses. The La Brie outfit just gave them one drink as an eye-opener and told them to get to hell out of there. For some reason they gave Beaver Tom whiskey again, and he was nearly drunk before we started. I had to get Henry Redman to help me put on the packs and all the La Brie outfit stayed to help. The bucks and squaws, seeing that they could not keep us here, were now bound to steal anything they could put their hands on. The La Brie outfit was too tough for them, however, and we drove off, taking the trail up the Big Timber.

I was at last on my way to the Musselshell! After we got a mile or so from camp, Reynolds, Red and La Brie left us and rode up in the hills. La Brie told us to make camp ten to twelve miles up the creek; they would come along behind and find us. We trailed along and soon the country got rougher and more broken. Beaver Tom was so drunk that he could hardly keep in the saddle. They must have given him a bottle, because he got drunker the further we traveled. He looked like a big gorilla talking to himself. Whenever the trail allowed it I would ride up to Brock Davis and give him and the bunch hell in general about giving Beaver Tom the whiskey. I wanted to know where I was going to come out. He said, "I know that it is not right, but cannot help it, for it is the others who give it to him. He is bothering them all the while and it makes me think that you are in for some time with that stiff.

"I want to tell you again," Brock Davis said, "if Reynolds and the others want you to join our outfit, stay out of it. You might as well know it now, for you will know it tonight anyway. The boys are bringing eighty-four head of horses behind us on the trail. We picked them up between Big Camas, Idaho, and the Gallatin, including eleven head we got from the Crows for whiskey. We came along through the foothills away from the trails in the Yellowstone so that we would meet no one. The reason we got you to travel along with us from Bozeman was because everyone knew that you are all right. We have been just using you as a blind so that whenever anyone saw us on the trail or in camp with you, they would think we were trappers. The others are going to try tonight to get you to come in with us.

"I told them to leave you alone, but they are bound to try. We want to steal some more horses and are shorthanded to handle them. If anything should turn up we want someone like you, who is supposed to be on the square, to handle our stuff in camp. We have a long drive and have got to know where our grub is. This is a good proposition for you if you want to be crooked. You can make some quick money, for we have a good place to get rid of those horses at a good price. We are now out of danger of running on any white men, and La Brie knows all the Injuns and the country.

"In one way I would like to have you come with us, but am telling you that crookedness does not pay in the end. I ought to know it, for I have a good wife and two nice girls back in Nebraska and used to be on the square till I got in with a bad bunch. Then one day I got in a racket with a fellow and shot him full of holes and while he did not die, still I can't go back for they will send me to the pen. Since then, instead of getting better I have gotten worse. I am now hoping to make enough so I can send for my family and start again on the square, someplace where I am not known."

I said, "You need not be afraid. I am not going in with your people and you can tell them so."

Then he said, "I can't very well tell them this because I am not supposed to let you know. Don't make them mad at you. Just tell them that you won't have anything to do with it, but that it is all right and that you will not squeal on them or tell what you know. Reynolds, La Brie and Shinnick are bad numbers. I don't trust them. Red is a good boy. He is too good for the bunch; however, he just can't keep from stealing horses."

CHAPTER FIVE
I Will See You All in Hell First

Shinnick was the lead on the trail and he could not see or hear what we had said as we drove along. I thought, "This is what I get for not leaving this bunch when I had the chance yesterday. They could not stop me and I knew that in some way were crooked. I have been told all my life to shy clear of crooked people, but I was afraid that the people I know would give me the laugh and say, 'We told you so!' Now I have got to like it or lump it."

We made about twelve miles further up the Big Timber and went into camp early. It was not long till the others of the bunch came along with their plunder. They had what looked to me to be about ninety head of horses. They were all fine saddle horses—no scrubs in the bunch. They drove them through camp and up the trail and then they started them up a ridge to feed for the night. Now the country was rough. They had to drive on the trail and could not run them on the foothills as they did in the Yellowstone. When they returned to camp they appeared friendly with me and wanted to be real friends.

Reynolds said to me, "What do you think of our men— are they not dandies to go trapping with in the Musselshell? A fellow ought to be able to trade one of them for a squaw any day."

I did not say much. I was wondering how this would all come out. They got their supper. I had to cook for only myself. Beaver Tom was living on whiskey. We all got around the fire and Reynolds began to tell the whole works. They knew I would keep my mouth shut. They wanted to give me a chance to make some quick money because they were getting shorthanded. They could use more help. They thought

I should come in with them. They could get more horses and handle them, if they did not have to bother about their camp. If there should be any trouble, they could run the horses up in the hills and could always be sure of having their grub when they wanted it. There would be no danger in it for me, I could play the innocent and prove that I had nothing to do with it. The rest of the country was only Indian and La Brie knew them all. I would be foolish to go trapping as there was nothing in it but trouble with the Indians and hard work, while if I came along with them I could make all kinds of money as they were taking those horses over to the Northwest Territory in Canada, where the Mounted Police was starting up and needed horses badly. We could get $100 to $120 apiece for a cayuse that was only worth from ten to fifteen dollars here. The Mounted Police would not buy horses from strangers, but La Brie had it fixed with a fellow that sold the Mounted Police many horses, and he could pass them off on them as straight stuff.

Instead of saying "no" I said, "Sorry, but I can't do it as I have all this stuff bought and what am I going to do with it? What about Beaver Tom? Is he in on this too?"

They all said, "Hell, no, what use could we have for that drunken deadhead? We can leave him drunk here with a jug so when he wakes up he can go at it again until he gets out of whiskey. Then he can ride back to the Yellowstone. We will leave him his horse and saddle. The stuff you have got you can cache—what we don't want of it, anyway. You come back this fall and get it if you want to. You can go trapping in the fall, as far as we are concerned. In that way you would be hitting two chickens with one stone. Don't be foolish and pass up a good thing, for what we are offering you is easy as falling off a log. Besides there is more to this, for we have made a bargain with the half-breed and the Indian who stayed in camp last night. For ten gallons of whiskey, they will gather a bunch of horses that are running up on the Boulder and will meet us tomorrow night at the ford of the Yellowstone near the mouth of the Big Timber. They will help to drive them up here with us; then we will give them the whiskey. They say that those horses will not be missed for several days, as the half-breed and Indian who own them are at Sweet Grass for the powwow. Now we have laid our cards on the table, face up to you. What do you say?"

I said, "Is not the name of the half-breed who owns the horses Enis?"

He said, "Yes, that is the name, but what in hell do we care what his name is just so we get the horses? He can keep the mares as we cannot sell them. The Indian and breed are going to cut them out."

I said, "I don't know much, but I know enough not to go stealing horses. I will see you all in hell before I will have anything to do with those horses, for I am not low-down enough to help you run off and steal a person's horses, whose grub I have eaten many times and whose blankets I have slept in, even if he is a half-breed. As far as I am concerned, you can steal all the Crow horses you want except that bunch. I am going to give you all the chances you want. I will pull out tomorrow morning and go back to the mouth of the creek. I'll wait there until Old Man Countryman comes back from Bozeman and I'll try to sell him this stuff. I will make you a present of Beaver Tom since you like so well to furnish him all his high-priced whiskey, just to bust our outfit up."

La Brie said, "If you are thinking of turning back, I am afraid you will have to forget it this time."

I said, "How are you going to stop me?"

He said, "Just with this," and quick as a flash he pulled his gun and the devil was shining in his eyes as he said, "You just try once to sneak away and I will fill you so full of holes that your mother won't know you, you damn hissing adder. I have a good mind to plant you right here, you two-faced sneak."

I said, "I have got ideas of my own who the sneaks are. The people are not much who will try to use a fellow for their camper to cover up their dirt, because he is soft and tries to be white to a crook." I don't know what more I would have said, for I was foolish enough not to know that this one time in my life I ought to have kept my mouth shut and not given this human devil an excuse to kill me. I have no doubt that he would have plugged me, only that he knew the others were not mean enough to stand for his murdering me.

Now Brock Davis said, "You put up your gun, La Brie. I don't want any trouble with you. Remember that if you kill the kid, I will kill you like a dog just as sure as God made little angels. You know I mean it and that I am not afraid of you, living or dead." Then La Brie put his gun back in his holster. His face was as white as a half-breed's can get, but it was not fear so much as the evil hatred of the devil that was in him. "You have no reason to call him a sneak when we all know that he has been more than white and could have turned us in along the trail. All the thanks you fellows give him was to get his partner drunk as an excuse to get him to come in with us. I told you all to play square and leave him alone, but you have not done so. I am telling you all that I am going to see from this time on that he has a square deal and see that he gets through to the Musselshell. He can leave us there and go where he wants. If any of you don't like this and are out for trouble, your chances are good now."

Then he said to me, "I am sorry, kid, but I think like the rest of us that we would be foolish to let you go back to the Yellowstone, knowing what you do about us. You come along with us until we come to the Musselshell. Then you can leave us and go trapping with Beaver Tom if you want to. None of us will bother you. All we ask you is to say that you will do this, and that you will not try to run away back to the Yellowstone."

I said that I would do so, for they had everything that I had in the world. Besides I owed Walter Cooper in Bozeman three hundred dollars and had no other way to pay him but to do this. I was beginning to find out that it was too late. I ought to have taken the advice of those who were older than I.

Reynolds said, "What is the use of us fighting over this? If the kid don't want to do this it is no reason why we should make it hot for him. I believe that he will keep his mouth shut and it is better to have him for our friend than an enemy anytime. We are all friends again so let us forget this and see what we are going to do with that other bunch up on the Boulder."

La Brie was sulking and didn't want any friendship. He got his blankets and rolled up to sleep, letting them call him when his time came to guard the camp. The others talked it over and Reynolds was going to ride back in the morning to the Yellowstone and find the Indian whom the half-breed said would be there to show them where to go—to meet them at the stolen horses. Reynolds would tell the half-breed to turn them loose as they could not handle them. They had found out that it was too dangerous and they thought they had better send the half-breed two gallons of whiskey so that he would not be sore at them for going back on the deal. It was now in my interest to tell them that, while they might think they were the losers, in the end they would be the winners. The 2nd Cavalry would, when the horses were missed, chase and follow them to the British line if it had to. Just as soon as the half-breed got drunk on their whiskey he would give the whole thing away to his friends, and what one Injun knew they all knew. I knew this bunch of horses and they were all very wild and not much better than elk. They could not drive them through this rough country with the help they had. If they did, the horses would probably take to the hills and take their other bunch with them. They would find out they now had more horses than they could handle until they came to the Musselshell country. Then they would be in the open country again. They were all good riders and, knowing their business, now admitted it was so, and did not want this bunch as a gift.

We rolled up for the night, leaving Shinnick to stay up and guard the camp. But I could not very well go to sleep after what turned up. I was now up in the silent hills of the

Big Timber with what I knew for sure was a bunch of desperadoes. One of them, La Brie, was only too willing to
commit murder at the drop of a hat. Reynolds and Shinnick,
although not evil, had a kind of rough honor. Still I knew
they would not hesitate to send a bullet through my head if
they thought I would endanger their safety or squeal on
them anytime to come. Those men had it figured out not to
meet another white man on this trip. They planned to go
clean through to the British line and on to old Fort McLeod
near Bella River in Northwest Territory. It would be an easy
matter for them just to give me a shot in any of those silent
canyons and I could lay there to the judgment day and none
would be the wiser. I have met and known men that would
think nothing of doing a thing like this if they ever thought
one stood in their way. Through no fault of mine I sometimes was with and even slept under the same blankets of
men that I knew were horse thieves, road agents and even
murderers, who held life so cheap one had to keep his
mouth shut and let well enough alone. I knew better than to
try and betray them to a Law that could not protect me.

They certainly put the fear of God in me. Many of them
whom I knew died some kind of a violent death. They used
to say, "Died with their boots on." I was never good, but I
was not bad either and I sure to God had all the chances in
the world to be a crook. I came through a tough mill, but I
always turned down anything that was not on the square.
The reason I came through clean was probably not due to
my honest disposition, but to my deadly hatred of whiskey
and of them that used it. I know only too well if I had drunk
whiskey it would have got me as it had gotten many a man
before. I would not have been here on earth long except for
my people and the stern way they had in raising their kids.

I am wondering what my people would think tonight to
see their hopeful in camp, running around with a bunch of
horse thieves and maybe worse. While my people may have
been bitter and revengeful in their hates and would think
nothing of sticking a knife in a person in anger, still there

were some things they did not tolerate, and they were drunkenness and stealing. I can remember just a few years ago when as a small boy going through El Paso one day with my father we met several drunkards—desperadoes with some women that were no better than they were. After they went by, my father grabbed me by the arm and shook me, saying, "Say it, muchacho, that you will never be like those vile men, for I would rather see you lying dead at my feet; and so Cristo I would do it with my own hands, rather than see you grow up and be like one of them."

The cold shivers ran through me as I thought of what would happen to me if some of my people should run down this bunch and find me with them as I was that night. While I might have been able to show a stranger that I was innocent, I could expect no mercy from my people. They would have given me the benefit of the doubt and hung me with the rest of the bunch, thinking that they were only doing their duty, and that I was better off dead.

CHAPTER SIX
Horse Lifters Limited

Now my happy musings were interrupted by several oaths from Shinnick, who, on coming in off guard to wake up another one of the bunch, stumbled over Beaver Tom. He was lying a little way out of the camp where he fell down last night, and had been sleeping off his jag in the cold frosty dews. He must have had the constitution of an ape not to feel the cold. Nothing happened during the rest of the night. We were all up early. I went out and ran in my horses with the ones they used. We did not run them with the stolen bunch.

After we ate, the La Brie bunch began to argue about the Enis bunch of horses. They told La Brie that they didn't want anything to do with them. They did not want any trouble with the soldiers or have to handle a herd of wild elk through those hills. At this La Brie got all the madder and said, "What does that damn kid know anyway? I thought you fellows were all cowpunchers and out to make money. Why, you damn fools, every one of the horses over in Canada is worth a hundred dollars at least. I thought you fellows said when we started out that you would leave everything to me. Here you are letting this sidewinder buffalo you out of the chance to make a lot of good old Queen Vic's money."

Brock Davis said, "We are with you in anything that can be done, but we know that the horses are a long way from Canada, and with the bunch we have got, we can never get them through those hills. We have plenty of whiskey left and wherever there are Indians we can swap for horses." La Brie raved and swore, but they stuck to this. Now I knew there was one fellow called the kid who had better steer clear of Mr. La Brie after this.

Reynolds said to La Brie, "We are thinking we had better bring the breed two gallons of whiskey so that he won't feel sore at us. I am going to ride down to the Yellowstone and find the Indian that is waiting for us and give it to him and tell him to go and meet the half-breed and tell him to turn that bunch loose. We cannot handle them now. I will be back here sometime late tonight and we can pull out tomorrow morning." But here La Brie queered the deal when he said, "You will do no such thing. I have something to say about giving that whiskey away. To hell with the breed and you. We are going to pull out of here now and keep a-moving."

During the morning Beaver Tom, a very sick man, was begging for whiskey. They refused to let him have any, so he said to me, "Which pack is that keg of whiskey of ours in? I am going to open it. I can't stand this and have to get some."

I told him, "If you open that keg, sure as God I will blow your head off, you drunken stiff, for I bought and paid for it and you are not going to swill it down your rotten guts. Keep your mouth shut about that whiskey to the bunch and, if you want whiskey, you go and get it from them who have made a total wreck out of you."

He kept at them till Davis said, "He is so far gone and sick that we will have to give him a drink or he will go under."

I said, "Give him a barrelful if you want, for the quicker he is dead the better."

We started saddling up and were nearly ready to pull out when we heard a horse running up the trail toward camp. The half-breed rode into camp all covered with dust and his horse with foam. He motioned the bunch to follow him a little way away. They left Beaver Tom and myself holding both outfits.

After some talking, Brock Davis and Reynolds came back to me and said, "The breed could not take the bunch of wild horses, but he and three Indians have rustled fourteen head on the side and are holding them down the trail. They want to trade them to us for whiskey, but are afraid of you. We are putting it to you: is this any of your business or not?"

What else could I say, but that I had no horses stolen that I knew of and it was none of my business. They went back and the breed soon rode back down the trail and then the bunch came back to camp and unpacked a five-gallon keg of whiskey from one of its packhorses.

Reynolds said to me, "Red will help you today on the trail. You can pull out and make what you think an easy drive. Don't get too far; we will probably have trouble trailing that bunch today. Camp near the trail so we can find you."

I could not help but notice that La Brie, who always told me where to camp before this, told Reynolds what to say to me and did not want to talk to me. I led off and Red drove the bunch behind with Beaver Tom riding in the pack train. He did not care whether he was in the U.S.A. or in China. We trailed along with my bunch and their pack horses making quite a string on the trail. I did not talk much with Red, so I had all kinds of time to figure out the profit and loss of the La Brie and Company Horse Lifters Limited with all capital subscribed and paid. I had to admit that if they would only leave out the tribulations that go with this kind of business, then horse stealing on this Canadian route would be a pleasant and paying proposition. They were getting fourteen head for a five-gallon keg of whiskey, which was worth fifty dollars. La Brie said this morning that a horse of this kind would bring at least a hundred dollars in the Northwest Territory.

I thought it was a good thing that the horse thieves down on the Rio Grande did not know of this great monopoly, for the bunch from down there would steal all the horses in Montana for the price they could get for fourteen head. They'd even throw in several murders for good luck if they had to. As we rambled along, the country kept getting rougher. The trail now left the Big Timber and went over a low divide; we followed it until we came to Otter Creek. We thought it best to camp here and wait for the horse wranglers, who were coming along somewhere on the trail behind. We fixed up the camp and waited. They did not show up right away, so Red and I had quite a confab.

Red didn't seem at all mean. It was too bad to see this jovial young man an out and out, all-around horse thief. He said these were not the first horses that he helped to run off. When I asked him why he took these chances, he said that there was nothing else for him to do; all the sheriffs had his number from Utah to Montana. I knew better than to ask him, but of his own accord he told me he was raised in southern Idaho. He said he was on the square until he got in bad by stealing a horse or two to get out of the country. He was caught and then got away, so it was all off with him. As we sat by the fire chewing the rag, I really did not know who this Red was.

He happened to be one of the most daring horse thieves in Montana and Idaho. Later on I was discussing with a man from the Madison Valley how this Red looked, when the man said, "Why I thought everyone knew of Red Murphy. From your description he cannot be anyone else." A few years after this he was hung on a tree someplace near Helena in the Boulder Valley.

It was nearly sundown when the bunch arrived with the herd. As they were driving them by camp to start them up a ridge to graze, I could see that they had quite an increase in their family. They had, if I counted right, 109 head of good saddle horses and not a single mare. They had found out today that the ways of the transgressor were hard—that over one hundred head of horses driven over a rough trail by three men was no joke. One of the four had to stay far enough in the rear to guard. It was a tired bunch that sat around the fire eating its supper that night.

I had been thinking all day that, since they got the four-teen head from the Crow half-breed and his dusky partners in sin, and because they could not take the Enis bunch any-way, La Brie would get over his mad fit at me. But it was not to be. This gentleman still gave me the bad eye good and plenty, and would not even speak to me. This was agreeable to me in one way, but I knew that La Brie was as bad as they make them, and no one likes to help advance the date of his own funeral. I did not say anything, and listened to the bunch, which was cursing the Crow half-breed for not telling them until after they took the horses and gave him a keg of whiskey, that they had better be on the lookout, as the war party of Crows, which was after the Piegans for stealing its horses, had not got back yet.

He thought that they would come down the Sweet Grass, but still they might have taken this trail and met us. If such was the case then hell would have been popping for us, as those slippery friends of the white man, who recognized the Crow horses, would have used them as an excuse to take all the horses and rob me besides, and leave us afoot. This was providing they did not do worse. Although some writers extoll the Indians' virtues and friendship for the white man, still it was well known, to the sorrow of the old-timers, that whenever those copper-colored gents caught a white man out in the hills they did not hesitate to rob and plunder. In a case of this kind, they were firm believers that dead men tell no tales. The bunch was not feeling any too good, and hoped we would not meet this Crow party.

They doubled up the guard and sent Red and I with our rifles to the point on the ridge where they turned up the horses, telling us to keep a sharp lookout until about midnight when two more of them would relieve us. Red, since the ice was broken that day, was out to get all the news about Bozeman. He wanted to know if I knew any people from the Madison or Jefferson valleys around Bozeman.

I told him that I did meet some of them, but that I was not very well acquainted with that part of the country and asked him, "Since you like Bozeman so well, why did you not come in with the others when they came in?"

He said, "I guess not. I would have probably met someone who knew me and got what was coming to me."

I found out from him that La Brie did not dare come into Bozeman for the same reason. Also, some of them had to

keep the stolen horses moving and get them into the
Yellowstone, where they would be much safer. We talked on
in a low whisper as Red told me the whole works. He wanted
to know if I had a girl in Bozeman. When I told him I kind
of thought I had, but could not swear to it, he told me that
if it was not for the generosity of some of the prairie queens
in Utah, Idaho and Montana, he would have gone hungry
many times when the law was shaking the country up for
him. He seemed to think that the time would come when I
would be an outlaw like himself. After cautioning me and
making me promise to keep it under my belt, he told me the
right people and where they lived in Idaho and Montana. He
said I would be sure of help and sympathy if I told them that
Red sent me, and that I would find them all right.

He said he had just met Brock Davis this spring and they
were coming along through the country looking for something to turn up when Reynolds and Shinnick, who had
come from Wyoming, caught up with them. They became
friendly with each other and tried to hold up some of the
Utah-Montana stages. After giving it the once-over in several
places along the trail they found that the stages had been
held up so many times that the stage drivers and shotgun
messengers had learned all the spots and places on the trail
where they could be held up. They were leery and harder to
hold up than a flock of wild geese. They seemed able to smell
a road agent five miles away, so they kept riding up toward
Montana, still hoping for a chance to hold up a stage.

Here they ran across La Brie, who had already ridden
from the Northwest Territory in Canada in quest of the
Golden West. Soon they found out, through a kind of
freemasonry known only to that kind of gentleman of the
road, that they were all kindred spirits. It did not take La
Brie long to unburden his soul and convince them that his
layout was far superior to stage-robbing and not nearly as
dangerous. In faraway Canada hid the Golden Eldorado of a
horse thief's dreams. They only needed the horses to start
the golden shower. But the rest of the bunch was worldly-

wise and told La Brie that, while his scheme was flattering, he must remember that Canada was some distance off and their Treasury Department was about flat broke. The horses could make the trip on grass, but he could not expect them to live through the long trip to Canada on this kind of grub. La Brie, the Renowned Magician, made a few passes with his hands; then ran them under his shirt at his waist and pulled out a money belt; he poured out on the ground fifteen hundred dollars' worth of Uncle Sam's gold twenties.

With a benevolent smile La Brie informed them that there was honor among thieves. He asked of them only to find the horses, and for each one at the end of the trip to pay him back his share of what he would spend. All would share alike in what was left. The bunch was only too willing to take him up on this layout.

Under the skillful management of Red, who knew every trail, hole and corner between Corinne, Utah, and Virginia City, Montana, better than he knew his prayers, they had gone through the Milad and Big Camas country and on through the Madison, Jefferson and Gallatin valleys. They were foxy—old hands at this business. They let the people down light as they came along. Being good judges of horse flesh, they only took a few of the best ones out of each herd. They kept increasing their bunch as they came through. By traveling on foothills and on out-of-the-way trails, they had made it through to near Bozeman without any trouble or anyone the wiser. The eighty-four head of horses only cost them their time and the grub they used on the way.

This was the way we put in the time until Reynolds and Shinnick came and relieved us. Then we went back to camp to sleep. Nothing showed up to bother us in the night. I was up at daylight and started out to round up my bunch and their pack and saddle horses. But because horse thieves never use bells, and at this time no one would be foolish enough to put bells on their stock in Injun country anyway, I had some bother in finding two of their saddle horses that had strayed from the band. It took some time to find them;

it was rather late when I got back to camp where La Brie, who I know is wanting to pick a quarrel with me, starts in and calls me a slowpoke. He said I could not trail a horse through two feet of snow. After this they would build a fence around me to keep me from getting lost when I went out in the hills. He again called me a sidewinder and as I was not in any too good humor I told him if he did not like my way of rounding up the horses he could go plum to hell and get them himself, as this was the first time I knew that I was hired out as a horse wrangler for a bunch of horse lifters.

One word brought on another and it was not long until I had him frothing at the mouth, for I had thrown all caution to the winds and had made up my mind, die or not, I was not going to be called down at every turn by this half-breed horse thief. Besides I had learned it is not so hard to die after you get used to it. I remembered that a Scotch Canadian named McGregor, who used to be a Hudson Bay dog-driver and who had put in many years in the Canadian Northwest among the half-breeds, said that they would stand for everything except to be called a woods Cree. I never thought La Brie would take it so hard.

He spit out the words at me, "I am going to kill you for that the first chance I get, even if it is the last act of my life." Then he walked off and roped his horse.

Brock Davis and Reynolds told me it would have been better all around if I had kept my mouth shut; I ought to have known how it would turn out. I had no breakfast yet and they wanted me to eat some of their grub on the fire. But I told them, "I ain't eating no horse thief's grub today." We got ready to pack up and they helped me. Beaver Tom was now half dead; he had eaten nothing since yesterday morning. He could keep only whiskey on his stomach and was as sick as a dog. I have had to do everything, even the cooking, since he started drinking.

When we were ready to pull out, the bunch changed things and said that Red and I were to trail behind them and follow them up on the trail. La Brie would scout ahead as there was no telling what might happen in this Injun country, and Brock Davis and Shinnick would drive the stolen bunch. They told Red to wait until they got started, and to keep about a quarter of a mile behind them. If anything turned up we were to shoot twice. They rode off to drive the stolen horses down from the ridge and start off on the trail. This left Red and I together again and, as we would have to wait a little while to give them a start ahead, he wanted to know what kind of a damn fool I was for not plugging La Brie when I had the chance. I ought to know, said he, that La Brie would do it to me the first chance he got. He told me to watch my step, and to plug La Brie even if I had to do it in the back, "because if you don't, he is going to get you, and Brock Davis will not be able to stop him. When that time comes, he will think nothing of giving it to you in the back."

When we were packing up, I knew that I should have shot him down while I had the chance. What Red said was so; when La Brie got the chance, he would have shot me in the back if he had to. But I had not the heart to do it that way. This killing business may seem easy to do on paper, but no one whose heart is any good wants to stain his hands with human blood if it can be avoided. I know that according to blood and thunder writers, who write from a deranged brain back East, and manufacture such stuff, that I ought to have pulled my gun at the start, and at the crack of both our guns, the villain La Brie would lay dead on the ground.

Such things did occur out here many times, but most of the time they occurred among the cutthroat and heartless desperadoes, who always had murder in their hearts. That kind was always willing to commit cold-blooded murder, if for nothing else than to keep their hands in practice and to cut another notch on their gun. If a person got in trouble with one of them he had as good a chance with him as a snowball in hell. Those kind never give a square chance to a person for his life as they have the best of it from start to finish and only play the dead cinch. I have no doubt that Mr.

La Brie would have been only too glad to see me make the break at him. In fact, I know that he would, as they say, spot me a few balls to do so. This morning was the first chance I got at him, but I was not low-down enough yet to take it that way.

CHAPTER SEVEN
Very Short on Law and Order

So Red and I hit the trail. Again we had to put Beaver Tom in the pack string on his horse and drive him along that way. It was an awful sight to see this big husky man helpless. His love for whiskey had brought him lower down than a brute. He was now of no use, as he was as helpless and weak as a child and could hardly hold on to the saddle.

I bitterly thought, "What am I going to do if he dies? If this bunch will do as they say and let me leave them at the Musselshell, I will be alone with this pack string of stuff, and because I have *aparejos,* I cannot put the packs on alone. Now I got sweet thoughts that La Brie is going to kill me anyway so why worry about the future, for I am as good as dead now."

In this happy frame of mind, we followed the trail which ran up Otter Creek for a while, then crossed another low divide and followed on down to the Sweet Grass. The way this trail kept winding and running into ups and downs made one think that he who laid it out thought that time and steep climbing were no object. Upon coming to the Sweet Grass I thought they would expect to camp here, but they still kept on going, and when we came to the forks of the trail that went down the Sweet Grass, I could see that a large bunch of horses had gone down that trail, probably early that morning. It must have been the Crow war party; and so it was. In a little while we came to where they had camped last night. Now we were safe from them, and the trail to the Musselshell should have been clear, if a bunch of Piegans were not following them up for revenge.

It seemed that La Brie had wanted to take it out of us all that day. He kept on going till near sundown. We were a hungry and tired bunch as we sat around the fire eating fat venison, except Beaver Tom, who now seemed worse than this morning. The bunch said that he was going to get the snakes, and didn't seem any too glad for what was done, because now they had to feed Tom their valuable whiskey.

They had run the stolen horses up in the gulch past the camp where there was plenty of grass and they would not be bothered all night. Those horses were good and tired, besides sore-footed from this rough country. They did not feel like rambling off.

None of us had much to say. It was almost too quiet to feel good. La Brie rolled up in his blankets and had not spoken a word to anyone. Red and I had to go on guard together again, but before we left camp Reynolds came over to where I sat and told me to be careful and watch every move La Brie made. He was awful mad at me. There was no telling what that crazy half-breed might do. He was going to say some more to me but saw that La Brie, though rolled up in his blankets, was watching us with his beady eyes. Reynolds got up and left me. Now Red and I went on guard at the mouth of the canyon where the stolen horses were. Neither of us had much to say; he thought that Beaver Tom was going to croak, and that La Brie was a bad one. In this silent way we sat out our watch.

Reynolds and Shinnick came and relieved us. They cautioned me to watch out for La Brie in going into camp. But he was in his blankets when we got there and everything went all right. At daylight Brock Davis and La Brie woke the camp up and sent Red out to bring in the horses. This gave me a chance to cook breakfast and get some grub ready for the trail today. Beaver Tom did not want to get up any more. They were giving him hot whiskey and soda as he was shaking like he had chills and could hardly keep the hot whiskey down. Red brought in the bunch and it was not long till we were saddled up. La Brie told Red to pack up and stay behind like we did yesterday, and to keep a sharp lookout behind. Brock Davis, Reynolds and Shinnick would round

up the stolen bunch in the gulch and start out and La Brie
would have to scout on ahead to see if everything was all
right so we wouldn't run into any jackpots. Then the four of
them rode out of camp.

It took Red and I some time to pack up. We were about
ready to go, but Beaver Tom did not want to move or go as
he was too sick. He did not get any sympathy from us. We
pulled the blankets from him and put them in the packs and
he soon changed his mind when we told him to climb on his
horse or stay. He was so weak that it took both of us to get
him into the saddle and to make sure that he would not fall
off, we lashed him tight and fast in the saddle. He bent over
the saddle horn in a half-dead stupor.

I led off, driving some of the pack horses ahead of me
and Red put Beaver Tom where he could watch him. When
we came to the gulch where the stolen horses had fed all
night I could see that they had got them and had taken the
trail ahead with them. I kept on going. After traveling a mile
or so, I was surprised when I caught up with Brock Davis,
Reynolds and Shinnick, who were holding up the stolen
bunch near the mouth of another gulch. When I stopped,
they rode up to me and Brock Davis said to me, "We are
sorry to do it, kid, but you have got to pull out from us here
when you have the chance.

"You don't want to let the grass grow under your feet in
doing it, for that Injun louse La Brie told George and Al yesterday that as soon as we get through this tough country, he
is going to kill you and take your outfit. He wanted them to
come in on the deal with him, and said it would be foolish
for us to let you pull through with you knowing so much
about us. When we came back, he said, we would have
always to be on the lookout for you and he is not going to
take any chances on you squealing. He says that he holds the
edge on us: If we kill him for killing you, we can never make
it alone through to the Northwest Territory without him to
guide us. He said the Injuns would get us all, and even if we
did make it through we could never sell those horses

because we are strangers. George and Al strung him along and fooled him into thinking that they would do it with him to throw him off. We talked it over and it is as he says. He does hold the edge on us. It would not do you any good if we killed him after you are dead and though we are bad enough we don't stand for any murder or robbing a friend. La Brie is liable to come back if we don't move soon, and find us all here, and he will suspect that something is wrong.

"We will just have to plug La Brie," Brock Davis said, "but bad as he needs it, we don't want to do it if we can help it. Red will help you to start up this canyon; then we will drive the bunch over and cover up your trail. Go as far as you can; then camp and try to get Beaver Tom well again. Then you can both take the trail for the Musselshell. Here is a bottle of whiskey; give him as little as he will stand and try to get him eating again. We think he will pull through in a few days. We intend to take care of La Brie so that he don't come back tonight after he finds you gone. Still, don't be foolish enough to stick around your camp any more than you can help. Get away a distance and lay low. Keep a sharp lookout for two or three days. If he should try to sneak back, remember—kill him with the first shot, or it will be the last of you. Besides, should we meet any Indians, he is devil enough to send them after you to do you in. Keep your eyes open until you get out of here. Don't be mean enough to leave Beaver Tom and ride off. Stay with your outfit. We are going to tell La Brie that we started you back for the Yellowstone."

I shook hands with them all, and while they had done me dirt by roping me in with them at Bozeman, I still had to be thankful that they were not all like La Brie. I was sorry to leave them and had good cause to feel sorry for myself. They cut out their four pack horses and put them in the stolen bunch. That was the only way they could drive them along. I started my way up the canyon; they started the stolen horses and went on their way.

In the end their trail was to bring two of them, Reynolds and Henry Redman, or Red Murphy as he was called, under the hangman's tree. La Brie and Brock Davis shot it out when La Brie tried to double-cross the bunch out of its share of the plunder after they reached Canada. Brock Davis shot La Brie, but when he was on the ground dying, he still had enough of the devil left in him to shoot Brock Davis so that he died a day or two later. It all goes to show that the good old adage that crime does not pay still holds true. In the years to come, I was to hear more about some of them, when I was in the country where they had been. Except for Al Shinnick, from whom most of this information came, we were never to meet again.

Sitting here tonight, many years later, with more time than money, I think about those faces that pass before my eyes like it was yesterday. They remind me of the chances and temptations to become an outlaw. I sure came through a tough mill. I see those men as they stood in those old days of the Golden West—some of them in the springtime of their manhood, so beautiful and strong that it makes you wonder, because their hearts are black as night, and they are cruel, treacherous and merciless as a man-eating tiger of the jungle. Others are ruffians, with the stamp of evil so plain on their whiskered faces that they make you shiver.

All of them died some kind of a violent death. It seems more real and horrid, because I knew them, and now stand like the sexton in the funeral train, for they have gone— all—all—all.

When I left Bozeman, how was I to know that the gent who called himself George Reynolds was one of the most notorious outlaws, and soon was to make history as Big Nose George in one of the most daring robberies in Montana?

The only thing that I picked up while I was with the bunch was that he had spent some of his younger life around St. Georges, Utah. Some writers have written about the career of Big Nose George and the Cohn Coulee Robbery. They leave the reader in doubt. The story was told to me by one who said he was not in this hold-up, but everyone knew that he was.

Old Man Cohn ran the sutler's store in Old Fort Keough. He was not very well liked. It came to pass that he acquired many of the soldiers', and some of the none too honest civilians', hard-earned dollars. He had to buy more goods, but, unfortunately for him, the East where all the goods were wouldn't come to Old Man Cohn, so Cohn decided to go back East.

There was an army ambulance and some officers going through to Bismarck and they would travel with an escort of fifteen men, because the noble red man still had decided ideas of his own about his white brothers. Everything was lovely, safe and sure for Old Man Cohn so he girded up his loins with all kinds of money. But in some way it soon came to be known to the shining lights in and around Old Miles and they communicated this valuable knowledge to the rest: that Cohn was going to take this trip, and take his money back to the predatory rich of the East. With righteous indignation they came to the conclusion that Old Man Cohn was not the proper person to take care of it. It would be a burning shame on this community of buffalo-hunting saints, for they could put all this money to better use in drinking redeye rotgut and playing draw poker. They were all firm believers in patronizing home industry; this way, they would keep it in the family.

The hell of it was how to get it with fifteen cavalrymen guarding it; but a little thing like that did not bother those master minds. Undaunted, they called a council of war with Big Nose George in the chair, and vowed they would get that boodle even if they had to draft the only preacher in the town.

This bunch took no chances on the ambulance not stopping long enough in Miles. When with a flourish of trumpets the ambulance pulled out of Keough with a front and rear guard in regulation style, the Big Nose George missionaries had seen to it that every soldier in the guard was the proud possessor of a full quart bottle of Buffalo Hunter's Delight, which was also good for soldiers. The soldiers had been told to spare it not and, if the ambulance stopped long enough in Miles, their many friends would see that each soldier got another bottle of the Buffalo Hunter's Delight. It was not every day that the buffalo hunters got the chance to show how they appreciated the noble soldiers' friendship like they did that day.

The ambulance did stop, for who ever saw a trooper good and true that would refuse a shot of good old red-eye. What they put under their belts then and there, only themselves and the devil knew. Off started the ambulance on its long journey, and in it were the officers and Old Man Cohn, not forgetting the boodle. The guard was in the right position, just as a matter of form of course; for what danger could have come from the innocent buffalo hunters. This being an awfully dry country, the troopers, one by one, fell out of line and trailed along behind to sample the Buffalo Hunter's Delight.

It went this way until the ambulance came to a coulee, said to be located about eighteen miles from Miles. At this point the escort was scattered behind along the trail as drunk as lords. Before the driver went down in the coulee, he thought that he saw a man's head on the opposite side of the coulee. He thought nothing of it until he drove to the bottom of the coulee, where he found out there was something in it, for now through the crisp Montana air came the words that all ambulance and stage drivers knew better be obeyed, "Hands up—light and hit the ground right side up." He pulled the four mules to their haunches. The head he thought he saw now turned out to be a determined road agent standing in the middle of the road with a cocked Winchester leveled at his manly bosom, and four more road agents, two on each side of the ambulance, with an awe-inspiring display of firearms in their hands. They told the occupants of the ambulance to come out the right side of the ambulance with hands up, and no monkey business about it either.

They promptly disarmed them and lined them up, but in no other way did they molest or do anything to the officers.

They went after Cohn and were soon in possession of every dollar that he had with him. The amount he had with him was never rightly known to outsiders. Some writers say forty thousand dollars, others say more and some a little less, but the man who said that he was not there, but whom everyone knew was, said that they were all damn liars and were only talking through their hats, for he had heard that all the cash the cashier for the Big Nose George company could make out of it was $16,218.75.

But the worst was still to come, and it showed that the cutthroats who did this robbery were well informed before of what Cohn intended to do. He had put in the ambulance a small keg of peach brandy for himself and the officers to drink on the trip. At the same time he put a small keg of whiskey in the boot of the ambulance for the soldiers to drink. Those hellions, after robbing the man of every cent, reached in the ambulance and brought out the keg of peach brandy. Cohn kicked on their taking that. He told them to take the keg in the boot, as it was the same kind of stuff. They promptly told him that he was a liar and that he could drink his own rotgut whiskey in the boot and see how he liked it, as they knew of the peach brandy for some time before this.

While the perpetrators of this crime were well known to most of the citizens of Miles City and the sheriff, nothing was ever done to bring them to justice. Not because those good people wanted it so, but they were powerless in one way; the cutthroat friends of Big Nose George were too strong for them. They could not help knowing who those rascals were. All of this money was spent in Miles City with lavish generosity in gambling and drunken debauchery. It soon became a common joke. When you wanted to treat a friend, you said, "Come up, old boy, and have something on me, for I still have one of old Cohn's dollars left." Down the river from Miles City about eighteen miles there used to be a coulee, called Cohn's Coulee by the old-timers. Maybe it still goes by that name yet. If it is not, the good people of

Miles City should put that name back on it. I know that it would please Old Man Cohn up in heaven. He sure to God paid enough for it.

After Big Nose George blowed in his share of the Cohn holdup he lit out with some more of his own kind. He went back to his old trade of stealing horses. Down in Wyoming he rustled a bunch, but in doing so got into a fight and killed a deputy sheriff. He got away with the horses and made the drive through into Canada. Where he blowed in the money of this raid, no one knows.

Again he went to Wyoming where there was now a reward on his head, dead or alive. Although they were after him good and strong, it did not bother this knightly gentleman with a big nose, who rustled another bunch of horses. But his old-time luck went back on him. In some way the law got wise to George's aspirations, and the result was a fight in which one of his men got killed. In this fight Big Nose George and his youthful partner in crime managed to wound a deputy and kill another and get away with the bunch.

Now he found himself with just this young fellow who had no experience in whooping up a bunch of stolen horses, although he was pretty good at plugging deputy sheriffs. Big Nose found out that he had bit off more than he could chew. He dropped most of the horses with a squaw-man friend and started off with a small bunch that the two of them could handle. He headed for Miles City to rustle up another crew. There lived the genial Al Shinnick of whom I have already told you so much. While it did not bust up their friendship, Al had let a female come in between him and George. He was now the possessor of a highly cultured lady, even if she was somewhat careless and liberal with her virtue.

George showed up at Miles City on the quiet. He was not long in finding out that it was different robbing Old Man Cohn, who had real money to pass around, from bringing in a few stolen horses that were a drug on the market in Miles at the time. All friendship had ceased anyway as George's hide was now worth more to the uplifters of the law than his friendship. They were out to get him and earn the fat reward that was offered for him by the Territory of Wyoming. The honest and law-abiding people were getting stronger and putting it up to the upholders of the law that the time was coming when they would find out that they did not intend to stand for outlawry much longer. Big Nose George laid low at Al Shinnick's, but it was not long until it leaked out that Big Nose George was in and around Miles again. When the uplifters of the law found this out for sure, did they go and take this murderer and horse thief to his face? They did nothing of the kind and for some days Big Nose George could have left and gone his way of crime and destruction and none would have stopped him.

Their scheme was to get a hooker, or harlot, of the town, to go and visit the Shinnick place and coax the young man who was with Big Nose George uptown with her. She did this for several days. Then the law got a man who had the guts to go and get the drop on Big Nose George, which he did as the two of them stood in the corral looking over the stolen horses. This man got a horse between him and Big Nose George, who had left his gun at the house, and told him to hold them up. Then the uplifters of the law, who were hiding in the brush nearby, bravely rushed over and captured Big Nose George, after this man had done the dangerous part. This was a brave act, for if Big Nose George had had his gun, the man never would have taken him alive, and probably would have lost his own life. It was an easy matter to capture Big Nose George's young partner uptown, and the law had both of them.

You may not understand that just because the good people called their town Miles City, it was not the beautiful city it is today. It was only a small town with a few houses and some shacks, for in those days anything was called a city and some of them had high-sounding names, like Ruby City which contained one magnificent lean-to shack. At that time Miles City had only trappers, buffalo hunters and what was spent by the soldiers from Fort Keough to depend on.

While there were some good, honest and God-fearing men and women there, the majority were the kind that the less said, the better. They were gamblers, tinhorns, and strong-arm men, with their prostitute partners who catered to the wants of the buffalo hunters and soldiers or anyone else, and what the gamblers did not get, those snuff-dipping vultures finished the job. In regard to the buffalo hunters and trappers, no one could tell who or what they had been. Some were good and a whole lot of them bad and as a rule stood in with the lower strata, as most of them were booze hounds who blowed in their money by gambling, and were very short on law and order. After the buffalo were all killed off, many of those gentry promptly took up horse stealing and cattle lifting as the next best job to buffalo hunting, and cost the stockman many a bloody battle and the loss of many thousands of dollars in stock before they got them hung upon trees, or run out of the country, and a few in the pen.

When the above kind of people are in the majority, they always see to it that their own kind of people are elected to enforce the law, and when they are not, they always seem to be able to elect them who will play on both sides of the fence. Where they had all the say in the election, you can imagine what chance for an honest deal the people got. It is no wonder that the justice you sometimes got was crooked and rotten as hell; and again those kind of people sure knew how to hold an election and get the full strength of them votes.

After letting every man and what few kids there were around vote two or three times, they now remembered that Phoebe's Baby Kid did not vote. This estimable lady was one of the four hundred and run a checkerboard house of prostitution where low-down white women and nigger wenches held out under the high-sounding name of Phoebe's Exchange. Two drunken brutes brought this little boy, maybe three or four years old for he still wore dresses, up to the window at the polls and made out a ticket for him to vote. To anyone but this drunken crowd of ruffians, it would have been a pitiful sight to see this little kid who had been raised in hell's cauldron, with a burly ruffian holding him by the hand.

The three judges were pretty full like the rest. The Republican judge now leered at them and said, "You Democrats have voted every man and boy two or three times in this burg today and I did not kick, but I'll be damned if I am going to see you vote Phoebe's Baby. I challenge this vote." Then two others amid the cheers of the crowd proved that the kid was twenty-one years old and of legal age, and voted him over the judge. And this goes to show that even Democracy can sometimes cover a multitude of sins.

After the Miles City capture of Big Nose George and his partner it was not long until officers from Wyoming came and took them to Rawlins to stand trial for their crimes.

The law was slow and Big Nose George got converted to religion to kill the time. So well did he play the hypocrite that he fooled the jailer and other officers. They did not take enough care in watching him. This desperate cutthroat took the steel shank from his boot and made a knife out of it. George watched like a cat for his chance which the careless deputy soon gave him. He repayed the man's kindness to him by springing on him and cutting him badly. He would have killed him only someone heard the racket in time to save his life. When the people of Rawlins heard this, they came that night and took Big Nose George out of the jail and hung him until he was dead. Big Nose George got what was coming to him.

It made me think what would have happened to me in the end if I had listened to him that night on the Big Timber, when he coaxed me to become a horse thief like himself.

CHAPTER EIGHT
Bear Grease and Pepper

In that summer of 1878, little did I know what fate had in store for those men I had been traveling with, nor how lucky that we went our separate ways. Now, except for Beaver Tom, I was alone in the broken country between the Sweet Grass and Musselshell, driving ten pack horses and a couple of extra saddle horses. Worse still, I had to drive along in the bunch a half-mad, drunken maniac with the snakes, who was tied down in his saddle. Without much trouble, I made it up the canyon though it was pretty rough going. After going about three miles, I thought it far enough and stopped in a good camping place.

I tried to get Beaver Tom out of the saddle. I untied him and tried to help him down, but he was too heavy for me so we both went down on the ground together. I left him there and started to unpack and take the rigging off the horses. I turned them loose up the canyon where there was plenty of good feed for them. I kept the saddle horse on a picket rope to use for rounding them up. They say in case of fire, it is always good to go to bed wearing your pants. I was fixing the stuff I had in camp and was not paying much attention to Beaver Tom. I found him crawling around like a dog on all fours. Every once in a while he picked up an imaginary snake. He kept this up for some time and occasionally asked me to look at the big fellow he caught and to watch him catch the rest of them. It sent the cold chills running through me. It made me wonder what I would do if this large, strong man should go crazy like they sometimes do, and take it into his head to go at me.

I got his gun and hid it. I never had any experience with anyone who had the horrors of snakes. I coaxed him to come and lay down on his blankets. Then I gave him a drink of whiskey and soda, but he no more than got it down than up it came again. I thought of giving him something to eat, but what we had was not what a sick man would want.

The only delicacy we had was some black-strap molasses and several pounds of dried apples that were quartered and put on strings like prayer beads, then dried as hard as rocks. The apples had been several years in making their way out here and they were surely dry and hard. When three or four of them were put to soak in a water bucket their swelling capacity filled it up. One had to be careful not to eat more than one of them raw; even with one, he was taking a desperate chance on his life, for it could swell up and bust him. There were plenty of prairie chickens and grouse, so I made up my mind that if they were any good with whiskey and soda, then Beaver Tom is going to swim in them and his worthless life is as good as saved. I started to hunt up some chicken, but as I already said I had respect for a gent called La Brie, who might have felt sore at me if I did not tell him I was in the vicinity; so I was not going to shoot them. I had good luck, cave-man style, and knocked three young ones over with rocks and lost no time in starting back to camp.

I resolved that, because of Beaver Tom's delicate condition, it would be dangerous for his constitution to feed him chicken when he cannot even hold his beloved whiskey down. I had had nothing to eat since morning and, being of a generous disposition, I made out our bill of fare—chicken for me and for Beaver Tom three varieties, including chicken broth, whiskey and soda. I had to be careful to make no smoke when I made a fire. I cooked them and made out a fine meal. Then I gave Beaver Tom some of the broth, but his ungenerous stomach refused to be placated and up it came. After trying it three times, I had to give it up as a bad job and put the rest away until his stomach would appreciate it better.

While all this was going on I kept wondering how the bunch on the trail was getting along. When they came to the open country again they could handle the stolen horses with ease. While I was with them, I could not help hearing some of their plans. La Brie told the bunch they would cross the Missouri River at or near Cow Island where he had friends who ran a wood yard. If they could run across some of the Blackfeet or Piegan Indian war parties that had been on a horse-stealing raid, they could get all kinds of horses from them for whiskey. They would be safe with them, for he knew them all and could talk their language. At Cow Island he could get all the help he wanted if the band got too large for them to drive on to Canada.

If La Brie started back to where we had camped that morning, he could have gotten there in no time on the fast single-footer he was riding. One glance back at the trail to the Yellowstone would have told him that I did not go that way. The rest would have been easy. In no time those Injun eyes of his would have been following the trail back to the canyon I went up, and although my trail was covered at the mouth, it would not have fooled La Brie. He would know I had not gone up in the air. It would have been no time until he was sneaking up the canyon on a fine plain trail made by fourteen head of horses. Fear and terror soon got the best of me, for La Brie might have been around there right then. It was not long until imagination did the rest. I could see his beady eyes peering at me from every clump of brush and rock.

The novelist always manages to cover up the trail on the Indians or villains who are pursuing the hero with the red-headed maiden in his arms on horseback. I never had such luck. They could always find my trail dead easy and run the hell out of me. It was always a matter of speed with me. We all like to see the hero and fair damsel make their get-away from the villain and for her to live happily with the hero until some nigger in the woodpile coaxes her to fly the coop. I am sorry to have to dispell the beautiful hallucination and tell, in most cases, that is B.S. In the many years that I have lived I have seen more heroes get it in the neck from the villain than were left to go around. If it was not for the strong Arm of the Law and the brave men who enforce it, there would not be a hero left to tell the tale, and the woods would be full of grass widow heroines. Many flourishing jails and penitentiaries will bear me out on this.

It was not long until I bolstered up my cowardly disposition, and remembered that I was not raised for nothing in that glorious country down on the Rio Grande, where they would cut a throat twice for a dollar. I kept getting braver all the time. Because of the location of my camp, there was not a half-breed or Injun on this side of hell that could come within two hundred yards of it without being seen. La Brie with his forty-four pea-shooter of a Henry carbine could not hurt much at that distance. Besides nothing could be seen inside the camp. As afternoon went slipping by I came to the conclusion that La Brie had not found out yet that we were gone from the outfit. I had until next morning before my funeral would come off. I rode up the canyon and drove the horses further up, so that they wouldn't drift down too much.

This was a great rattlesnake country. When I was hunting chicken and driving the horses up the canyon, I saw all kinds of them—more of them than I like to see. I was wondering if Beaver Tom's snakes were contagious and if I had caught a dose of them from him. I went back to camp and got something to eat, and tried again to feed Beaver Tom, but it was no use. He was in pretty bad shape. Most of the time, after he got tired chasing snakes, I could not get a word out of him.

But when he saw me get my blankets and rifle, he had sense enough to want to know where I was going. He took it into his head that I was going to sneak away and leave him alone in the hills. He whined and begged me not to do so. He swore that he would never touch whiskey again, if he could only pull out all right this time. I had some time to convince him that I was only going down the canyon to watch for La Brie. Then I started off down the canyon and kept as good a lookout as I could, to be sure no one was coming up or hiding behind the brush or rocks. In about a half mile I found a good place on a point where the canyon narrowed. I could watch both ways and could look down and see if anyone tried to sneak up in the night or day.

It was getting kind of dusky after I had sat for a while. I reached around behind me for my blanket and nearly put my hand on a large rattlesnake, which must have crawled there in the little while that I was sitting there. It rattled and struck at me, but missed. I did not give it time to strike again, for I sure made good time in getting out of its reach. Being superstitious, I now christened him La Brie, and I went at him with rocks. When he lay dead at my feet, I felt much better. This was a good omen that I would triumph over La Brie.

La Brie could not get there until morning so I tried to get some sleep. I would doze off and wake up with a start, wondering if any friendly rattlesnakes had crawled in the blankets with me. In this manner I put in a real enjoyable night until the gray streaks in the sky warned me that daylight was coming and to get busy and watch. This was the time when the Injuns would strike. If La Brie was going to do anything he would have showed up soon; but the sun came up and still no La Brie. I waited until about eight o'clock in the morning and became pretty sure that La Brie had given it up. He probably could not leave the bunch. I started back for camp and, being a natural-born kicker, I then felt kind of disappointed and thought that La Brie should have come and taken a shot at me.

It was a good thing that I did not wait longer. When I got back to camp it looked like a family of cannibals had torn it up. All the packs were lying around, and Beaver Tom had found the sacred five-gallon keg of whiskey and was going to burst in the head with an ax. In his half-crazy way he could not get the bung out of it. I had some time in getting him to give me the ax. When I got it away from him, I rolled the keg out of the way and found out that he had drunk the bottle the bunch gave me and spit it up again on the ground. But he was burning up and said that he had to have whiskey or die, so I told him he would have to die that time.

I started to get something to eat. I tried to get him to drink some of the broth from yesterday, which I warmed up for him. But he said to hell with it—it was only whiskey that would save him. He did not get any of that either. It was going on three days since he ate anything. I had to do something desperate or my patient was going to croak or at the best would get hidebound on me. I wished that I had some of that good cure-all, castor oil, that my people used to say was the only panacea for all ills. They used to pour generous portions down us kids, even if they had to hold us by the nose and choke us to make us swallow it. It is with sorrow that I had to admit we had none. I always knew that I missed my calling and that I ought to have belonged to the medical profession, because this problem did not stick me long. I remembered that in the few possessions of Beaver Tom was a large bottle of somewhat ancient bear grease, which this mighty nimrod used to grease his gun with when he was sober. I had no trouble in finding it and poured out three or four large tablespoonfuls of it in some whiskey, then I put in plenty of black pepper and boiled the whiskey, bear grease and pepper in a skillet. I stirred it up good and plenty. Beaver Tom was watching me, so I let this cool off until I could stir it with my fingers and then I took a large tin cupful to him and told him to drink it. Although he was shaking like a leaf and burning up, he refused this well-intended mixture. They say you can lead a horse to water, but cannot make him drink, but I made this drunken soak swallow down the whole cupful. I had stood enough of this old sinner's dirt. I grabbed up the ax and told him to drink or I would smash his head in.

He thought I did not mean it, and said, "Holy Gawd, kid, you dassent do that," but I soon convinced him that it had come to where I would do anything. He shook so badly I had to steady his hand when he drank the cupful in three or four gulps. It must of had a little too much pepper; it was a while before he got his breath. I thought one time he was going to choke to death. When Beaver Tom got his breath he said, "By Gawd, I am going to get you for this if I ever pull through and get well again!"

I thought that this stuff was a success and told him that he would now get all right, because this batch did not come up like the other stuff. But he said, "How in hell can it come up when it went through me like quicksilver and is now down in my boots?" This fiery dose done him good, or something else did, and while he did not get well that day, the next morning he was able to eat a little. He kept on getting better every day. We had to stay eight days in that camp before he got well enough to pack and take the trail.

I had to look after the horses, which were getting restless. That night I did not take any chances of having only their tracks left, but drove them into camp and tied them up. They had plenty of feed all day. When I went down the canyon to watch, I made sure to take the whiskey keg away and hide it. I did not expect La Brie to come back; still I had to do some watching as the bunch might meet some Indians and La Brie, to get square with me, would send them after us. I put in the night—not even a rattler showed up—and went back to camp early to find that Beaver Tom was much better, although he was still weak and shaky.

I knew I had to give him some whiskey so I went and filled a bottle out of the keg and gave him a hot drink. This time it did not come up. When I gave him some broth he took it meekly and drank it. He did not tell me to go to hell this time, for he had enough of the dose he got yesterday. I was glad to see that this stayed down. After I ate, I ran the horses back up the canyon and came back and had nothing to do. Beaver Tom was still sick, but he was coming back to his senses. He told me and swore by all the gods that are holy and them that are not, that he had taken his last drink and that it was good-bye to whiskey forever with him. Being young and a damn fool I joyously believed him, but I soon found out that this was just like a fellow burying his first wife, who howls and moans that there will never be another. It means not until he can take on another.

Beaver Tom rubbed the soft soap in me good and plenty until pretty soon I kind of pitied him, but I thought if he was a damn brute it was no reason that I should be one too. I knew that he had never taken off his boots or clothes, nor washed his face or hands since that night on the Big Timber nearly a week ago when he danced the grizzly-bear tango with Leather Belly. He was now only a fit subject for an old-time scavenger to tackle. An Injun should have been able to smell our camp two miles away. I got clean clothes for him out of his war sack and coaxed him to come to the little creek in camp and I would clean him up. The old hog did not believe in baths, but I made him come and helped him to the creek. I went at him like a house on fire, and for once, since his mammy quit washing him, Beaver Tom was clean. Then I washed his blankets in the creek the best I could. Our camp did not smell like a slaughterhouse any more. So the day passed; it was getting kind of monotonous. I was over the La Brie scare, and even the rattlers had gone back on us.

I was just about ready to slip down where the trail was in the opening when I learned it was a good thing that I had not gotten there a few minutes sooner. I thought I had heard horses coming; and after listening a little while, I knew for sure that someone was coming on horseback on the trail from the Musselshell country. Four Indians came in sight and as they came opposite me I could see that they were painted up and stripped for action. They had nothing but their guns. I knew they were what Injuns call the dogs or scouts, and that the rest were not far behind. Those four Injuns would not go on the warpath alone. Now I was in an awful fix, for the four of them pulled up their horses on the trail and looked at the ground and could not help but see the tracks of La Brie's stolen horses. They had seen them along the trail as they were coming, but they did not ride into the mouth of the canyon, which was a good thing for me; they would have struck our trail up the canyon. They just slipped off their ponies and squatted down on the ground and I knew that they were waiting for the rest to come. In a few minutes thirty-five more painted devils rode up. All were naked except for their war bonnets and breech-clouts, and painted up for the warpath. They had nothing but guns and cartridge belts, and were riding barebacked.

They slid off their war horses in a bunch and were hold-ing some kind of a powwow. The slobbers of fear and terror dripped out of my mouth like a hungry hound dog. I thought to myself, "You damn fool. You wanted some excite-ment—well, here your chances are good for all kinds of it. After La Brie scared you hell, west and crooked, you had to come in just the right time to put your foot in more trouble. What are you going to do if they look around a bit and go in the canyon? They will find our trail and at the same time see me where I am."

I regretted I did not hold onto the prayer beads my mother gave me, for I would have needed them badly if they saw me. Two more Indians rode in, each one with a deer in front of him on his horse. They were talking of whether they would make a fire and eat their venison there or go on. It was with gladness that I saw the four scouts get their horses and hit it off down the trail. In a few minutes the whole bunch got on their horses and pulled out after them. Because the place where I was hidden was not fifty yards from where they had stopped, I had to wait until I was sure there were no more of them behind. When I went, I sure burned up the grass and got my horse. That was one time that horse made good time in going up the canyon to our camp.

It was still early in the morning, but I found Beaver Tom sitting up. He was too shaky to do anything, but he said he was hungry. I told him of my narrow escape with the Indians and how they pulled out down the trail. He said that it must have been a Blackfoot war party. It was a good thing that they did not run into us. We put in the remaining days and I lost my curiosity about what was going on below, at the mouth of the canyon.

Beaver Tom soon got his old appetite back, and, since he had sworn off whiskey forever, he was not a bad fellow. He tried to do what he could and blew about what a good cook he was. I did not encourage him in this—told him he was still too sick. His ideas of cooking were simple; he put large chunks of buffalo meat or venison on sharp sticks around close to the coals and fire. After they cooked a while, he would cut off a place which was half raw and eat it like a hungry dog. He could live the year around on this kind of diet without bread or anything else.

He had done some growling in Bozeman at my getting so much flour and other stuff. It was surely little enough, but he claimed we did not need it. Most of the trappers and hunters took along very little, if any, grub with them as they killed what they ate. Most of them were as destructive and wasteful as a pair of cougars and did not think anything of shooting a fine big elk or buffalo just to take enough for a meal and leave the rest to spoil. It was wonderful the appetites they had. They could eat more meat than a buffalo wolf and it was nothing for three or four men to cut a large fat deer for their supper and breakfast. They would sit around the fire until late in the night swapping lies and eating half-roasted meat. After their breakfast in the morning, there would be nothing but the bones left.

While that kind of men were in one way shiftless and lazy and despised common work, their life was still harder than any kind of work. Only those who were made of steel could stand the hard knocks they had to go through. As a rule, most of them were hard drinkers and in some ways they could not be blamed for this. They lived out on the wide prairies and in the silent hills and sometimes did not see a white man in a whole year. In this life a man soon forgot his father and mother, and even his God. When they came into a trading post they just went wild and everything went for the vilest kind of whiskey. It certainly was a savage scene to see a lot of them drunk and many drunken Indians with them.

Nearly all traders depended more on the power of whiskey and rum than they did on their own ability. Under this system the trappers and the Indians were under the mercy of the trader. In a few days the trapper and hunter would be dead broke and had to accept the trader's credit at his terms. There were many risks in this, for his prices were more than high. The trapper found himself bound in debt in bands of steel which he knew better than to try to break by defrauding the trading company. Its power was greater than any old-time Czar of Russia, and it did not hesitate to use it.

The trapper and hunter had to take desperate chances on his life with the Indians. He had to go through blizzards of wind and snow, and ford through warring streams of boiling foam, and lay out in the rain and cold. After all this hardship and toil, if he did not get killed, he would come back to the trading post where the trader told him that furs had gone on the bum, and that he had nothing coming to him. Do not blame him if he filled up on rum.

Many of the trappers had squaws. In this way they could sometimes get along with the people of her tribe, but this did not keep other Injuns from killing him and her if they got the chance. The Blackfeet and Sioux were known to kill a white man who had a woman of their tribe. Sometimes, they committed the murder in her presence. Generally they had women who belonged to more distant tribes. Then the trappers could trust them better. There was also a hatred between the women of one tribe and the women of a different tribe. Many times a despised Indian squaw was known to stand and fight to the death by the side of her man, sometimes even against her own people. Many of them proved their devotion and faithfulness and made good honest wives. Sometimes the squaws were too good for the drunken and dissolute white brutes who were no credit to their race. The Indian squaw, if her mistrust could be broken through, and she could be convinced she was really cared for, was willing to give a beautiful love and affection, of which no white woman would be ashamed.

I have said that some of the squaw men were drunkards and dissolute brutes; but some of them were good, honest

and respected citizens. To their eternal credit, they were true
and good to their Indian wives, and were not ashamed to
live and die with them. But as a rule the fate of a squaw who
was married to a white man would be desertion by him in
the end. Not much could be expected from a drunken blackguard, but still they were not the only ones who took French
leave of their dusky better halves and half-breed progeny.
This was done by many who were called honest and whose
word was as good as gold otherwise.

Some honest men thought nothing of leaving their
squaw wives and families to rustle their own living. This was
the case of Big Finnen McDonald. He deserted his squaw
wife and family in Manitoba and went back to the county of
Glengery in Ontario to live. However, she was one squaw
who would not have it so. Indian style, she trailed Big
Finnen and landed at his door with four beautiful little half-
breed McDonalds. Back East near Williamstown, Ontario,
she found Big Finnen among his Scotch friends. Big Finnen
was a good squaw chaser and Catholic. What else could he
do but take in his lawful wife and children? This good
woman lived with him until her death. She raised their family, which was good; its members became respected citizens
who lived and died there. Today this wild squaw from the
plains of Saskatchewan sleeps at the side of Big Finnen as
she should in the churchyard of St. Mary's Church in
Williamstown. It is a just and fitting reward and at the same
time it goes to prove the beautiful love and devotion an
Indian woman can have for an ungenerous white man.

CHAPTER NINE
One Squad, One Fight, No Funeral

The Beaver Tom Trading Company Limited was all hooked up and ready to hit the trail for the Musselshell early next morning. Beaver Tom had foresworn his old love, whiskey, and was going to ride on the water wagon for the remainder of his life. A wonderful change had come over him. He recognized his importance in the financial world as the senior member of our immortal company. His beautiful whiskers, which gave him the resemblance of a Rocky Mountain goat, had ceased to exist. I had given him the artistic haircut of the day with the aid of a sharp butcher knife and our sourdough crock. When I attempted to give his whiskers a Russian duke cut, which is a military appearance, I am afraid it did not become him for I got it a little too top-heavy on one side. A butcher knife is not what it is cracked up to be at haircutting; besides, I was green at the business.

Beaver Tom's drunk had nearly cost him his life and kept us there eight days while he recuperated from its effects. Under the soulful silence of the last few days I was beginning to be a philosopher and began to recognize that maybe it was for the best. Perhaps I was under a special dispensation of Providence, for if I had gone with the La Brie outfit as intended, La Brie would have found a way to kill me. There were some points in favor of that place where we had been. It was certainly a good place for a person to meditate on his past sins and deviltry. It would have made an excellent place to start a monastery, but I am afraid no such thought entered the head of either of us. While there were no buffalo there were plenty of deer and elk. They came and mixed with the horses like tame cattle. In the morning when I went to round up the horses, it would be nothing to see twenty-five or thirty elk around the horses. They hardly would pay any attention to me on horseback.

That night I went down to the trail at the south of the canyon. Beaver Tom said I should go to see if there were any new signs of traveling on it. I was not stuck on the job, but I knew better than to tell him that the Injun war party had taken all the curiosity out of me about who was passing on the trail. I put it off until near sundown in case I should run into any of the noble red men who might not like my looks and challenge me to a foot race. I meant to have the friendly shades of evening not too far away to help me make my get-away from them. I went and looked at the trail and found there had been several horses over it going both ways since the Injun war party went by. It showed there were several Injuns somewhere in this part of the country, as there were no white men but us.

In the morning at daylight I got the horses. After one of Beaver Tom's delightful breakfasts of half-raw elk, and cof-fee that would float an iron wedge, we were soon packed up. We started down the canyon for the Musselshell with better hopes than the day I came up it with Beaver Tom lashed in the saddle half dead and seeing snakes. Beaver Tom may have been a good hunter and trapper, but like all of his kind he was not much as a horse wrangler. He went in the lead and I trailed, driving the horses behind him. They were fresh and feeling good so we made stage time down the canyon to the Musselshell trail.

I thought he would stop the outfit to see whether the trail was all right, but he kept going and struck the trail. It was all right so far, and we were off for the Musselshell country at last, somewhat behind schedule. We kept pounding along and Beaver Tom had nothing to do but look wise and hold his Betsy Ann, a buffalo gun which weighed sixteen pounds without her nightshirt. I had to drive ten pack horses and two empty saddle horses, but I had the consolation of knowing that, if anything happened, Beaver Tom was going to get it in the neck first. After traveling about three hours to where a little creek joined the one our trail was following, Beaver Tom, the death-dealing Injun scout of the plains, ran us into a bunch of buck Injuns before he knew it.

Our horses and theirs were mixed up along the trail. I expected to hear the deadly war whoop and I was trying to think up a long-lost formula of prayers. I soon gave up that idea. My heart gave a bound of joy as my eagle eyes discovered that most of them were not bucks, but were what some people who are vulgar called squaws. Highly educated highbrows of the plains like Beaver Tom and I called them lady Injuns. Except for their female deviltry, they were harmless and never chopped you up until the buck got through scalping you. They were accompanied by several old bucks and good-sized boys, some children and papooses and the usual number of dogs. It was not long until we found out by signs that they were Blackfeet and then the rest was easy to guess. They were the women of that war party and they were hanging around until their men got back from their deviltry. I hoped they would stay away for some time. It would not have been any too pleasant for us, if that war party showed up.

I had to tell Beaver Tom to get a move on and try to get past them, but that old cockeyed buzzard had forgotten that he just missed death by a few inches the other day. He was making sheep's eyes and was trying to make a buxom young squaw. She was on to him and knew he was easy meat and that he was the big Medicine. I had to call to him twice before he would jar loose. With a lot of trouble I managed to work the pack horses through the Indians and get in the lead. It did not do any good; they were going our way. I pounded the pack horses on the tail and told Beaver Tom that, if he could not do any better, to get out of the lead, but still that bunch followed up and stuck to us like the paper on the wall. We finally went into camp, because the pack horses were loaded pretty heavy and we did not want to make a long drive with them.

We had to make camp early with the whole bunch of Siwash camping with us. I counted thirty-three grown-up squaws and several young ones, besides several good-sized boys and two old men. There was not a warrior or fighting man in the outfit. They were not mean or sassy to us, but they began to pester us by telling us they were hungry. They were bumming us for anything we had. I turned out my horses with theirs; there was no other way. We talked it over and came to the conclusion that one of us could go out and kill a couple of elk. This would be cheaper than being bothered by them the way we were. There were many deer and elk around, but it took quite a lot to feed this outfit. There were only two old men and boys with some old-fashioned guns to do the hunting, and they sometimes had to go hungry in a land of plenty and wait until the warriors got back. Beaver Tom went out and knocked over two large-sized elk, and the squaws went out with pack horses and brought them into camp. The Injun camp was happy that night and all of them would go to bed with a full belly. We had some troubles in keeping the many squaw cooks, who thought we were the white-headed boys, from foundering us with large chunks of broiled elk meat.

Beaver Tom, being a great philosopher although he got most of it out of a whiskey barrel, started one of his lecture courses on the congenial bliss of matrimony. He told me he hoped that I would not be foolish like him and remain single, for I would regret it all my life like he had. He pointed out with pride our full shift of cooks that night, and how nice and handy it would be to have a lovely little better half, even if she was copper-colored and had a smoky smell, to broil my venison, chop wood and pack water while I laid by the fire enjoying myself.

He had to admit that they were not up to a white woman's standards on education, but he said, "Don't let a little thing like that bother you, for you will find that if the squaw has not the white woman's reading education, she is strictly up to date with her in everything else. She can give the white woman cards and spades every time when it comes to woman's deviltry. There is such a thing as a woman

knowing too much," he said, "so why jump on the wild
Indian squaw and kick her just because she is down? Even
Caesar's wife was not above suspicion."

We had no trouble of any kind during the night, and we
started off again early in the morning with our admiring
friends still sticking to us. The trail ran up a creek which kept
getting smaller as we went along. Then it went over a low
range of hills. When we came to the top of this hill, we could
see that we were coming to our promised land at last. As we
stood up there, Balboa gazing on the Pacific did not have
anything on us. The Musselshell country was a beautiful
land. A person could stand in the same place and see buffalo,
deer and elk, all at the same time without turning his head.

It was business before pleasure so we started down the
trail with our dusky escort. The nearly naked younger boys
had by that time lost their fear and shyness of Beaver Tom
and I. They loped their ponies around us, yelling and cutting up like young monkeys. Everything was going fine and
dandy, but we were not feeling so good and even Beaver
Tom, the squaw Beau Brummell, was saying we had to get
away from this bunch of brunettes. The other day I saw at
the mouth of the canyon, and counted with chattering teeth,
forty-one painted devils, from whom not even a fool would
expect any mercy. They were the bona-fide owners of the
same outfit which was so friendly with us.

We kept jogging along until we came to where the trail
forked and Beaver Tom kept on the straight one. Then with
a great hullabaloo, our admiring friends rushed their horses
around us. They tried to convince us that we were taking the
wrong trail. Long life, joy and happiness laid at the end of
the other trail, the way they were going, so why were we not
going to go along with them? Were not the Blackfeet good
friends of the white man? One old warrior then showed a
surprising knowledge of Piegan English and by signs, which
Beaver Tom understood well, he asked us, if we were going
to trap and trade with Indians, why not go along with them?
In two days more they would be where they were going to

hunt buffalo that fall and winter and they would have all kinds of furs and robes to swap. Besides, were not the warriors all off on a raid among the Crows? They would soon be back with plenty of horses and robes to swap, and they would remember how good we were to their old men, women and children, and how we killed meat for them when they were hungry.

So well did they argue their point and paint it in glowing colors that I forgot all caution. I said to Beaver Tom, "Let's go it awhile anyway."

But Beaver Tom with withering scorn in his eyes said to me, "I thought you said that you were raised around the Comanche and Apache Injuns and that you savvied them. Why be a damn fool now? We want to get away from here as quickly as hell will let us. We don't want to let the grass grow under our feet, either. I have had good cause to know the Blackfeet, and if I am here today, it is through no fault of theirs." He argued to pull away from that bunch right there, and hit the trail for where we intended to go.

I have told about the deviltry of the Comanche and Apache Indians and of the deadly hatred that existed between them and our people, who had fought the red man since the days of the conquistadores. In the beginning they enslaved the Indian with hellish brutality. But they could not make a success of that because the Indian was different from the Negro; he was always a free man and would die rather than be a slave. Then the Spaniards did their best to exterminate the Indian. The English and French were not any too good either, and under the names of Christianity and civilization always gave the Indian the worst of it. Bad as they were, however, they were angels compared to the people I came from.

The Spaniards, in brutality, cruelty and treachery, outshone them all, and were known, hated and feared more than all others by the Indian. Having this deadly hatred born in me and having seen the cruelty and deviltry of the Indians, it could not be expected that I would have had any love for the Indian. Before, I had always helped those who were hunting them down. In their camps I saw them herded like cattle and their women abused after they were run down and captured. The same men who were doing the brutality would say among themselves that they did not blame the Indian, that they would have done the same thing themselves if they had been in the Indian's place. The Indian was only fighting for his life and liberty and a square deal, which he knew, from past experience, that he could not get from a white man. If some of the white men had not been so ready to start the dirt first, the Indian would not have been made the goat, and in the end get blamed for the others' dirty work.

That was the first time I have ever slept in an Injun camp. I did not feel any too good among the wild and savage faces, still I could not help but feel sorry for them in one way. When Beaver Tom killed the elk for them, they tried to show us how glad they were. In gratitude they would not let us do anything. But I am sorry to say that the more friendly and sociable they got, the more suspicious I became of their kind actions. I figured that they were up to some deviltry. What else could be expected from the Indian but treachery, deceit and lies?

Still, they did their best to coax us not to go. When they saw that we were bound to leave them, an old warrior, White Grass, pointed out to us eight or ten elk not very far away on the side hill. He wanted us to kill some of them, so they would have some more meat. He said as soon as the warriors got back they would have plenty of meat. I said to Beaver Tom that this was fair enough. Even if they were Blackfeet, they had used us all right, and it would be mean for us to go off and leave the women and children hungry. The elk were close, and he could knock them over easily.

Beaver Tom, who the night before was praising all womankind and not forgetting the squaw, now changed around about the squaws and did not practice what he preached. He said that he would see all the squaws, and especially the Blackfeet squaws, in hell before he would shoot them some

meat. He was done with the black-hearted hussies and it all
came about this way:

After we camped the night before, Beaver Tom killed the
elk for them and our stars were shining high. Then that
Cock Robin, who had the manners of a billy goat and, when
he was not drunk, thought he was pretty, got poetical and
said, "When the bucks are away, the squaws they can play."
He started in a fatherly and playful way to give some of the
squaws his famous grizzly-bear hugs and squeezes when our
dusky hostesses were going around by the fire, seeing to our
comfort. Some of those prairie matrons were built to stand
hard knocks, but even they soon gave a surprised grunt.

They took it in a friendly way as a white man's joke, but
I noticed that whenever he got a hold of one of the slender
willowy reed kind and turned on the hydraulic pressure, and
began to reduce her girlish form and to shove her liver up in
her eyes, she did not take it as a joke. That morning when I
went with some of the young Injuns to run in the horses, I
left Beaver Tom to watch our stuff in camp. He tried it again
on one of his slender victims of the previous evening, who,
as soon as she got her breath, playfully ripped Tom's arm
open with her skinning knife. When I got back to camp with
the horses I found it much upset and most of the old men
and squaws giving this young woman the dickens for carv-
ing up Beaver Tom's arm. I had to fix up his arm with a slice
of sow belly on the cut, which us prairie scientists knew was
a cure-all for cuts, bruises, broken heads and legs and, if the
patient would eat enough of it, it would cure broken hearts.

Meanwhile I told him that a man of his age ought to have
known the fair sex better and to be a good boy like me. I
would not touch a squaw with a ten-foot pole. He refused to
appreciate my golden advice and said that Adam was caught
in the act, and lost his job in Eden for squaw chasing.
Anyway that was the reason Beaver Tom changed his religion, and did not want to shoot more meat for the squaws.

After much coaxing and telling him that I was not the
shot he was, he rode off and, in a few minutes, shot two big

elk in the neck and they dropped like rocks. He shot another in the shoulder; it gave a few jumps, then lopped over. Such was the power of Betsy Ann; it shot a 45-size bullet with 120 grains of powder behind it. Although Beaver Tom may have had his faults he sure was a crackerjack with the rifle. As Beaver Tom started back to us I saw him make a sign to me with his arm. I looked behind us and I saw four Indians coming on the trot not a hundred yards away. I did not have to look twice to know that they were the four dogs of the war party I saw at the mouth of the canyon. The rest of the party would not be far behind them. Mother Carey's chickens were coming home to roost and it looked as though our name was pants. The old bucks, squaws and kids were whooping it up with war whoops and shrill cries welcoming them back. By the time Beaver Tom rode back, they were up to us, and giving us anything but friendly looks. While they were holding their powwow, Beaver Tom was blaming this all on me. He said that if we had pulled out when he wanted, we would have got a start on them, and could have gotten away from them. I told him so would the dog have caught the rabbit if he did not stop. I hoped we had some new friends who would help us out.

But he said, "You are welcome to all the consideration that you will get from this lousy bunch of old bucks and squaws now that the bucks are back. It is good-bye to all our outfit and we will be lucky if we don't lose our hair with it too." We were not given any more time to grieve, for the main bunch was coming along the trail in a cloud of dust. We were soon surrounded by a bunch of yelling devils. They were expressing in savage war whoops their joy that they meet again. Some of the bucks crowded their horses around us in a threatening way; I thought that the fandango was due to start.

The old warrior White Grass and some of the squaws came up and told them to leave us alone. There was quite a powwow over us. In the end they did nothing to us. The old warrior told us that it was all right; they wanted to swap

horses. He said we should not make the warriors mad, and
it would come out all right. What could we do? We had no
choice. They started off with us.

It was not long until they pitched camp. We piled our
stuff in a pile and let our horses go with theirs. We could see
that they had gotten quite a bunch of horses from their raid
on the Crows. They also had eight or nine young Crow
squaws that they picked up in the raid. The Crows did not
seem any too sorry. They knew that they would be traded
back soon to their people for the Blackfeet women the
Crows had.

White Grass, who had been a war chief before he got too
old, said there were also nineteen Piegan warriors in the
bunch. They had been picked up after the Crows gave them
the run. They were in bad humor, and it was a good thing
for us that we had the Blackfeet for our friends. He and
some of the old people would see to it that the warriors did
us no harm. He then went off and left us, giving us a little
time to do some thinking and talking. We realized that we
were in bad shape, but as long as they did not start any trouble we would meet them halfway. It would be useless to try
to stand them off. If trouble started, they were not going to
rob and do us in without some of them getting hurt. If they
should get at our keg of whiskey in the packs, which Beaver
Tom had left alone since his last close call, it would be all up
with us. I told Beaver Tom that maybe it would come out the
way the old warrior White Grass said, and they might not
harm us or find that keg of whiskey.

Beaver Tom, with a sigh that came from his heart, said, "I
say 'amen' to that, although I have poor hopes of getting
away so easily from this bunch."

The squaws finished fixing up the camp and the warriors
were through blowing about their great deeds on the raid.
They began to come around us in small bunches; they wanted
to know if we had any whiskey. We lied to them like a preacher,
telling them "no," that we did not swap whiskey. They wanted
to see what we had in the packs to swap for the horses and buf-

falo robes they had stolen on the raid. Beaver Tom told them that we were sorry, but we had all the horses we needed. We could not swap for buffalo robes because we did not yet know where we were going and we had no place to put them. This made them mad. More and more of them started coming around us. Again they wanted us to swap for horses, but we told them as before that we did not want any horses, besides they were stolen and the soldiers and Crows would take them away from us and put us in the skookum house.

They said, "You can come with us. We will trade with you this winter and no soldier or Crow will bother you."

We told them we could not do that—we had to meet some friends who were waiting for us. They got mad in the right style. It was no fun. We stood surrounded on all sides by this crowd of naked and painted devils in their war bonnets. At any minute they might have turned loose on us. Then some of the old men of the camp came and gave them a good talking to, and they let up on us.

I had a forty-four Winchester carbine which I carried on my saddle. A young warrior saw it and wanted to trade for it, but I would not give it to him to look at. It was loaded and all ready for action. He got mad as the devil and offered me five horses for the gun and belt of cartridges. I told him "no." Then he offered me ten head of horses. I told Beaver Tom to tell him that I could not trade it; I had to keep it for myself. Besides the horses were stolen and would not be mine. Off he went as mad as hell.

I thought I was through with him for good, but I soon found out that there is a calm before a storm. He came back again pulling along with him one of the youngest of the Crow squaws. With a triumphant yell, he told Beaver Tom to tell me he would give me the ten horses and the Crow squaw for my rifle, and no questions asked. Before Beaver Tom could stop me, I shook my head "no" and hugged my rifle to let him see I loved my gun better than the horses and the young squaw. At this the young buck went up in the air in right style. He tried to knife me, but one of the bucks caught his arm and held it. This was not all the trouble that act brought on my head. The young Crow divinity started in wailing and raising hell with me. It showed just what a woman is when you try to do her a good turn.

Beaver Tom said, "After this—if we pull out alive—you are not to be hasty and should leave this kind of diplomatic business to me. You have committed a terrible breach in Injun etiquette by insulting the young buck and worse still you have cast a slur on the worth and beauty of this dusky goddess."

She was telling me with her best signs and the Crow language what she thought of me for saying her beauty and loveliness plus ten head of horses were not worth my rifle. Besides, the young buck was liable to beat her up as the cause of his failure to get the gun.

I never knew how it happened. I must have turned my head away and not been watching as I should have. The first thing I knew, this young buck sprang at me and wrenched the carbine out of my hands and gave me a push that sent me sprawling backward over our packs. With a satanic shout of glee the crowd of warriors pushed the young squaw over on top of me in no gentle manner. Before I could get that dusky charmer off of me, the young buck went off with the admiring crowd and my carbine. He left me in undisputed possession of the young Crow squaw, who was using me for a camp stool and playing monarch of all she surveys. I soon wiggled out from under her. I was mad as they make them, and breathing maledictions against all Injuns. Then, to make matters worse, Beaver Tom, although we were in a dangerous position, could not resist the temptation to give me the horse laugh. He said, "It could have come out much worse. You might as well keep her today as some other one tomorrow, for it is bound to come in the end. Because you are such a good little Friar Tuck you might as well have the game as the name."

The young Crow squaw did not try to go off. She proudly sat down on a pack. I did not understand the Crow language much, but in this kind of business one did not need to understand any language because there was the good, old and reliable language of the soulful eye, which every man and woman can talk and understand without any interpreters to spoil the works. Although we said nothing to each other, her lovely, soulful eyes said in a very short time that she had forgiven me for insulting her, and that, as far as she was concerned, she hoped it was a trade. She was ready to start keeping house without any honeymoon. I could not help but notice that she was good looking, and not over seventeen or eighteen years old.

There is no use in denying that in the couple of days I had been running around with those Injuns and squaws, they had raised the dickens with me. I had got used to them and kind of liked their ways. If it were not for thinking about the bucks coming back, life would have been fine and dandy there.

I had been watching several young squaws in the camp on the sly. Beaver Tom had been throwing it at me. He said that I had developed a serious case of squaw fever. He did not have a thermometer, but from past experiences he swore my temperature went up to one hundred and five degrees. When it got that high, the case was hopeless unless the victim got a squaw to nurse him out of it. Then he would like it so well that he would hate to part with her, and to please her, he would begin learning her Injun language. About the only way you could learn the grunts and twists that go with most Indian talk is from a sleeping dictionary.

I watched the little wild Crow squaw sit there. She had always been with her own tribe. Even there she had never been treated much better than a dog, and probably not as well as some white ladies' dogs. She was valued by her own people like a brute to be traded to the highest bidder for horses or whatever took their fancy. Her master would be someone for whom she would have to get the wood and keep the fires burning, tan buffalo robes, pack water and do every kind of drudgery. Most of the time instead of getting a smile from her lazy lord and master lying by the fire she would get a good beating. The Indian buck was a firm believer in the more he beat his squaw the better she would be. To make matters worse those red devils in camp had pounced on her and other Crow squaws in their camp like a hen hawk and stole them off. She was, before he snatched my gun away, the property of that enterprising young buck.

My meditations were interrupted by several shots. I could see that a bunch of bucks were trying out my carbine. It held only ten shots and it was not long until I knew it was empty. The Indians did not have any cartridges to fit it. I had made up my mind that those Injuns were not going to do anything to us, or they would have cleaned us up before this. Squaw or no squaw, I was not going to let that lousy Siwash snatch a gun out of my hands and get away with it. I started off, but Beaver Tom called me back and wanted to know where I was going. I told him, "To get my gun."

He said, "Holy Gawd, kid, don't be foolish. Let well enough alone, and don't get us killed over that lousy gun. Everything is coming all right. Take the horses and the squaw, even if they are stolen. Don't let a little thing like that bother you. No one will take the horses away from you where we are going, and any fool can see the squaw is willing to call it a go with you. She knows that she will be far better off with you than with the Blackfoot devils."

I said, "I thought you said you savvied Injuns. You know that if I let that young buck do that, every Injun in camp will come and take anything he wants, thinking that we are easy. Those Injuns don't intend to do us any harm so I am going to get my gun or get a licking."

I started off for the bunch of bucks, leaving Beaver Tom and the squaw in camp. I went to the young buck who still had my gun in his hands. By signs I told him I wanted my gun, but he only grinned at me and pointed to the squaw. With his fingers he told me he would give me the horses in the morning when they drove in the band. Then he wanted me to give him my belt and cartridges.

I knew better than to try to take the gun away from him and get smashed with it on the head. I made signs that I wanted the gun, or it was to be a fight; but he did not want to understand it that way. The others did understand. The war chief of the raid went up to him and took the gun away from him. He pulled his hunting knife out of the sheath and pushed the brave up to me. I wanted a fight or my gun and it looked as though I was going to get a fight. Get it I did, for the warriors began ki-yi-ing at him.

He came at me like a wounded buffalo bull, and, before I could bolster up my cowardly disposition, we were clinched in a deadly embrace. I wore a buckskin shirt, and while it saved my hide, it gave him a good hold of me. I found myself in a bear hug that was making my ribs crack. He was doing his best to trip me and lift me off the ground. Then he would come down on me like a ton of brick. He had nothing on but his breech-clout, and he was as slippery as soft soap. I tried to gouge a hole in his side with my sharp fingernails for a handhold. For all the good it did me, I might as well have tried to get a hold of a frozen quarter of beef. That was my first work of that kind. I never thought that fighting was such hard work, for, as I said, I was a woolly Texan and despised work more than an Injun. I felt kind of sorry that I did not stay in camp and let well enough alone as Beaver Tom had wanted me to do. I could have talked to the little squaw in the language of the soulful eye and found out if she believed in alimony.

That buck Injun was keeping me so busy that I soon forgot about the little squaw and all my other regrets. As the sun was still on the job, I was soon sweating like a Brewery Dutchman. There were no rules or time set. It was every man for himself, time being no object. I now realized, when it was too late, that as a wrestler the honors and the gun were going to go to the Injun. So far, I had not fazed him. I had only scratched the Stars and Stripes on his back, and got him bleeding like a stuck hog. When I managed to get one of my arms free I quit wrestling, and proudly entered the arena of

pugilism by landing several underhand swings in his bread
basket below the belt. They did not bring the results I had
hoped for, but still I had the consolation of hearing him
grunt every time I hit him. Next he had his hand wound up
in my long hair and had taken a bulldog grip with his teeth
on my other arm. He was chewing on it like a hungry dog
and at the same time pulling me so close to him I could
hardly move. I could thank my stars that I had on the buckskin shirt and that his mouth was only full of buckskin.

Just the same he was reaching deep enough to make me
want to yell with the pain. I saw that the hair business was the
right medicine so I had no trouble in reaching with the arm
he was chewing on and getting a couple of turns of the long
hair hanging down his back. I pulled his head back and could
just manage to smash him in the face with my other fist.

How long we would have kept at it that way I don't know,
nor who would have won the fight. I did know one thing, I
was more than glad when the warriors took a hand in the
game and pulled us apart. I had a suspicion that I was not a
safe bet for my friends in a fight. During our racket and the
endeavor to spoil each other's face to the best of our abilities, the warriors and squaws had crowded around us and
were as silent as the grave. They did not even hoot for their
own man. I thought some of his friends might take a hand
in it and rip me open with a knife. I soon began to think of
what the bunch would do if I should beat the buck—would
they take revenge on me? I knew that if I had been alone
fighting a white man under the same conditions, and had no
friends, I would have had my head kicked off before that.

The warriors and squaws stood around us. Whenever we
got close to them, they moved back and gave us all the room
we wanted. Although those same red devils of warriors
thought no more of committing murder than killing a fly and
were as treacherous to an enemy as anyone could be, they did
nothing against me. I had to give the devil his just dues.

I had good reason to be thankful to White Grass and the
old men who made the warriors pull us apart. The young

warrior had had no right to take my gun in the first place.
We stood glowering at one another in a kind of one-is-
afraid and the-other-dares-not way. The warriors held quite
a powwow, and then the war chief handed me my gun. I lost
no time in getting back to camp. Even if I did not lick the
buck, I had my gun, and the squaw was still in my camp. I
was tired, my arm was chewed up some and a lot of my hair
was pulled out; otherwise I was not much hurt. The little
squaw was down in the mouth as she noticed the gun in my
hands. She knew that the deal must be off, and it was back
to the Blackfeet with her.

Then Beaver Tom took up her cause and said, "You surely
ain't going to turn down this nice young squaw for a gun,
are you? Trade him one of the needle guns you have in the
packs. She has been telling me that she doesn't want to go
back and get abused by that Injun. She wants to go with you.
She says that she will be a good woman to you. We are liable
to run into some missionary preacher and you can marry
her if you want. I really do feel sorry for her."

But I said, "Why don't you hook up to her yourself, if you
are so stuck on her?"

He said, "I would, but I know that I am a bad one. But,
bad as I am, I ain't mean enough to take her, knowing only
too well that I would abuse her. Besides, I have only my buffalo gun to trade. It is up to you to take her."

"I am sorry for her too," I told him, "but I ain't going to
take her and that settles it. I ain't gone so far yet as to go to
hell for a woman!"

I was not too good to join in this business, and wanted to
take her bad enough. Just the plain fear that I would go to
hell if I did take her without marrying her kept me from her.
Though I was kind of tough and had lost some of the
respect for God that my people had pounded in me with a
club, I had not been able to get the belief in hell out of me.
This belief called for a special process and was put on me
with a branding iron by my people and the padres. It still
stuck to me, so well did they do their job. After all these

many years I have still a kind of regard and fear for hell. Why should I not? It has kept a man like me, who was never any too good, from listening to them who said there is no God or hell, and that Jesus was a fraud, and that there was no hereafter, to hell with the laws of God and man, we take what we want, the easier it comes the better, and some of them would boast they had broken every one of the Ten Commandments several times and wished to hell they would make some more so they could break them too. Some of those men were my friends. Most of them, bad as they were, were good to me, and never done me a wrong. But I saw them shoot each other dead for almost nothing, saw some of them left hanging on trees dead and riddled with bullets, others of them lying shot full of holes by some sheriff's posse. Anyway, they all went in a short time the way en route they had sent some other poor devil. If I had not had this fear of hell there is no doubt that I would be with the bunch long ago and would now be holding up stages in heaven or some other hotter place today.

White Grass, the war chief and some warriors put up quite a powwow with us. They tried to get me to give the gun to the young buck for the squaw and horses. They said that he was giving me the best of the bargain and more than the gun was worth. I was a better diplomat or liar than they thought I was. I told Beaver Tom to keep his mouth shut about the guns I had in the packs. Then I told him to tell them that I had to keep my gun because it was so short and light. I had to have it to carry on the saddle. I did not want a woman yet, but I soon hoped to. She would not be a Crow woman, but a beautiful Blackfoot woman, as they were the prettiest and best among all the squaws. This pleased them and they were glad to hear it. They said that now I should do as they wanted, and should come with them and trade with them—that if I took one of their women, all Blackfeet would be my friends.

I soon saw that I had better get this squaw talk done, or, the first thing I knew, I would have my foot in it in the right style. The war chief was beginning to wax eloquent on the virtues and beauty of a young sister in his lodge. (This must have been good news to Beaver Tom, because this same angel was the young squaw who ripped his arm open with her hunting knife.) He was looking with loving eyes at our packs and at my carbine. It was a good thing that some other warriors came and wanted to trade for horses and buffalo robes. Too bad the La Brie bunch missed this outfit, for it was surely hungry for whiskey. We told them we might meet them later that fall and go with them when the buffalo got good, when it was colder. After wrangling among themselves the Indians took this philosophy and said it was all right.

During this time the young Crow squaw stayed with us. Soon the young buck and some of his friends came up. He said something to her. She did not say anything to him or start to go, so they held another powwow. The war chief asked Beaver Tom if I intended to keep her and not give her back. I felt sorry for her. It was a pitiful sight to see her among all those devils, but what else could I have said? I told them that she was his woman and to take her if he wanted her. I had a nice large silk handkerchief which I sometimes wore around my neck. I got this and gave it to her as an offering to show her I was sorry for her. I put it on her neck. Bad and tough as I was, I really believe if there had been a preacher of some kind in camp, I would have married her. Probably, as Beaver Tom said, I might get a worse one the next day.

The young buck told her again to get back to his lodge, but she had her Injun up and didn't budge. He tried to grab a hold of her, but she fought him like a wild cat and clawed him. In the end one of his friends came and helped him. Each one got a hold by the arm and pulled and half drug her off. When they got away, he took the handkerchief I gave her and tied it on his own neck, so my well-meant gift did neither her nor me any good. Then he gave her several kicks that sent her sprawling. The poor thing got up and walked off to his tepee to a life of hell, unless her people would buy her back or she could run away.

While this was going on, Beaver Tom and I just stood there and cussed that buck to ourselves. I got square with that buck although it did the Crow squaw no good. I told the war chief that if he wanted the handkerchief it was his for good, so he went and took it away from the brave. I supposed the squaw would get another licking for that.

We packed up and were ready to pull out. It was wonderful. We could hardly believe it, but it was so. The squaws were pulling down the tepees. The Blackfoot camp was soon ready to pull out. Several of the warriors and women bid us good-bye when we left them. White Grass and Two Dogs, another old warrior, rode along with us as, they said, there was no telling what the Piegans might do. Maybe they thought the same of their own warriors. Anyway, it was not long until we came to the forks of the trail at the same place where we tried to leave them the day before. We followed the trail and the two Indians kept with us for some time. When they said they would have to turn back I gave each of them a good woolen blanket and some tobacco. The presents were not much, for there was no doubt if it were not for those two and some more of the old warriors we would not be here on earth today. It was only them who kept that cutthroat bunch from murdering us.

So White Grass and Two Dogs rode off and Beaver Tom and I were alone again. I ought to have been thankful for us getting away with our stuff and our lives, but I felt lonesome as we trailed along. I thought if I had the fellow who invented hell it would go hard with him, for it was as Beaver Tom said—the mischief had been done. My mouth was watering and I was hankering to go back to the Injun camp and take some of the higher degrees in the soulful eye from those wild and woolly nymphs of the plains. No matter what they might be lacking, they were adept at that and slick as greased ice.

If I came back alive, I was going to write to our Church on the Rio Grande to see that a thirty-day clause was put in the rules of the Church to give enterprising proselytes a chance to try out the companionate marriage business. Then if it wasn't worth going to hell for, we could pull out in time and not have to go there to find it out. If it were not for this, I could have taken the little squaw along to sympathize with me in my tender years.

We left the trail because we wanted to get away from it and took to the foothills in an easterly direction. We traveled that way up and down until we camped for the night. We stopped early so we could turn out the horses to feed because we were going to tie them up that night, just in case the Blackfeet or Piegans came to run them off. That way they would not find it so easy. Beaver Tom's arm was hurting him where the squaw slashed him with her knife. He was as cranky as a sore-footed bear and snapped at anything I said. I said that some Injuns were not as bad as painted if the right thing was done by them. He would only believe evil of them and said it was still not too late for that bunch to clean up on us. It would be just like an Injun if they did.

Nothing happened that night and we pulled out early in the morning and crossed several little creeks along the foothills. We traveled until early in the afternoon when Beaver Tom said that we were in the good beaver country. We decided to camp for a day or so; it was an out-of-the way place at that time of the year. We looked the place over for two days to see if anyone had cleaned it out. It was a good all-around country to trap and hunt, being just lousy with beaver. There were good signs of mink along the creeks, and also wolf, coyote and some bear. At that time there were plenty of deer and elk and soon there would be buffalo.

Beaver Tom said there would be more Injuns around that fall and winter than I would want in order to get rid of my stuff. He was willing to stay there that night, but in the morning he changed his mind and said we should pull out and go over to the Judith Gap country. Maybe even go on into the Judith Basin to see if we could find anything better, although we would be liable to have plenty of trouble with the Indians over there. At first he wanted me to pick up everything and take it with us, but I told him that the stuff had gone as far as it was going. We would cache it and then go over there. I was not going to take any more chances on losing everything, or maybe having to pack that stuff all back again.

We had quite a racket and he said that he had a notion to pull out and leave me and what would I do if he left me? But I held the winning hand when I said, "Go after that Blackfoot bunch and get some of them to help me out of here. They cannot be half as dirty or rotten as you."

He had to pull in his horns. It took us nearly all day to pack our stuff into a ravine where we cached it. The next morning we started with two light pack loads and the rest of the horses empty, with just their rigging on. Early in the afternoon we crossed the Musselshell and camped early. We had not been in camp long when three white men rode into our camp. They were traveling with just one pack horse. Two of them were old-time trappers and hunters named Hubbel and Kennedy. I had seen them sometimes in Bozeman. I guess no one knew the name of the third man, but he was known far and near as Lonesome Joe. He poked around, generally alone, and was more of a prospector than a trapper or hunter. He was only traveling with the other two until they came to Fort Ellis. Hubbel and Kennedy were working for the Government as guides and scouts. They were carrying some kind of dispatch from Carrol on the Missouri River.

They were the first white men we had seen for some time and we coaxed them to camp that night with us. But they were in a hurry and wanted to push on until dark. When I got the chance, I told them of my troubles with Beaver Tom and I said that I would go back if they would help me. They said that they were in a hurry and could not go out of their way to where my stuff was. They told me to stay with my stuff and to keep a stiff upper lip. They said, if Beaver Tom got gay, I should show him where to get off, and in the end it might come out all right, as there was no telling how a fool's luck might turn out.

Early the next morning they left us and we pulled out for the Judith Gap country. We did not want to meet any Injuns, but our old luck was once more with us. It seemed that every kind of Injun in the country had turned out to meet us and wish us god speed on our way. We met bunch after bunch of them. The Injun holds the record as a liar, but the white men were no slouches at it either. Beaver Tom was busy lying to them in sign language. His arms and fingers got tired asking the Indians about the band of soldiers we were going to meet. Having all the empty pack horses, they believed us and just gave us the bad eye.

We finally arrived in the Judith Gap country. There we found the camp of two French squaw men, named Bulleau and La Rue. They were old-time squaw men of the days of the American Fur Company; at their best they were a tough bunch. There were many Indian relations camped with them—enough to entitle them to a reservation of their own. Both of those bewhiskered gents had served their country in a patriotic way, to the best of their ability. This being a healthy country, they had succeeded beyond their wildest dreams. Bulleau had a regalia of three squaws. La Rue had two squaws, but as he was some younger than Bulleau, there was still time for him to reach the high-water mark. From the number of all sizes of half-breeds that came hobbling out of their tepees, it looked like a prairie dog convention. They sure to God had gone the limit, and could not be accused of practicing race suicide.

Both of them had received us with open arms and Western hospitality, until they found out that we did not have a jug of whiskey or rum with us. Then their ardor cooled several degrees. After we set up our camp and they found out we were looking for a place to do some trapping and a little trading with the Indians on the side, they threw several buckets of icy water on our ardor.

They asked us if we were going to be Sam Pepin* men and trap and trade for him in the Judith Basin country. The genial Sam claimed the whole country—its prairies, hills, creeks and rivers, and all the buffalo, game and fur in it—by the divine right of God and the rifle. I christened Bulleau, Three Squaws, to myself on the quiet, and La Rue, Standing Bear, because his mug would pass for a bear anywhere.

He stood there with several cockleburs in his hair and wanted to know how it is that a man like him who had come to this country long ago and to get here had to pull and haul a keel boat and walk the whole way on the bottom of the turbulent Missouri River with the waters up to his head from St. Louis to Fort Benton and after that had given the rest of his life and energy to populate Montana's dreary wastes, and made the deserts bloom with seething life, and now in his old age have to live to see us *interlopers* from the Yellowstone country come in and deprive him and his friend of their just

* Probably the name of a local whiskey trader.

rights, when it took two buffalo a day to feed his family, not counting his wives' relations. No, *Sacré*, Three Squaws and his lifelong friend Standing Bear were not going to stand for it and sit meekly by and let us drive him out of the country and onto the howling prairies to wander away to die, when he had 280 aboriginal relatives who would be only too willing to lift our hair and dance on our graves if he told them to.

Then, with the combined dignity of Julius Caesar and Sitting Bull, Three Squaws and Standing Bear pulled their resplendent greasy buckskin shirts about them and departed from us in righteous indignation to enter their none too sacred harems, leaving Beaver Tom and I to chew and meditate on this.

We had to get ourselves something to eat. While we were eating, none of their Injun relatives came over to help us eat, which showed it to be a serious case. When an Injun willingly misses the chance to eat on someone for nothing, look out, for hell is soon going to pop. As we were eating, I could see that Beaver Tom was in profound meditation, for he had his ears laid back and was as solemn as a jack rabbit running on three legs and coaxing you to chase him. Then he said that it was a serious affair and there was no telling what that bunch might do. "It would require a diplomatic liar of no mean ability, like myself, to handle this affair. I had better go over to Three Squaws's buffalo-hide mansion and pour some oil on the troubled waters."

But I said, "I am not disputing your word about being a diplomatic liar of great achievements, still I think this kind of business should be left to me. My religious tendencies and piety would soon dispel the evil in their hearts, for one look into my innocent eyes can always drive away the anger and bring a smile to the lips of the fiercest squaw."

Beaver Tom said he had seen some of my diplomatic work in the Injun camp and it was B.S. stuff. He said I ought to feel proud of my record as the chump who shied away from the little Crow squaw who was as beautiful as Cleopatra's legs. Then he grabbed the oil can of peace and went off in disgust to Three Squaws's tepee, leaving me to watch the camp. I came to the conclusion that while I may have been a chump all right, as Beaver Tom said, there was one consolation—that only a damn fool would buy a cow when milk was so cheap. I said my prayers, rolled up and went to sleep. I had had nothing but doubts that night about Beaver Tom's diplomatic ability and kind of expected to wake up dead. It was way into the night when Beaver Tom got back to camp. He was praising Three Squaws and Company and was running around like a circus-day kid.

When I asked him the cause of all his hilarity and why we were not dead, he said that his soothing voice had done it all. He had quickly calmed the fierce raging waters of hate without having to use oil. It was no time that night until he had had the squaw men under his magnetic influence. It was all right. Once more we were under the beaming smiles of Three Squaws and Standing Bear stronger than ever.

We had to feel proud and honored to be allowed to associate with those blue-blood breechclout aristocrats of Judith Gap. It was not every day a fellow got the chance to mingle and rub elbows with the Great Muck-a-muck Bulleau. He was the boss squaw man between Forts Lincoln and Benton. Tom had gotten an invite over to Three Squaws's tepee, where they were going to hold a great powwow. All the warriors would be there of Three Squaws's and Standing Bear's wives' relations. They were going to hold a buffalo barbecue with him the guest of honor.

I said, "I suppose I am in this too?" But Tom said, "Well, I guess not. You stay and watch the camp. I had enough of the trouble you started in the Injun camp over that gun. I told the bunch all about the nice trick that young buck played on you and about the Crow squaw and we had a great time over it. Bulleau said that they were going to send the young squaws and breeds over to play with you this afternoon, so they won't be in the way when us warriors are eating at the feast. But I told them you might take to the hills and get lost if they did. A nice little breed said that you will never see the hills if she can get her arms around your neck once."

I said, "You mind your own business about what happened to me, and to hell with you and the Three Squaws bunch. They are only going to feed you on fly-blowed buffalo meat anyway, as that is all they have got. I supposed you told them of the squaw ripping your arm open with her knife?"

He said, "That squaw did not mean it; she was only playing and the knife slipped in her hand."

I told him I wished to hell she had slipped the knife in his belly. He asked me what the use was of feeling sore and jealous of him. Maybe he had saved my life the night before. Just because he was one of the Lord's chosen and was invited to the feast why couldn't I take a joke? I was to do like he did. What Rome did, he did. He added that he had better get his whiskers trimmed.

"All right, my hunting knife is as sharp as a razor. Shall I trim them for you?" He said that was the first thing I was not going to do. Maybe I would cut his throat besides. He had had enough of my last job of that kind. Every time he went near water or got down on his knees to drink in the creeks and could see his face in the water he said he looked like a Scotch terrier. He could hardly keep from barking at his shadow in the water. No, he was going to go over to Bulleau's, and one of his lady squaws was going to go at them with a scissors.

"I told Le-oh-hee last night to come over and get a little flour," Beaver Tom said. "Don't you be stingy like you always are. Let her have it as she wants to make some Rah Goo for the feast. What it is or tastes like I'll be damned if I know. It is made of chopped-up buffalo meat and cooked with flour."

I said, "Who in hell is Le-oh-hee anyway?" Tom said she was the sweetest flower that ever grew—Bulleau's daughter. I was not to get too inquisitive all at once. "Do you think that I am chump enough to swallow this: that a young woman will have anything to do with you, old granddad, even if she is a breed? If she did, she is only trying to pull your leg."

He said, "You need not get so sarcastic about my old age. I want to tell you I am a swift worker, I am, when I start in on the fair sex. I just keep them going and coming. Breeds are my specialty, but I am generous and will leave the squaws to you. If you stay around them you will find out that they can teach you a whole lot."

"I thought you said in the Blackfoot camp that you were too rotten to take up with even a squaw."

Tom replied, "I did not say that. If I did, I have reformed since then."

So I said, "When do we pull out of here? This is as far as I am going. I will go back to the cache, Injuns or no Injuns, tomorrow morning. If you have nothing to do but fool around Three Squaws's and Standing Bear's Injun chippies, I have."

Then Tom said, "Say, do you know I have been thinking it would not be a bad thing for us to go back to the cache and get the stuff and go partners with Bulleau and La Rue. We could give the fur and buffalo a whirl this fall and winter. What do you say?"

"Not on your life! You had better forget about it or there is going to be trouble." He said I made him sick and he started for Three Squaws's incubator, leaving me alone in the camp to curse Beaver Tom and the day I ever listened to him.

I was not left alone long. The first thing I knew, a vision of Injun loveliness in buckskin and fringe glided up to me. I had not seen her yet, but I knew that this was Le-oh-hee, who had turned over Beaver Tom's cracked nut. No wonder she did, for she was a whole country by herself, young and pretty, maybe twenty years old. I thought this must be some Injun saint, for Le-oh-hee, with all her beauty, was no breed, but one of the prettiest squaws I had ever seen. They might have called her a breed and Bulleau's daughter, but there

must have been something radically wrong with the con-
junction of the moon and the stars, for I surely knew a
squaw when I saw one.

Anyway, she was all the better being a squaw, but she
could not speak English. She could talk Piegan and a kind of
Injun French that came from the Hudson Bay men. The
only way this could be understood was to get a French and
Indian interpreter to help you out. I understood none of the
above and only some of the sign language. She said in
French that she wanted some flour. I knew from Beaver Tom
what she wanted, but I did not intend to understand her for
a while anyway. She would only go back and spread her
smiles over that worthless scamp Beaver Tom, who was old
enough to be her grandfather.

No, I would save the fair squaw from that villain, even if
I had to take to the hills with her myself. But how was I
going to get the fires of love started when I couldn't talk to
her? The answer was the language of the soulful eye, which
was made by Adam and Eve. She soon gleamed back with a
heavenly smile—don't be afraid, I ain't going to eat you and
am one of the boys, myself. It was wonderful the way she
could express herself in this mysterious and soul-stirring
language.

Who should then come to the camp but Standing Bear
La Rue. He was all smiles and in the best of humor. I said she
wanted something, but I could not understand what she
wanted. He said she wanted a little flour to make some Rah
Goo, so I gave it to her and with a shy smile she went to
Bulleau's tepee. Then Standing Bear said Le-oh-hee was one
damn fine girl. What did I think, wouldn't Le-oh-hee be one
damn good woman? *Sacré!*

And he said, "Beaver Tom he is one great man for kill the
buff. I heard for long time about him, but no see him till
now. He says he has got another new buff gun and plenty of
needle guns and ammunition, powder and lead, much traps,
blankets and tobacco and much kinds of stuff to swap to
Injuns this fall and winter, cached across the Musselshell

River. Beaver Tom, she says he and you come and stay with Bulleau and La Rue and we will be partners this fall and winter. We will shoot the buff, trap the beaver and wolf. Beaver Tom says he will bring plenty stuff here to trade to Injuns for robes and furs. Bulleau and me now plenty glad, for we are too old and no more can me and my partner Bulleau do like we did long ago when we came out here for the Hudson Bay Company. We were young men and poled and paddled the canoes. We made the long portages between Fort William and Fort Gary and were so tired we just laid down on the wet ground and sleep all night in the rain.

"Yes, Sacré Bliew Batice La Rue his head is now as white as snow and now no more will we follow the fire brigades for the Hudson Bay Company over the prairies and mountains covered with snow and up and down roaring rivers of swift currents and foam over and through the Muskegs of the Athabasc and on to the McKenzie River far away through blizzards, rain and snows and drive the dog teams through the gates of blinding snow with no mark to show the way, through boundless plains of nothing but snow to some trading post hundreds of miles away. Yes, Batice she is old and soon must go and maybe it is better so, for now the American Fur Company is no more and the steamboat now hauls the load we used to pull and pole the batteau and keelboats up the swift and treacherous currents of the Missouri from St. Joe to Benton and then trap the beaver and all kinds of furs on all the streams to the mouth of the Columbia River and fight with Indians every day. For all this work what have I got today, nothing but a bunch of half-breeds and my boys are worse than the Injuns. Yes, Batice is gray but they are all away on the go like the buffalo bull trying to call some squaw in their wallow and none now but the girls and women work, for the boys are too lazy to even hunt, but now it will be good again, for Beaver Tom will come and kill plenty buff with the big guns and then the women can tan plenty robes when you and I trap the beaver and catch the wolf." Then he got up and went off to his tepee.

I knew then how Beaver Tom pulled his lion-taming stunt on them. He told them that all my stuff was his when he had nothing. Then it was getting time for the feast and I could see the squaws around two large fires outside of Three Squaws's large tepee. The smell of broiling buffalo meat came over to me on the breeze and the warrior relations of Three Squaws's and Standing Bear's wives were strutting around in war bonnets, war paint and in breechclouts and gaudy colored blankets. Inside the tepee were Three Squaws Bulleau and some more of the higher ups with the redoubtable Beaver Tom as Medicine Man of this notable gathering of damn rascals and liars. They had left me, a great warrior like Horatio, out in the cold; and I swore revenge. Oh, yes, he would pay and retribution would overtake that vibrating and oscillating liar, Beaver Tom, who could put the liars of *The Arabian Nights* in the shade, together with Three Squaws Bulleau and Standing Bear La Rue.

The great feast at Three Squaws's tepee was on. If Bulleau was as good in keeping in his head that he would send over the young squaws and breeds to play with me, as he was with everything else, he would surely be a soul of honor and a credit to our glorious Territory of Montana. He must have had a very generous disposition, for he did not send only one, but enough lithesome copper-colored damsels and roly-poly half-breeds to satisfy the vanity of even a hog. I was resigned to my fate. I couldn't be a great warrior and wear a breechclout, instead of pants, to show off my manly form. I was not allowed to sit with great warriors like Three Squaws and Standing Bear and the vivacious Sodomite, Beaver Tom. They and their Siwash friends could eat half-raw, fly-blowed buffalo meat and lie to beat the band. Well then, I would follow Beaver Tom's advice for once. What Rome did, I did.

I bid them enter and received them with open arms. They did not come like a flock of sage hens all in a crowd. They bobbed up and squatted down around the fire like they had been there all their life. How they got there I'd be damned if I knew. Some seemed to glide out of the bushes, others out of the grass and I would not want to swear that some of them did not come out of the ground at my feet. Every one there was an artist in her own line. At first I was disappointed, but with a sigh of joy I counted them—my lucky number, thirteen, also the devil's number. All of them were young; how old they were I do not know. Every one in the whole bunch was old enough to sue a fellow for alimony and fair enough, on the brunette side, to bring tears to the eyes of a hardhearted jury. Most of them were dressed in squaw's buckskin dresses with fringes all over them and wore leggins, though a few had them made out of calico— all of them were worn up to the knee and seemed to say we are short on material at home. They looked at me as if I were a curiosity; they had never seen a white man as young as I was, though they had seen white men many times. All of them had a sainted and modest look and stare in their awk-ward inscrutable eyes. Their saintly looks did not fool me any more, as this was about the cheapest look they could wear and cost them less than it did to smile. I knew that every one of them was plenty sly. This was the first time in my youthful innocence that I had run up against the breeds, but I had to say that Bulleau and La Rue had sent over a very creditable display. It was with admiration that I admitted that both of those indefatigable gentlemen were worthy of their hire. Handicapped as they were without any of the modern appliances of civilization and considering the rough material they had to work on, they certainly did pro-duce some fine works of art, and when using the good old scenery of Montana for a background, their work was sim-ply superb. Two of them had blue eyes, and if it was not for their copper tinge, they were as beautiful young women as you could find in any man's country, even if they did not know what a table knife or fork was. All of them squatted around the fire, all of them fiery little savages, and wild and graceful as a bounding doe, and their Indian dress could not help but show the beautiful work of wild exuberant nature, their beautiful and perfect forms and lines of true beauty. Here was the work of the master hand all around, not a blemish, not a flaw. Here was Nature's greatest treasure, unpampered health, even to their beautiful and expressive eyes that centuries of abuse and drudgery under the cruel brutality of her master man, who has done his best to make a brute out of her, but has not been able to kill their expression of joy and gratitude or dim their luster. They had constitutions of iron that could stand out in raging blizzards without any more clothes on than the law allows (for the wild squaw was buried with the same suit of underwear she was born in) and skin buffaloes all day and not seem to feel any effects from the cold, while a white man all wrapped up was freezing to death. There were many hardships that made them as hard and tough as a rock and a picture of rugged health, a true daughter of the sun, living the way they did in the open. At this time the Indian and squaw out here had no disease of any kind and none of the diseases a white man was subject to, this was the wild squaw of them days fifty-two years ago and before the white man, with his low-down vices and unspeakable diseases and all other diseases that he is subject to, came to strike her down and lay low the magnificent work which Nature had taken centuries to build up.

As they squatted around the fire as solemn as owls it kept me guessing what they wanted. I knew they did not come over just to gaze on my beauty, but were sent over to pull some kind of deviltry. The Injun French they spoke was worse than Injun to understand, so we talked in sign and I soon learned what they wanted. They kept pointing to their mouths that they were hungry and wanted something to eat. But after some trouble I made them understand they would have to tell me something new, for whoever seen a buck Injun or squaw that was not hungry? This did not insult them any; they said they had heard that the white man's grub was heap good, and they wanted some bread as the most of them had never eaten any. I was foolish enough not to take into consideration the husky appetites of those copper-colored Junos.

I thought that if I couldn't leave camp and go over to
Three Squaws's festival, I would have one of my own, even if
the delegates are all squaws. I did know better than to cook
for this wild squaw delegation or do any squaw work, as they
would have despised me if I did any work like this. They had
been taught by their lordly masters that it was disgraceful
for a man or warrior to do any kind of work except hunt,
fish, gamble, steal and fight. Even when he did kill any kind
of game he just left it where it was and the squaw had to go
and get it with a pack horse and get it to camp the best way
she could. I let them understand that it was all right, but I
would not cook. This gave them just the chance they
wanted—to get their hands on my grub, so they told me
they were all *bon ton* chefs. (Some of them had not washed
their hands since the last time they fell in the creek, for the
wild squaw with all of her grace was a dirty cook and don't
get no recommend from me who has a truthful halo to
maintain.)

Then it was all rustle and bustle in camp. Some got wood
and it looked like business was booming. I started them off
on a large piece of sow belly that I had got in Bozeman
which had either come around the Horn or over the plains
several years before, and our packing it around with us in
the hot sun did not improve its flavor or aroma any—this I
gave to the boss cook to start in on and slice it up but she
just cut off a nice fat greasy slice and started in to sample it
raw, and it was no time til everyone had a slice and with
gusto were eating it raw and in vain did I try to tell them to
wait till it was cooked, but with withering scorn in their eyes
they gave me to understand they knew their business as this
was the proper way for an Indian maid to eat Chicago
chicken and it was no time till the whole chunk had disappeared and they stood around licking their greasy fingers
and ready for other worlds to conquer. So by this time I am
beginning to regret my kindness to them and that I did not
give them the run in the first place, for they now take me for
a long-lost brother and have lost their fear of me and are

trying to prowl through our stuff like a bunch of Barbary pirates, and we had a quart bottle filled with black-strap or nigger-heel molasses, which was as black as tar, which had started to work and get sour, when one of the divinities in some underhand way got hold of it and, without waiting to see if it was poison or not, pulled out the cork and took a good swig then smacked her lips. When the others seen this they wanted a treat too but this Queen of Sheba said, "No." When now they all start in on her to take the bottle away from her, and again my religious modesty was joyfully shocked by a free-for-all leg show that went the limit as they stumbled and fell over our packs, but anyway she managed to get the greater part of the bottle down, but still she held onto the bottle like grim death till what was left of it in the struggle went down to lubricate her husky breasts and I thought there is one squaw that will get what is coming to her. But I was doomed to disappointment, for though what she drank would have given a horse the St. Vitus Dance, it did not faze her in the least. Now I see that the way it is going they are going to eat me out of house and home and I am not going to get anything to eat with them for it is a feast for them and wind for me, so I get mad at them and tell them in the best signs I know to get to hell out of here. But this was the last thing they intended doing, for they all start in to give me the glad eye, which said come on let us kiss and make up, forgive and forget and start all over again, so they started in fixing up the fire and get ready for another round, and the breeds began to say in Injun French Du pan— Dopan (Bread), at the same time pointing to their mouth and I don't know now if it would have come out for I am beginning to get suspicious that in some mysterious way my family was increasing as there seemed more in it than at the start, so I started in to count my chickens over and what was my surprise to find that instead of thirteen there is now seventeen, four more that must have slipped in like spirits, including Le-oh-hee who was standing like a shadow behind me as I turned around, Le-oh-hee who was going to be Beaver Tom's cupbearer at the feast according to the latest reports—ah yes, I live again. The rushing waves of hellish joy go through me.

Now nothing is too good for the bunch and I dug up flour, coffee and other stuff and am going to learn them the civilized ways of the white man; no more are they going to stand for a straight buffalo diet. So I told them no more fooling and to get busy and I did not now have to tell them twice for they now seemed married to their job and, as the slab of sow belly has disappeared, a young squaw went over to one of the tepees and got a large chunk of buffalo meat. But they all don't know how to make frying-pan bread and it looks dark for them for a while when now the Peerless one said she heap savvied all the higher arts of breadmaking, so I gave her the flour and she started in while the others were getting ready the other stuff and it was only a few minutes till I knew Le-oh-hee as a delightful little liar, for while she has probably seen someone make bread that is all, for she is wallowing it around with the dough sticking to her hands, but I had forgotten to give her the baking powder so she made up a large batch of rubber dough of just flour and water and begins to hand to her apprentices pieces of dough to lie on the ashes till they got hard enough to stand up, so after they got this conglomeration all standing around the fire, Le-oh-hee rubs the dough that is left on her hands and now finds them cleaner than when she started in on the job. But here I almost came near losing Le-oh-hee, for an old squaw came over from the feast and wanted her to go back but she had a mind of her own and would not go back to be ogled by Beaver Tom when I could do it more polite and the way she liked it.

The other stuff did not require much skill, so the feast was soon ready even to coffee and I put the sugar in the pot and they boiled it with the coffee as I know better than to trust them with sugar that costs three pounds for a dollar, and squaw fashion they put everything before me to eat first and stood around so meek as angels, and they were soon gnawing the delightful grindstones Le-oh-hee made, every one seemed to be a coffee mill when they tried to chew it and when with pride in her eyes she gave me a generous chunk of this bread, love or no love, I knew better than to try to eat it for it was hard enough to cut glass and none but a cast-iron Injun stomach can get away with it. The way that bunch went at that grub they soon made it scarce and I could not help but think what would Solomon, that guy in the Bible who had a thousand wives all his own and nobody else's according to report, have done if he had a thousand wild squaw wives and a few breeds thrown in for luck, wise as he was he would have fallen down on the job when it came to feed them for they would have eaten everything up in the Jewish Nation of Palestine even to the leaves on the fig trees, and as they have cleaned up everything slick and clean and as I know Injun style is stay with it as long as there is any more in the house, so I turned them loose at another batch. Through the afternoon and into the night, we kept it up, as the warriors are still at it at Three Squaws's tepee and the beautiful eyes of Le-oh-hee gleam in the half darkness near the fire. The Squaw Kid learned much that day, fifty-two years ago. Finally the great powwow and the feast at Three Squaws's was over and I was now feeling kind of sad to have to pull out, but I stayed here too long now for my own good.

I was up at daylight. I rounded up the horses and drove them into camp where Beaver Tom had some grub ready. Then I started to saddle up, but Beaver Tom stood there with a look on his face that boded me no good.

He asked, "What are you going to do?" I said, "Get out of here as quick as hell will let me and go back to the cache. There has been enough fooling around here. You get a move on and pack up this camp!"

"I will tell you when I want to pull out," he said. "Now don't be foolish, for I think we had better go in with Bulleau and La Rue. They have a pull with the Injuns. We can make more this way even if we do have to trade for Sam Pepin. At the same time we can have some company and friends to

talk to. I am getting tired of living like a dog and ain't stuck
on going back to the other side of the Musselshell and putting in the fall and winter with just us two, dodging Injuns
all the time. I want to tell you I have already made the bargain with Bulleau and La Rue and what I say goes. Do you
hear my gentle voice?"

I said, "The hell you say. Kind of handy with other people's property, are you not? What right had you to lie to
them and say to them that my stuff, even to my buffalo gun
in the cache, was all yours? You know that by rights you have
nothing. Besides I have a debt to pay on some of it." He said
that he did not tell them that. "You lie, for La Rue told me
the whole works yesterday. The way I understood him was
that I had nothing and everything was yours. I am not even
in the deal, even if I wanted to be, for they think I have nothing and want no more deadheads. Sure to God they have
enough deadheads of their own."

He said, "You have got me wrong in this. I am getting sick
of you and your damn fooling with what don't concern you,
for it was your damn snake-in-the-grass, slippery tongue
which coaxed Le-oh-hee away from the feast yesterday. You
have been putting hell in her head against me right along. You
damn half-breed, American greaser, I ain't forgot that
drink you made me take with that ax when I was sick and
helpless."

I replied, "If that is all that is bothering you, I can tell you
this, you big whiskey soak: I made you take it sick and I can
make you take it sober. If you think because you are big and
strong that you can rub your dirt in one, and get away with
it, you have got it wrong. Listen to this, you big son of a
bitch, you are going back right now to help me get those
horses and outfit back to the cache. Then you can go where
you want. You'll go even if I have got to take you back dead,
for as sure as Jesus I will kill you like a dog and chop you up
in chunks, and put you on the *aparejo* to pack you out,
Injuns or no Injuns. I will do it now when I have you where
I want you, and have got the right chance!" I pulled my gun

on him and I suppose I was devil enough to have done it. I had had more than enough of that man and thought he had it coming.

But he threw up his hands and said, "Don't do it, kid, I know I got it coming." He made all kinds of promises to do the right thing by me. So by that time my mad was kind of over and I was sorry I had done it. The fear of him took hold of me, for I knew only too well that I had made a bad break and ought to have gone through with it, killing him after starting in to do so. Beaver Tom, although no good, was not a coward. If I took the drop off him and let him go and he took the notion into his head to lay his hands on his buffalo gun then it would go hard with me. For some time Beaver Tom stood as close to the hereafter as anyone could get and still come back.

I was not bad enough to commit murder, so in the end I said, "All right. See that you do it or something is going to happen. One or both of us are going to be sorry." Then I backed away from him and picked up his cartridge belt and hunting knife laying on the bed, saying, "I will keep these until we are better acquainted." I knew that his gun was empty and that those were all the cartridges he had with him. The rest of them and his reloading outfit were left at the cache and he did not have a six shooter.

We were camped near Three Squaws's and the others' tepees when the racket started. It was only a moment until their sharp eyes saw that something was wrong at our house, for a man doesn't stand holding a gun against the belly of another just for fun or practice. By the time I got through with Beaver Tom, Three Squaws and Standing Bear and several Injuns and squaws were standing around. Standing Bear La Rue wanted to know what right I had to want to kill their friend and partner, Beaver Tom. They knew him to be a good and square-shooting man. I must have had my gall to try to kill him. I could never get away with it when his friends were around. It was sure a lucky thing for me that I did not do it.

Beaver Tom whispered to me to say nothing and not to give him away to them. But I was still mad and said, "To hell with you. You ain't going to unload your dirt on me any longer." I up and told them the whole works, that except for his buffalo gun and the saddle horse he was riding, which a man in Bozeman had lent him, he had nothing. I had bought that stuff and owed some money on it yet. We were partners in the traps and some of the grub, but he had nothing to do with the trading goods.

Bulleau asked Beaver Tom if that was so and Beaver Tom said that was about the size of it. Then Bulleau said, "I don't see as this will make any difference, for you can come in with us just the same. It will be all the better with two buffalo guns. We will pay you out of what we get in robes or furs for our share of your stuff."

But I said, "I don't want anything to do with this. There will be too many in on this and nothing in the end for us all. I have got to make good because I promised Mr. Cooper in Bozeman that there would be no fooling. I am to do my best to pay him the balance. All I want is to get back to the cache. Beaver Tom must help me get the horses and other stuff back to the cache, then if he wants he can come back. He cannot take any of the stuff unless he pays his share, as he said he would."

Then Bulleau said that he asked no more than what was right and fair. No one could say that Joe Bulleau was not on the square. He didn't stand for any dirt. "If Beaver Tom wants to come back it will be all right with me, but first he will have to treat you white and do as you want. The quicker he does, the quicker Joe Bulleau will be his friend again. He will not have to lie to me the next time."

Our war was over and Beaver Tom and I shook hands in front of them, to forgive and forget and love one another until the end. Then they helped us in a friendly way to pack up and leave. They told us to be sure to come again any time we felt like it. We pulled out from their camp and started back to the cache. In the beginning I did not like them or their looks, but I took it all back. I had to admit that although they may have been rough and tough in their ways, still Bulleau and La Rue, with all their faults, were men who had ideas of honor and justice.

As I rode off Le-oh-hee stood there waiting to say good-bye to me. Her beautiful and mysterious eyes were somber. Le-oh-hee—that little squaw who was one of the most beautiful women I had ever seen.

PART TWO
Emporium on the Musselshell

We rode off on our way to the cache on the other side of the Musselshell River. Everything had come out all right and I was soon in a joyful mood, an unusual thing with me for some time. As we rambled on I kept getting all the more joyful and began to think that I was a combined lark and nightingale. I started to liven up the surrounding country with my melody. Beaver Tom snapped at me, "What the hell is eating you anyway, do you want to bring all the Injuns in the country on us?" Nothing could insult me, for was not the wind whispering sweet music in my ears? The little creeks and streams were all laughing and kept up a sweet, silvery song. The trees were fluttering their leaves and sighing to me in low whispers. My horse seemed not to touch the ground, for I was floating in the air. Overhead the sky was a beautiful silvery blue without a cloud in it. Little did the Squaw Kid know, as he was riding along so joyful and happy, that it was the beginning.

The time had come when he was leaving those whose faces were white forever; gone forever was the sweet face of a little girl in Bozeman, with her kind and gray eyes and a head of beautiful brown hair. In many ways she had shown her kindness to me, and when I was leaving on that trip she had come to me and had given me the little Bible to take with me, and with a shy smile, she said she would be glad if I read it, and when I asked her if she would be glad if I came back, she said she would. The Squaw Kid was shy and half wild and not used to her kind. I did not know what I know today or I would have asked her anyway. I probably would never have gone on that trip and would not have to write what I write today. When Beaver Tom was sick with the snakes and along the trail before I met those dark-eyed squaws, it used to be a great comfort to me to think of her. I wished I had a good home to ask her to and hoped to make good on that trip and ask her anyway. But now she was gone out of my life little by little on that trip, for they had driven her away and all I could see now in all this beautiful land I was traveling in were the swarthy faces of beautiful young squaws with their coal-black eyes glittering, and their lips were flashing tender smiles as they tossed their long and shining braids of raven-black hair and then voices came whispering and then rang out with silvery laughter as they put their hands cup-fashion to their lips and blew their wild love calls and sent them quivering and ringing far and near all through this beautiful land.

We traveled back to the cache and met some Indians, but did not have any bother with them. Beaver Tom seemed happy enough and had forgotten our little unpleasantness at Bulleau's. Everything was all right at the cache. We hunted around a couple of days and after much solemn deliberation we chose a place not far away from the cache. It was as good a place as we could find to start building, because almost everything was handy. We started first to build a corral to hold the horses at night as they were beginning to be too much trouble for me; besides, if we had any trouble with the Indians they were much safer shut up at night. The Indians around there generally chose the break of day to do the most of their deviltry.

To give Beaver Tom his just dues he, for once, seemed to have forgotten his folly for Le-oh-hee and had buckled down to hard work. We didn't say much to each other. He cut the poles and I snaked them like a squaw's travois, until soon we had a good strong corral. Then we started on a good-sized cabin of the dugout style in the side hill, that would hold everything we had. I spent a long time snaking in the small logs, but everything else went fine.

Thus far we had had no bother with the Indians although several small bands of Piegans visited us long enough to fill up, then with a "How" left us. Because they had their squaws along they were not out for trouble. We kept on working and in a day or so the Beaver Tom Trapping and Trading Company Limited, all shares subscribed but not paid for, started shoveling on the dirt of the roof of its Emporium of Merchandise. We were going to open in a few days with a grand bargain display. But then we decided just to open up the ladies' apparel department of latest Musselshell styles, and would give as a premium to every white lady—no squaws allowed in that deal—who purchased two hundred dollars' worth of our good and reliable merchandise, a pair of our special built to fit any leg, full-length stockings, warranted all pure silk except the weave and the woof. Every squaw who bought four buffalo robes' worth of our imported French-style lingerie, we were going to give, as an inducement to become civilized, one full-sized eight-yard fiery red calico dress, warranted to fit any bust, and adorned with two dozen large-size bright tin buttons, warranted to hold their color against everything but water. That guarantee alone would insure a squaw many moons' wear. They could avoid the danger of fading by taking it off when it rained and just running around in the lingerie, which they sure to God needed.

We could not make that sweeping price-slashing reduction in the magnificent garment except for the bright and farseeing sagacity of the senior member of our firm, Beaver Tom. So then the Squaw Kid was happy, and with the help of the squaw's paradise he indulged in sweet pipe dreams of the time to come when the root of all evil would come flowing in as buffalo robes and furs. But the Squaw Kid was christened wrong and should have been called the Kid of Sorrow, for once more old man calamity had landed at his doorstep for a long visit.

It was the old story once more and it came from our sacred whiskey keg. Beaver Tom had sworn off booze forever after his narrow escape with the snakes and he did not show any inclination to start in again. The keg had laid wrapped in a pack and everything had seemed to be going fine. But in the last few days I began to smell whiskey and wondered if Beaver Tom was hitting it again. The pack looked like it had not been tampered with. He seemed all right too, and nothing was wrong with him. It went that way for several days until one day I rode up in the hills, scouting around for some excitement.

When I got back Beaver Tom was at the campfire trying to cook something to eat. The first thing I knew he fell face down in the fire, and if I had not jumped quickly and pulled him out, he would have burned to death. He burned his hands and clothes even the way it was. Beaver Tom was drunk as a fiddler's bitch again. There was no use to say or do anything, he was so drunk. I went to the pack where the whiskey keg was and undid the mantas. I had only taken a quart bottle out of it and the rest of the five gallons was supposed to be still in the keg. Lo and behold it was over half empty. On looking around camp I found that everything in bottles had been poured out. We had a keg of vinegar, which I found gone. He had filled everything that would hold whiskey and had cached it some place, and had laid out a supply for a good, long periodical drunk. As I looked around and saw his dirty work after I had used him so well, I kept getting madder. I knew then there was no use in fooling with him any more, for he would only do something else to be in the dirt and in hell. It was just born in him. When he was sober he was too strong for me to fight. The devil in me said there was an easy way: "Just take your six shooter as he sleeps helpless on the ground and scatter his brains all around on the ground. You need not be afraid of the Injuns alone as they are my people and I will take care of you like I always do one of my own."

I kept getting madder at him. If I had had the six shooter on me I would have done it. I looked at it and I had a hell of a time not to take it up. But the little good in me got the best in the end. I walked out of camp leaving the gun on the bed, for I knew only too well that if I stayed around in camp looking at the gun, I was devil enough to give it to him between the eyes. I took my horse and drove the horses into the corral for the night and took the whiskey keg and cached it where not even a booze hound on the scent could find it. When I came back at dark Beaver Tom was sleeping his jag off on the bare ground and was good for the night. I felt so sorry and mean that I went to bed without eating anything and tried to sleep off the hell that was going on in me, but I laid awake nearly all night.

I knew one thing, that Beaver Tom had to go even if the Injuns did get me in the end. I was going to try to get rid of him on the square, but if it came to a ground-hog case I was going to do it crooked. When it came down to brass tacks, Beaver Tom was a little too strong for me. I got up and turned loose the horses and got something to eat. Beaver Tom was up and made no bones about it. He dug up a couple of bottles and started drinking. As he got drunker and meaner he grabbed his buffalo gun, Betsy Ann. He told me he would like to see the color of any half-breed greaser who was so close to him that he could spit on him and would still have the nerve to tell him not to take a drink or two when he wanted. Tom had his faithful, the great and handsome Betsy Ann, at his side. If I wanted to try any ax business on him again my chances were good. Beaver Tom was a cyclone and had a private graveyard of his own. He had trapped more beaver and killed more buffalo and Injuns than there were trees on the hills.

The Squaw Kid rode off leaving him in undisputed possession of the camp. I knew only too well that if I stayed in camp I would have a murder on my soul, for before he could raise his clumsy buffalo gun to shoot, Beaver Tom would be doing time in hell. I got back late, in time to round up the horses, and Beaver Tom was lying helpless. If any Injuns had come they could have packed the camp off without any bother as he laid there drunk with the empty whiskey bottles laying around him. I got busy and tried to find the rest, but search as I would I could not find the gallon keg. I had found a full bottle buried under his bed on the ground; we were still sleeping outside on the ground.

I knew that it would be no use to show my hand until I could get a hold of his cache or he drank his supply and was hungry for a drink. The next morning Beaver Tom was good and shaky. He looked under his blankets, but couldn't find his bottle. He scratched his head and started off. He soon returned, bringing the gallon keg. I rode off and gave him the run of the camp.

That day I nearly ran into a small Piegan camp, but I saw it in time to get out of sight before they saw me. While I was watching out for that camp, I ran slam-bang on two loose squaws. They wanted to know by signs where was my woman and camp? I told them I had no woman, and said nothing about where our camp was. But I knew I would soon have a visit, sooner than I wanted. They left saying that they hoped we would meet soon again.

When I got back to camp Beaver Tom was dead to the world. The Squaw Kid's day had come at last, for lying beside Beaver Tom was the gallon keg with quite a lot of whiskey left in it. He was a hog, but he could not get away with a gallon of good old red-eye rotgut before he got knocked out. I took the keg and put it where it would be some time before he saw it again. I got busy, for Beaver Tom would have no more booze, and then would come the show-down between him and me. I hoped he would be sensible, in fact I knew he would, so I went to bed. Early as I awoke I found Beaver Tom up and prowling around camp looking for his whiskey keg. But he could not find it so he came over to me all smiles and said, "Say, kid, where is that keg I had yesterday? Where did you put it? Hell, I am burning up. Come through with it or it will go hard with you."

I told him that if he wanted a drink he would probably reach hell in time for one if he did not heed my gentle voice. It was only a matter of choice with him, if he wanted to live on or go there. He started to go toward his bed, but I told him, "No, you don't. See, I have got something to say and even if you did get to your bed it will do you no good, for your redoubtful Betsy Ann, cartridges and reloading outfit, together with everything you have got except your blankets are now waiting your exalted presence over in that coulee nearly one mile from here. I want to know right now if you are going to get a move on or do you want me to give it to you between the eyes?"

He tried to soft-soap me and said, "Hell, kid, give me a drink and help me out of this."

So I said, "All right, I will give you a drink that will last you all your life—a nice little blue hole between the eyes." So he started his abuse and said I could be damn brave when I had him with his pants down, but his comeback would come when he got hold of Betsy Ann, and then he would perforate me with lead from a mile away. I told him he did not scare me a little bit, for I had Betsy Ann's twin sister Betsy Jane, and as sure as Jesus died, if he went and I got sight of him after that I would fill him full of lead or know the reason why. He said he would go but he didn't say that he wouldn't come back. "I ought to have known better than to trust your kind when I knew that you had enough greaser in you to be treacherous and mean. All along I kind of expected you to crawl up to me when I slept and stab me in the back. You would have done it before this only you were afraid of the Injuns."

I told him he would be lucky to get off that easy, for us, good, tender-hearted people of the Rio Grande country thought nothing of cutting a fellow's throat twice for a dollar, and for four bits more would lick the cut clean. I could see that this racket had done more to sober him up than anything else. He was only sparring for time and half a chance to turn his nearly six feet of bone and muscle on me. I was the runt with only a forty-four Colt six shooter between him and me. It was my only hope and salvation, for Beaver Tom who had come through all kinds of scraps with the Injuns wasn't going to have it said that a runt like me made him come through, if he could even get half a chance. I told him that was the last call and was he going to go or not? Then said he, "Now don't be too hasty with that damn gun of yours. I have got to go, but you surely ain't dirty enough to set me afoot with nothing."

I said, "That is up to you. You are the doctor and the happier you smile and the more sensible you take this the better you will come out. You had better try to eat something from on the fire. We can talk it over at the same time. Don't make any foolish breaks that you will be sorry for." He tried to force some grub and coffee into his burning stomach. His hands were shaking like a leaf from his three days' drinking.

He tried to scare me and wanted to know how I was going to get along without him. I would be alone among all those Injuns, he said, who would make short work of me when they found out I was alone. I told him it was hell with him anyway, so it could be no worse with the Indians. Was he so forgetful not to remember he had left me the squaws? Even if the bucks were bad, I could find all the consolation I wanted from the squaws, and a sweet place to lay my weary head on their motherly bosoms. Then he tried to bluff me into giving him a full half of all the stuff he agreed to pay for in Bozeman. I said, "All right, come through with the rocks, pay up and it is yours." But as he had nothing, he could not do it and it was doubtful if he would have done it if he could. In the end we agreed, because the six shooter had a whole lot to say. I was to let him have one dozen number four beaver traps, one dozen number two mink traps, some powder and lead for his reloading outfit, two hundred rounds of ammunition for Betsy Ann, a fifty-pound sack of flour, tobacco and a few other things he needed, in all enough to make one good pack-horse load, plus one horse and rigging. Then he said, "I will pull out with no hard feelings, you damn little snake-in-the-grass. I'm damn glad to get away from you besides."

He wanted to take his horse and saddle, but I said, "No, you borrowed them from Jim Hyatt in Bozeman and I had to promise him that I would make the horse and saddle good if you did not." It was not long until he was ready to pull out to where his gun and other stuff were. I was sorry to give him the horse as he was a damn brute to him, but could not help it. When he was ready to go I went and got the bottle of whiskey I had taken from under his bed. I poured out three or four large drinks in another bottle and put it down on the ground for him to drink if he wanted a drink. I did not have to tell him twice to come. He took a good swig and then another and in a few seconds he was another man. He did need it badly, and half crying he told me I was the only friend he had left in the world. He had no hard feelings, for I had used him white and better than he deserved.

He had it coming to him and wanted to shake hands and call it square, but the Squaw Kid wasn't taking any chances on Beaver Tom's long hairy arm or bear-paw hands, even if he had a gun in his hand. I told him to let the handshake go until some other time. I asked him where he intended to go and he said, "I will pull out for near the mouth of the Musselshell at Clagett where a friend of mine named George Robertson runs a wood yard. I may meet some old friends there and go in with him."

He was starting off when I told him I meant him no harm. "Remember that what I told you still goes. You keep away from me for good and don't be foolish and turn back to this camp." He took the horse and started off to where his gun and other stuff were and I was alone. Off went Beaver Tom, who was once a good square-shooter, a fine large man, but now useless and only a whiskey soak. The Squaw Kid was like the kid who cried until he got the moon, but didn't know what to do with the damn thing when he got it.

I had the works to myself and the way it looked all that stuff might as well be at the North Pole. Soon there would be all kinds of roving bad Injuns. I felt good and blue, but what was the use of howling before I was hurt? I had to do one thing and do it quick. I had to trail Beaver Tom to be sure that he would leave the country. I turned out the horses from the corral and saddled one. I did not take the time to cook anything and only took some dried buffalo meat on the saddle and plenty of ammunition.

I rode off leaving everything lying around on the ground. I had to get a line on Beaver Tom before he got out of sight, for should he have taken a notion to sneak back that night to get a stand up on the hillside in the brush and lay a half mile away, then saltpeter wouldn't have saved me.

I could see Beaver Tom putting what stuff he had on the pack and shouldering his buffalo gun. He started off toward the Musselshell River and I trailed him all day. When he camped for the night I had to camp without a fire and had only dried buffalo meat to eat. I nearly froze as I had only the saddle blanket. When he pulled out I still kept after him until he crossed the Musselshell River around noon and, instead of going on to Clagett, he headed for the Judith Gap country. That meant back to Bulleau's, so I turned back, and after riding what was left of the afternoon and all night through the dark without any trail, I got back to camp at daybreak with my horse all in.

I laid down on the ground and went to sleep, not caring if all the Injuns or Beaver Toms in the country came or not. I slept until the afternoon and then I got something to eat. I rounded up the horses. I was lucky and found them all right and corralled them for the night. When it was getting dark the Beaver Tom Trading and Trapping Company Limited was sure to God a sad-looking dump, but the saddest thing around was the Squaw Kid.

I put in one delightful night in hell, for I was all alone and my nerves got the best of me. I put in nearly the whole night watching with my carbine in my hand. As I sat on the bed I could see all kinds of imaginary Injuns and Beaver Toms stealing down around camp to do me in. The sweat would pour off me when a horse tramped in the corral; it sounded to me like a company of cavalry was charging the camp.

Near morning I was worn out and went to sleep, thinking I would saddle up in the morning and leave the whole works in that hell-hole forever. But when the bright sun came I knew my fears were only imaginary. The Squaw Kid got brave and wasn't going to leave even if he had to kill all the Injuns in the Musselshell. I had to do something so I chinked up the shack and fixed the top of the fireplace. The day went all too soon. I went for the horses and scouted around to see if there were any Injun signs, but there were none around.

I put in another pleasant night watching imaginary foes, although it was not as bad as the first night. I was beginning to believe they were there, but that they were afraid of me. Anyway, I came through alive as usual, so in the morning I got foxy and made three dummy beds on the ground near mine as though there were four men sleeping there. I was beginning to break into the elite society at last, for that bunch of Piegans of the two squaws I met the other day pulled in and stayed until they got their guts full. There were eight men and twelve squaws, several papooses and plenty of dogs. I was talking signs pretty well. They wanted to know where the other men were, after they saw the beds. I told them they were up in the hills.

It seemed that the warriors didn't take as much stock in this as they should have. They didn't give a great merchant like me the respect that was coming to me, but it seemed that I was a mark for the squaws who appreciated me and knew my worth. One of the squaws I had met the other day would talk the soulful eye to me every time she got the chance. She sent me S-O-S that she was a grass widow, first trial, and out of a job. It was a shame to let a sweet prairie flower like her waste her fragrance on the wind, if I could only know how sweet she was. She only weighed a little over two hundred pounds and was still a maiden. I did not give her any encouragement; my heart was about broke anyway.

They left saying they would come again. I was getting wise to Injuns, so after they left I followed them for quite a way. I pulled down one sign and turned around two more, all telling any Injun that might happen along where my camp was located. I had to keep busy doing something in camp, for I dared not go rambling in the hills with no one in camp. I had no visitors for the next two days and I was getting used to being alone and managed to sleep some every night.

CHAPTER TWELVE
With Le-oh-hee Comes Temptation

One day I had a close call from some visitors, who made up for the lost time of the others. A bunch of seven bad buck Injuns—anyone could see they were out for hell in big letters—came around. When they first came they were sassy and mean. It was a good thing I saw them before they got into camp, for it gave me time to get into the cabin door.

When they rode up and got off their horses and started to come up to the door, I made signs to stop and come no closer. Then, mad as the dickens, they made signs that they wanted something to eat and quick. I had better do it, for one of them, to show they meant business, drew his finger across his throat to let me know what they would do to me if I did not. I had to point my carbine at them to keep them from coming up to me. Even then they did not seem to scare much. When they noticed the beds on the ground they wanted to know where the ones who slept in them were. I made signs there was only me there and it was with gladness that I saw them tell me I lied. Again they pointed to the beds on the ground and held up four fingers.

After talking among themselves, they made all kinds of insulting signs at me and got on their horses, except one, who led his horse toward my saddle horse picketed nearby. I yelled at him not to go, but he kept on just the same. Before the others got between me and the Injun, I grabbed Betsy Jane and shoved her through a chink in the wall. I was so excited I don't know whether I sighted at the Injun or not, but anyway Betsy Jane went off with a roar that shook the dugout. The bullet hit so close to that Siwash that it splattered the dirt all over him. At that he jumped on his horse and the whole bunch went off on the lope. It was a good

thing they did not see my other horses or that would have
been the last of them.

I could not tell then what tribe they belonged to, but
after I got to know Injuns better I knew they were Gros
Ventres, a mean bunch. I watched them as far as I could, to
see if they did really leave for good. However, I was afraid to
go far from camp as there might be more of them cached
nearby, watching for a chance. I put in the day in no joyful
mood and hated the job of going out after the horses. It was
a ground-hog case and I had good luck finding them close.
I sent them a-flying, and with a sigh of relief got them in the
corral.

As night came on I kept feeling more afraid that those
Injuns would come back and do me up. I cached several
things, including Betsy Jane, my buffalo gun. When it got
dark the brave Squaw Kid took his saddle horse and left his
camp deserted with his horses shut up in the corral. I picketed my horse close to me where I slept and watched from
the brush all night, thinking if they came they might get the
stuff, but the Squaw Kid never. Nothing happened so I was
back in camp at daylight, braver than ever.

Toward night an old Piegan buck and his squaw rode
into camp. He told me they were friends of that bunch
which was there the other day. They were my friends and
wanted to camp with me all night. I gladly told them they
could, for misery always liked company and wasn't particular what it was. Instead of staying one night, they stayed
three days. I would probably have them yet, but another
band of Piegans came into camp. After the usual visit, they
pulled out together. They told me they and other Piegans
knew that I was camped there to trade for buffalo robes and
furs that winter. It was heap good, but that didn't do me any
good then, because the Injuns had nothing to swap yet.

Besides, I would have to watch more closely, for what one
Injun knew they all knew. A bad bunch may have come and
cleaned me out just to keep their hands in practice. I was a
philosopher and was getting over the night sweats. I had

come to the conclusion that I had to die sometime anyway. Things were coming along fine again.

I was eating my dinner by the campfire when a pair of soft hands covered my eyes from behind. I nearly jumped up to the sky I was so surprised and scared. How she got there I didn't know, but large as life and twice as natural stood Le-oh-hee, the Peerless, all covered with dust and looking somewhat the worse for her long ride from the Judith Gap country, and having to camp out alone on the way. Yes, there stood Le-oh-hee in her squaw dress of buckskin with fringe, her of whom I had been thinking so much since it had been so lonely there—her the most beautiful in all the squaw paradise—but there she was with her shy smile and her beautiful eyes, one minute showing shame and the next a light that a man likes to see in a woman's eyes, and it was with joy and gladness that I realized that it was not every day that a nice young beautiful woman, even if she was a squaw, thought enough of the Squaw Kid to risk the ride all alone from the Judith Gap to where I was.

At first all the bad in me was rushing through me with brutal joy, but as I looked at those sad, pleading eyes, what little good I had got the best of the evil. It pleaded to me, saying, "You surely to God are not going to harm her. She is the only woman in your world who thinks enough of you to do this for you. Now come and be good to her. You must take her right or leave her alone and send her away. It will be better for her to be sorry now for a while, than to be sorry all her life."

The good in me won the day, and while I let Le-oh-hee know that I was more than glad to see her, that was all I done. I could see she expected a different reception and didn't know what to make out of all that. I got her something to eat and went to picket her horse for her. The Squaw Kid was in an awful fix. He started out to wear an angel's crown, which didn't seem to fit into the occasion. The good and the bad were at it hammer and tongs, fighting it out inside my crooked soul. The good said, "Now, kid, ain't she just sweet and beautiful, like she was made for you, to bring joy and gladness to your rotten heart and comfort to your old age? It is so seldom lately that you will let me advise you, so you must not blame me if I strike while the iron is hot. Saddle up and take your dusky darling to some mission, even if it is far away. My true light will lead the way night and day until you marry her, then you will see a better day." So the Squaw Kid said to the good, "Whatever is the best thing, we will do."

But the evil said, "Are you going to go back on the one friend you have got, who always is with you when you want to raise hell in general. Do not listen to that punk, who calls himself good and wants you to marry that dusky Jane. You will never trust her anyway. She is a bad one, I tell you, remember what Standing Bear La Rue told you about her. Besides, she is only a squaw and no white man marries a squaw. You just roll her over and all will be well, because she doesn't know any better." So it went that way all afternoon.

Le-oh-hee didn't say much, but started to fix things up in camp. She was making herself pleasant and useful. When I went for the horses, she came along and things were surely going fine. The Squaw Kid had risen in dignity, for he had a fine camp cook. Le-oh-hee seemed contented over the way things were going and so was the Squaw Kid, even if everything looked too good to be true. She said that she heard Beaver Tom telling where my camp was and Injun style she had no difficulty in reaching it, though she had to camp out three nights and find her way alone. She ran the chance of meeting some bad Injuns of other tribes.

I found out that Beaver Tom was at his old tricks again and wanted Le-oh-hee. He had the help of the whole outfit to make her take him. He was old enough to be her father and then some, and worse still he was of no account and not worth the powder to blow him to hell. Beaver Tom, when it came to flopping the buffalo over with Betsy Ann, was on deck all the time. It was buffalo they wanted, for plenty of buffalo killed meant happiness for the women and money to live on.

What was a squaw to them anyway, for had not Bulleau and La Rue, with their wives' relatives, a whole raft full of young squaws and breed girls? They were running around their tepees as wild as the wild broncos on the hills. They were wishing to God that someone who was good with a rope would come along and rope the pick out of the band, even if he should leave only the culls. Alas for them, Beaver Tom was only a booze fighter and besides was no good with a rope.

Meanwhile the Squaw Kid camped on one side of the fire and on the other side was camped Le-oh-hee, her eyes telling the Squaw Kid his chances were good.

The Squaw Kid, who had promised his good part to play square with her, swore that if he came out of that alive, never more would he sign any contracts to play to a willing squaw. The next morning Le-oh-hee saddled up her horse and said she would have to go back, and with sorrow in my heart I did not know what to do. I did not want her to go, but I said nothing to her. She changed her mind and said she would wait until the next day if I would say I was glad. I told her those were the easiest words I ever said. I was wondering how I was going to get along if I let her go away. For sweet were Le-oh-hee's smiles, and squaw style, she wouldn't let me do anything but sit by the fire and look wise. To give the Squaw Kid his just dues, for once in his life he played square with Le-oh-hee and Le-oh-hee played square with him. Well she knew that just a loving touch of her little hand would set off the dynamite.

It went that way for five days—Le-oh-hee kept on her side of the fire night and day and the Squaw Kid did the same. Nothing about love was said. There was no need to say anything, for Le-oh-hee had told the Squaw Kid her story only too well when she first came and it was the Squaw Kid's first move in the game. Like two happy kids we went around in sweet dreams. Twice more she saddled up to go, but every time changed her mind and said she would stay another day. The Squaw Kid still said nothing to her; whether he would make her his wife or pull her down with him to hell.

Le-oh-hee was all rigged up in bright calico and red ribbons and looked ten times more beautiful than when she came. The Squaw Kid liked her ten times better than he did before, but still he tells her everything but the word she would like to hear. On the fifth morning Le-oh-hee, with gentle reproach in her beautiful sad eyes, said she would have to go. She meant business that time for she cooked herself some grub to take with her on her way back. The Squaw Kid stood in doubt and terror because he knew that she was giving him his last chance.

But poor little Le-oh-hee never heard the words she hoped to hear. She stood with her little hand held out to shake hands and say good-bye with her head bowed down to hide the shame of her love and sorrow they showed. Le-oh-hee climbed in the saddle and, with a sweet, forgiving, sad smile I have never forgotten, she rode off. The Squaw Kid was left standing in the dark again as the bright light of Le-oh-hee—a sweet sun—faded away from him. I liked her only too well, and wished to marry her one minute, but was narrow and bigoted enough to heed the whispered words of evil from the foul mouth of old La Rue. After all those years that are now gone forever, the face of Le-oh-hee is once more smiling at the old Squaw Kid. It is to me a beacon of hope in my none too good a life.

CHAPTER THIRTEEN
Lessons in Pend d'Oreille

So the Squaw Kid General Merchandise and successor to the Beaver Tom Trading and Trapping Company Limited was ready for business, but so far he himself was his only customer. I would have to wait a long time until fool's luck would turn up something, for it would be late fall and winter before the Siwash had anything to swap. Plenty of Injuns were going by, but all they wanted was to bum something for nothing. The last few days since Le-oh-hee left the Squaw Kid had been living on love.

Since I had left the Bulleau outfit I had not seen a white man. But one day a bright change came and I had a visitor. He was not a white man, but a half-breed, who talked like a cayuse Frenchman. At least he had on a pair of buckskin pants—I was sure to God fed up and had seen all the breechclouts I wanted for some time—and I didn't have to talk like a dummy with my fingers.

He said his name was Gabriel Depew. He was an old man somewhere in his sixties, tall and straight as an arrow. He said he was with a large band of Injuns who belonged in the Colville Valley where he now lived. Some Spokanes were with them, but most of the band were Pend d'Oreilles from the Kalispell Valley not far from where he lived. They were camped about three miles from where I was and had come there the day before to get ready to kill young cows. They needed young buffalo cow hides for the winter, because the old cows and bulls were too thick and heavy to make tepees.

They had come over the year before and had hunted buffalo in the Musselshell country the previous winter. He said they had had fair luck, but the Injuns from west of the mountains generally stayed two or three years before they went back home. Last spring they all went to Fort Benton to trade their furs and robes and to get ammunition and the other stuff they would want for the winter. But it was the old story, for the traders, like they always did, first filled the bucks with whiskey and rum and then got their robes and furs for almost nothing. Most of them went for whiskey and in a few days the camp was broke with all their robes and furs gone and nothing left to get what they wanted for the winter. Unless they could in some way get ammunition some of them would have to hunt again with the buffalo lance and bows and arrows, so they left Benton and had been rambling all over the country.

He said he was a half-breed Cree from the Northwest Territory of Canada. In the days of the fur brigades, when he was young, he had worked for the Hudson Bay Company at many places until he came to old Fort Colville. There he married a Colville woman and stayed. He had been to Alberta that summer on a visit to his relations among the Bloods and the Crees. He was expecting some of them to come and visit him soon and maybe stay with him all winter, for if the winter was bad most of the buffalo left Alberta and came south and wintered in the Musselshell country.

You may be sure I gave him the best I had and soon we had a good meal. He wanted to know how it was that I was alone there. At first he would not believe that I was alone, but he said nothing and only shook his head. Then he asked, "Say, have you got one drink of whiskey for me?" But I had seen enough of whiskey drinking with Beaver Tom so I shook my head. I suppose he saw I was lying, but he did not get mad at me; finally I went in the cabin and brought him out a good drink. It seemed to warm his heart toward me, for he got very friendly and was willing to open his mouth. He told me many things that I knew were only too true. He said I ought to have known better than to stay there alone, for many kinds of bad Injuns came in there to gamble at playing hands and to hunt buffalo. They would run off my horses and clean me out slick, for even the Injuns themselves had plenty of fights and troubles with other tribes. To keep their horses they had to watch close all the time, for the Blackfeet and Gros Ventres, who were generally the Pend d'Oreilles' enemies, were bad and thieving outfits.

He stayed for some time, but did not ask for any more whiskey. When he found out I wanted to do some trapping and wolfing besides swapping what stuff I had, he soon put me in despair when he said, "You will sure have some job watching your traps, for the Injuns will steal them on you faster than you can set them out. If you put out poison for wolves you will poison all the Injun dogs and they will kill you for that. It will be better for you to sell them than to have them stolen." He went away saying that he would come back tomorrow. He left me not feeling any too good, and wishing I had listened to the good people of Bozeman. If I could not trap and wolf with what stuff I had, I wouldn't be worth much and would have to hang around camp.

He came back the next day and told me he had told the Injuns in camp that I had some guns, ammunition and other stuff to swap and wanted to know if I would give them jawbone credit. They would pay me a good price in robes when they got good enough to tan. But I remembered what Old Man Countryman had told me, trust not an Injun on jawbone, for that was the last of it if I did. I told him no, that I would not do that. Then he wanted to know if I would swap for horses, but I had to tell him I had more horses than I knew what to do with. I had some myself to swap for almost any old thing, but he did not get mad like the Blackfeet and other Injuns and said he was only asking me for them in camp.

I got him something to eat and, without being asked, got him a good-sized swig of whiskey, which went to his head right away. Again he told me that I was foolish to stay there alone. After some more talk he said that he would have to go because the chief of the hunt, Co-quay-ah-tam-a-la, and some others had not made up their minds for sure that they would stay there for the winter camp. They would make up their minds that day. He thought they would stay there, as that was a good sheltered place for a winter camp. There was plenty of wood handy. When it got cold and the blizzards came, the buffalo would come to those sheltered places where there was good feed for them. He left and said he would return the next day.

In a little while a large band of Piegans and their squaws came into camp. That bunch was pretty sassy and mean to me and tried to bluff me into feeding them and giving them tobacco and sugar. They said it was their country and if I wanted to stay I had better be good to them—my only friends. But I made signs I would not do it; then they all got mad and some of the bucks drew their fingers across their throats to show what they would do to me. I stuck it out with them and made signs that some of them would get what was coming to them while they were doing it, so they changed their minds and rode off. Both bucks and squaws made all the dirty and insulting signs they knew to let me know what they thought of me.

I had to watch my horses pretty close every day, besides corralling them every night. I dared not go far away from the camp and, while I had had fool's luck so far, it did not mean that I was going to have it all the time. When Gabriel Depew came the next day I was glad and told him about the bunch of Piegans and of my trouble with them. He said that generally when Injuns had their squaws and papooses along with them they were not too mean or out for trouble, but a bunch of bucks on the lookout for something to steal or run off would not hesitate to take life if they could. If the Injuns had wanted to get me, I would never know what struck me.

Then he told me that they were going to camp there for the winter. They would camp where they were or someplace close by. Again I cooked him the best I had and gave him his regular swig of rotgut. He was soon in good humor. I thought that he was just coming to get his belly full and the drink, but I was wrong in that, and time proved it to me. Old Gabriel Depew had a good heart.

Before he left me he said, "I feel kind of sorry for you. You are young and have used me fine; if you want, I will move my outfit here with you. It is close to our camp and other Injuns will not be as liable to bother you if I am with you. The Injuns of our camp, in which there are some bad ones, will not steal on you or bother you." I was more than glad, but wanted to know if he expected me to give him anything for doing that. He told me that he wanted nothing and he would be glad to get away from the large camp.

Near noon the next day they pulled into camp. I had thought there was only one tepee; he had not said anything about his people, but I found out there were three large lodges of them, he and each son had a tepee and a squaw with family. A brother of his squaw and his squaw and family were with them.

Old Gabriel rode up all smiles and said, "Well, here I am at last with my Hinjuns."

After that he always called them his Injuns, and not without good reason. He said himself they were worse than Injuns, for although they were a quarter white they wore a scalp lock and Injun leggins with a breechclout. They could talk some Piegan English, but never would do so except when they wanted something. Both of them had full-blood squaws, one was Petol and the other Samwell. In old Gabriel's tepee there were his old squaw and an old woman, who was some kind of a relation to his squaw. She was named Chus-sh-meops, which means Short Tail in Pend d'Oreille.

There were also two young women, daughters of Old Gabriel. The oldest was maybe twenty-one and named Kat-a-lee (Kate), and the younger was about nineteen and was called Sow-set (Josephine). Both of them had no men at that time. I did not know it, but they were married and had left their men when they refused to go along on that hunt. They had gone anyway and were now camped in the parental tepee. When I first saw them I thought, "There are two sweet angels, even if they are copper-colored." But I was soon to find out that the both of those estimable young lady squaws were frolicsome young hussies and as crooked as mink. They would rather turn over a trick than eat ice cream. The Blackfeet houris could not hold a candle to them when it came to crooked deviltry. Their men had lost nothing when they left them.

It did not take the squaws long to get the tepees set up and everything was rigged up in Injun shape. The Squaw Kid's outfit took on a Siwash appearance. He had now broke into the four hundred and was now an Injun at last (though he did not know it). They pitched their tepees right beside my camp. When old Gabriel came over I offered him something to eat, but he said no, but did not refuse a drink of forty rods. Then he said, "Remember, I don't care to who you give or sell whiskey, but take my advice and never give or sell the Injuns any. In the end you will be sorry. Whatever you do, see that you do not give my girls any whiskey even if they should want you to."

My camp was a gay scene of buck Injuns and festive squaws coming and going from their camp to visit old Gabriel's outfit and to try and get stuff on jawbone. They might as well have asked a rock, for they got nothing. I had nothing to do, for even my horses were running with old Gabriel's bunch. They were taking them in and out with theirs. All I had to do was prowl around. Because old Gabriel's sons didn't seem to care much for my society and were a surly bunch, I had to go back to my old trade of herding squaws. Old Gabriel's sweet and fair daughters, whom I began to think were sweet swamp angels, were at first kind of shy with me. Soon they were as friendly as pet monkeys.

Two or three days after they moved next door they roped me into going with them on a visit to the Injun camp. We rode over there and found there were twenty-two lodges still left. Injun style they took me in several tepees to let the squaws see what they had found. Most of the bucks were away. The squaws offered us boiled buffalo meat as that was all they had anyway. It was all bloody from chasing the buf-

falo, and was the way an Injun wanted his meat. It was hard
stuff for a white man to eat. I had to do the best I could not
to insult them. That happened in every tepee we went into.
Soon I was as sick as a dog from trying to force that stuff
down. They could eat that way all day, and a full meal every
time.

Under the instructions of those two angels, who had
time to burn, I started to learn the Pend d'Oreille language.
It was no easy job. I used to write down the way a word
sounded and soon could get off quite a lot of stuff.
Whenever a bunch of young bucks or squaws would come
over to camp, my saintly teachers would hold an examina-
tion and I would proudly recite for them what I knew. With
shrieks of laughter they would tell me something else, and I
would faithfully write it down so I could say it again without having to ask them. It went that way for a few days until
I started to say what I knew in Injun to old Gabriel to show
him how fast I was learning. Instead of being pleased, he got
mad as hell and asked from whom I was getting all that kind
of stuff. I told him from Kat-ah-lee and Sow-set. Then I
found out those two she hellions had only been teaching me
blackguard words as something else. Instead of saying what
I thought I was, I had been blackguarding in Injun, a thing
that all wild Injuns were adept at.

He said, "If you want to learn, I will learn you, and can
tell you the good from the bad." So I had to start over again
and soon could talk quite a little Pend d'Oreille, and, with
the sign language, began to get along well with the Injuns.

Then one day Co-quay-ah-tam-a-la, chief of the hunt
and chief of the Pend d'Oreilles who belonged around
Chewelah, came to my camp. He was a fine middle-aged
warrior and old Gabriel came over to interpret. Co-quay-
ah-tam-a-la wanted to know why I would not give his warriors guns and ammunition on jawbone. They were straight-
tongued men, for did not the Pend d'Oreilles always keep
their words and were they not better friends to the white
man then he was to them?

He had come to give me his word as a good chief that I would get my pay in robes when the buffalo got good to tan in the fall. But I said that I could not do it. Old Gabriel got kind of mad and said he thought that they would pay me, so why didn't I let them have the guns and ammunition so they could hunt better? I said, "Because Old Man Countryman, a man who had traded with the Injuns for years, told me never to give jawbone to an Indian, for if I did it would be the last of it. Besides, the chief might mean all right, but an Injun, when it don't come his way, don't give a damn for his chief. I saw that the squaws in camp have plenty of dry hides from last winter to tan." Co-quay-ah-tam-a-la went off mad and I still had my guns. When I gave old Gabriel a shot of forty rods, he soon got over his mad. Then I told him I could not take a chance on losing my stuff.

I found out that those two grass widows in Gabriel's tepee could talk some English if they wanted to, for that same day Sow-set said to me, "Heap good boy, you. Come now you catchem whiskey. Sow-set heap good to you. Kat-a-lee watchum old man. You savvy Kat-a-lee and Sow-set no tellum old man on you?"

I told her I would not do it, then she left with a look on her face that meant me no good. I soon saw the both of them ride off to the Injun camp.

Along in the afternoon I had another surprise, for old White Grass and four Blackfeet warriors in paint and feathers came to my camp driving two pack horses with them. Old White Grass held out his hand with a "how." I was glad to see him and let him see that he was welcome. They got off their horses and I gave them something to eat. Then they started to unpack the pack horses and I could see that they had buffalo robes on them. They had, Injun style, invited themselves to stay all night. By signs White Grass told me that they had come from their camp where they were going to stay for the winter. They had plenty of robes to swap and had brought some with them, which meant that they had been on some more raids and had had good luck. One of the bucks brought

me a nice large robe and wanted whiskey, but I shook my
head no. Then he wanted to swap for sugar. I knew that a
good robe was valued by traders at three to five dollars, but in
Bozeman they easily sold to the ranchers and miners for ten
dollars. That was the Squaw Kid's first sale and I thought I
would be generous. After much deliberation, I valued the
robe at five dollars. I gave him a very liberal exchange—ten
pounds of brown sugar, composed of four tin cupfuls to the
pound. I had no scales and my customers were supposed to
bring their own paper so they could not accuse me of dis-
honesty by selling them the paper. I put it in a pan for them
and told them I wanted the pan back. They all squatted
around and it was not long until the five had eaten the whole
ten pounds of sugar and were licking their fingers for more.

I could see that old Gabriel and the Pend d'Oreille bucks,
who were about twenty-five yards away, were taking it all in.
They did not like the way I was so friendly to the Blackfeet.
Then White Grass wanted to know if I would swap some of
the needle guns and ammunition and how many buffalo
robes did I want for a gun? I did not know what to ask for
them. I had picked them up in Bozeman for ten dollars. I
told him I would let him know in a little while. I slipped over
to old Gabriel, thinking he could tell me better just how
much those Siwashes would stand. I asked him, but he and
the Pend d'Oreilles only gave me the bad eye.

Old Gabriel said, "I thought you did not know any Injuns
and that you had been here alone? How is it you know those
Blackfeet devils so well? They seem to know you well. You
and them are good friends."

I had to tell him all about being in the Blackfeet camp. "If
it had not been for White Grass and some of the old warriors, I would have been dead long ago. I know that old
White Grass is a good Injun. He was a friend when I had
needed one badly."

He said, "You may think so, but I and many of the old
Pend d'Oreille warriors know that old cutthroat devil only

too well. Many a Pend d'Oreille warrior has lost his scalp to him and there was always wailing in the Pend d'Oreilles' lodges, whenever the bunch he used to lead came around. They ran off many horses, and that old devil himself only knows how many white women and men he helped to murder in his time. Yes, I have good reason to remember old White Grass, for long ago I had a friend, Pierre Bonnville. He was a half-breed, but had blue eyes and long dark brown hair. I was at a trading post on the Pend d'Oreille River when a war party of Blackfeet came sneaking up to the post. The Injuns who were in the post told the factor that they were Blackfeet and that one of them was a chief.

"The Blackfeet had killed many of his trappers and the factor was going to shoot the chief dead from in the post. We told him not to do it as there might be many of them nearby and they would come and take the post. They made signs of peace and said they were friends. They came up to the post and wanted to come in, but the factor would not let them. They had nothing to trade so he told them to go away. Like a fool he told them he had a man out hunting meat for the post and they must do no harm to him. If they did he would follow them with his men and Injuns and kill them all. The Blackfeet chief said they were good Injuns and the white man's friend. They quickly rode off.

"We told the factor that he should not have told them that and wanted him to send some of us out to follow them. We thought they might find the hunter, who was my friend Pierre Bonnville, but the factor laughed at us and said they knew him too well to do that. Besides, he said, Pierre knew enough to take care of himself. Pierre did not come back to the post and it soon got dark. We dared not go out of the post and knew it would be of no use anyway. The devils of Blackfeet had killed him. We took his trail at daylight and about four miles from the post we found where the Blackfeet had surprised him when he was coming back with a pack horse loaded with meat. They had killed him, scalped him, and stripped him of everything, cut and slashed him up and left him lying on the ground. When we got back to the post with him, the factor wanted to go after them, but we told him that it was no use as they would be miles away. It would have been better if he had listened to us; then Pierre would not be dead.

"About a month after that I was at Fort Benton trading post when a very large band of Blackfeet warriors came in. They wanted the factor to give them many presents or they would make trouble, but the factor would not do it and told them to go or he would shoot them up. Then a Blackfoot warrior started to dance the scalp dance where we could easily see him and to insult us. He waved a coup stick with a scalp of long brown hair. We thought at first it was from some white woman or man, whom that devil had killed. I watched him as he danced through the hellish actions, showing how he killed that man. I knew it was the scalp of my friend Pierre Bonnville, so I took my gun to kill him. But the trader and others would not let me do it, because there were too many Blackfeet. If they got any madder there would have been a bloody fight. The one who danced then and who had killed and scalped my friend is that old devil sitting over there by your fire, White Grass, who you say is a good Injun and your friend.

"Three times I thought I killed him, but he always pulled through. I would do it now only my friends and I are camped in the Piegan's lands with our women and children. We will have to watch our horses more closely as the Blackfeet are only spying around to see if there is a good chance to do some deviltry to us."

I had to leave them all mad at me and went back to my camp where the Blackfeet sat. I made up my mind that if I did not know how to charge enough without asking a buck Injun, then I had no business being a one-hoss trader. I told White Grass that in the morning I would swap them one needle gun for eight good buffalo robes and the cartridges, twenty in a box, for a robe, and the Henry cartridges, fifty in a box, for the same price. They kicked, but I told them they could take it or leave it. They said nothing and we rolled up and went to sleep on the ground, the Blackfeet cutthroats and the Squaw Kid side by side.

Early the next morning old Gabriel signs for me to come over to his tepee. I went over to find he had gotten over his mad and wanted to know if I had made any trade with them yet. I told him what I had asked, but thought they would not give me it.

He said, "You need not be afraid. They will give you what you ask, for they know better than to take robes into the large trading posts at this time of the year. No Injuns have robes to swap now unless he steals them on a raid. But that need not bother you, for most of the time you can never tell where an Injun buffalo robe comes from."

I traded them two needle guns for sixteen fine robes; they left five robes for five boxes of fifty-caliber cartridges for the needle guns, which cost me one-fifty per box by the case in Bozeman. White Grass wanted to know how many guns I had left and while I still had thirteen of them I told him I had only six left. He said they would come back and get them and swap for heap cartridges. There was no law against it at that time and I told them it was all right. They rode off for their camp, past old Gabriel with the devil shining in his eyes.

He came over to me and like a fool I had to blab the whole thing to him. It was not long after until I saw his Siwash son Petol ride off to the Injun camp. About noon there were more than thirty Pend d'Oreille bucks strutting around old Gabriel's tepee and my camp like turkey gobblers. All were mad as wet hens. Old Gabriel and the bucks called the Blackfeet cutthroats and murderers, but, to give the devil his just dues, there were quite a few in that gentle bunch of Pend d'Oreilles who were pretty handy at throat-cutting themselves. There was no doubt if they had a few shots of whiskey in them, they would have cooked the Squaw Kid's goose for him good and brown. What hurt them the most was that I should turn my friends down, and

swap guns and ammunition to their enemies the Blackfeet
when they wanted the guns and ammunition so badly
themselves, and would be only too glad to take them all. I
was only a crooked-tongued snake in the grass for the
Blackfeet. Like a fool I got mad and told old Gabriel to tell
them that the Pend O'Oreilles were liars and did not intend
to pay me in the end, for I had seen that their women had
plenty of dry hides from the last winter and were tanning
them. There sure was a hell of a racket.

I don't know how it would have turned out as they kept
getting madder and sassy all the time. Then one of them, on
his own hook, started to abuse old Gabriel. The whole
bunch went at him and said that it was him who was the
cause of it all, for getting them to be my friends. He was as
treacherous as I and was getting stuff from me through his
two girls' buttocks. Old Gabriel got his Injun up too and
started into the tepee to get his gun to kill the buck that had
said that. To pacify them I said I would give them a needle
gun for seven robes, one robe less than the Blackfeet paid
and three boxes of cartridges for two robes, but that they
still had to bring in the robes first as there was going to be
no jawbone.

The powwow ended in peace after all; they went to their
camp leaving old Gabriel and I alone. He said they were no
better than a band of wolves and would tear a friend to
pieces when they got mad. I gave him a shot of the elixir of
life, but he was so downhearted I had to give him a second
dose before I could get the desired results. He went off to his
tepee saying where else could he find a friend like the Squaw
Kid and if they tried to bother me again he would shoot that
lousy bunch of Siwashes full of holes.

In the morning two Pend d'Oreilles came and I robbed
one of them of seven buffalo robes for a second-handed
needle gun and for two buffalo robes I gave him three boxes
of fifty-caliber cartridges, and I got two robes from the other
buck for three boxes of Henry cartridges.

CHAPTER FOURTEEN
The Call of the Wild Squaws

Strictly cash business was slow, but it was the right dope. Business was slack and I had time to burn. Lately I had gotten to prowling around in the creek bottom where the trees and brush grew. I had an awful experience one day, for I knew someone was trailing me with evil and deadly intent. Along came some grim avenger silently through the brush, but, do as I would, I could not see anything. I could not throw him off my trail. I thought it must have been one of the Pend d'Oreille warriors who was trailing me, and was going to do me up on the quiet.

There was a large cottonwood tree nearby that the wind had blown down. I drew my gun and crawled up aside of the tree, resolved to sell my life as dearly as possible. I made the tree without any noise, and after a few seconds that seemed a hundred years, I carefully raised up to see if I could see what was on the other side of the tree and got the surprise of my life. I know you are going to say there he goes again, the same old story, for from the other side of the fallen tree, with just the tree between us, rose up the sweetest little squaw I ever saw. She was not so beautiful, but her eyes and face had truth and honesty in them. She was as surprised as I was and she tried to bolt, but I was too quick for her and got a hold of her hand. She let on that she was awfully mad like they all do. She was the squaw I had been looking for and I was not going to lose that chance. I could not talk enough Pend d'Oreille and had to use sign language with the fingers. I was afraid to let her go so I could talk to her that way, but in the end I had to let go of her. Then she didn't seem so anxious to go.

She had been trying to make me believe she was mad, but when I let go she stood still with a smile on her face. I could see that she had one tooth broken off on the upper row in the middle of her mouth and she was about eighteen years old, and sure could not claim anything fancy or gay on her much worn buckskin Injun dress, for that little squaw, as far as Injun wealth went, was sure down and out. I asked her why she was trailing me, but the little liar denied it and told me that I was the one who was trailing her, for whoever heard of a squaw trailing a man. It was always a man who trailed up the squaw, for did I not hold her by the hand to keep her from going on her way. If I had let her alone, she would have been far on her way.

I tried to find out her name, but could not understand it; it did not seem like Pend d'Oreille. She said it was Kot-kot-hy-hih, but I could not understand her. I was sitting down on the fallen tree so she sat down a little way off and still tried to tell me what Kot-kot-hy-hih was. Then she said in Pend d'Oreille, E-pick-ca-pu and I knew it was White Feather. She said, "Mission Lapwai Sw-zan." I could understand that her Injun name was White Feather and that she was christened Susan. She said she was not a Pend d'Oreille, but a Sapah-tan. I could not understand what that meant and said it to myself several times so I could ask old Gabriel what it meant.

We could hear some squaws talking in the brush not far off. She started to go, pointing to the place the squaws were. I made signs for her to return there the middle of the next day and I would be there, but she shook her head no. The Squaw Kid saw in her eyes and smile that she would be there or know the reason why. She slipped through the trees and brush as silently as she came. I got my horse and rode back to camp.

Something told me that little White Feather or Susan, or whatever her name was, with all her poverty, was a good straight squaw and not of the kind like Kat-a-lee or Sow-set. I tried to be foxy with old Gabriel. I had noticed her a few times in the Injun camp so I said, "Who is that little, young squaw with the broken tooth? Is she a Pend d'Oreille? She don't look like one of your women."

But he was suspicious and said, "You surely are not gone on that young woman now, are you? You had better let her alone, for she is as good a girl as is in camp." I thought, "If that is all, she has not much to brag about." Then he said, "She has had plenty of sorrow and trouble. Enough without you trying to make her more. She does not belong to us, but is a Nez Perce woman that got away last fall when the white men caught Joseph and his band and took them prisoners at the Bear Paw Mountains. She stayed last winter with some Assiniboines and we picked her up this spring when we met them. She is staying in Cha-ki-a-ki's tepee and is going to go back home with us when we go, unless she can get some better chance. She came from the Wallowa Valley.

"Our women don't like her and are kind of mean to her and that is why you always see her alone. When they start the buffalo hunt, Cha-ki-a-ki and his women will take it out of her skinning and tanning buffalo robes, for she has no home and no one to give her anything and has not even a horse of her own. She says her name is White Feather, but our women have given her a new name that will stay with her for some time. They call her In-who-lise, because she has a broken tooth, which she says she got in the Battle of the Big Hole when a white man hit her with his gun on the mouth after she was shot in the shoulder. She and some others were running out of the tepees to get away at the time. I am telling you this so you will leave her alone. I mean what I say, I always married a woman or let them alone."

But I fooled old Gabriel, foxy as he was, and said, "You need not be afraid, for I thought she was the greasiest and toughest-looking squaw in the whole bunch," and poor little In-who-lise, when I found her, was that.

The next day I was at the cottonwood tree on time as near as you could tell by the sun. I had not been there long when In-who-lise, as I will always call her, glides out of the brush with a sheepish smile on her face. I could see that she had made improvements within her limited means. Her face was as slick and clean as river sand would make it and her long raven hair had been combed and braided in the latest squaw style.

We sat down on the fallen cottonwood about eight or ten feet apart—I guess she thought that was close enough for the beginning—but I tried to edge closer. It did me no good because she moved away every time. The Squaw Kid had not been rambling in the squaw paradise for nothing and knew the only way to get anything from a squaw was to make her believe you didn't want it. I started to widen the distance between us, which took her by surprise and I soon had the beautiful In-who-lise steadily pursuing me to lessen the distance.

I told her that I heap savvied Sap-tan, which is what the Nez Perce tongue was called, but I knew better than to tell her I was at the Bear Paws the day Chief Joseph had surrendered. I had been with them when they went as prisoners to Fort Keough and had helped to drive their large band of horses along with them; the horses the Nez Perce never got back. I had seen her people driven on flatboats in the cold like cattle to be floated down the Yellowstone to Fort Buford without any shelter from the storms.

Anyway, before we left the Squaw Kid sat four feet closer to In-who-lise, and in her affections, which was not so bad for a start, considering that we had to do the most of our talking with our fingers. We agreed to meet at the same old place and time the next day, rain or shine.

I went back to camp wondering what I could bring to In-who-lise that would help to grease the skids of love and make things slip along easy and quicker. Alas, I had no candy and the only delicacy I had was some old-fashioned dried apples and some nigger-heel molasses. I decided to bring her fruit as my first offering on the altar of love, but remembered that the swelling capacity of the dried apples after they got wet was enormous. I knew that even dynamite would not hurt a squaw's stomach from when I had tried the apples on the squaws and breeds at the feast at Bulleau's.

Before I would take any chance on killing the only squaw I loved, I thought I would try a string apiece of them on Kat-a-lee and Sow-set. If they swelled up and burst, then it would be nothing lost. When they came around my camp, I went and got them a string of dried apples apiece and they ate them. They said they were lovely and I watched to see them swell up and bust, but they never fazed those squaws' Injun rubber stomachs. They even helped me to eat a hearty meal on top of them. So I decided to take the lovely In-who-lise some of my famous dried apples and give her the bene-fits of the white man's civilization. I knew if she would give them a fair trial they would melt her savage little heart and then she could see that I thought a whole lot about her. Besides, it would come cheaper than having to pack her a diamond ring and two-dollar-a-box chocolates.

When I left I found a good large string and took them along with me and was soon at the fallen cottonwood tree on time loaded for bear, when now out of the brush like a sweet spirit without wings came the lovely In-who-lise, her divine presence wafted to the breeze like the sweet scent of—it was not violets. But what is there that is sweeter and tempts the appetite, tickles your palate and imparts a deli-cious scent more than the delightful aroma of someone fry-ing good old-fashioned sugar-cured ham? It just makes your mouth water and hungry, so you could not blame me when I say I was ready to eat the lovely In-who-lise when she came up to the tree and sat down four feet away, and her eyes said this is as close as you are going to get for some time. We talked in Injun and made the rest with signs on our fingers. I tried to get closer but In-who-lise was heartless and mean and would not respond to my soul-ripping appeals, so in a forlorn hope I drew forth the string of dried apples. I pulled one off the string and took a risk on my life and started to eat with relish. Soon I see my charm has started on its deadly work, and while In-who-lise did not know a dried apple from God's off ox, still this made it all the better and easier for me, for now I had an ally in old curiosity, for now there came in her face a cautious look, then she starts to rub her chin like a fellow rubs his whiskers when he is in profound meditation. Now she throws caution all over the woods, and was standing up pleading and smiling and wanted me to let her sample those dried apples. I took the bull by the horns and sat the lovely In-who-lise down in my lap. Now In-who-lise, the little Nez Perce squaw who has been eating nothing but bloody buffalo meat and sometimes a few choke cherries, is now munching them old hard dried apples and thinks they are about the finest thing she has ever eaten and now playfully offers me some. As she was eating them I could see that she was busy thinking, for sometimes her face would show gladness then she would steal a look at me. Then I could see terror and doubt for the white man, and In-who-lise has had already more than just reason to be afraid and not to trust any white man, for young as she is, she carries a hole in her right shoulder made by a white man's bullet, and a broken tooth from the white man's gun butt on her mouth one year ago in the bloody Big Hole battle. Her people who are not dead are now prisoners in the old Indian Territory, so this was why old Gabriel took pity on her and had told me to keep my hands off her and how well I have done so you have already seen. When she got through eating her treat and wanted to leave, I let her go as I was beginning to find out that she was of athletic build and must weigh 150 pounds and while this cottonwood tree would do in a pinch, it was not built for this kind of work. Besides there was no use in scaring her the first time, so we soon left, both satisfied with the day's work and will continue the program at the same time tomorrow.

As I rode back to camp I come to the conclusion that if I have got to take a squaw it will be In-who-lise, and I will take her on the square and meant it. I had enough of hand-blowing squaws, but when I got back to camp Sow-set came over and wants to know in an underhanded way, what I am finding so interesting those last few days that is depriving her and Kat-a-lee of my enjoyable presence. I told her the truth when I said that I had only been prowling around through the trees and brush to pick out a good place to set out some traps when the right time came. But the vixen laughed and said, "That is right, but say, wise one, you want to be careful when you do that you are not sometime caught in one of your own traps and have to call for some tender-hearted squaw to let you out."

That morning business had picked up some and I swapped a needle gun to a Pend d'Oreille buck named In-ti-ya for seven buffalo robes and three boxes of fifty-caliber cartridges for two more robes. So far I had only swapped guns and ammunition, but for no other stuff.

Later, cautiously peering to the four corners of the earth to see that none of old Gabriel's divinities were watching me, I rode off to meet In-who-lise. She came out of the friendly brush all smiles and this time right up to me. She was sure intelligent and easy to learn and I will yet make something out of her, for when I showed her that I had not forgotten her and had brought her another string of dried apples, she now thought that the only way to eat them was sitting down in my lap and with a sigh of content she lit there as graceful as though she already had some practice. What else could I do but to hold her with both arms from the danger of slipping off and hurting herself and I intended to give her a few lessons in strangleholds. She was beginning to feel as heavy as a house, but as she eats she also gets busy and wants to know why am I holding her anyway, so I told her because she was going to be my squaw. Then she chewed some more dried apples on this, then wants to know if I like her, then she came out flat-footed and wants to know if it is just going to be a roll over Injun style or is it going to be a mission with a ring on her finger, so I told her that it would be that way, that I would marry her and put a ring on her finger, a thing very few of them got those days from a white man, but before we got any further we thought something was wrong and on looking around, there in the brush stood the inseparable grass widows Kat-a-lee and Sow-set who have been taking in the whole works and I ought to have known that even the devil could not hide anything like this from them two experts. They came

over to us and soon there was hell to pay among the three of
them and as they talked and spit out the Injun so fast at one
another I could not understand much that was said but could
tell they were trying to give In-who-lise the run and make her
leave for the Injun camp, and when they could not do this,
Kat-a-lee now starts in on sign and Injun oratory to tell me all
about In-who-lise and for me not to let her fool me as she was
a bad and tricky Sapah-tan (Nez Perce) girl and they were all
bad ones and that none of them in the Injun camp knew anything about what she was except what she wanted to tell
them, but everyone knew that the Sapah-tan women were all
crooked and this was the way she was paying the Pend
d'Oreilles who had been so good to her, when they found her
with the Assiniboines and she wanted to come with them,
Cha-ki-a-ki had taken her in his lodge and had given her a
horse to ride as the Assiniboines kept her horse when she left
them and one of Cha-ki-a-ki's squaws' brothers named Spel-
a-qua (Mud Turtle) was going to take her for his squaw, but
here they caught the little crooked-tongued Sapah-tan snake
coiled up in my lap, and was only fooling me and now that
she had told me everything for me to give her a kick and send
her back to the Injun camp where Spel-a-qua would give her
what was coming to her, and if I wanted a woman, there were
plenty good Pend d'Oreille girls left in the lodges.

Then In-who-lise, who has been sitting down on the tree
and has not said anything, now jumps up with fire in her
eyes saying it is all lies she has been saying, that Cha-ki-a-ki
had taken her into his lodge and had given her a horse but
she would help the women to skin the buffalo and to tan the
robes for that, but it was a lie when they said she was going
to be Spel-a-qua's squaw, for she was a Christian woman and
as Spel-a-qua had plenty of horses and now had two squaws
in his tepee now so she had made up her mind to be my
woman when she was sure that I liked her the way I said and
would marry her and take her back to where her people
came from, and wants to know of me if this was all right and
I told her it was.

Soon there was another fight in right style this time. For now Kat-a-lee and Sow-set go at In-who-lise who promptly pulled a wicked-looking knife and starts in slashing at Kat-a-lee, who now backs up out of the way and falls backward over the fallen tree. If I had not jumped and caught In-who-lise she would have ripped her open, but I made her give me the knife and had no more than got it when now I have just time to catch Sow-set coming at In-who-lise with her knife and murder in her eyes and I had to flop her on the ground and get on top of her before I could get the knife away from this husky lovely tiger cat, which now makes one thing that this squaw love business is sure fierce going. As we left this love nest, In-who-lise is telling them that if they tell in the Injun camp what they saw today she will kill the both of them, and Kat-a-lee and Sow-set are reading the riot act to her and telling her that this is the first thing they are going to do and that they would cut her up in buffalo strips and hang her up to dry when they got her right.

I made signs on the quiet for In-who-lise to come here tomorrow but she shook her head that it would be no use to come here any more, then she left for the Injun camp so I went off with Kat-a-lee and Sow-set and as we rode back to camp they now get as sweet as honey to me and say they are not squealers and are not going to tell the Injuns and only wanted to scare In-who-lise. But just the same, they were going to see to it that In-who-lise that Sapah-tan girl is not going to get me for her man, for they are going to get me a nicer girl than her and for me to wait till I see their friend Nancy, whose Injun name was Squis-squis (which means one of those little drumming pheasants).

I did not say anything about this as I did not want to make them any madder. But I had already seen the lovely Squis-squis and she sure was some squaw, and I also knew that if she was a friend of theirs she was of their own kind— a hand blower.

I have mentioned this hand-blowing business to you several times and I might as well tell you a word or so about this

refined art, a side line of the wild squaw and one of the
under workings of the squaw's paradise, for the wild squaw
when she made love wanted to be chased over the prairies
and through the brush. That would not have been so bad if
it was in daytime, but as most of this hand blowing is done
by crooked women and young squaws, they chose the night
and made the one who was after them do some running
when this was going on, for she could, by cupping her hands
over her mouth and blowing through them in a way that
takes much practice to learn, blow a shrill mournful sound
that on a still night could be easily heard a mile away. When
the lovely sly little squaw is ready for business, she silently
crawls under the edge of the tepee and is now out in the
night when all good squaws are supposed to be sleeping so
she now goes quietly away from camp and now bugles with
her hands, calling for the buck she wants who knows the
sound of her call, for each woman has a call of her own for
they can make different sounds when blowing by working
their fingers like a cornet player, and unless she learns you
her call, you cannot tell who the woman is, though you can
surely hear her and know that some woman is out for blood
and as there may be several of them rutting squaws out at
different places at the same time it would be useless to try
and there would be a mix-up if you didn't know. But the
dusky amourites have taken care of that and each one has a
tune of her own to blow, for the wild squaw makes no mis-
takes and has this down to a science that would make some
of their white sisters who play this game in different ways a
four-flusher and piker, so when the buck hears this sound of
boots and saddle ringing through the air, he silently sneaks
off to where the sound is coming from and now thinks she
is there; but alas, for the dusky Beau Brummell now hears
the bugling coming maybe a quarter of a mile in another
direction, for the fairy nymph who is watching him has
made a run for it and is off when he gets there and is now
encouraging him over there with beautiful bugling that
would make a bull elk die of shame and envy, so, as he is no

fool and some player at this game himself, he now uses all the stealth and low-down trickery known only to an Injun and soon it is a race o'er vale and dell with her bugling and encouraging him to keep it up when now she may have been only fooling him and quietly slips back into camp leaving him there to ponder on the trickery and deviltry of woman and to get square with her and the next one, but most of the time she takes good care that he will catch her as most of the time this kind of work is only done by crooked squaws who don't like their men and by young squaws who know that any day may bring a warrior who has the horses to buy her, while the one she likes has none.

So, as we rode back to camp, I tried to soft-soap Kat-a-lee and Sow-set as I was afraid for In-who-lise in the Injun camp, and to leave In-who-lise alone and if they would do so I would give each one of them enough to make a fine dress of calico of five yards, but they would not agree to this and as we rode into camp this ended the racket for a time at least.

CHAPTER FIFTEEN
Not the Only Fool on the Musselshell

I had not been in camp long and this is sure a day of surprises, for now old Gabriel rode into camp bringing with him a curiosity to me, a white man, who said his name was Webber who old Gabriel had run onto while out hunting afoot and looking for my camp, which he said he had heard of from some Injuns, and this man had a tale of woe to tell that went to show that the Squaw Kid has no more the monopoly of being the only fool in the Musselshell country at this time. As I got him something to eat I tried to cheer him up and console him with good fatherly advice, that if it was not for us fools then how would the smart ones live, and that he should not get down in the mouth and take it so hard, for in this we were not alone for they said there was born a fool every minute. This man I could see was a plain and simple tenderfoot and, as he told his story of how he came to be here today, it went to show that them who are on easy street sometimes do not know when to leave well enough alone, for he said that he lived in St. Louis, Missouri, and as he had heard so much about our glorious territory he thought it would be the proper thing for him to see it and have some excitement with the buffalo and noble red man, who he had been told was always willing to furnish all the excitement you wanted free of charge. He had no trouble to get a friend of his named Harris to come in with him in this undertaking and they bought a good supply of goods of the kind to trade to Injuns and in this way thought they could see this country and make it pay at the same time, killing two birds with the one stone as they went along.

They had bought a shuttler prairie schooner to hold and haul their stuff and had come up the Missouri River on the steamboat *Helena* to Fort Buford, where they bought four condemned army mules to haul their stuff and were told by some of the old-timers coming back on the boat that the best place for them to get off was at Carrol, as they would be sure to find all the Injuns they wanted in the Musselshell country and could easily go on through to Bozeman with their wagon and the captain thought the water was too low to make Benton. They unloaded their stuff at the government cantonment at Carrol and had no trouble to find a Cree breed as guide and interpreter who could talk English and knew the country on the way to Bozeman or to Helena, where they intended to sell what was left of the outfit and take the stage to Corinne, Utah, and then take the railroad back home.

So they started out with this breed paragon of many virtues leading the way and everything went along well enough, only they found the Injuns had nothing to trade for at this time of the year and they were elected to haul their stuff through to Bozeman as there were no white men to trade with and as they came on the breed gets more sassy and three days ago when they camped for the night by a large camp of Injuns, the breed on his own hook stole some of their whiskey and proceeded to get drunk with some of his Injun friends in the camp. When they found out from the breed that there was more whiskey in the wagon, they soon find all kinds of Injuns howling around them in a threatening manner wanting whiskey. They got so mean and ugly that they had to give them a ten-gallon keg, about all they had left and the Injuns had an awful drunk on the whiskey and sometimes they had to stand them off with their guns in the night and thought they were going to be killed. So after the drink, the Injuns pulled out the next day, after they had stolen their harness from under their wagon. They also run off their mules and left them with their wagon full of goods standing on the prairie afoot, and the breed went off with the Injuns.

The breed had found out from the Piegans there was a white man camped not far off, so Webber had started afoot to try and find my camp, while Harris stayed at the wagon to try and watch their stuff. He had taken a chance on finding me and was lucky enough to find old Gabriel and was here now to see if I would not buy their outfit and give them a chance to get out of this God-forsaken country as they had now more than their belly full. They had goods in the wagon that cost them over nineteen hundred dollars wholesale in St. Louis, not counting the wagon which cost them a hundred dollars. The freight and fare on the boat had made the costs nearly three hundred dollars more, but I could have the works for just what it cost them in St. Louis.

I was sorry for them but still I could not help laughing and saying where did he get the bright idea that I could dig up nineteen hundred dollars in cash? The outfit I had did not show much prosperity and I was like himself and wished to God I had never come here and wished I could break even and get away, for the Injuns had nothing to trade except a few stolen robes till late this fall and before that there was some chances that I might be dead. He was candid and said, "I don't blame you for that but as you have got to stay and are used to the country, come over and look the stuff over and tell us what you will give us for it anyway as it is of no use to us the way it is now." But I told him that I could not buy it if I wanted to, as I did not have that much money. The best thing for him to do was to get some of the Pend d'Oreilles to go back to Carrol on the Missouri River and the chances were that he might pick up four more condemned army mules and harness, and to come back and try again for Bozeman where they could easily sell all their stuff for cash.

But he said, "I guess not, I have now got all I want of this glorious West and your friend, meaning old Gabriel, has been telling me that we were lucky the way it came out that the Injuns did not rob us of everything we had and that the worst is yet to come, as there are a bad bunch of Blackfeet camped near here and, if it had been them, they would have cleaned our outfit out slick and clean and probably murdered us as well. So here is the chance of your life and don't be foolish and mean and turn us down for you surely have some money and riding horses that will help us to get out of here and back to God's country."

But I told him all the money I have got is $250, but that I still owe $300 in Bozeman on the stuff I got. I thought more of the $250 than of his outfit.

He had to stay all night. Old Gabriel asked me to come over to his tepee alone and there told me, "I think you are one damn fool for not trying to get that stuff in some way as you cannot lose now and the stuff is here. Just wait till the buffalo and fur gets good and you could sell much more stuff than this as you will be right here among the Injuns and get everything from them as quick as they will have it."

I went back to camp and put Webber in the dugout to sleep; then I went to sleep by the fire outside and don't know how long I had slept when I woke up with a jump. Someone had threw a small rock on me on the bed and on looking around I seen a woman standing in the shadows of the camp and I could see her beckon to me to come over to her and, think of the devil and he will appear, for here was my honey squaw In-who-lise, who tells me she had sneaked out of the Injun camp and stolen some warrior's horse that was picketed out handy, bringing all of Cha-ki-a-ki's dogs with her for company and had come through the three miles alone and she now tells me she is afraid that if Kat-a-lee and Sow-set tells on her then will be much trouble and that Spel-a-qua might catch her and make her his squaw Injun style. I found out that In-who-lise can say more English words than she will admit, for I had no trouble in understanding her in Injun and some English that she wants me to say to Colon Suten (Jesus Christ) that I am going to marry her and do what I said I would and that if she has to run away from the Injun camp and come to me, I will take her off and marry her. I told her it was all right, I would do so, and that Sow-set and Kat-a-lee said they were not going to tell and for her to keep out of their way for a few days as I had to go away in the morning with a white man and see his goods and would be gone tomorrow and maybe next day. If she thinks that anything bad is going to happen to sneak off and hide till I come back, and, if necessary, to tell Spel-a-qua that if he does anything to her I will kill him, and that I will ride through Injun camp tomorrow. After some more talk she rode off in the dark.

In the morning, against my better judgment, I went back with Webber and old Gabriel and rode through the Injun camp and saw In-who-lise as I rode through and can see that so far nothing is wrong with her. As I gave Webber a horse to ride, we were back at his wagon in less than half a day, where we found Harris somewhat white about the gills, but otherwise O.K. and damn glad to see us. They sure had a fine three and a half shuttler wagon with double boxes and wagon sheets, complete; it was loaded up above the top of the double box with goods and a good four-mule load it looked to me. After wrangling all that day, old Gabriel talked me into it; but I still did not want to buy this outfit, which goes to show just how bright the Squaw Kid was at this time, and a fool for luck every time, for I got the whole works. The goods alone cost them over nineteen hundred dollars wholesale in St. Louis. I got the wagon and everything the way it stood except their bed and a few cooking utensils and some grub. The stuff, being here, was worth nearly double what it cost in St. Louis and for all this stuff I paid in cash $240, one pack horse and load of fifteen buffalo robes, two saddle horses to ride and one pack horse to pack their bed and camp outfit, and when they were ready to leave, would furnish them an escort of two Injuns and one guide to the mouth of the Big Timber on the Yellowstone where the Bozeman trail ran. In their stuff, now mine, was two cases of Spencer rifles, six rifles in a case, two cases of Henry carbines, six rifles in a case, several cases of ammunition, powder and lead, three dozen eight-pound Hudson Bay blankets, three dozen fancy all-wool Indian blankets, two dozen fancy-colored wool shawls, bolts of calico and red flannel,

some squaw axes and butcher knives, traps, tobacco, one box
notions like ribbons, thread, needles and silk handkerchiefs
and other knicknacks, one barrel of sugar and many other
things, and last but not least, about a peck of phony jewelry
and near five gallons of rum, one good four-horse load and
more stuff than many one-horse country stores have in
them. Webber and Harris agreed to camp there until all the
stuff was moved. It took ten pack animals two trips to pack
it to my camp. The price paid for this was no better than
highway robbery. I never could get a bargain like this since
then. But I was so disgusted because if it had not been for
old Gabriel who had to knock some sense in me I would not
have bought it at any price.

I had no harness or horses that were broke to haul the
wagon into camp, still I knew that I had to get it here some
way or some of the wandering Injuns would wreck it and
take out the spokes to make war clubs and squaw whip han-
dles and then maybe burn the rest of it, so I told old Gabriel.
He went to the Injun camp and when he came back said that
Pa-kal-k who had a raft of squaws said that he thought that
he could haul the wagon with them travois horses, and
would do it for a needle gun and two boxes of cartridges, so
as I could not help myself as the wagon was no good twenty
miles away and they had to come across several creeks to get
here, still they made it in two days and it sure was a sight
worth going many miles to see them as they came into camp
with a cayuse lashed on each side of the tongue and a squaw
riding them to steer the wagon and two squaws on their
ponies on each side of the wagon and all of them pulling to
beat the band and leading the outfit on his dancing buffalo
horse rode Pa-kal-k (Young Eagle) as proud as Napoleon the
day he crossed the Alps with his elephants on snowshoes.
Though the squaws done all the work and he just looked on,
I gave him his gun and cartridges but felt so sorry for the
squaws who were all mud from having to get down when
they would get stuck in the creeks and had to pull and push,
so for once in my life I opened my hard heart and told

Gabriel to give and to keep for me a free pass through the Golden Gate for I gave each one a cupful of sugar, about a yard of red ribbon and a brass ring with a thousand-dollar glass diamond in it that never did sparkle or never will and Pa-kal-k thought I ought to give him the same as his squaws, but when I refused, went off anything but pleased, and you need not be surprised if you see it in the papers as I think he is going to sue me for alienating his squaws' affections, so now the Squaw Kid has his white elephant in camp with everything but the harness and horses that will pull it.

When going back and forth from the wagon to camp, I seen In-who-lise every time I went through the Injun camp and could see everything was all right so far, but if you think that old Gabriel's inseparable Kat-a-lee and Sow-set have reformed and entered a convent to leave the vanities of this wicked world behind in prayer and holy meditation, you are wrong, and have got another guess coming, for they are still on the job and going strong and while they did not give In-who-lise away in the Injun camp, it was not through any pity or generosity on their part. Those two master minds knew of many better ways to hurt and prolong her misery, and at the same time, though there is no doubt that they thought a lot of me, they gave me a lesson that I will remember for some time. I started with my pack train to get this stuff at the wagon with two young Injuns to help me. To my surprise as we struck out from camp, Kat-a-lee and Sow-set, on prancing squaw ponies, fell in line in the outfit saying that they were going along as a guard to keep away any bad Injuns or squaws from trying to do me any harm or wrong, and in vain did I protest that they should not come as I thought I could not make it back to camp today and would have to camp at the wagon tonight and besides, I did not want In-who-lise to see them going with me through the Injun camp, but they only laughed at me and said, "Foolish, brave, noble squaw-chasing warrior of the plains, we shriek with joy when we hear you say that, and know that your broken-tooth Sapah-tan buffalo heifer In-who-

There was some change when we started again, for Kat-a-lee paired off with the buck in the middle, leaving me behind driving the rear with the lovely Squis-squis riding at my side. Every time she got the chance she accidentally, but lovingly, crowded her horse against mine. She would reach over and pull my long hair, all the playful monkey antics that the lovely Squis-squis could pull off, even on the back of a horse. I thought it was a good thing this little whirlwind did not have me on the ground.

Another interruption came to the Squaw Kid's hopes of making the wagon in time that day, for Kat-a-lee reined up with the buck and in Injun hog grunts they argued about the wonderful speed of their horses. Kat-a-lee was saying to the young buck, even if the other Injun did beat Sow-set, that didn't say that he could beat her, for she knew that she could run away from him and leave him in the shade, even if she was a squaw. No buck would take that from a squaw. I knew there was no use in trying to hurry an Injun, so with a sickly smile I realized that I was elected to camp out under the bright stars with them that night.

I was wishing that old Gabriel had knocked them in the head the day they were born, or that he would whale the hell out of them and keep them at home. So after much slick fooling around, the young Injun beat Kat-a-lee easily as I knew that he would. No buck Injun would have it said that a squaw beat him.

Then we struck out again, but I didn't care how fast we went as it was too late to make it back to camp that night. We trailed along and the lovely Squis-squis was helping me behind, driving the horses along. That kind of work only seemed to make her all the more affectionate. So I said to Squis-squis, "Nay, fair squaw, not today. Alas, I am on the water wagon now and must be good today, and would be on my way."

But the lovely Squis-squis seemed not to be dismayed, and laughingly said, "Sweet warrior, An-ta-lee"—as she called me, "be not afraid, for you are going to see a better day. Come now and let Squis-squis ride with you on your horse. She still has many beautiful words to say to you, then you can know that she is the sweetest squaw of all the Pend d'Oreilles."

Then Kat-a-lee and Sow-set, who seemed to think that things were not going right, rode back to us and Sow-set said, "Lovely Squis-squis, how comes your day? Why does not your voice ring out with laughter and song? Sweet life to us is short, and the night soon to come is long."

Squis-squis said, "Oh, that I should have to say it, she, whom the warriors greet with songs, now smiles no more. The white-faced warrior, An-ta-lee, his heart is dead to me." Kat-a-lee called out to the two young bucks ahead, in a silvery voice that rang with deviltry, saying, "Stay, brave warriors. Why hurry on your way? A race, a race, to liven up the day, when the night is still far away, and the sweet prairie was made for play. Yes, a race, between the pale-face warrior, An-ta-lee, and our lovely Squis-squis, sweetest maiden of the Pend d'Oreilles. An-ta-lee surely will not say nay to her or us and have the warriors and squaws in camp say that the white warrior, An-ta-lee, was afraid of a squaw, our lovely Squis-squis."

To make matters worse, Sow-set started on me, saying, "A great warrior is An-ta-lee, the white brave. But no one ever saw him come back from the war trail, with the scalp of his enemy, whom he had slain, nor have they seen him wave a scalp from his coup stick as he danced and sang his glory before the warriors and squaws. An-ta-lee, the white buffalo bull, holds his head down in shame, and will not answer our bawls or bellows, when we paw the ground around him. All our misery is in vain, for it is only that evil Sapah-tan In-who-lise who can bring back the fire to his eyes. Evil was the day she came to our tribe and when An-ta-lee said that we ought to be good like her." The two bucks sat on their horses as solemn as owls, and what they thought only themselves and the devil knew, but I knew that this tongue-lashing from a squaw didn't raise me any in their estimation. I saw that I had either to go at Kat-a-lee and Sow-set and give them a good beating Injun style, a thing they knew that I would not do, or I had to shut my mouth and race Squis-squis as they wanted, for if I did not they would spread it around that I was afraid of a squaw.

I thought it would only be a short race, like the other two had been, but Squis-squis, had ideas of her own and said that it was to be over the prairies and far away. The rest of them could keep on going; they need not have any fear when Squis-squis led the way, for she would find them before they could reach the wagon. After much wrangling, I told her to light out. She was off like a streak of wind and the race was on as she headed for a ridge nearly a mile away.

I kept gaining on her, which she intended anyway. She started up the low ridge and, with the caution that was born in her, she stopped when she made the top, to see what was on the other side of the ridge. All at once she wheeled her horse around and got off, making signs to me to be careful. I thought that it was only a squaw's game, but when I got up to her, she said to get off and not to ride any further. There was a bunch of Injuns on the other side, at the foot of the ridge, and they would see me. If I did not believe her she would hold my horse and I could crawl up to the top and see them. I crawled up to where I could observe with safety, and saw eleven buck Injuns about four hundred yards away at the foot of the ridge holding some kind of a powwow on their ponies. I could not tell what kind of Injuns they were. I thought they were Piegans, but when I got back to Squis-squis she said, "No, Cha-qua [Blackfeet]." She said we should light out and catch up with the others, as the Blackfeet were bad friends of the Pend d'Oreilles, and tough on their squaws when they got the chance.

We lost no time in getting out of there, and it was easy to see that the bulling fever that had been burning up the lovely Squis-squis all day along the trail had now dropped to zero, and she was back to normal again. All she wanted any more was to be on her way and put all the distance between that Blackfeet bunch and us. We had not gone a mile when, sure enough, over the ridge the buck Injuns came. When they saw us, they let out a whoop, to let us know that they were on the way.

I could not help but say, "So the sweet squaw of the Pend d'Oreilles wanted to race An-ta-lee over the prairie and far away to a sweet place, and it will surely be a sweet place the way it looks." But the divine Squis-squis is now too much occupied in throwing the rawhide in her pony to say anything, and it sure was a race in earnest, and when Kat-a-lee and the others saw us coming and what was behind us, they now sent them pack horses flying along the way with a zeal that if they had done so in the first part of the day, then it would have been much better for the Squaw Kid in the end.

We landed at the wagon in a cloud of dust. Webber and Harris stood there with their hair standing on end, as they seen them charging and whooping Injuns coming behind us.

It was lucky for us that two of the Injuns in this bunch of Blackfeet were some I had traded with. When they found out that the wagon and stuff was mine they got on their war ponies and rode off leaving us all feeling much better. Webber and Harris said that if God would only let them pull out alive and get back East to God's country, with their hide and hair, that never more would they come on a trading trip among the noble red men in the beautiful Musselshell.

We made camp and Kat-a-lee and the other Junos came in handy, to rustle wood, make the fires and broil an antelope that one of the bucks shot. Webber wanted to know how it was that I was traveling around with such a display of females when he thought I told him I had no woman. I was truthful and told him that they did not belong to me, but to the bucks who were too lazy to work and had brought them along.

We sat around the fire eating broiled antelope and had a good time. The Blackfeet seemed to have put the fear of God in Kat-a-lee, Sow-set and Squis-squis. They sat there and did not try to bother the Squaw Kid any more. He sat there in

glee, as he thinks this one time he has got the best of the wild
squaws at their own game, and that the Blackfeet do a good
turn once in a while, even if they can't help it.

In this happy frame of mind, I said my prayers and rolled
up in my blankets, my cherubic face reflecting a halo of
purity and modesty. With a sweet smile on my lips, I went to
sleep murmuring, "In-who-lise," who was twenty miles
away in the Injun camp.

Next day as the morning's light now came, so the Squaw
Kid woke up to view its magnificent splendor, and to view
the beautiful Squis-squis, who now reposes in his arms, with
an arm around his neck, and a triumphant look in her eyes.
With a silvery laugh she reminds me of what she told me
yesterday: to tell her this tomorrow, and wants to know how
I like the color of her hair.

Yes, there was no doubt about it, there she was, and In-
who-lise, the sweet little truthful squaw, is out in the cold;
and Kat-a-lee is sure some prophetess after all, and is entitled to a full life-size bas-relief of herself on the gate of hell.

The Squaw Kid missionary to the squaws, who had said
to Colon Suten and to a squaw that he would be good and
meant it, was mad. I had fallen under the skillful management of Squis-squis. She had proven herself a worthy pupil
of Kat-a-lee and Sow-set in the dark hours of the night.
Squis-squis had become afraid to sleep alone because some
of the Blackfeet were around, so she crawled in with the
Squaw Kid. The Squaw Kid had finally taken and had been
put through all the degrees of the squaws and now knew all
the cards in the squaws' cold deck.

With the help of this jovial bunch in the morning, it was
not long until I had the loads packed on the horses. I started
back to camp, leaving Webber and Harris there, because
there was another pack-train load left, and the Squaw Kid,
who had been preaching to you about his fear of hell, but
alas, like many others, now does not practice what he
preaches, for as he now goes on his way back to camp, he is
headed for hell with a downhill pull (and seems to like it). I

planned to be back the next day. We trailed along, and Kat-a-lee, Sow-set and Squis-squis were more than gay. They were trying to give the Squaw Kid a better day with their laughing eyes and songs of joy, but he hears not their laughing voices, for he is now doing some thinking that dampens any gaiety on his part, for now a grim and merciless hand is pointing and showing him the way back on his trail.

When not so many years ago but that he can still remember, and see himself as he stood down on the Rio Grande, when his heart and soul were pure and good, as he went down on his knees in old Isaleta, and with holy reverence bowed down his head, and prayed to God Jesus and the Madonna with a holy light on his face and tears of pity in his eyes. As he went around those somber and silent walls on his knees, praying to Jesus where hung the stations of the cross, that portrayed the cruel suffering and sorrowful journey of the Nazarene, carrying with him the cross as he goes to his death on Calvary hill, that man might live an eternal and better life. And the Squaw Kid shivers as he now can see and hear the old padre, pounding the pulpit, his eyes flashing and face stern; he is saying, "Woe be unto you Jezebels, mend your ways or hell shall be your lot, and to you sons of Belial, hell was made for you." And the Squaw Kid is thinking he is meaning him, and can smell the brimstone and sulfur. So the further the Squaw Kid goes along the trail, the worse it gets, and why should it not be so, for not even a decent squaw would touch him today. And what is Squis-squis going to do, who, though a kind of a bronco Christian, can claim that she is now my woman, as this roll-her-over ceremony is as good to her as though all the preachers in the universe had done the job? So the Squaw Kid resolves that if he can only get out of it this time, with his hide and hair, to be good again, and to give Kat-a-lee and her bunch of festive squaws the run, and to put a lock on the stable door of love, even if the horses of love have been stolen.

By the time we got near the Injun camp Squis-squis was now pouting at my funeral looks, and when we were going through the camp, I seen In-who-lise sitting outside the tepee but she held down her head and would not look at me, and when she finds out the whole story it will be worse.

We nearly got through the camp, when two burly squaws stood in the way, one with a good long stick in her hand. When the first Injun that was on the lead came up to them, the one with the stick who was Squis-squis's mother gave him a good whack, and as the pack horses went by she struck them. But the buck who rode in the middle seen what was coming and rode out of the way. This sent the horses flying. Then I came up from behind with the Junos. The squaw without the stick caught hold of Squis-squis's horse and held it. Squis-squis's Amazon mother smashed Kat-a-lee on the wrist and nearly broke it, then wheeled around and gave Sow-set one on the leg, and before I could get out of the way, managed to give me one on the leg that left a blue ridge there for some days. Then she started in on the three of us and gave us a tongue-lashing of blackguarding oratory. I thought Kat-a-lee and Sow-set had stretched the female limit, but this dusky lady put them in the shade, and was a professor and bachlor of arts next to them. In vain did old Gabriel's two Sodomites try to tell her that she ought to know that nothing wrong could happen to her innocent daughter when they were along to protect her.

But she was probably on some of the same kind of trips in her youthful days, so she would not swallow this. Squis-squis, who was old enough to have a mind of her own, now slashed the squaw who was holding her horse on the hand with her whip, and took her by surprise. She let go of the rawhide whang that was tied on the horse's lower jaw for a bridle. Then Squis-squis gave her horse a crack with her whip and was off, but the horse stepped on the trailing whang and stumbled; then the squaw caught the trailing whang and held the horse till Squis-squis's mother came up and pulled her out of the saddle by the hair braids. Even then she put up a good fight with her husky mother, but the other squaw came up and helped her mother, when now this sweet little daughter of the sun quick as a flash pulls her knife and rips the squaw down the arm, and if she had not taken it on the arm, would have had her belly ripped open, such was the sweet affectionate nature of the Squaw Kid's gentle houris in the squaw paradise. But they took her knife away and got the best of her, and though she had busted it up between In-who-lise and I, I could not help but feel sorry for her, as she was a good little squaw.

After we got a little way from the Injun camp, Kat-a-lee and Sow-set rode on ahead to camp. We soon arrived and old Gabriel met us all smiles, glad that we made the trip in safety. If he knew that they were with me he said nothing.

I put away the stuff and got something to eat. I told the two young bucks not to go back to the Injun camp because I would need them to go back to the wagon in the morning with me. They went over to Petol's tepee.

I sat by the fire thinking of the fine mess I had got into, and of the many more to come, as long as Kat-a-lee and Sow-set and their bunch were around to help me on my way to hell. But even those sweet thoughts were denied me, for soon both of old Gabe's limbs of Satan came over. Kat-a-lee started the ball rolling about something I wanted to forget. That was: What was I going to do about Squis-squis, and our fishing trip to the river Jordan? She wished me joy and happiness and launched out like a female evangelist to praise the virtue and modesty of Squis-squis over In-who-lise. I was lucky that I had two good friends like her and Sow-set to save me from getting gored by that buffalo cow In-who-lise, who was a bad one.

Where could I find a sweeter maid than Squis-squis or one who loved me like her? Had she not proven her love to me, and was it not up to me to make it right with her people? Only ten horses stood in the way. If I would say that I would marry her the first time a Black Robe came that way, then they had no doubt that I could have immediate possession of the lovely Squis-squis, who was, according to Injun law and custom, my squaw.

"Hark, you are not going to see that Sapah-tan snake any more. If you do not take Squis-squis, we are going to tell Spel-a-qua and Cha-ki-a-ki's women everything on her and you, then that Sapah-tan snake will be Spel-a-qua's squaw before tomorrow night. When we tell Spel-a-qua that we caught her coiled up in your lap, then Spel-a-qua will take the coils out of her."

I threatened her in vain with what I would do to them. I said that I would kill Spel-a-qua the first chance I got, if he harmed In-who-lise in any way. But I might as well have talked to a rock as to them. I told them that I had given up all hope of getting In-who-lise. She had never done them any harm. They should leave her alone and I would give them many pretty things. But they only laughed at me and said, "You take Squis-squis, your woman, or we tell." It must have been the devil who put the next notion in my head, for I said to them, "You can do so, but Kat-a-lee and Sow-set must know that I have plenty of friends in the Blackfeet camp, two sleeps from here."

Sow-set said, "Yes we do, for do not some of the Pend d'Oreille warriors say that An-ta-lee is a snake-in-the-grass for the Blackfeet, or else why are they his friends?"

I told them to go ahead and tell Spel-a-qua, but they could not do In-who-lise any harm in the Injun camp. In a few days some of the Blackfeet warriors were coming to camp to swap. I would show Kat-a-lee and Sow-set to them, and tell the warriors to watch and catch Kat-a-lee and Sow-set and cut their throats. I would give the warriors two new rifles and plenty of ammunition after they did it. It was a hard thing to knock a squaw speechless, but both of them turned a sickly white, with terror in their faces, but those two unholy diplomats were too case-hardened for it to last long.

Kat-a-lee said, "So this is An-ta-lee, the friend of my father and the Pend d'Oreilles. When we tell the warriors this it will be An-ta-lee who will have his throat cut; he is so good a friend of the Blackfeet."

But I said, "Shut your mouth, squaw of evil. If you are going to tell on In-who-lise, you should know I am not afraid of the warriors doing that. I know that the good squaws in camp, when they know the Blackfeet have cut your throats, will not have to fear and dread Kat-a-lee's and Sow-set's love calls in the night any more. Why do the old warriors say that it would be better for the Pend d'Oreille camp if Kat-a-lee and Sow-set were dead or far away? No, that will not save you from the Blackfeet warriors. Their hearts will sing with joy, when they know that the Blackfeet warriors are watching and trailing you like the cougar trails the deer. Just as sure as anything will come the time when they will spring on you. And the good squaws in camp will comb their braids as they laugh and sing, when they hear that the Blackfeet have cut your throats and that you are dead.

"Why does not Kat-a-lee, the wise one, say that she will tell her father on An-ta-lee? Maybe she knows that he would want to know why An-ta-lee was going to get the Blackfeet to cut her throat, something they don't want him to know. Yes, go and tell your father on An-ta-lee, so he can ask me why Sow-set has a cut on her thigh and Kat-a-lee a burn on her side. Maybe he would ask An-ta-lee how he knew."

Then Sow-set said, "But sweet An-ta-lee will not tell him that, when I tell him that Kat-a-lee and I shall die and An-ta-lee with us. Sow-set is not afraid of sweet An-ta-lee, for though his tongue is lying to me, his eyes are telling Sow-set that he will never harm the squaw whose arms he had felt, nor have her throat cut by the Blackfeet. An-ta-lee cannot know how well Sow-set loves him and because of that he will do her no harm for telling on In-who-lise in the Injun camp.

"Sow-set's heart is singing with joy. She knows that In-who-lise covers up her head and cries in the Injun camp. Sow-set will not tell Spel-a-qua on her, but she will go to In-who-lise and wring the last drop of blood out of her heart to make her cry some more. Then she too can feel and know what Sow-set feels and knows: the pain and hate that burns like a roaring fire. Sow-set can reach up to the bright sky, caring not for the Black Robes' fires, for the man she loves. An-ta-lee need not think that Sapah-tan snake has forgotten him, for the squaw who covers up her head and cries and says that she has forgotten and doesn't care, lies." So in that way we kept it up, and when they saw that they could not get what they wanted, they got as sweet as honey to me.

Kat-a-lee said, "Sweet An-ta-lee. You know how well we love thee, so we will not tell on In-who-lise. Tomorrow we are going to go back with you, then you will surely know that we did not tell or do her any harm, when we are both with you."

But I told them they had done the deviltry already, and as sure as the white man's God they were not going to go back to the wagon with me and pull off some more of their Squis-squis games on me. I was done with them forever. When they saw that they could not soft-soap me any more and were leaving, Kat-a-lee said, "Then if sweet An-ta-lee will not let us go with him any more, and if our love makes him cry, then we promise him nothing for In-who-lise, and he will have to get the Blackfeet to cut our throats."

At daylight I ran the horses in and was soon ready to start back to the wagon. The two young bucks who were helping me wanted to know if I was going to let Kat-a-lee and Sow-set come too. When I said no, the both of them rode off for the Injun camp, leaving me alone with the outfit all saddled. I did not know what I would have done, only old Gabriel came up and said that he would go with me. Old Gabriel, the only friend I had and the man that I was low-down enough to stab in the back. I swore to God, and to all the angels of heaven and hell, that I would never do a thing like that again, no matter the color of the squaw's hair.

We were soon on the way, and in passing through the Injun camp I seen In-who-lise, but she covered up her head and would not look at me. Old Gabriel said, "I wonder what is the matter with that Nez Perce girl. She seems to be in some kind of sorrow. I suppose some of the women have been mean to her." I could have told him, but I said nothing. We rode on to the wagon without any trouble. We camped there for the night. There were no high jinks or squaws this time. We made it back to camp early enough to fix up the outfit for Webber and Harris. For an Injun blanket apiece and two boxes of Henry cartridges I got two Injuns named Charl and Petoe to go along with them. Old Gabriel's son Samwell went as guide, though he had never been over the trail, for two blankets and two boxes of fifty-caliber cartridges. Early in the morning, the fifth day after I bought the outfit, they started off for the Yellowstone with Webber and Harris, who I hope that in whatever they undertake they will have better luck than they had on this journey, as they were two nice and generous men to me, even if they could not help it. Five days later the Injuns got back without any trouble, saying that they had left them on the Bozeman trail and had helped them to start off for Bozeman.

After Webber and Harris left I spent the day looking over the stuff I got from them. The shack was full nearly to the roof, but it did not bring me any joy, for after the events of the previous couple of days, like all crooked acts, I realized I had to pay for them dearly in the end, and was down in the mouth.

I put in the day passing good resolutions. Toward nightfall old Gabriel came over and noticed my sorrow. He wanted to know why I was not happy after getting all that stuff for almost nothing. I told him that I would probably live through it, so I went and got him a couple shots of redeye. They made his Injun eyes grow bright, and then to relieve my conscience for the dirt I had done him, I dedicated the five-gallon keg of rum to him that I had gotten from Webber and Company. It was great stuff for I had tasted some of it, and it tasted and smelled like the horse liniment that Uncle Sam used on his mules, called Four-X. So he started to tell me about the great time they had at Kamaloops when he was young and was working for the Hudson Bay Company.

Being out for many months in the hills and over the prairies, they met here to have a good time all together, but what was his sorrow when the factor put him and a Frenchman in as cooks to prepare the feast while the rest of them were having a good time and a glorious drunk. This made the Frenchman and him so mad they wanted revenge. There was a bitch with a litter of pups where they were doing the cooking, so they killed all the pups and cut them up, hair and all, and cooked them in a large pot of soup or bouillon that they were making. The others were so drunk they did not notice it, or know what they were eating till they sobered up the next day, when they told them and gave them the laugh. With a chuckle old Gabriel said that factor never tried to make him do any more cooking after this. Then he got up and went over to his tepee, to sleep off the three shots of red-eye I had given him.

Kat-a-lee and Sow-set came over to camp the next day and wanted me to kiss and make up, but I was a frigid monument of virtue to them. I would not speak to them and gave them the bad eye good and plenty. They left, but they did not fool me any. Their eyes said, "We go, but we will try again when the moon is right and the stars are bright, we will slip back into your life."

Along toward night five Piegan bucks rode into camp and I knew that they were Three Squaws Bulleau's Injun wives' relations. I had seen them in his camp. So after the usual handshaking they started to make themselves at home. That left me no doubt that the Squaw Kid was elected to feed them that night and maybe longer. I decided I would try to get some information from them about Beaver Tom. But more than that I was going to try to find out from them if Le-oh-hee had made it back all right, and where she was.

I badly wanted to know where she was, but did not know that I was going to get the jar of my life. A young buck in the bunch came to me and gave me what looked like a tassel of black human hair. There were five small braids all put together in a tassel and bound around the top with beads. It had a buckskin loop to hang it on a button or anywhere else a person wanted to carry it. I did not know what a squaw's love token was, at that time, but just as soon as I took it in my hand something seemed to tell me that something was terribly wrong. My legs began to tremble and I shook like I had the chills and fever, and the hair tassel dropped out of my hands on the ground. The buck picked it up and hung it on a button on my shirt.

I could not talk Piegan, so he began in signs to tell me about Le-oh-hee. I sure to God got it in a way I never want

to hear again as long as I live. He told me by signs what I
understood only too well. It made me want to cry out in terror as I stood shaking like a leaf. But still hoping against
hope that I might be wrong, I made a sign to old Gabriel to
come over from his tepee where he was standing. I told him,
"Ask that Injun what he was saying with his hands and fingers, and what the hair tassel meant."

"He says that a Piegan breed girl Le-oh-hee sent you this.
It is to let you know that she remembered you while she was
living. She hopes that when you see this, you will think well
of her, now that she is dead." He told old Gabriel that when
Beaver Tom came back to the Bulleau camp, they said she
would have to take Beaver Tom for her man. She ran away
and they did not know where she had been. Nearly two
weeks later she came back to camp. Bulleau was awfully mad
at her, but she would not tell him where she had been. He
told her that she would get no more chances to run off
again. She was to get ready to take Beaver Tom for her man.
All that she would say to them was that she would never run
off again.

A couple of days after she got back, she washed herself in
the creek, combed and braided her hair, and put on her
Injun finery. She told Bulleau to tell Beaver Tom that he
could be glad, for he could have her for his woman that
night. When she got the chance in the afternoon and no one
was in the tepee, she took a buckskin string and tied it on a
tepee pole and the other end to the trigger of a rifle. She
tried to shoot herself through the heart, but only wounded
herself. She lived nearly two days before she died. Le-oh-hee,
with her beautiful misty, somber eyes, and with a heart and
soul that were good, killed herself rather than be Beaver
Tom's woman. Before she died, she asked the warrior to
come and give me the braids, and to say that I had thought
wrong of her, but would know her better now.

I stood there in sorrow and I saw that Kat-a-lee and Sow-
set and some of the Pend d'Oreilles were listening to all this.
And old Gabriel's eyes were blazing at me in anger, as he

asked, "How comes it that this breed Piegan girl who shot
herself sends you her hair as a keepsake of her love for you?
What deviltry have you been up to with her? You told me
then that you were a stranger here and did not know any
Injuns. I am finding out some more of your lies to me. I
want to know how it is that she knew you so well, if you had
not been with her some time?"

So I said, "Yes, I knew her. If you think that I ever harmed
her you are a liar. She was a good woman, better than a full
country of she devils like some of the squaws the Pend
d'Oreilles have. It would have been better if I had taken her,
then I would not be like I am today, a damn snake-in-the-
grass to my best friend." It was a good thing that old Gabriel
did not fully understand what I meant. He still raved at me,
but I would not tell about Le-oh-hee being in camp with me
all those days, because he would not understand and only
think all the worse of me. I told him that he could think
what he wanted. So he went to his tepee as mad as hell.

That night the five Piegans laid around the fire with me
and slept. But I did not sleep, for across that same fire I
could still see Le-oh-hee laying rolled in her blanket as she
did when the Squaw Kid fought with the devil them nights
to keep from doing her any harm. When it was too late, he
understood Le-oh-hee and why she came to him, and now
the Squaw Kid was silently crying.

Early the next morning the Piegans from Bulleau's camp
left to go back to the Judith Gap. I was alone in camp all day,
because none of old Gabriel's bunch came near me. It
showed that old Gabriel must have been good and mad at
me. To make it worse, that tassel of Le-oh-hee's hair was still
hanging on a button on my shirt, in plain sight; every time
I looked at it or touched it, it sent the cold chills through
me, but I would not take it off. So it went for a couple of
days. They all shunned me like I was an evil spirit.

I could not find out anything about In-who-lise, and was
beginning to wish that old White Grass and the Blackfeet
would come, as they said they would, to swap for more guns

and ammunition. Then, maybe I would pull out with them, because I had not swapped anything to the Pend d'Oreilles for some time. If old Gabriel stayed mad at me, they would soon clean me out. I knew there were a few in that bunch who would be only too glad of the chance to give me a shot in the back. They were afraid of old Gabriel and the chief of the hunt, Co-quay-ah-tam-a-la, who was a good man.

CHAPTER EIGHTEEN
The Logic of In-who-lise

I got sick of hanging around camp and saddled up. I rode off not caring much where I went. Everything was busted up with In-who-lise, and the only thing I had gotten out of it was that I now talk Injun, walk like one, and had got the Injun smell from the squaws. Now the Injun dogs no longer tried to bite me like they do all white men. I rode along by the brush and trees on the creek, toward the Injun camp. I had gone a mile or so—they say that if you will think of the devil he will appear—when the dusky and wingless angel appeared, In-who-lise, and waved her hand for me to come to her. I had been wanting to see her for a few days, but then when I had the chance, I didn't feel any too good. I knew it was going to be a hard job to meet those honest eyes and to look her in the face.

The Squaw Kid knew that he had done her dirt, and there was no use for his oily tongue to lie out of it. Kat-a-lee and Sow-set had taken care of that, and they had wrung the last drop of blood out of her heart. They probably milked her dry to make her cry some more, as they said they would, even if they had not told Spel-a-qua yet. That was one kind of joy that a squaw would not miss, even if the heavens fell, nor could Black Robe's fires of hell scare her away. However, In-who-lise was a squaw herself and she did not meet me with bitter reproaches.

Instead she was all smiles as she said, "Do you know that I have been trying to see you for some days? Why did you not come to me? I thought that after you told me all those beautiful words that you would be sorry to know that I now cover up my head and cry. Sow-set now laughs at me, because you will say no more sweet words, or come back to me no more. She says that I will never be your squaw in your lodge. She calls me the Nez Perce buffalo cow, when she and Squis-squis and some more of the beautiful Pend d'Oreille maidens are around. You had found out that their arms were softer and their lips sweeter than mine. But I told her that maybe it was so today, but when you found out their evil ways you would come back to White Feather tomorrow, whose love for you is as sweet and true as a bright day. Why sit there on your horse? Do you want me to believe that what they say is so?"

I got off the horse and went up to In-who-lise. A look of horror came into her face, and she points at the braided tassel of Leoh-hee's hair hanging on a button on my shirt. She started to back away from me, and at the same time she said, "So it is just as the women in camp are saying today. An-ta-lee is bad and evil like all white men are. They say that Kat-a-lee heard the Piegan warriors say that An-ta-lee ran away and left his Piegan woman before he came here. She killed herself in her sorrow for him, so the Piegans came and brought An-ta-lee her hair so that her spirit will come from the land of the dead and haunt him night and day."

Then I knew why the squaws in the squaw paradise got out of my way and gave me the bad eye. Kat-a-lee had taken care of that. I tried in vain to coax her to come up to me so I could explain to her that there was never anything between Le-oh-hee and me. I had never harmed her and she did not kill herself on account of my leaving her, but because they tried to make her take a man she did not want. But in the end I only made a bad job of it.

I only got her jealousy and suspicions of me all the worse, for she said, "So this is how I find you out. Evil was the day when some evil spirit put your face in my heart and a smile of joy on my lips, to think that you cared only for my smiles. Sad is the blow when I know that another face was always sweeter to your heart than mine, when she was living, and is still whispering to you her sweet words from the land of the dead. If this is not so, why do you carry that love token of hers in plain sight, to let every squaw know that there never was another like her living, and it is still so after she is dead? I can fight the evil love of Sow-set and others who are living, for their evil love will fade away before my sharp knife like the snow in the hot sun. But she who is dead will stand there as a misty form in that hair, and she will mock me all day. It will lie between you and me in the night, for she will come and keep your heart away from me with her sweet dreams. If you care for me as you say, put away and destroy that woman's hair."

I said that a Piegan warrior had put it there, and there it was to stay. I told her that Le-oh-hee never did her any harm, and it would be wrong for me to destroy it, after the way that she sent it to me to remember her. It was of no use, for in the end she said to me, "Then if you think more of that woman and her hair than you do of me you can keep her to comfort you with her love." She had a look of sorrow on her face as she glided off in the brush, leaving me there alone.

I rode back to camp in sadness, to think that In-who-lise would think that way about it. As I looked at the hair braids of Le-oh-hee, they did not terrify me any more, and they now gave me a kind of comfort. They were all that the Squaw Kid had left. Something seemed to tell me that Le-oh-hee's sad, somber eyes and sweet face were smiling in a better land.

I was sitting by the fire when it was getting dusk and old Gabriel glided up to me with his silent tread. He was smiling again, and wanted to be friends. He said, "Why should you and I quarrel over a squaw? It is only the devil that under-stands them anyway." I felt so good over this that I went in the shack and got him a good three-horn drink of Webber and Company rum. It was enough to kill a horse and anything else but an Injun. It just brought a smile to his lips as he drank the whole batch down at one setting. Then he rolled up his eyes and smacked his lips. I thought he was going to croak at first, but it was only an Injun smile, thinking of the happy hunting grounds. I asked him if it was good.

He said, "No, it is better than that. It is great. That Injun whiskey that you have been giving me is pretty good stuff, and a fellow can feel it burn from the mouth to the toes. But this one is much better. It makes a fellow's toenails turn up. Where you catch 'em?" I did not tell him that it was part of the stuff I got from Webber and Harris, nor that there were five gallons of it for him to drink, if he could only live through it. He stayed for some time; then he went off to his tepee, his eyes and heart beaming with joy.

A hand touched me in the night and I woke up with a start, to see In-who-lise at my side. She grabbed me by the hand and made me come away from the camp with her, to where there was no danger of anyone at old Gabriel's hearing us. And though it was dark I could tell that a change for the better had come over her, for she was as sweet as honey to me. She seemed to have lost all fear of the hair braids of Le-oh-hee. She was as playful as a kitten, and wanted to know if I was mad at her for what she had said that afternoon.

When I said no, she asked, "Why do you not tell me nice words so I can smile again? Have I not cried enough already? I have done nothing but cry for many moons. I cried when the white men came and shot and killed our people in the Big Hole and shot me and killed my sister and my father who died afterward. I cried along the trail as our wounded people died on the way. I cried when I seen the soldiers drive our people off, as some of us stood on the Bear Paw Hills and saw them go. They made me cry in the Assiniboine camp and now Kat-a-lee and Sow-set make me cry here. Oh, say not that you are sorry I came to tell you you are my man still. Who is there in the Pend d'Oreille camp like you, who has said before Colon Suten that you loved White Feather, that you would marry her and take her back to where she came from? Yes, An-ta-lee was good to White Feather. Her heart sang with joy to him, when you told her that you would put a ring on her finger and make her your squaw by the Black Robes, and not like Spel-a-qua and the warriors, who think that a squaw is only a bitch to pull into their lodges to work for them and just to use her when they want her."

I said that she ought to know now that I was bad and was no good for her. If it was not so, why did Sow-set and some other squaws make her cry every day? It would be better for her to forget me and let me go my way. It could only turn out like the other day, for how could she stop Kat-a-lee, Squis-squis and their kind, who hated her? They knew that their lips were sweet and their arms soft and warm, and they had smiles as bright as the sun. I had told her before Colon Suten that I would be good and true to her. I had tried to, but it was no use, for Kat-a-lee and Squis-squis had seen to that. She could see how it was.

Like a woman she said, "Sweet An-ta-lee is not the bad one. It is them squaw bitches, who prowl around night and day. An-ta-lee must do as he said to me, for who has White Feather got but thee? And An-ta-lee, after he gets me, need not fear them bad squaws no more with White Feather at his side. When Kat-a-lee laughed at me in scorn yesterday, I told her: Yes, laugh at White Feather today and steal her man away like you did the other day. But harken, if An-ta-lee leaves me for you, some night when Kat-a-lee lifts up the tepee flap to go out, and as she stands there in the light, White Feather, the Nez Perce, will stand there in the dark and her knife will feel your heart!"

I said, "I have friends two sleeps from here, in the Cha-qua [Blackfeet] camp. Let us leave the Pend d'Oreilles and go with them. Some of their warriors will be here almost any day to swap, and they will help me pack my stuff to their camp."

But she said in fear, "Don't go to the Cha-qua. They are bad Injuns. Foolish An-ta-lee, don't go to them. For the Pend d'Oreilles say that the Blackfeet spare not, and they kill every white man they find. Every Blackfeet warrior has to hide his hands when they talk their lies to the white men's chiefs, saying that they are the white man's friends, so the white chiefs cannot see the white men's blood on their hands.

"Don't go to them. When they get you in their camp they will make you sorry. Their squaws don't care for or know Colon Suten and they will make White Feather cry more than she does here. Sweet An-ta-lee, see White Feather is afraid of the dead Piegan woman's hair. Take it off and put it away where I will never see it again, then I will be good and sweet to thee again."

I took her hand and put it where Le-oh-hee's braids had been and I said, "See, they are gone. You are the sweet one; it is for you that I have taken them away." Then the Squaw Kid and In-who-lise started back for the Injun camp hand in hand. I found out that Spel-a-qua and some of the Pend d'Oreille bucks were on a gambling jaunt, playing hands among the Piegans, or any other kind of Injun they could find. She had gone to the chief, Co-quay-ah-tam-a-la, and he said that he would tell Spel-a-qua to leave her alone. We agreed to meet the next day to figure out how we are going to get married when there is no preacher in the country.

In-who-lise left me near the Injun camp, saying that there was none to her like An-ta-lee. She rubbed her head on the Squaw Kid's breast to show her joy that he had put away forever Le-oh-hee's hair braids. I prowled around nearly all night with In-who-lise.

CHAPTER NINETEEN

A Few Guns for the Blackfeet

Next morning old Gabriel came over and said, "Do you know that this Siwash is hard up and would like to get some things and ammunition from you on jawbone, as I have nothing to pay you with now? I know that you would not like to do this, but thought I would ask you anyway. There is no other way, because you do not want to take horses."

But I said, "You thought wrong, for Gabriel Depew can have anything I have got, whether he ever pays me or not." So he got from me three boxes of Henry cartridges, also some calico, tobacco and two blankets. I owed him much for his kindness and good acts to me. I made him a present of a Spencer carbine, with two boxes of cartridges, and a Hudson Bay blanket to keep him warm. Old Gabriel went back to his tepee with joy, and knocked cold with surprise.

Then as I looked and seen what was coming, I thought that it was a good thing that I had placated old Gabriel's heart by giving him jawbone. His good friend and best enemy, old White Grass, with eleven more Blackfeet warriors and a half-breed with them to make the devil's dozen, were headed my way. They were all dressed up, except White Grass and the breed, in regulation style with paint and feathers on their heads, and the rest of them naked in mortal sin, with cartridge belts on them and their guns in their hands. They rode into camp driving seven pack horses loaded with buffalo robes. They gave me the glad hand like I was a long-lost brother. It was not long until they had the robes unpacked and had turned the most of their horses out to feed. I was wondering how much I would have to up the price on what they swapped, so I could break anywhere near even, after I had fed twelve hungry Injuns and a breed. Their stomachs were open at the top, and had no bottoms in them. They asked me the usual question, did I have any whiskey or rum? The Injun thirst for booze is as eternal as the sand hills of Arabia is for rain, but I told them I had none.

After they filled up the breed said to me, "They have brought me along so they could talk to you better. They want to swap you those robes for guns and ammunition and some other stuff."

I asked the breed, "What is your name?" but all I could get out of him was that his name was Joe and that he was a half-breed Blood. Some Bloods and he were visiting in the Blackfeet camp. A buck gave me a robe and wanted sugar for it, but as sugar cost money out here, I only gave him about ten pounds. It did not last them long. Then another buck said, "Boys, this one is on me," and he gave me another robe, for another shot of sugar for the gang. They went through this like grease through a horn; then they licked their fingers, and thought they were sweet enough to last for some time. Then they wanted to see the guns and other stuff I had to swap.

But I said, "How is it that the Pend d'Oreilles say that White Grass and his band of warriors are thieves and robbers, who steal their robes in their raids like they do their horses and squaws? They say that their tongues are like a crooked stick; no one can trust where it will go when it is thrown in the air. Is it because the robes are stolen? Is that why the Blackfeet are my friends, and bring them here to me to swap?"

Then White Grass said, "This is not so. The Pend d'Oreilles and their brothers the Salish are the liars and sons of evil. Why are they here, far away from their own land, in the land of the Blackfeet and their brothers, the Piegans, killing our buffalo and saying that we are thieves? No, it is the Pend d'Oreilles, the crawling snakes, who steal all day and say the Black Robes' words at night. The Blackfeet are great warriors and the Pend d'Oreilles were always cowards, who sneaked off the trails like coyotes, whenever we came their way. You can tell the Pend d'Oreilles that White Grass,

who they know well, is here to hear them say that the
Blackfeet are liars and thieves."

I thought I would be foxy and swap them the new
Spencers and Henry peashooters that I got from Webber
and Company. Because they were new, I thought that I
could raise the price on them. I found out that they only
wanted the needle guns, which tore a hole big enough to put
your fist in, and were not bad to knock down a buffalo with.
With the Henrys and Spencers, half of the time the buffalo
did not know that you hit them, and had to be shot so full
of holes that their hide was no good; for it took a bullet with
some force to kill a buffalo.

I swapped them four needle guns at the price of eight
robes for a gun. I would only let them have the four, unless
they took Henrys or Spencers, but they did not want them.
They got twelve boxes of ammunition for twelve more
robes, and they still had nine robes left. They were wrangling about what they would take for them when one of
them saw the phony jewelry that I had got from Webber and
Harris. With shining eyes, the buck picked out a pair of old-
style woman's bracelets that looked like a pair of leg irons. I
showed him how to clamp them on his wrists and with the
pride of a peacock he paraded before them to show the gang
their magnificent splendor. He wanted to know the price,
but I told him that I did not want to sell them because the
big chief of the white men wanted them for his squaw, who
was crying to get them. But I loved the Blackfeet so well, I
would take a chance on the white chief having me shot and
would let him have them for five robes, which was giving
them away for nothing. He said that only three of the robes
left were his and for me to prove my friendship for him by
letting him have them for the three robes. So with tearful
eyes and my devotion to the altar of Mammon, I let my
avarice get the best of my generous heart. With a sigh that
came from my toes, I let go of this unreplaceable, meteoric
splendor and priceless treasure which was worth a king's
ransom in brass, tin, glass and crockery. And the only con-

solation I had left was that I knew that I would get thirty dollars for them three robes, if I could get out of this land alive with them. I had found the price list among this stuff, with the address of an enterprising Yankee, in Bridgeport, Connecticut, who was willing to make this kind of stuff for five dollars a bushel. So now, with the reckless generosity of drunken sailors, they forgot about the other stuff they wanted, and blew in the remaining six robes for the Squaw Kid's fully warranted-to-turn-black jewelry. Not to be out-done by their generosity, and to show the Squaw Kid's heart was in the right place, I made my bosom friend old White Grass a present of a magnificent and beautiful brass ring with a sparkler of red glass, that put the Kohinoor in the shade in size, if not for brilliancy.

When I was swapping for those robes, I could see that old Gabriel and some of the Pend d'Oreille bucks were squatting around Petol's tepee, holding some kind of a powwow. It did not take a clairvoyant to tell that their thoughts were anything but holy about the bunch of Blackfeet and the Squaw Kid.

I sat with the Blackfeet around the fire that night, and the breed Joe said, "White Grass wants to know where you came from—where you was a papoose?" I said that they could not know. It was a place so far away to the south that it took a horse nearly all summer to come here from there.

He said, "White Grass asks if it was a place where the cactus is a tree, the sun hot and the ground dry? Do the people live in strong tepees and have the men long black hair, and are their faces nearly as dark as an Injun, and had big hats and plenty horses and cattle?" He heap savvied that land, and had been there long, long ago. When he was young and the first time he went on the war trail as a warrior, it was there he went to raid for horses. Many Blackfeet warriors and him started from their land afoot in the spring when the grass got good like they always did, but they did not stay that way long. For in the land of the Shoshones, their enemies, they soon surprised some of the camps and got horses to ride.

Then they started off for the land of their friends the Utes, which was a long way off. They were on the trail many days and they had many fights with their enemies the Pawnees. Finally, they came to the land of the Utes. They stayed with the Utes all winter, and danced and made medicine with them. Then early in the spring a large war party of Utes, including the Blackfeet, started off south on the war trail, to the land of the black-haired white men.

It was not long until they came to the land where the Injuns lived who had strong tepees, with no doors. They went to the top on a ladder, which they pulled up so no one could get at them. Then they went down in their tepee through a hole in the top.

After they left there they began to get in the white man's land, but the Utes who knew the country said, "Not there, the best land is still far away. When we come to a river where many of the white evil spirits live, they will have as many horses as the Great Spirit has buffalo on the prairies." Like the wolves in the night, they went through this land, so no one would know that they were there, until they came to a large river, where white men with strong tepees and plenty of horses lived. But those people had many guns, and they had many fights with them. The Utes said, "Why should we only take their horses when those white devils have many beautiful things in their tepees? Those things will be ours if we kill them all, then we can take them back with us to let our old warriors and squaws know that we are great warriors. Our women will greet us with songs and dance with joy, when they see the many beautiful things and the many scalps and horses that we bring back to our land."

They came through that land like a blizzard from the north, and every day they had fierce fights with the black-haired white men and plenty warriors fell before the white men's guns and their long knives. But many times they took the white men's tepees and the Utes, who were bad Injuns, would kill all the men, women and children. They would take what they wanted, then set fire to the long grass and burn up the whole land, but the Blackfeet were good Injuns and they would not do a thing like this to their friends the white men. As they went north, the horses taken were many, and they got more beautiful things out of the white men's tepees and the bad Utes killed more white men, women and children.

After being gone nearly all summer they came back to the land of the Utes, where there was much joy. The Blackfeet again stayed all winter with their friends the Utes, and in the spring they started back for their land in the north, with many scalps, horses and other things. They were not to get back without plenty trouble, for the Pawnees were watching for them on the trails. They had many fierce fights with them, and killed many of them. Some of the Blackfeet warriors got killed, but they got many of the Pawnees' horses. So they came on their way; and after raiding in the land of the Snakes and Shoshones, they still got back to their land before the snow came. There was much joy and dancing in the Blackfeet camps, although many of the Blackfeet warriors lay, and their spirits stayed, in that land that was far away.

I sat there and looked at old White Grass's face, with a benign smile on it, still as inscrutable as a rock. Shivers went through me when I remembered old Gabriel's words, "You may think he is your friend and a good Injun, but I and many of the old Pend d'Oreilles know that old cutthroat devil only too well. Many a Pend d'Oreille warrior lost his scalp, and there was always wailing in the Pend d'Oreille camps whenever the bunch he used to lead came around. Many were the horses that they stole, and that old devil himself only knows how many white men, women and children he has helped to murder in his time."

Many times since that night I have wondered if there was more truth in old White Grass's story than a person would believe. Not long after that I heard old Hudson Bay and American Fur Company men say they knew of the Blackfeet to go as far east as Minnesota and as far west as Walla Walla.

But how far south they went on their thieving and plundering raids, they did not know. I used to listen with fear and terror, when I was a kid, to my grandfather and some more of the old gray-haired men tell of when they were young men. Large bands of strange Injuns would sometimes come sweeping through the land from someplace up in the north, and many were the bitter fights they had with them. Many the hacienda they took, destroyed and plundered. One time they left the whole country, from near El Paso, Texas, to Socorro, New Mexico, and up along the Rio Grande in New Mexico a blackened waste of ruin. Not satisfied with that, they stole hundreds of horses, they murdered every man, woman and child that fell into their hands and spared nothing. While the Comanches were sure to God bad enough, they were still gentlemen aside those red devils from the north.

As I sat by the fire with this bunch of cutthroats, I could not help but think what my people would think if they could only see me sitting there as one of this savage band. Every man of my people either had a knife scar, a bullet hole or lance stab on them from their bitter fights with the Comanche and Apache Injuns. Every one of them either had a father or brother, or perhaps a mother or sister, who was butchered by the merciless red hands I was with. It was no wonder that they thought a good Injun was a dead one. Whenever an Injun fell into their hands, they seen to it that he never bothered them any more.

So we all rolled up around the fire and were soon asleep, the Blackfeet cutthroats and the Squaw Kid. Early the next morning old White Grass and his bunch pulled out for their camp two sleeps away. They said they would soon come back again, and bring a lodge or so and their squaws. They would stay a few days to swap for blankets and other stuff I had. Then they rode off leaving me alone in camp.

It was not long until old Gabriel came over. I was wondering how many shots of Buffalo Hunter's Delight I would have to inject in him to get him to forget the visit of those

Blackfeet so he could forgive me and take me back in his heart. I knew well that he and the Pend d'Oreille bucks had been watching the Blackfeet and my camp like hawks. They also knew that I had swapped their enemies, the Blackfeet, guns and ammunition. I predicted they would go up in the air and be as mad as hornets.

It was the way I thought, for he started in on the Blackfeet, saying they were cutthroats and devils, and the Squaw Kid was worse. I was a double-crosser and a snake-in-the-grass to my friends, the Pend d'Oreilles, and him. If I thought they were going to stand by and watch me swap the Blackfeet guns and ammunition right under their nose in their camp for the Blackfeets' stolen robes, then I need not be surprised if some of the Pend d'Oreille bucks took a shot at me on the quiet. I told him that, while the Blackfeet might be as bad as he said, still they came to me like men and did not try to cheat and swindle me.

"As bad as old White Grass was, still there must be some truth in him, for he said last night that those robes were not stolen. He wanted me to go and tell you and the Pend d'Oreilles that he was in your camp and that he wanted to hear the Pend d'Oreilles say that the Blackfeet were liars and thieves. If the Pend d'Oreilles wanted the guns on the square, they could easily rustle up the robes to pay for them because their women were still tanning dry hides."

Instead of making up our friendship, old Gabriel and I parted bad friends. He went back to his tepee without a peace offering of Injun elixir of life, red-eye rotgut. I knew that there was going to be some trouble if I stayed there in camp. I thought here is one time I would fool them and get out when the chances are good. I would steal away to find and make love to In-who-lise, a more pleasant occupation. There were three miles of trees and brush—and jungle—between the Injun camp and my place. How was I going to find her in all that jungle of brush and trees?

Such thoughts of despair did not bother me long, for I knew from past experience that the lovely In-who-lise was not born a wild squaw for nothing. I would only have to ride along the edge of the trees and brush and she would do the hunting. That is, she would if she thought anything of the Squaw Kid. I knew that she did, this squaw who had the nerve and ability to steal out of the Injun camp in the dead of the night, where they all slept like the weasel with one eye open and the other shut, and take desperate chances on them catching her. Then she would walk three miles in the dark night, believing that all kinds of evil spirits were promenading around, to tell me that I was still her man and that everything was all right. She was worthy of a better fate than the somewhat slippery honor and the love the Squaw Kid had given her so far in return.

I put my blankets in the shack and other stuff, as there was no telling what some of the Injuns might do to it if they saw it laying around outside. Then I rode off, taking the side of the creek and edge of the brush and timber where the Injuns did not travel much. It was as I thought, for I soon came to where In-who-lise was hidden in the brush, watching for me. I lost no time in going to her. She was all fear for me because she heard some of the bucks in camp say that they ought to run me out of the country to my Blackfeet friends.

But a buck called Kute-a-nal-a-quay said, "No, the best way is to watch him go off someplace and leave him laying there in some hole. Then we could have all them guns, ammunition and other things of his without having to give him our buffalo robes for them."

I tied the horse in the brush out of sight, and to make sure that we would not be seen we went further in the brush. She said that Spel-a-qua and the other bucks, who had been gambling at playing hands, had gotten back the night before. Spel-a-qua, who was always lucky at playing hands, had won thirty head of horses from a band of Gros Ventres. He and the bucks had traded some horses for whiskey and other stuff to two white traders, who came through where they were gambling and that they were all drunk when they got back the night before. Worse still, they had brought whiskey back to camp with them, and several of the Injuns in camp got drunk and raised hell all night, and were still drunk.

That was why she was afraid that they would do me harm. The whole camp was mad at me for giving the Blackfeet them guns and ammunition. Spel-a-qua had tried to catch her that night, but she stood him off with her knife and got in the tepee of Mas-a-qua, who gave Spel-a-qua the run. Then Co-quay-ah-tam-a-la, the chief of the hunt, had come and told him to leave her alone. But Spel-a-qua told him that he was only the chief of the hunt and that In-who-lise was none of his business. He then went off to his drunken friends, saying that he would catch her yet and take the evil out of her.

When she had returned to Cha-ki-a-ki's tepee that morning, Cha-ki-a-ki's squaw called her all kinds of evil names. She wanted to know what In-who-lise wanted anyway when she would not be Spel-a-qua's squaw, and he, having all those horses, and she, only a Nez Perce who had not even a horse of her own to ride. The warriors in camp were saying that many Assiniboines, Gros Ventres and Piegans, with their squaws, were coming to visit, dance and play hands for horses in a few days. I had to watch out as the most of them were bad Injuns.

We sat there and I knew how much the little squaw cared for me and how nice and sweet she was to me. She still believed everything that I told her, even after all the dirt I already done her. I thought it was time that I done right by her, and try to find some way to marry her as she wanted me to do.

However, there was no place to take her to get married unless we went too far away; I could not leave my stuff to go. My only hope was that some missionary might come preaching into the Injun camp, like the Injuns said they did sometimes. But preachers had been scarce so far. I tried to get her to leave the Injun camp. I would get old Gabriel to take her in his tepee and I would pay him for keeping her. But she said that she would die first, rather than stay in the same tepee with Kat-a-lee and Sow-set. As far as the other matter went, the first thing that Spel-a-qua knew she would rip his belly open if he tried anything.

So In-who-lise, the wild squaw, and An-ta-lee the Squaw Kid, sat there and made love, and the Squaw Kid promised her, this time for sure, to love her till the cows came home.

The foolish In-who-lise and Squaw Kid, instead of keeping their eyes and ears open, kept on dreaming and like all sweet dreams that are too good to be true, theirs had a cruel and rude awakening. Suddenly, like a silent evil spirit, Spel-a-qua sneaked out of the brush and stood before us. It was a good thing that we saw him in time to stand up and face him, for he was mad as peccary. There stood Spel-a-qua, resplendent in a new flashy breechclout, colorful blanket leggins, and a gaudy white man's shirt, which he wore like all buck Injuns do, à la shirttail. Besides he had a vicious-looking hunting knife and there was no longer any need for Kat-a-lee to tell what she knew, for Spel-a-qua caught the Nez Perce maid dead to rights, sitting in the Squaw Kid's lap.

He stood before us a good-sized, husky Injun. Worse still, he was just drunk enough to be mean and full of Dutch courage. He said, "This is how I find In-who-lise, the Nez Perce slut. She thought she was too good to be Spel-a-qua's squaw, and told him that she was not a bitch. She said she had a sharp knife for his belly, if he made her his squaw. Her, a squaw, said that, yes, the Nez Perce slut said that to Spel-a-qua, who is a great hunter and warrior. Who in the Pend d'Oreille camp has more horses than him? There is none. No more will she look at him with scorn in her evil eyes, for Spel-a-qua will lead In-who-lise, the Nez Perce slut, back to camp and tie her up in his lodge. He will see to it that she will not have to go running off after An-ta-lee the white dog. He is the friend of the Blackfeet, and a snake-in-the-grass for them against his friends, the Pend d'Oreilles.

"No more will the warriors and squaws in camp laugh at Spel-a-qua or speak like that old hag Mal-tiene, Pal-las-away's squaw, said to him today. 'Alas, Spel-a-qua, how comes it the buffalo cow Sapah-tan In-who-lise's smile does not brighten up your lodge? Her trail leads into the thick brush and trees, where the sweet murmuring water lay. Cha-ki-a-ki's squaw says that she tans the robes no more, and like the bounding jack rabbit is on the go day and night.' An-ta-lee, the white brave, knows the sweet words that a squaw likes to hear better than Spel-a-qua. The rainy day or dark night cannot keep her away from him."

Then Spel-a-qua tried to grab In-who-lise by the hand, saying, "Come, squaw of evil, it is time that you are on your way back to camp with Spel-a-qua."

But she stepped back out of his reach and, with her knife in her hand, she said, "See Spel-a-qua, the Pend d'Oreille boasting warrior whose only glory is to fight a squaw; the Nez Perce White Feather now says to you nay. I will surely be glad to put my knife in your belly, if you put your hand on me, to take me away with you. I know which way the camp is and do not need Spel-a-qua to lead me like a bitch to his lodge. I have told An-ta-lee that I will be his squaw, and he said that he will put a ring on my finger and marry me by the E-qui-lix and take me back to where I came from."

"So the Sapah-tan squaw stands and shows her teeth and fights. Spel-a-qua will take the Sapah-tan squaw back to camp, knife or no knife, and will make her rue the day she came here to listen to the evil words and lies of the white-faced dog, An-ta-lee. It makes Spel-a-qua laugh to hear her say that she is going to be his squaw by the E-qui-lix, and Spel-a-qua does not hear An-ta-lee say that is so."

I could talk Injun now, so I told him to leave her alone and to go on his way. He had heard what she said. She was going to be my woman and he might as well know it from me. I was going to marry her as soon as I could find the Black Robe. Why was it that he was so mean to her and still wanted to make her his squaw so badly, when he had two squaws already and could not take care of them? If this was not so, why did the young bucks who were wise say that Celcha-pee, the one that was young and pretty, had said that there was only wind in Spel-a-qua's belly anyway and that she blew her hands and would romp and play whenever Spel-a-qua turned his back on her or was away?

But he got all the madder and said, "Yes, marry her—that is what all the white dogs say, but the foolish squaw never sees that day. Soon they are gone and far away. Yes, An-ta-lee is a white man and a liar when he says that, for why do the young squaws say that An-ta-lee is a bull elk and only plays with one of them today and is off with another tomorrow? The old squaws in camp say that it would be much better for them if that whinnering white stallion, An-ta-lee, was gone from here and chased back among the white squaws where he came from. Then they would not have to watch or tie up the young squaws in camp to keep them from running off with him, to romp and play in the brush in the creek bottoms."

I told him that I wanted no trouble with him, and to get back to camp and stay there because he was not going to get her.

But he said, "See Spel-a-qua has his knife. If An-ta-lee the white-faced dog stands there like a fool hen in the way and says to Spel-a-qua 'nay,' then it will feel your heart. Spel-a-qua will leave you here for the coyotes to feast on."

I said, "See An-ta-lee has his gun, and Spel-a-qua's knife will make him sorry. He will be in the land of the dead before tonight. His squaws' wails for the dead will come from his lodge if he does not go on his way and leave In-who-lise alone."

"Spel-a-qua laughs at An-ta-lee and his gun, for he knows that An-ta-lee knows better than to kill Spel-a-qua for this squaw of evil. If he does that, Spel-a-qua's friends in the Injun camp will soon know it. Then An-ta-lee will not be long in joining Spel-a-qua in the land of the dead, and the Nez Perce In-who-lise with him. Spel-a-qua will be fair and throw his knife away. An-ta-lee cannot now say that he is afraid of Spel-a-qua. An-ta-lee can put his gun away and then Spel-a-qua will wrestle him for this squaw of evil. If An-ta-lee bests Spel-a-qua, then he can have her."

In-who-lise said, "No, no, foolish An-ta-lee. Do not do so. Do not put your gun away. Don't trust Spel-a-qua in any way or we both will rue the day, if you listen to what his evil voice now says. Spel-a-qua well knows that you are too small for him, and that he will win the day. The Pend d'Oreille warriors say that there is no warrior in camp who is more tricky or mean in his ways when he wrestles with them, and none of them will play with him."

I was not foolish enough to take Spel-a-qua up at his own game. I still had good reason to remember my wrestling match with the young buck in the Blackfeet camp, where I got more than my belly full. That young buck was a baby in size and strength beside Spel-a-qua, who must have weighed one hundred and eighty. I said to him, "Spel-a-qua is wise and knows when his sun shines for him. An-ta-lee still says for him to be on his way. This place and day could be an evil one for him. Why should I wrestle with him for In-who-lise, when I had her already and she would not go with him? Did she not say herself that it was so?"

Like a fool I stood arguing with him, although I knew better. Suddenly, like a flash he made a spring at me, and I seen it coming, but I was not quick enough. As I pulled on the trigger to let him have it, he got me by the wrist, and the two shots that I got went wild. Instead of hitting him they came near getting In-who-lise. The next thing I knew I was lifted up, and came down on the ground like a ton of brick with Spel-a-qua on top of me still holding my wrist. I could smell and feel his hot whiskey breath in my face. He glared at me like a big black bear, and struggle as I would he still held me down.

I seen that it would not be long until he would get the gun away from me and then the Squaw Kid's name would be pants. I flipped the gun away the best I could so that he would not get it anyway, and I was more than glad to see In-who-lise coming at Spel-a-qua, with her eyes blazing with fury and her knife ready in her hand to rip Spel-a-qua down the back. She picked the gun up before he had time to get it.

Spel-a-qua was not idle, for when he saw that I got rid of the gun he let my wrist go and got a stranglehold on my throat. He started to push my head down in the soft dirt, and it was not long till I began to see all kinds of rainbows.

Then that sweet little squaw of mine brought the butt end of the heavy forty-four Colt down on Spel-a-qua's head. She had to smash him several times before Spel-a-qua sprawled out as good as dead. At first I thought he was dead. In-who-lise said, "Evil is this day for us. Now the Injuns will kill the both of us for this." I saw that he was not dead and told her so. I said for us to light out when we had the chance, and that she would have to come with me to my camp. She could no longer go back to the Injun camp. She said, "Yes, White Feather will go with her man An-ta-lee, for where else can she go now?"

We headed for my horse and I thought that if Spel-a-qua found him, then it would surely be an evil day for us. We had gone just a short way, when the creek bottom began to sound with Spel-a-qua's war whoops calling for help. He was still a long way from being dead. We got to the horse, and I found my carbine in the brush. In-who-lise leaped up behind me and we started back for camp. We rode back to camp, with anything but pleasant thoughts, for In-who-lise kept saying that Spel-a-qua and his bad Injun friends would surely kill the both of us.

Then she was afraid that I would not marry her. "See, sweet An-ta-lee, White Feather has raised her hand and struck down her own kind for thee, and for that they will never forgive her. Say that you will surely marry her now that she has no other place to go." And I said again and again, by Colon Suten, that I would marry her.

It was not long until we came to camp. If I thought by leaving camp that I would get rid of that bunch of Injuns, I was badly mistaken. There must have been twenty of them squatting around camp patiently waiting until I came back, so they could give me hell for swapping the Blackfeet the guns and ammunition. When they saw me bring In-who-lise back to camp it did not improve their temper or good thoughts toward me either. Nor when they found out what happened to Spel-a-qua; that was not going to make them love me any better. It was surely one time that a bride and groom got a chilly reception to their homecoming.

Old Gabriel came up looking anything but pleased and asked, "What are you doing with that Nez Perce woman? I thought I told you to leave her alone? Surely you are not bad enough to coax her away from her own kind of people before you are married to her."

I told him that I was going to marry In-who-lise. There was no use in him getting mad. What I wanted to know now was he my friend, as he had been saying he was? Then I told them what happened to Spel-a-qua and how he came on us in the woods. I said I expected him and his friends here at any minute, and I wanted to know if they were going to let them do us up when we were not to blame. In-who-lise wanted me to marry her, but Spel-a-qua would not have it so. He had done his best to kill me. If they were going to let Spel-a-qua and his bunch clean us up, then we would go in the shack and shoot the hell out of them as long as we lasted.

The chief Co-quay-ah-tam-a-la said, "Spel-a-qua is a bad Injun, for I told him to leave this woman alone. She did not belong to our tribe and did not want to have anything to do with him. But he would not listen to what I said, and so he must take what he got. If An-ta-lee says that he is going to marry her, then I see nothing wrong in that. The Pend d'Oreilles here will not let Spel-a-qua and his friends make any trouble for An-ta-lee, or do him any harm. But An-ta-lee must give Cha-ki-a-ki pay in horses for keeping In-who-lise all summer and for giving her a horse to ride."

I thought that this was more than fair and promised that I would do so. Now there could be heard the bloodcurdling war whoops of a bunch of Injuns coming our way. In a few minutes Spel-a-qua, with his head all swelled up and bloody, rode into camp, with five more bucks with blood in their eyes and their guns in their hands. And there sure was murder in their hearts as they sat there on their war ponies and howled like savage wolves. But the Pend d'Oreille warriors stood around us and the chief asked, "What brings Spel-a-qua here with his head all sore like he was coming back from the war trail?" Spel-a-qua said, "It is that white-faced dog, An-ta-lee, but more so that Nez Perce squaw of evil, In-who-lise, who did this to me. We are going to kill them even if you say nay."

Co-quay-ah-tam-a-la said, "Spel-a-qua will do well to heed the words I say to him. Leave this woman alone, and go on your way back to camp. The warriors who are here say that An-ta-lee and In-who-lise are not to blame and that you and your friends shall not do them any harm or wrong, when they are here to say nay."

Then the worst one of them all rode into camp, Madame Cha-ki-a-ki, Spel-a-qua's sister, who nature intended in the beginning for a Roman gladiator, but got sick of the job and turned her out a squaw, forgetting to take away her fighting disposition. Now, as graceful as a swan, she let her nearly two hundred pounds of bone and muscle light on the ground, proudly brandishing her squaw whip, which had a wagon spoke for a handle and was heavy enough to brain a crocodile.

"This is how I find out the Nez Perce strumpet, In-who-lise," she said. "Wait until I get through with her; then she will know better the next time than to play the snake to those who were good to her. If Spel-a-qua and his friends are squaws, to let that white dog, An-ta-lee and his Nez Perce coyote slut get away from them, then I am not."

The chief said to her, "Harken, squaw of wind and trouble, you are not the loser for what she has done today. An-ta-lee is going to give Cha-ki-a-ki horses to pay for keeping her in your lodge and for giving her a horse to ride. Then no one can say evil of her or him."

When Cha-ki-a-ki's squaw heard that, she changed her tune and said, "Then, if this is so, An-ta-lee can have the Nez Perce strumpet, In-who-lise, and an evil day it will be for

him." When Spel-a-qua and his friends saw that the Pend
d'Oreille warriors would not let them do me up, they did their
best to get them to let them take In-who-lise back to camp
with them. But the chief, old Gabriel and the others would not
have it so. In-who-lise, the wild squaw, and the Squaw Kid had
much to be thankful for that day. Those Pend d'Oreille warriors, who were wild and savage and did not pretend to follow
the white man's ways of honor, still, when it came to grim justice, they stood there and barred the way and would not let
men of their own tribe commit wrong. There is no doubt if
they had let them have their way they would have made short
work of the both of us, and the Squaw Kid would not be writing this today. After abusing us as only an Injun can and
knows how, they rode off for the Injun camp, still saying that
they would have their vengeance on us some other day.

Then the chief, Co-quay-ah-tam-a-la, said, "It is now too
late today to have the powwow about you giving the
Blackfeet the guns. An-ta-lee must promise the Pend
d'Oreilles not to do it again; then the Pend d'Oreilles will be
his friends again. An-ta-lee ought to know that they were his
friends today." What more could I do but say that I would
not swap them guns any more? I would not promise them
not to swap for other stuff, as I had to sell it some way. They
agreed to that; then they rode off to their camp, leaving old
Gabriel and In-who-lise sitting with me there.

Old Gabriel said, "Now that you have got In-who-lise,
what are you going to do with her? You, now that you
coaxed her away from the Injun camp, are not going to
make her live with you without being married to her?" I told
him again that I was going to marry her as soon as I could.
He would have to take her in his tepee and let her sleep there
at night until I could find a way to marry her. I would pay
him for doing so. He said it would be all right, but he
wanted no pay, for he was glad to hear that I was going to do
right with her.

Old Gabriel said that we had to be careful for a few days,
and shouldn't go prowling around away from camp. There

was no telling what that Spel-a-qua bunch might do if they caught us right. He went off to his tepee and White Feather and the Squaw Kid are alone together.

In-who-lise said, "Is not An-ta-lee, her man, now glad, like I am, that I am here with him to stay for good? No more will I have to fear Spel-a-qua, and what the bad squaws in camp say." I said that it was so. Then she said, "Why did you ask old Gabriel for a place in his lodge for me to stay? You know that Kat-a-lee and Sow-set stay there. They will make me rue the day, if I have to stay in the same tepee with them."

"There is no other way," I told her. But she said, "No. White Feather goes not in that lodge to sleep or stay. She shall stay out here by the fire with her man until An-ta-lee can find a way, or a Black Robe comes this way." She said she would stay on her side of the fire and that I could stay on my side of the fire.

In-who-lise was wary and afraid of me at first, but that soon wore off. She had only a squaw's short buckskin dress on, buckskin leggins up to near the knees. Under that was nature's underwear. At first she was careful with herself, but squaw style the more I met her, the more affectionate she got, and she became careless and generous with her scenery.

When she was sure that I was going to marry her, she did her best to keep me frothing at the mouth so that I would not forget her, as the competition was keen. I had not run free and wild among the wild squaws in the squaw paradise for nothing, so now knew all their symptoms from A to Z. In-who-lise thought that she could stay good, but I knew better than that. A layout of that kind only works on paper. I knew that it would be only a short time until she would get a case of squaw fever like they all did. The first thing she knew, she would wake up rolled up in the same blanket with the none too good Squaw Kid and then it would be good-bye to marriage for her.

I said, "White Feather must know that Kat-a-lee, Sow-set and the others will say evil of us if it is that way. Why did you

make me say to Colon Suten that I would be good and
marry you? No, you shall go to old Gabriel's tepee to sleep
in the night, then they cannot say evil of us. White Feather
ought to know what might happen to her if she stayed that
way".

Then In-who-lise said, "Why should my man An-ta-lee
want his woman away from his fire and in old Gabriel's
tepee unless it is to do evil with the two strumpet squaws?
Surely it must be so. You want me away from here so that
one of old Gabriel's hussies can crawl under the edge of the
tepee and come and lie with you while foolish White Feather
sleeps in the lodge out of the way. But White Feather, who
has left her people for you, is here to stay. I shall keep you
good. No more shall I run away and let the strumpet squaws
steal my man away. The squaw who tries to make me cry
shall die, and the dark night shall not hide her from White
Feather's knife."

I told her that she was wrong about what she said, and
that I did not go near Kat-a-lee or Sow-set any more. I only
wanted her to go in old Gabriel's tepee for her own good.
There was no other squaw for me but her. Talk to her as I
would, I found out that In-who-lise could be as bullheaded
as a rock and did not intend to go in old Gabriel's tepee no
matter what I said. In one way I could not blame her. She
had only too good a reason to believe what she said and
thought.

I found out that she had had nothing to eat since that
morning so we started a fire and got something to eat. Then
we sat by the fire and I thought there was going to be
another mix-up. Was I not deep enough in hell without having to go still deeper? What was the use in trying to be good,
when In-who-lise has planned these nights by the fire?

My good angel old Gabriel came over and after talking
for a while said, "Come, In-who-lise, it is time for you to be
on your way to the tepee, for the nakedness of night is here.
All good girls should be rolled up in their robes to sleep." In-
who-lise, to my surprise, meekly got up to go with him,

without saying a word against it. I got her two blankets to take with her and then she followed old Gabriel off to the tepee.

I was awakened by In-who-lise at the break of day, making a fire like a sweet dutiful squaw should. She seemed to have turned over a new leaf. She was as sweet as honey to me, and things were looking brighter. The Squaw Kid at last had a sweet, dusky cook, and soon we were in a happy frame of mind. But the blue skies of love soon darkened when I saw Kat-a-lee and Sow-set coming over to pay us a call. I saw that it would soon turn into mix-up of knives and screams. After some jealous taunts, those two Jezebels glided off with the majesty of Cleopatra and caught their horses. They rode away in the direction of the Injun camp, probably to rustle up some more deviltry against In-who-lise. Injun love-making was sure fierce; no one but the devil could tell how it would end. I talked to In-who-lise like a Dutch uncle about her dread of water, and said that I would expect her to wash her hands and face at least once a week.

She asked, "How can I be clean when all that I have is on me?"

I showed her some calico and she took a piece that was mostly red. She worked all day like a beaver, and made herself a swell dress of the latest squaw style, called in Injun, swoop-a-whop-a-can. That kind of a garment required great skill to cut out and make. It was like a sack with holes for the head and arms and two flaps hung down about six inches and protected the arms, and it was minus any buttons.

She had never used soap before, so I showed her how to use it and told her to get her courage up and not let the water scare her any more. That night In-who-lise was as nice, clean and sweet a little squaw as you could find. The bright colors of her dress made her look like a pinto. I gave her a shawl that had the seven colors of the rainbow in it, and she laid her face on my manly bosom and cried with joy. She said that her man, An-ta-lee, was the truest, sweetest and most virtuous man that ever lived. My joy was shortened by the silvery laugh of Kat-a-lee and Sow-set. They had been watching us from behind old Gabriel's tepee.

Bright and early in the morning Cha-ki-a-ki came to camp and wanted to know how many horses I was going to give him for keeping In-who-lise. I was beginning to savvy an Injun and put it up to him as how many did he want? After much dodging he went whole hog or none and said that I owed him ten head. I told him to guess again as I never would give him that number. In the end I ageed to give him three head, and Cha-ki-a-ki went off with them. In-who-lise was free from all claims of Cha-kia-ki, and all the Pend d'Oreilles, except for putting a head on Spel-a-qua.

Along in the afternoon I heard a squeaking sound some distance away. I thought I must be back on the Rio Grande again, because there could be no other sound on earth or hell like the squeak of a Mexican cart. A whole bunch of breeds and squaws rode in, and with them six Red River carts, those were the simon-pure ones, the wheels made out of the trunk of a tree, everything was wood and there was not a nail or piece of iron on them. On they came with four cayuses on a cart, and a noble squaw riding each cayuse. But what made it greater than Barnum's parade was one breed had four buffalo hooked up to his cart; buffalo was not so hard to domesticate if they were captured when calves—and to capture them was no hard job, for I have seen many of them stand bawling beside their dead mother, as she lay there on the prairie, the victim of some buffalo hunter. So those breeds and squaws who arrived went up to old Gabriel's tepee, and I soon found out that they were nearly all old Gabriel's Cree relations on a visit from Canada, excepting two families of Scotch breeds, named McDougal and McLeoud. It seemed funny to meet a breed that talked like an old country Scotchman.

This jovial bunch that arrived did not disappoint me; all of the men lived up to the traditions of the breeds, who, instead of trying to marry a nice little breed girl, always seems to prefer a full-blood squaw. The breed women also lean heavy toward the buck Injuns, probably knowing that full-blooded stock is the best every time.

The Squaw Kid's dump had taken on a spurt of prosperity and I swapped with some of the breeds for several articles, such as tobacco, calico, red flannel and blankets. I took buffalo robes as legal tender. One breed woman came over and gave me a surprise when she asked in good English, "How many yards of calico will you give me for five dollars?" She dug up five iron dollars out of a buckskin sack. It had been a long time since I seen money, but I could still remember it. I wondered if I knew the soldiers she had gotten it from. After much deliberation I said that calico was going up in the Musselshell lately so five yards was all I would give her. She said, "I cannot make a dress out of that." I said, "I don't see why not, when all the other squaws use is three yards to make a swoop-a-whop-a-can, and some of them have enough left to put frills on them." But she got mad.

I said that I would give her six yards though I knew that it would ruin me. She said all right, and because I had no yardstick I gave her six squaw yards—a yard being from the point of your nose to the tip of your fingers, with your arm stretched out. I could see that she was still mad at the price and took it just because she had to have it. To appease her anger I offered her one of my priceless heirlooms of phony jewelry. At the sight of that stuff, which usually brought the luster to the eyes and a happy smile to the lips of the fiercest squaws that ever lived, that doubtful hussy seemed to know the value of the beautiful brass ring with glass rubies that I told her was once worn by Catherine of Russia, and that it was worth fifty hugs and all the trimmings that go with them in the squaw paradise any day. But with haughty scorn she refused my generous offer, and went away saying she did not have enough to make her dress and I was a damn robber.

The cabin was now too small; with the stuff and buffalo robes that I had, it was full to near the roof. I had to sleep and cook outside, which was all right as long as it did not rain or storm. If it rained I had to go in the wagon, which had a good wagon sheet on it, to sleep. I didn't have any place to go when the cold weather came and I would have no place to put my unblushable bride In-who-lise, when that day arrived. Mas-a-wa's squaws were making me a beautiful rawhide mansion out of buffalo hides, in trade for a Spencer rifle. In-who-lise would feel more at home there than in a brick one. She can soon give a smoker for the short skirt and breechclout Siwash four hundred, as they discuss the latest society news and chew a delightful luncheon of buffalo guts. It took several young buffalo cow hides to make a good-sized tepee or lodge, and much hard work for the squaws. They had to take the hair off first, then tan them and sew them with sinew.

Many of the tepees in them days were ornamented with life-like drawings that made you wonder where those wild squaws got their training at drawing, for the wild squaw was born a true artist of nature, and needed no years of training. I used to watch them reach in the fire and get a piece of charcoal and draw the most beautiful designs of flowers, vines and leaves so true and perfect in shape that you wondered how they did it.

That night old Gabriel came over to my camp and said that his relations were going to stay a while. There was a large camp of breeds and Crees, camped a day's ride from there. His friends thought that Père Landre was with them. He was an old priest and who had been a missionary among the Crees in Canada, and lived with them most of the time, and followed their camps, and said Mass and preached to them in their own language. The Crees thought much of him because he was such a good and holy man. Gabriel was going to send his son Samwell to the Cree camp the next day to tell them to send word over when Père Landre was coming. We would go over to church, and bring along Kat-a-lee and Sow-set to be bridesmaids for In-who-lise. Père Landre would marry us there. I saw the devil come in In-who-lise's eyes as he said that, but I shook my head at her to keep her mouth shut. I knew that In-who-lise was going to raise hell over this, and I also knew that Kat-a-lee and Sowset would see In-who-lise in hell many times before they would help her get married.

I told him that I would do it anyway, and the sooner the day came, the better. Since she had been in camp old Gabriel did not get any eye-openers, because I did not want her to know that I had the whiskey and rum in the cabin. I put her through the third degree and found out that she had never tasted whiskey and thought it was bad stuff. I made up my mind that I would see to it she always thought that way, and she could never say that she learned to drink from me.

I gave old Gabriel a good shot, which I knew he had been missing very much lately. He got jolly and said that I ought to do better as his relations had plenty of robes and the Injuns had started to visit the Pend d'Oreille camp to gamble and race horses. The Piegans and Gros Ventres always had robes, because, he said, they were like the Blackfeet and did nothing else but raid and steal. The next morning the breeds were going to kill a few young buffalo cows. They would make pemmican and sell it to the Hudson Bay Company across the line in Canada.

All Injuns go to bed when the hens go to roost, so Gabriel told In-who-lise it was time for her to be in bed. They went off together to his tepee, leaving the Squaw Kid there to meditate on just how many shots of whiskey and rum he would have to give old Gabriel to make him forget he was going to take Kat-a-lee and Sow-set along to stand up with In-who-lise in the Cree camp when we were married.

CHAPTER TWENTY-TWO
Not the Last of the Blackfeet

This morning things brightened up some, for many bucks and squaws are going by to the Pend d'Oreille camp to visit and to race horses and gamble at their great game of playing hands. On they came, Assiniboines and Crees, Bloods, Gros Ventres and Piegans.

I got my Dutch courage up enough to visit the Injun camp, where since my little unpleasantness with Spel-a-qua, I gave him a wide berth, being a firm believer that a live coward is worth the woods full of dead heroes.

In-who-lise said that it would be better for her not to go to the Injun camp for some time; she did not fool me any, as she only wants to stay in camp to watch Kat-a-lee and Sow-set, who were tanning a buffalo robe outside of old Gabriel's tepee.

In the Pend d'Oreille camp now is all a gala day, with all those bucks and squaws here and arriving to visit them. But all of them have the good intentions of cleaning them up at gambling and at horse racing, and if they lose their horses to the Pend d'Oreilles, to sneak back a few days later and steal them back. When those slippery gents were around, a horse was harder to hold than your money.

Talk about the reckless abandon and nerve of the gamblers of Monte Carlo, they are pikers aside of the wild Indians of them days, who were born gamblers. For here you can see an Injun have more then a hundred horses at noon, but before the middle of the afternoon, he has been stripped of everything, even his breechclout is gone, and he is going around as naked as when he was born, with just a strip of buffalo hide for a G-string, though this is not compulsory. The Indian did what I never seen a white man do;

he would strip himself and put up everything till he was naked, and thought nothing about it. And when this happened he was a philosopher, and did not whine about his loss, but now bums something from a friend to put up, and maybe next day he is again on easy street, with a large band of horses and many other things. Things move fast and furious in their games, and there is no such a thing as trying to hold them close to your belly, if lady luck is agin you.

Rows of seven or eight warriors are squatting on the ground here and there; facing each row of warriors are their rivals; they squat five or six feet apart. They are gambling at the Injun game of playing hands. The warriors in one row are singing an Injun chant, and the warrior in the middle of the row has two sticks grasped in his hands. Those sticks are skillfully made, usually of bone, and about an inch and a half in diameter and about two and a half inches long, so that a person can grasp them all around. One of them is plain, but the other one has a ring cut around it in the middle that can be seen easily. As the warriors chant, the one who has the sticks in his hands keeps time to the chant with his body, and going through gyrations with his arms that would make a juggler die with envy. As he opens his hands and throws the sticks from one hand to the other, then he closes on them and moves his arms in and out toward his opponent. He whirls them around, then under his armpits, or any place where he can change them without being seen. All this is done swiftly. Then he brings out his hands and holds them out toward his opponent, still keeping them on the move. The opponent, after feinting and faking several guesses, points to the hand he wants. If he gets the hand with the marked stick, he wins that point. Between the players on the ground is a ring in which two sets of sharp sticks are poked in the ground. Each team has the same number of sticks. If a player guesses the stick with the ring on it, he takes one of the sticks out of the other side of the ring and puts it on his own side of the ring. If he did not guess the stick with the ring on it, then the other side takes one stick

out from the other side of the ring, and puts it on their side
of the ring. They are entitled to keep the sticks they play
with, or, as the gamblers say, they hold the deal till the other
side guesses the right stick, and, with changing songs and
much shouting, they play till one party wins all the sticks
and whatever they have been playing for. In some games
every stick represents a horse.

With joy in our hearts, old Gabriel and I seen our people, the Pend d'Oreilles, winning all the games today. Spel-
a-qua and his bunch seem to have forgot that they promised
to shoot me up the first chance they got. Today they were all
smiles.

When we returned to camp, I found In-who-lise with her
face all scratched up, and her hair all down, and with two
black eyes and a couple of knife cuts on her arm. The beautiful calico dress that she had made is now hanging from her
in strips. Before this I did not think Kat-a-lee was devil
enough to commit murder, but today there is no doubt of it.
I told In-who-lise that she could leave old Gabriel's tepee,
that we would have to get along some way, and that I would
give her some nice stuff to make some more clothes.

Several bucks and squaws came over from the Injun
camp that had been lucky gambling, and I got several robes
from them and one dozen elk buskskin moccasins from a
squaw. And if I would have taken horses in trade, I could
have sold them all kinds of stuff, as those gamblers were
offering horses for almost nothing. They came drifting in in
bunches and were dying for whiskey, and if I would have
sold them what little I had, I could have cleaned them out of
house and home. It was probably a good thing for me they
did not know that I had any, or they would have taken it
away from me anyway.

Most of them were Gros Ventres and most of their
squaws were a tough bunch of hussies. Some of them (right
before In-who-lise) make no bones about it, that they were
good-hearted and generous with anything they had from A
to Z, and that I ought to meet them halfway and do some-

thing for my country to liven up trade, which they claimed was on the bum proper here, as there was only Injuns here and no white men around.

But with righteous indignation, I told them they were only bringing their coals to New Castle on the Tyne, that our output far exceeded the demand, and as charity should begin at home, that I was a protectionist of the home guard, who believed in patronizing home industry, and that at Fort Ellis not so far away, were many kind red hearts and free traders who would not say them nay.

They came and went till about noon, when they all pulled out for the Injun camp, to try their luck again with lady chance, when now old Gabriel wanted me to go with him to the Injun camp to see and bet on the horse race this afternoon between the Assiniboines and Piegans. I thought I had better stay in camp and take care that Sow-set and In-who-lise did not come together in the battle arena and do each other up.

It was a good thing that I did not go with old Gabriel and his bunch, for it was not long after they left, when in a cloud of dust rode into camp Lieutenant Clark, with nearly a troop of the 2nd Cavalry which were the first white men that I had seen since Webber and Harris had left camp. They were as much surprised to see me here as I was them. They dismounted and started to make some coffee and eat their rations. The troopers wanted to know how I was getting along trapping and where was Beaver Tom? I told them that he was gone long ago and that trapping was on the bum and no good. They said, from the looks of things, the squaw trapping must be awful good, for anybody can see that you have a supply with you. In-who-lise was sitting by the fire sewing and did not have time to get out of the way as they rode into camp. When they seen her scratched face and two black eyes, they began to rake me over the coals, saying that they never thought that I was mean enough to beat up my squaw like that. I tried to tell them that I did not do it, but they said to come off, for who in hell else could have done it?

The Lieutenant then questioned me and wanted to know if I had seen or knew anything of a large band of Injuns, some thought they were Piegans, but others said they were Blackfeet. They had been raiding the Crows at different times and places all summer, and were a bad bunch all around. The last raid they had gone over as far as Tongue River and raided some Cheyennes. They had run off many horses and killed several Injuns.

I knew it was old White Grass's bunch they wanted, but I told him that I never seen them or knew anything about them. I found out that they were going to turn back here, as they were out of rations. He wanted to know if there was any other Injun camp around here. I told him no, that the closest camp I knew of was a Cree breed camp, nearly a day's ride toward the Musselshell River from here. I thought it was a good thing that old Gabriel and his breed friends had gone to the Injun camp, as old Gabriel would go to hell to give them away if he was there.

After eating their rations and drinking their coffee, they mounted and went back the way they had come, leaving the Squaw Kid standing there an Injun in everything, to even his name. The reason that I lied to them was not for any love I had for the Blackfeet, but for a hatred I had for the Crows, like many others in them days.

One night after midnight and all was quiet as I was sleeping by the fire, I woke up. Something seemed to tell me that everything was not all right. It was moonlight and I had not long to wait, for now a dark shadow came toward me, and before it got up to me I heard the Injun hiss to keep quiet. At first I thought it was some Pend d'Oreille warrior, but I got the scare of my life as he glided up to my side and squatted down, whispering in pidgin English, "It is me, Blackfeet from White Grass your friend, see you come away from here. Blackfeet want to talk to you, here maybe no good, Pend d'Oreille in tepees hear and see us."

I whispered to him that was one thing I was not going to do and I had my six shooter in my hand under the blankets, ready to shoot him through the blankets if anything went wrong. I whispered to him, "What does Blackfeet want?" and for him to go away, as old Gabriel's tepee was close. I was scared bad enough, but that was nothing to what I was going to be, for now they came gliding out of darkness up to me one by one till twenty-one Blackfeet stood scattered around me and in my camp. I thought they were here to do old Gabriel's bunch up, or raid his horses and the Pend d'Oreilles. I could see they were stripped for action, with their guns in their hands.

The first Injun who came whispered, "Blackfeet want cartridges. Hurry quick so we can get away from here. Blackfeet Injun has plenty robes on horses in the dark to swap for the cartridges."

I knew they were out for some deviltry, and was not going to give them any, and whispered to them that I could not get the cartridges in the dark now as there was plenty stuff piled on top of them in the shack, and that I could not find them and would have to make a light, and they would soon notice the light in old Gabriel's tepee even if they were now asleep. After I refused them two or three times, they began to get sassy and say that I must get them the cartridges. It began to look as though they did not care whether they roused the whole camp. As afraid as I was of them, I was more afraid of someone in old Gabriel's bunch seeing them Blackfeet in my camp. I knew that they did not intend to harm me; if they did, no one could stop them. So I got up and went in the dark with them to where the horses with the robes were. Again I told them I could not get them the cartridges, and for them not to raid the Pend d'Oreilles or old Gabriel's horses, as mine were with his, and they would blame me for being mixed up in it, as the Blackfeet were my friends. But they said, "Blackfeet no want Pend d'Oreilles' horses tonight. Blackfeet want cartridges to go far away." Then they wanted to know what the soldiers wanted in my camp yesterday and if they had seen or talked with any of the Pend d'Oreilles in camp, and every few minutes would

say, "See Blackfeet your friend; you must catch 'em cartridges." When I would say, "No can catch 'em," they kept
getting meaner all the time and I do not know how it might
have turned out in the end. Suddenly the large band of dogs
of old Gabriel's outfit came by us. They must have been filling up on some buffalo carcass, and were returning to camp.
They began to bark and growl at us. The Blackfeet tried to
quiet them with the Injun hiss, but still they came at us
snapping and yelping. Then I made a runaway from the
Blackfeet and most if not all the dogs took after me; and it
was a good thing that my camp was not far and that those
Injun dogs, which were more or less wolf, now found out
that they knew me and let up on me. When I lit in my bed,
they wanted to play with me instead of eating me up, and
then old Gabriel and some more Injuns came up silently
with their guns in their hands. Gabriel wanted to know if I
had seen or heard anything wrong, and why was I playing
with their dogs at this late hour of the night, and why the
dogs had been making all that racket if nothing was wrong?
But I told him I had not seen or heard anything wrong, that
maybe the dogs were lying anyway. Then I was sorry that I
said this, for if old Gabriel and them Injuns start to look
around, I will be in a hell of a fix. What if I have to tell them
to get away from here quick, as there is twenty-one Blackfeet
about fifty yards from here, who are watching you all, and
who will be only too glad to fill you all full of lead, if you
give them half a chance? Then he said them dogs do not
make a racket like that for fun, and were not playing with
you when they did and I hope that it is not some of them
Piegans or Gros Ventres in the Pend d'Oreille camp who are
out now to raid our horses, for it is just their way. Then he
went back to his tepee with the others and the dogs, mut-
tering in Injun as he went.

After waiting for a long time and everything was quiet
and still again, I still knew that I had not seen the last of
them Blackfeet. Soon the Blackfoot Injun that first came
sneaks up to me again and pleads and begs of me to get

them cartridges. I whispered to him to get—that if they wanted the cartridges, to come tomorrow and they should have them. He whispered, "Blackfeet must be far away from here tomorrow; now Blackfeet must go, and we will leave the robes where the horses were, and before daylight you go and get them. Keep them until White Grass comes. He is soon coming again to swap. Give him what he wants for them." Then he went off as silently as he came, leaving the Squaw Kid in a hell of a pickle and wondering what old Gabriel and the Pend d'Oreille warriors would say and do if they find out that the Squaw Kid, their friend, was holding powwows with the Blackfeet in their camp in the night.

At the break of day, I went and got the robes where the Blackfeet left them and shoved them in the shack. When In-who-lise came at daylight, she had to wake up the Squaw Kid who was pretending to be soundly sleeping the sleep of the just, that he was far from feeling. She started a fire and I could see that she was watching me with reproachful eyes all the while. When she seen that I did not intend to tell her, she said, "Since when has An-ta-lee, White Feather's man, got afraid to tell his woman? Why like a snake-in-the-grass, he makes powwow with the Cha-qua in his camp in the darkness of the night, and why them sons of evil come to him, like evil spirits in the night when his friends the Pend d'Oreilles are asleep?"

But I said this is not so, and no Blackfeet have been here, and White Feather must have had a bad dream when she thinks so. She said, "Dreaming, is it? Maybe I am, but why are all those Cha-qua moccasin tracks all around in the dust where I stand. An-ta-lee had better hurry and help me tramp them out, or old Gabriel might ask him why they are here. Then maybe he will tell me why he has to lie to his woman, who has never lied to him." Then we tramped all the Blackfeet tracks out in camp. But there were too many where the pack horses stood with the robes; we had to let them go.

I told her how it was, that I could not help it if the Blackfeet came to me in the night the way they did, and she might as well know that they had left me four bundles of robes that were in the shack, and that old White Grass was soon coming to swap for them; that there was nothing wrong with that, for the Pend d'Oreilles had said, though they did not like it, that I might swap the Blackfeet anything except guns. Then she said, "If you will only listen to White Feather, you will have nothing to do with that old evil warrior White Grass or the Blackfeet no more. It will only bring us trouble with our friends the Pend d'Oreilles in the end."

After we ate breakfast, she said, "I have to go over to old Gabriel's tepee and tell him how close the Blackfeet were to camp in the night, for as soon as Petol and Samwell bring in the horses, they will find the tracks anyway. They all think that something was wrong with the dogs last night, and think that some of the Piegans or Gros Ventres who are staying in the Pend d'Oreille camp were prowling around camp last night, looking for some mischief to do. It will be better if we fool old Gabriel than to let him know that the Blackfeet came to see you." Then she went to old Gabriel's tepee. Soon every buck Injun came back with her and In-who-lise took great pride in showing them where the Blackfeet had stood in the night watching our camp. Petol and some of the others trailed them for quite a way toward the Yellowstone country. Old Gabriel said, "See, did I not tell you that the Blackfeet were sneaks and no good? They were here to murder us all and run off our horses only they were afraid that there are so many Pend d'Oreilles camped so close to us." To this I heartily agreed, knowing now only too well that if it was not for In-who-lise's Injun shrewdness and sharp eyes, old Gabriel or some of them would have seen them Blackfeet moccasin tracks in and around my camp; then he would have had a different song to sing to me.

CHAPTER TWENTY-THREE

A Ring for In-who-lise

Along in the early part of the morning I seen a wagon coming toward camp, with four cayuses hauling it, and Mexican Joe and Pete rode into camp as the advance guard, while their Piegan squaws drove the four cayuses some way. Their wagon was an old army wagon that must have been abandoned by Noah, who after he left the ark, tradition says, got lost in the badlands of the Little Missouri. And after here losing seven of his favorite wives from drinking alkali water for their complexion, after filling up on buffalo berries. In despair, he abandoned his wagon trains and then getting his camels sharp-shod, and hiring Paul Bunnion to guide him on the way, after an awful and harrowing journey of privations, succeeded in crossing the Rocky Mountains and discovered and colonized the Barbary Coast in the land of Frisko…. For this old-time war chariot that the Emperor Caligula never rode in was bound and wrapped with rawhide in so many places to hold it together that it was hard to see any wood about it. Even the wagon tires were wrapped with rawhide around the felloes to hold them on. But as time is nothing to a buck Injun or to a son of sunny Mexico, they seemed to get through the country some way. They put their tepee close to my camp.

They had quite a few half-breed kids that were blacker than Injuns. This went to show that I have been right in trying to impress on you the fruitfulness and fertility of good old Montana, as a healthy country to live in.

A Mexican and a squaw take to each other as natural as ducks take to water, and there is nothing wonderful in this. The reason for this is only too plain, that birds of a feather flock together, and the offspring of this union is a product of delicious deviltry, of an amorous intensity that is only equalled by billy goats. For the half-breed of a squaw and a Mexican are in a class of their own, and while they show the Circassian features more than any other breed and have beautiful blue-black hair and melting sloe-black eyes, still they are of a complexion on the brunette side that makes a squaw look like a white woman.

Both of their squaws were estimable ladies of a build and grace that showed Joe and Pete were shrewd buyers, out to get all the squaw they could for the money, even if they did waive all rights to slimness and beauty. Both of them were a ravishing dream of oriental beauty that would satisfy the most exact requirements of any Arab—for an Arab beauty is a load for a camel and I can tell you that a camel's load is from six to eight hundred pounds according to their size.

It did not take their squaws long to put up their tepee; then the whole caboodle of them started over for my camp. I said to In-who-lise, "You might as well get busy. We will have to feed them anyway." But I was mistaken and heaved a sigh of relief, when they all got around my white elephant, the new prairie schooner I had gotten from Webber and Harris. Pete and Joe start in caressing it lovingly at the same time murmuring Spanish words of endearment to it that would have made any of our swarthy limpid-eyed señoritas fly to the end of the earth with you any time. Then Joe said to me in Spanish, "Friend of all my friends, it is glad we are to see that you still have got it. May all your noble ancestors and you [of which there was much doubt till today], may you all dwell in paradise. For now no more will we have to wait till the rawhide dries out after a rain or fording the creeks, so that our old wagon will not fall to pieces."

Then I knew that they came to get my wagon, and began to wonder if they had the money to buy it and how much will they stand if they have; so I put out a feeler: with tears in my eyes, I met my dusky countryman's flowery eloquence, with heartbroken whispers, that I too loved that wagon, and that nothing but death could part us. When I

seen that this was an awful blow to them, I started to console them with Spanish sympathy, that all Spanish are so
good at, though they don't mean it. So, not to have them
heartbroken there on my hands, I said that being such good
friends of mine, I would die and they could have the wagon
for that friendship, and the only thing they would have to
give me was just a mere bagatalle—did they hear that? Just
one hundred and seventy dollars in gold, so that I could
have prayers said for my wicked soul after I was dead.

When Pete said, "Friend of all friends, I weep for you
when I hear you say that. Now don't place your trust in the
preachers after you are dead, and don't take any chances on
going to hell, when José and I with our Piegan squaws can
pray so much better for your benighted soul, night and day,
and on to and from the Musselshell to the Yellowstone, and
when you now know that our prayers are more effective
than a preacher's any day, you will say that wagon is ours
right now." But I told them friendship or no friendship, it
was the gold or no wagon, that I was not taking any chances
on them changing their minds about praying for me after
they got the wagon, as that would be awful on me after I was
dead.

But they said, "Friend of all friends, what is gold between
a friendship like ours, and besides you have the word of
honor of us whose noble ancestor was a Castelian Cavelero,
who leaned so heavily on the squaws four hundred years ago
that we have not been able to get the blood of the daughters
of Montesuma out of us yet, and are still an Injun."

But I said I was not taking any chances on an Injun, who
was as slippery as an eel, and some said that Mexicans were
more slippery still, and that the best brands of honor that I
had seen turned out to be a poor thing to live on in the end,
and if they wanted the wagon, to come through with the
money. But they said, "How can we when we have not got it
and what good is that wagon to you out here, with no harness or horses to pull it with?" Then I told them, "If you
want a wagon so bad, why don't you go over to the Crow

reservation and each of you take on a Crow squaw with the
Piegan one you have got, and mix the breed up." That Uncle
Sam was giving his Crow squaws all wagons as a dowry, just
as soon as they could rope in some damn fool of a white
man to live with them. Besides he would feed her and him;
then they could have two wagons instead and their bellies
full all the time.

But soon I got to feel sorry for them, being tenderhearted
and charitable. A bright idea for once entered my head. Yes,
I would perform a worthy and charitable act, even if I did
see to it that I received a little more than the value of the
wagon, for what is the use in giving charity unless it brings
in ten percent or better? That would be foolishness and not
the simon-pure brand of charity. I had been thinking for
some time, "What am I going to do if I get mostly buffalo
robes, which are bulky though light, how am I going to get
them to Bozeman without using large strings of pack
horses, when if I could use this wagon it would be simple?"
I had nearly two hundred robes already and they were getting to be quite a pile. So I told them if I pull out alive from
here in the spring, and if they would then haul this wagon
loaded with robes to Bozeman, then the wagon would be
theirs. And when they seen that they could not get the
wagon any other way, they readily agreed to do it. José said,
"But suppose you should be dead before spring, then where
do we come in for the wagon?" I said, "Then I will have no
use for it and it will be yours just the same."

Every day is now a bright and gay scene around my
camp, gaily colored bucks and squaws are going and coming
to and from the Injun camp, where they are still whooping
it up. I asked old Gabriel how long those visiting Injuns were
going to stay and keep it up. He said, "As long as they can get
something to eat and there is a chance to win what the Pend
d'Oreilles have got." I have been picking up anything I
wanted, which was mostly robes, buckskin hides and elk
moccasins. Near noon today several breeds and Crees with
their women came into camp from the large Cree camp on

the Musselshell River, to visit old Gabriel's bunch and the breeds who are here. It was a good thing for old Gabriel and the others that buffalo meat was easy to get, for if he had had to rustle his Injun relations ham and eggs, spuds and white bread, it would have bankrupted the Empress of India to feed this bunch, who have appetites like a hay press.

In-who-lise (who is raring to go) asked them if they knew or heard of the Black Robe that was coming to their camp to preach; one of the breeds told her that he would soon come; he was now some place on Milk River preaching to the Crees who were camped there. This breed also told her he had seen White Bird and some of her people who were with him last winter in Canada, but did not know if they were still there.

It had been bothering me, where to get the right kind of a ring for the sweetest squaw that ever lived. I asked her which ring she wanted out of my priceless treasures of brass, tin and glass that I had got from Webber and Harris. With shining eyes she picked out the pride of all that was left— this was the ring I had told the breed woman was once worn by Catherine of all the Russians, but she had refused my generous offer, saying that I was a liar and that it was not even good brass. In-who-lise, who is just a simple sweet little wild squaw, went into raptures over this beautiful tiffany with a cameo setting, representing a Roman sunset, in resplendent colors of red, green and yellow glass, backed up with a background of glittering tinfoil. This magnificent setting reposed in solid walls of brass, which if they did not shine were guaranteed to last, and when I laughed at her, she got mad and insulted. I told her she could not have it, as it was no good. I would get her a better one, because that one would turn black before she could turn around. She said, "What care I for that, when there is plenty river sand to keep it shining and bright?" So you may know how much a wild squaw knew or cared about gold. Brass suited them just as well, even if it did keep them scouring it to keep it bright. But I was not lowdown enough to give the woman I was going to marry a brass ring, even if she did not know any better. I decided to get reckless and extravagant and try to make her a ring out of the ten-dollar gold piece I got from the breed woman. It was all the money I had in the world, except for the five silver dollars I had gotten at the same time.

When Mexican Pete came over, I asked him if he thought I could make a ring out of the ten-dollar piece. He said, "Yes, but why do you want to waste good money to do that?" I had to tell him that I wanted it for In-who-lise when I married her, that I thought a lot of her and was not going to give her a brass one. He thought at first I was joking and roared with laughter, but when he seen I was not, said, "A ten-dollar ring for a squaw? I would see all the squaws in hell and back again before I would do that. Why don't you do like I do? Just tie a buckskin string around her wrist, then give her a good licking; then she will like you all the better. You will soon find out that little sawed-off runt of a squaw that you are crazy enough to marry can run like an antelope and she will run the hell out of you trying to catch her, for the slim ones are always either pouting or sulking. When they are not doing this, they are off on the range bulling the rest of the time. You should be sensible like José and I, who have tried all kinds of them. If you must marry a squaw, then get a big fat one like my Isidora, who is too large and fat to run off. I want to tell you she is some woman I have got. And though José thinks his woman the best of the two and an angel to boot, still she is nothing compared to my Isidora, even if she is as big as a Congo elephant and he calls her Buena Ventura."

Then I started in on the ring with a jackknife and a small file, and after some trouble managed to get a hole through the center. Soon I was sorry I tackled the job, but Mexican Pete said, "Give me that. If you have got to have a gold ring, I will make it for you." Then he went to his old wagon and got a bolt out of it about the size of In-who-lise's finger. After he got the bolt through the center, it was not long till he had it hammered into a fine ring, which, though a little rough, was the pure thing.

An Injun named In-qua-la came from the Injun camp riding a fine-looking horse and says that he came to swap his buffalo horse to me. I thought it funny that he would want to do that, as that was the last thing an Injun would do and, though I had never seen his horse, I had heard that it was one of the best buffalo horses. I told him, "You know that I don't swap for horses," but he said, "See, he is a great one; no buffalo can get away from him. See, he can go like the wind." He began to show the horse off. He sure could go. When he came back, he said, "Is it not so, and since An-ta-lee is now an Injun like us, he will want a horse like this when he comes with us to hunt the buffalo. So In-qua-la his friend brings him his buffalo horse, so An-ta-lee can have a good one." This tickled my vanity to think that he thought so much of me and thought I would give him what he wants for the horse.

But In-who-lise came up and spoiled my beautiful dream. I told her, "See, is he not beautiful? My friend In-qua-la is going to swap him to me." In-who-lise said to In-qua-la, "Since when has In-qua-la got to be so poor a liar? He says that is his buffalo horse, when he knows I have seen his buffalo horse when I was in the Injun camp, and know him well when I see him. This horse is not your buffalo horse, besides he does not belong to the Pend d'Oreille camp." Then he hung down his head and said, "That is so, but this one is mine now, and a good one too, which I won from a Gros Ventre playing hands yesterday."

Old Gabriel came up, and after telling him the nice trick In-qua-la had tried to turn on me, I said, "Is this what you call Injun friendship?" Old Gabriel said nothing to this, and starts to give In-qua-la the dickens. Then he said, "If you want the horse, why not buy him and take a chance on the Gros Ventres stealing him from you. We will picket him in the camp at night, where the Gros Ventres cannot very well get him. If you want a good buffalo horse, you may not get a chance like this again." I asked In-qua-la, "What do you want for him?" He said, "Ten good blankets." I laughed at him, saying that he would have to let the Gros Ventres steal him on himself. In the end I got him for one good blanket, knowing that I was foolish to give him that.

Then he went off with old Gabriel to get a horse from him to ride back to the Injun camp, leaving us standing there and in possession of this buffalo horse of somewhat doubtful title. The horse is now snorting and pawing the ground, trying to get away from me. I have already told you that I had got the Injun smell from the squaws so bad that it fooled the Injun dogs, and they now take me for an Injun, but this wild Injun horse was not to be fooled. When I tried to get on him, he struck at me and jumped to one side and in no way could I get on him.

Mexican Pete and José, who seen the racket, came up, saying, "Fool, don't you know that you are trying to get on him on the wrong side? All Injuns get on a horse on the right side, and the white men get on from the left." But even this way I could not get near him without getting my head smashed by his front hoofs. Mexican Joe said, "Give him to me; he knows that you are afraid of him and has you buffaloed. Just watch me who can ride anything that wears hair. See me make him eat out of my hand and bring him back to his milk." But all he got out of him was a good smash on his shoulder from his front hoofs. Then he got his Spanish up and told Pete to go to their camp and bring him his saddle and lariat. They would choke him down and put his saddle on him. Then he would let the Injun son of a bitch see that he did not care where he went or what he did after he got on him and had his spurs jabbed in his guts. But I would not let them abuse him, for I knew he was only in terror and before this had only been handled by Injuns. I told In-who-lise to take him off a ways and to be sure to picket him good. He meekly let her lead him off. In a few days he got used to me and I could do what I wanted with him, and soon had a horse that was the envy of the Pend d'Oreille camp.

The next day some Gros Ventres were in my camp, and this Injun who lost his horse gambling with In-qua-la was with them. I said to him by signs, "Is this horse yours or mine?" He said, "Yes, he was mine, but is not mine no more." I told a half-breed Cree who could talk Gros Ventre to tell him I was sorry he lost his horse. "I am going to give you this Spencer rifle, cartridges, and this nice blanket to keep you warm, if you will say in your heart that he is mine." Those cutthroat Gros Ventres stood around speechless. The breed had to tell him again, before he or the others would believe it. Still he stood there silent. Then their war chief picked up the gun and blanket and gave them to the buck, saying to the breed, "You tell An-ta-lee, for doing that, no Gros Ventre will steal his horse or harm him, as far away from here as the eagle flies."

PART THREE

In-who-lise and the
Nez Perce Movement

CHAPTER TWENTY-FOUR
Why Should I talk of my People?

Early in the afternoon old Gabriel came over with a bunch of his Cree and breed friends, saying, "We have declared the rest of the day a legal holiday and are going to have a buffalo barbecue, a little later than the middle of the afternoon. You got to come and be there with us. Petol has killed a nice young buffalo cow and, as there will be too many of us to get in one tepee, we will have the women build a large fire outside where they can roast the meat and we can have a good time. My friends and us have come to get In-who-lise to tell us the story of her people, and of the fights they had with the white men along the trail on their way out here. We have heard much, but would like to hear it all from her. She can talk to us in Pend d'Oreille and at the same time talk by signs to my friends the Crees, as they do not understand the Pend d'Oreille talk." In-who-lise at first refused to do so, saying, "Why should I talk of my people and the many of them who are dead? I have been sorry many times; why should I be sorry again tonight telling you that? Besides it is too long a story for one time." They kept at her, saying, "Then we will come again till it is done." Still she did not want to do it. Old Gabriel and the others kept at her till at last she consented to do it the best she could. Then old Gabriel invited Mexican Pete and Joe to the feast. They said, "No, we will pull out in the morning for the Pend d'Oreille camp; our women want to see some of their Piegan friends before they go back."

It was not long at old Gabriel's tepee before the squaws began to bring in wood for the fire. I saw that Kat-a-lee was well again, going around helping the others; she had been staying in Petol's tepee, and I hoped she would stay there for

good. Soon the smell of roasting buffalo comes through the
air; all around the fire are large chunks of meat sticking up
on sharp sticks. Squaws are busy turning them around so
they will not burn. Soon the feast was on. It was a wild sight
to see all them buck Injuns and breeds with their women
and papooses squatting around the fire. An old gray-haired
Cree starts the ball rolling by saying grace, and asking a
blessing on us all in the Cree language. Even in those days,
those Injuns and the Pend d'Oreilles were bronco Catholics
and prayed every time they ate, and when they went to sleep
and got up in the morning. Their religion did not take very
deep, for even Kat-a-lee, Sow-set and Squis-squis, with
other beautiful Pend d'Oreille maids, would solemnly roll
their eyes heavenward and respond to good old Gabriel's
prayers morning and night, with a look of sanctity on their
faces worthy of the prophets and saints of old, but they soon
forgot this, and would sneak back to the squaw paradise, to
blow their hands, buck and squeal and kick over the traces
every time the whiffletrees touched their heels. There is no
use denying the fact that the wild Indian christianized was a
died-in-the-wool hypocrite of the slickest kind. And how
could you blame him, when at this art he was only excelled
by his white brothers, who brought him the cross of Christ
in one hand and the whiskey bottle in the other?

We were soon eating, everyone for himself, cutting off
slices and chunks of sizzling buffalo meat. Injun etiquette
and the process was simple. You ate the piece as soon as you
could, then licked the grease off your fingers, then cut off
another chunk, not forgetting to give some to your favorite
dogs, who were sitting behind you on their haunches. You
kept at it this way till you got tired eating, then layed off for
a while to give you the required determination to start in
fresh again.

Although the language of each tribe of Injuns was different and they could not understand each other, they had a
sign language that was the same among all Injuns, no matter where they came from. By sign, they could talk with one

another just as well as if it had been done with the tongue. In this they had it better than the white man. When In-who-lise squatted down inside this circle of eager faces to tell her story in Pend d'Oreille, it was no bother for her to talk the sign language to the Crees and breeds who were there. Most of the Injuns, even if they talked with their tongue, kept their hands going with the sign language, even among their own people.

The story told by In-who-lise would be incomplete if I did not tell the beginning. I am compelled to bring the bitter past to life in the Wallowa Valley—the country of Joseph's people.

In this land lived a part of the Nez Perce tribe called by the other Nez Perces Wal-lam-wat-kin. Those Injuns had lived in this valley as far back as they knew, but in time the white men seen this land and wanted it. In this valley the grass on the hills was never known to fail stock in the winter in the memory of Injun or white man. Stock could winter out without need for hay, and this was the only valley in this part of the country where this was possible year in and year out. Those Injuns did not want to leave this land, but the white men started to come in small numbers at first and later more and more of them. They said why should those lazy buck Injuns have this land when we can use it ourselves? Let them get out of here to Lapwai where they belong. When they seen that the Injuns would not go, they started to make trouble for them in many underhanded ways. It went from bad to worse and, when the white men still could not get those Injuns out, politicians done the rest. General Howard was ordered to remove these Injuns out of the Wallowa Valley and force them on the Lapwai reservation.

After several bitter councils with him, Joseph, with the most of his people, agreed to leave the Wallowa Valley to the white men to save trouble and bloodshed, though they were not given time to round up their stock. Those Nez Perces were not the wild savages that some would have you believe.

Many of them had large bands of horses and cattle and were peace-loving and progressive, and far exceeded most Injuns in intelligence. But among those Nez Perces were several young bucks and some others who had been beaten up by the white men, and others who had brothers or friends killed or injured by the white men. Those Injuns were very bitter against Joseph for agreeing to go on the Lapwai reservation and were out for trouble. If Joseph and the older warriors would have held in check those young hot bloods and injured ones, there would never have been this Nez Perce war. A white trader sold whiskey to several of those young bucks, whose minds were inflamed with their wrongs, and the devil in their hearts and whiskey done the rest. They began to murder and burn, and while it would have been bad enough if they had picked the ones who caused their wrongs, still this is not the Injun's way. The first ones that come his way get the benefit of his vengeance. He does not care if the guilty ones are there or not; any white man, woman or child answers the purpose. His belief is that all white men are brothers, and if he hurts one, he hurts the guilty one and them all. He is out to make them all sorry and he sure to God does.

A white man's war is horrid enough, and when the white man is inflamed with hatred he will commit acts of brutality of which he should be ashamed. But, as a rule, the Indian does put the white man in the shade, and is in a class of his own when it comes to low-down deviltry and brutality. It is not the main body of them who does this deviltry but the small bands of stragglers who prowl around sometimes miles away from the main body of them. They are the bad and evil ones.

After those young Nez Perce bucks in their drunken fenzy started to butcher and burn, then the other discontented ones broke loose from all restraint of their chiefs and wiser people and would not listen to reason, and promptly took the warpath. They left a trail of blood and fire behind them that forever closed all hopes of pardon for their acts. It left the whole of Joseph's people with no choice but to fight it out to the bitter end. And fight they did, and in the first two battles they had with the soldiers and citizens, they attacked them with such fury and bravery that those two battles were nothing more than a butchery of the soldiers. It is well known that the white men outnumbered the Nez Perce. Though the soldiers were well supplied with ammunition and rations, and using artillery, cavalry, infantry and volunteers in the battle of the Clearwater,* for two days they were unable to dislodge the Nez Perce who finally left of their own accord, and had to move their families and large herds of horses and cattle with them. They took their time doing this and crossed over to the other side of the river, leaving the white men in possession of a battlefield they never won.

General Howard, with all the faculties at his command, could not do what those simple Injuns had done, that is move his command over this swift water, and by the time he got around and after them, they had struck the Lolo trail and were on their way to Montana, and were now willing to give up the land of their birth to the white man. The old settlers in the Wallowa Valley—through their greed and avarice—have handed the soldiers a bunch of bad trouble, for many of them are lying in none too deep a grave.

*July 11 and 12, 1877.

CHAPTER TWENTY-FIVE
The Story of In-who-lise

Now at Gabriel's barbecue, this is how In-who-lise told her story: After our people had their last fight with the white man in the land of the Nez Perce, they left and went to Kamiah, and now the chiefs In-mut-to-ya-lat-lat (Joseph), White Bird and Looking Glass had much trouble with some of them. They still wanted the warriors to stay and fight the white man and drive them out of our land far away and not to run away the way they did. The old men and some of the warriors with them who were evil say they do not want to fight the white men no more, who are now too many for our people. We should leave our land to the white men and go to the land of the buffalo and to King George's land far away. Then our chief White Bird said to them, "Is this what you now do to my warriors and people who are here ready to fight and to die for their lands and against the white man's wrongs? You sons of evil who wanted and made for us all this war, you are going to stay here with us and fight till we kill the white men, or die like Nez Perce warriors in our own land."

Then Looking Glass said to them, "Yes, cowards who hold down your heads and hide your hands behind your back, red with the blood of white women, children and men, and who leave a trail of blood and smoke behind to darken the Nez Perce warriors' name, you who are the cause of your brothers and friends lying dead on the battlefields, you wanted to fight, this is war, the war you wanted, and the war you get my people in. We will not run away from the white men, when we are in the right and the white man in the wrong, and give them our country. Here we will stay. We will put our women and children away in the hills, then come back and fight the white men, for it has now come to where the white men or the Injun has got to die. The right place to live is in the land of our fathers, and it is the right place to die in. No Nez Perce warrior shall run away, as some of them say they will. Here they shall stay, with White Bird's warriors and mine, and fight and drive out the white men away from our land. We made them run before this, and we can do it again, for it has now gone too far to turn back. My people have now lost their lands and most of their horses to the white men. No Nez Perce warrior has ever run away from the white men, and you shall not do it now."

But there were too many of them for the chiefs and the others who wanted to stay and fight the white men. They and the old men said, "No, this shall not be so. Have we not got enough of our sons and friends dead now? And still the white men come, and they will soon be like the sands in the river and no matter how brave we fight, and the more we kill of them, the more they come. And in the end will kill the most of us, and them that are not dead, the white chief now says that he will hang them. Then who will care for our women and children after we are all dead? For how can we now stay and fight the white men, when our brothers from Lapwai have left us and the others there are now helping the white men, like the snakes they are, to kill and fight their brothers from the Wallowa. Besides, the warriors of Hush-Hush-Cute who were with us have left, and only the warriors of Joseph, White Bird and Looking Glass are left to fight the white men. It is as the chiefs say, the white men's wrongs to us have made some of our men bad. Because of that we will give up the land of our fathers to the white men and go to the land of the buffalo and to King George's land far away. The white men will surely be glad and leave us go on our way in peace. But to stay here and die or give up our sons and friends to the white chief in the end it shall not be, and we will fight the white men to the bitter end, if they want it this way."

Not till then did the chiefs Joseph, White Bird and Looking Glass say that they would go with them. Then when

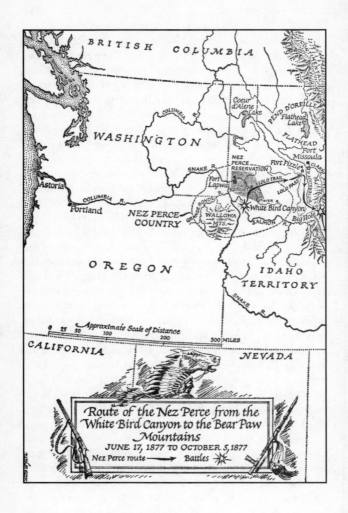

Route of the Nez Perce from the White Bird Canyon to the Bear Paw Mountains

JUNE 17, 1877 TO OCTOBER 5, 1877

Nez Perce route ⟶ Battles ✷

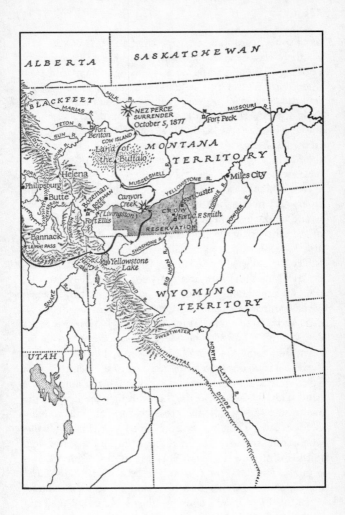

our people heard that the white chief and his soldiers were on their way here to fight and bar the way, Joseph sent Looking Glass and some warriors to fight them and keep them there till our people could start on their way; which they did, leaving all our cattle behind, but taking the most of their horses with them, and were soon on the trail going to the land of the Salish, and to the land where the buffalo stay. In the last fight with the white men, our people left many of their lodges to the white men, and now some of us did not have any tepees.

As we went along the trail to the land of the Salish,* the chiefs and our people had much to say each day. Which would be the best trail to take, when they came to the land of the Salish, going from there to the land of the buffalo far away? Joseph with Looking Glass and their people said, "We will go the old way, the Salish way, to where the buffalo lands do lay." But White Bird and our people said, "No, not that trail, for much danger to us does lay along that trail, when we have our women and children with us. There will be soldiers and white men to bar the way and fight us nearly every day. White Bird and his people shall not take that trail, for when they come to the land of the Salish, they will not take the Salish trail, nor turn to the right to go the Bannock way. They will turn to the left and go through the land of the Pend d'Oreilles, our friends, then through the land of the Skal-a-says [Kootenai], and cross over the big hills to King George's land. There on the other side lay the buffalo lands, where our friends the Sioux and Ec-mut-a-sute-a-lem [Sitting Bull] now does stay. This trail to King George's land is only a few days' travel from the land of the Salish, and there are no white men or soldiers to fight us on the way."

But still Joseph and Looking Glass said, "No, it shall not be that trail and White Bird knows not what he says. For are not the Salish our friends? They will help us on our way, and

*"On the morning of July 16, 1877, the non-treaty Nez Perces filed eastward upon one of the roughest adventures in military annals."—p. 80, Beal, *I Will Fight No More Forever*, University of Washington Press, 1963.

when the white men see us so many warriors and know that we will do them no wrong, as we are only on our way to the buffalo country, the white men will be only too glad to see us pass quickly through their land and go on our way without wanting to fight us. The soldiers, they are not many, and if it is fighting they want, we can fight and whip them every day. We done it in Idaho and can do it here again."

Then White Bird said, "Yes, Joseph and Looking Glass are wise when they say the Salish are our friends and that they can trust the white men. Maybe they can tell White Bird why the white men now stay in our land in the Wallowa, and why we have now no land or homes in which to stay today. And why the one-armed chief follows us behind with soldiers and white men, who say that our hands are red with the blood of white women, children and men." So the warriors and their people talked this way on the trail on their way to the land of the Salish. And when White Bird sent off three runners to ask the chief of the Salish if White Bird's people can go through the land of the Pend d'Oreilles, Joseph and Looking Glass said to him, "Surely you and your people are going to leave us, your brothers and people, and go by that trail. Then if we should have trouble with the white men and soldiers on our way to the land of the buffalo, how can White Bird and his warriors help us, when he is far off on another trail?"

Then White Bird said, "What good will White Bird and his warriors do Joseph and Looking Glass and their warriors when like them they will all lie dead, leaving our women to wail and cry, as they see the ravens pick our bones, as we lie there to rot in the hot sun on the prairies along the Salish trail, if Joseph and Looking Glass with their people still say that they will go by that trail to the land of the buffalo far away?"

When we came near the hot springs, the runners came back, and say that the Salish chief says, was not he and his people always the Nez Perces' friends? Then why should White Bird, his friend, ask him if his people can go by and through the land of the Pend d'Oreilles, when he knew that the chief of the Salish and his people are sorry for them, for they have heard and well know the white men's evil ways to them. And that they will be glad to help them through any way they want to go. Then our people left the hot springs and came down the trail to the land of the Salish, but before we got there the scouts ahead came back to us and say that there were soldiers and white men not far from there, who bar the trail on us to the land of the Salish and on to the land of the buffalo still far away.

We did not go far when Joseph said, "We camp here, till we can find out what the chief of the soldiers and white men want and have got to say to us. When they know that we come this way not to harm them, they will let us go on our way in peace. If not, we had better find out first what the Salish chief and his people are now going to do, if they are our friends or the white men's."

Before the women got the lodges of the camp up, the white chief of the soldiers and white men came near, and by signs and talk said they wanted our chiefs to come with them for a powwow, and wanted to know why the Nez Perce warriors were in this land. Then our chiefs and some of our warriors went off with them to the powwow with the chief of the soldiers and the white men not far off.

When the chiefs and warriors came back to camp from the powwow, now tell the warriors and people that the chief of the soldiers and white men now say that the Sapah-tan warriors cannot pass on through the Salish land, and that they must give them their guns and go with the chief of the soldiers to their skookum house near In-ola-a (Missoula), and stay there till the one-armed chief of the soldiers (Howard) comes with his soldiers, who will talk on the click-clack with the great white chief far away, and he will say where the Sapah-tan warriors shall go to stay.

But the warriors in camp were mad and said, "No, it shall not be that way. If it is war they want, then they will have it. We will make the Salish trail run with their blood, if the soldiers or white men try to bar our way to the land of the buf-falo, or try and take from us our guns."

But Looking Glass said to them, "Stop your tongues, warriors of evil, for we have already told the chief of the soldiers that this could not be so, that if they did not let us go through in peace, then we were going to go through anyway. And that the Nez Perce warriors are only on their way to the land of the buffalo and not here to harm no one. But the white chief said nothing to this, but that he will come tomorrow and make powwow with us. And as we want no trouble, we said that it would be so, and now all Nez Perce warriors shall stay in camp, and shall not prowl around. Then the white men cannot say evil of us."

Then some warrior scouts who were watching the white men's camps came back, saying, "Evil for us in this land, for we seen Salish warriors, they who say they are our friends, they had their war paint and war bonnets on them and their guns in their hands, and now stay with the white men and soldiers in their camp."

Then our chiefs went into council and In-mut-to-ya-lat-lat (Joseph) said, "Alas that this is so, that the Salish warriors hearts to us are bad, when our people and I am sad, and they make us sadder when they lift their guns and hands against the Sapah-tan people who were always their friends. There must be something wrong, for did not the chief of the Salish tell White Bird's warriors that the Salish were our friends, that they would help us on our way? That all trails were open to us any way that we wanted to go to the land of the buffalo?"

Then White Bird said, "Did I not tell Joseph and Looking Glass and their people that bitter for them would be the day, if they went to the land of the buffalo by the Salish trail, where they will have to trust the white men on their way, whose friendship for us is like the snow that falls on a summer day? Alas for us, my brothers, you must now know, to your sorrow, that it fades away as quickly as it comes, under the heat of the glaring sun. Yes, the white men, with their voice as sweet as murmuring waters, but alas for us, that this is so, their tongues are crooked, and they are snakes that bite and sting the Indian whenever he stands in their way. So now Joseph, Looking Glass and their people can see that the trail through the land of the Pend d'Oreilles and the Skal-a-says is the safest way for our people to King George's land far away."

Then Joseph said, "We will wait and see, and send three wariors who know the way to where the Salish chief does stay, and they can hear what he now says about why his war-riors are with the white men today, when yesterday he said he was our friend. The white chief can talk to us till we know what to do, then we will leave and go through to the land of the buffalo, even if we have to fight our way." Then three warriors who well know the land of the Salish and the white men's ways, at dark sneak out of camp on their way to where the Salish chief did stay. So our people can know for sure what he will say and some more warriors went and watched the white men's camp all night, so if the white men came in the night then the warriors would know in time to fight them.

Next day before the sun was in the middle of the sky, the warriors who went to powwow with the Salish chief came back to camp, and with them came a half-breed of our peo-ple, who lived in the land of the Salish. The chiefs asked the warriors, "Did you see the Salish chief and is he well?" The warriors said, "Yes, he is well, but alas for us, he is mad and like the rattlesnake when he is blind, now strikes at the sound of our voice, and does not see or know his friends of the Nez Perce any more. For he now says that evil for him was the day that Joseph and his cutthroat warriors came to the Salish land. That we had better listen to and do what the white chiefs say to us today. For if the Nez Perce chiefs and their people do not, then they will know early tomorrow what the Salish chief and his people will have to say to them. Yes, this is surely war for us, for we seen that the white men have left their lodges and have taken their women and chil-dren away, and they now stay in their strong tepees." Then the chiefs and half-breed went off and talked by themselves, and what they said to him or what he said to them none of the people know. Then he takes his blanket like an Injun and goes on his way, so the white men or Salish may not know that he was with us today.

Soon some white men came near camp and say for the chiefs to come to the powwow, that the chief of the soldiers and white men are again there to hear what the Nez Perce chiefs have to say today. Then the chiefs and some of the warriors rode off to them not far away, where the white men were waiting for them. The white men and chiefs powwow for a long time, and when the chiefs and warriors came back to camp, now say, "Alas, it was only the same as yesterday, that we must not go through the Salish land, and we will have to give them our guns, and go with the soldier chief to his skookum house near In-ola-a. But we told them that as the Nez Perce had done them no wrong, it could not be so today that they should come back tomorrow. Then surely the Nez Perce chiefs and warriors will tell the white chief that they are not going to give up their guns, or go with him to his skookum house near In-ola-a (Missoula) to stay. For we would first know what the Salish chief will say tomorrow. We do not want trouble with him or the white men, if it can be helped."

Some of the warriors were mad and said, "Why do we stay here and powwow with them soldiers and white men who are afraid of us. Let us away at the break of day tomorrow and fight our way through them. Has it come to this, that a Nez Perce warrior has got to ask the white men and Salish warriors if they can go by on the trails?"

But Looking Glass said to them, "Stop your tongues, sons of evil and cowards, who ran away from the white men in Idaho, and why do you want to do it here now? Have you not made enough trouble already for us, without making more here? You shall do as I say, even if I got to kill you with my own hands." And not till then did the bad warriors become quiet.

Next morning before the sun got high in the sky, five Salish warriors came near the camp and made signs of

peace. Then some of our warriors made signs of peace, and
went to meet them to see what they wanted. Then a warrior
came back and said to the chiefs, "They are the warriors of
the Salish chief. One of them says that he knows the words
the Salish chief told him to tell the Nez Perce chiefs, and the
other four warriors are here with him to see that he is not
afraid, and to hear that he says them right, and that he does
not lie. Shall we hear them where they are or in camp?"

But some of the warriors said, "No, the Salish snakes are
only spies for the white men. When they are telling us the
words, their eyes will know and see everything in our camp.
Then if the white men come to fight us, they will know just
what to do, like they did in Idaho." Joseph said, "We care not
for their evil tongues, or what they say to the white men,"
and made signs for the Salish warriors to come to camp to
say the words of the Salish chief. Then he said to the warriors in camp, "Hide your looks of evil when they stay with
us, so that the white men cannot be glad if they hear this."
Then the warriors came back to camp, with the Salish warriors and while the Salish warriors knew many of the warriors, now they knew them not, and the Nez Perce warriors
knew them not. Joseph said, "What brings the Salish warriors here, his friends of yesterday, but who are now the
white men's friends today? What has the Nez Perce people
done to them, that it should be this way, that they stay in the
white men's camp, with their war paint and war bonnets on
them and their guns in their hands?"

Then the Salish warriors said, "The chief of the Salish
says to In-mut-to-ya-lat-lat [Joseph] and his people, that his
people and him—their hearts are sad, when they have to say
to the Nez Perce warriors, who have always been their
friends, but are not so today, for our chief now says that the
white men are now his good friends, and that he is their
friend. That Joseph and his warriors are now bad men, that
their hands are red with the blood of white women, children
and men, of their white brothers in Idaho. That the white
chief and his soldiers now comes behind after them, and

that they shall pay dearly the white men's way, for the evil
they have done, and if the Salish help them on their way, or
shall be friends of Joseph and his people, they shall pay
dearly with them. For now Joseph and his bad warriors only
come this way for evil and they will leave a trail of fire and
blood behind them, of weeping white women, children, and
men, along the Salish trail to the land of the buffalo, where
they say they are going. The white men say they lie about
going to King George's land to meet Ec-mut-a-sute-a-lem
[Sitting Bull] and his bad Sioux warriors, where the white
men cannot harm them for their crimes, and they can make
more trouble for the white men. Then hear again, Sapah-tan
warriors, the words of the Salish chief, who was always a
good man and kept his people from doing wrong, who
believes in Colon Suten the white men's God, and does not
believe in staining his hands in the blood of sleeping women,
children or men. That he now believes Joseph and his warriors guilty, or why do they run away from the white men's
anger? And again he says to the Sapah-tan warriors, that if
they lift their hands against or harm or wrong any white
women, children or men in the Salish land, they will have to
answer for this to the Salish chief and his people, and they
shall pay dearly if they do so, and that the Nez Perce warriors
may surely see and know that the Salish are the white men's
friends. The Salish warriors will dance the war dance at their
friends the white men's camp tonight. To White Bird and his
warriors the Salish chief now says that they shall not pass or
go through the land of his people the Pend d'Oreilles, as he
now believes like the white men, that they only want to go
that way to make trouble and to put evil in the Pend d'Oreille
warriors hearts (who are now evil enough) against the white
men, and like the Sapah-tans would have them stain their
hands with white men's blood, and in the end like them only
to lose their lands to the white men."

Then Joseph said the Salish warriors can tell the Salish
chief the words of Joseph, that his heart is sad to hear the evil
words the Salish chief now says against them who have never

wronged or harmed him or his people. While it is so, that
some of his people's hands are red with white men's blood,
and the Salish chief surely knows that they had never been so,
till the white men's wrongs made them the way they are today.
But when the Salish chief says that Joseph and his warriors are
only here for evil and to leave a trail of fire and blood behind
them along the Salish trail on our way to the land of the buffalo, then he knows that his evil heart and tongue lie. For have
not Joseph and his people given up their homes and the land
of their fathers to the white men, so that they would not have
any more white men's blood on their hands and now only
want to go on their way through the Salish land, at peace with
the Salish warriors and white men, and to harm or wrong no
one. And when the Salish chief now knows this, if he or the
white men in the land of the Salish shall now lift their hands
against In-mut-to-ya-lat-lat (Joseph), his warriors or people,
then the blood of the white women, children, men and Salish
people will be on their own heads. For the Nez Perce warriors
and people are going to go on their way through the Salish
land, even if the Salish chief, his people or the white men shall
bar their way. In-mut-to-ya-lat-lat has now spoken.

Then Looking Glass got mad at the Salish warriors and
said to them, "Hear me, Looking Glass, war chief of the
Chute-pal-lu Sapah-tans. Tell your chief and your people
who were once men, when their chief Victor led them, but
now, like our brothers at Lapwai, snakes that strike their
brothers down and crawl like a tepee dog up to the white
men's feet, and lick the white men's hands, who robs and
strikes them every time. Yes, Salish warriors, dance your war
dance in the white men's camp, to show them your bravery
and friendship, and as a warning to the Nez Perce warriors.
Could the white men only know that the Salish warriors are
boastful braggards who dance their war dances only behind
the white men's guns, when Looking Glass and his Sapah-tan
warriors are around, and that when they hear the hoofbeats
of the Sapah-tan war horses and war cry, they will turn away
and fly like the ravens they are. Then the boastful words of

the Salish chief and his warriors shall not save the white men
nor them from the wrath of Looking Glass and his warriors,
who now would pass in peace through the Salish land. Yes,
tell your chief, people and white men that one blow struck or
one insult offered to In-mut-to-ya-lat-lat's warriors or people—then Looking Glass with his Sapah-tan warriors will
make the river and creeks in the Salish land red with the
blood of Salish warriors and white men."

Then White Bird said to the Salish warriors, "Harken,
you can tell the Salish chief that White Bird has heard his
words to him, and now knows his evil heart and crooked
tongue—of him who says that he is the friend of the white
men, and that they are his friends. That the day will soon
come for him when the Salish chief with his people shall
leave their land, with tears in their eyes.* Then shall the
Salish chief come to White Bird and say the white men lied
to me, and I wish I could forget them words, said to you and
your people. Yes, on that day the Salish chief would forget,
but not I, White Bird."

Then the Salish warriors left camp to tell the Salish chief
what the Nez Perce chiefs say. The warriors who are now mad,
say to the chiefs, "Why should we powwow with the soldiers
and white men today, when them and the Salish warriors
know what we are going to do and say. Let us tell them to go
away and let us go by in peace, or they will surely rue the day."

But the chiefs said, "No, we will keep our word to the
white men and will tell them today that as sure as the sun
rises, the people of In-mut-to-ya-lat-lat will leave here
tomorrow morning, as the sun rises up in the sky, to go on
their way, and no Nez Perce warrior shall leave camp today,
and they will do well to heed the words we say, when we
powpow with the white men, that here they stay."

When the chiefs went to powwow with the soldiers and
white men they did not stay long with them there, and soon
came back to camp. They said the chief of the soldiers still
says the same words that he said the first day and yesterday,

*This prophecy came true.

and we seen the chief of the white men, who is now there with them. The white men now know the words of Joseph's warriors and people, that they will leave here in peace tomorrow morning, as the sun rises up in the sky, and want no trouble with the white men or soldiers, but if the soldiers or white men shall bar their way, they will fight their way through them to go on their way, then the blood of the soldiers and white men will be on their own heads.

Then the chiefs tell the warriors to get ready their guns and cartridges, and the women to see that everything is ready and all tepees down at dark tonight, and to be ready to go from here when the sun rises up in the sky tomorrow morning.

Again our chief White Bird said to Joseph, Looking Glass and people, "Brothers hear the voice of White Bird again and, for the last time, do not go on by the Salish trail, nor through their land on our way to the land of the buffalo. You can now see the trouble we are having already with the soldiers and white men and now it is the Salish. This would be nothing to us if we were only warriors alone on the war trail. But now we have our women and children, besides many horses to watch and take care of. It is soon going to be like in Idaho, the soldiers and white men will come more and more every day to fight us and bar our way. This is only the beginning and evil for us will be the end if we go through by the Salish trail to the land of the buffalo. We have now the one-armed white chief and his soldiers from Idaho coming behind after us. After we leave here and his soldiers come here, then if we meet too many soldiers and white men to fight them, then we cannot turn back to get away from them, for then the white chief and his soldiers from Idaho will be behind us. The white men are now talking and calling the soldiers from far off on their click clack. They may come now any day, and like in Idaho be too many for us. Then what will Joseph and Looking Glass say to their people when they see their warriors lying dead along the Salish trail every day? My brothers can see what White Bird says is so, and that the only and safe way for us to go from here is for us to go down the river in the Salish land, and on through to them, who surely know they are our friends, the Pend d'Oreilles. Even if the Salish chief did say for my people not to go through that way, they, like us, do not care what him or his people think or say. White Bird has spoken. What do his brothers say?"

The spirits of evil are now whispering to Looking Glass and to most of the warriors, who are now very mad at the Salish chief and his people. Looking Glass now says, "White Bird and his people can go by the land of the Pend d'Oreilles if they want to leave their brothers and friends, who are not afraid of the soldiers, white men or Salish warriors at night or in the day. What White Bird said about the soldiers and white men that would meet and fight them along the Salish trail was only a dream of his. For if there were more soldiers, why were they not here now with the other soldiers and white men?" Now Looking Glass, war chief, and the warriors said with him, they would go through the Salish land and by the Salish trail, to the land of the buffalo, even if they had to fight soldiers, white men and Salish warriors every day.

White Bird said. "What does In-mut-to-ya-lat-lat say to this?" Then Joseph said, "It will be as Looking Glass said." Then White Bird said, "Evil is this day and place, for White Bird and his people, when he knows that he is doing wrong to them, when he now says that White Bird and his people will go the way that Joseph, Looking Glass and their people his brothers go, for White Bird would rather lie dead there rotting in the sun, with all his people along the Salish trail; then no Nez Perce warrior could tell the story around the campfires and in the tepees, that White Bird and his warriors were cowards, who deserted their friends and brothers and went their way to save themselves—leaving their brothers, Joseph with Looking Glass and their people, his people, when they needed them badly, which they surely will, since we are all going to go on to the land of the buffalo by the Salish trail."

Near night time, sometime before the sun went down, nineteen Pend d'Oreille warriors (one of them was a war chief) came close to camp, in a way that no white men or Salish warriors can know that they are here. Their war chief made signs of peace and says that they are friends and want to come into camp to powwow with our chiefs and warriors. They rode into camp, all in war paint with their war bonnets on and their guns in their hands, chanting in Pend d'Oreille, Haul-haul-pe-nunt-tem, Sincal-o-spetch-a-mien.

After they eat and talk to the warriors for some time, Joseph said to them, "What brings our friends the Pend d'Oreilles to us, and why are they on the war trail? I did not hear or know that they were at war with anyone."

Then the war chief said, "The Pend d'Oreille warriors have heard the words that White Bird sent to the Salish chief, that his people are going to go through our land on their way to King George's land, and on to the land of the buffalo. Our people's hearts are glad and they have sent us to lead and show our friends the way from here, how they can go to the land of the Pend d'Oreilles from here, and neither the soldiers and white men of In-ola-a (Missoula) nor the white men in the Salish land will see them nor will they fight them on the way. For the Pend d'Oreille warriors are sad, when they have heard and well know the evil ways of the white men to them, in their friends' land, and now well know that soon for the Pend d'Oreilles will come the day when they shall roam no more and go on their way through the lands of their fathers. For now already the white men are saying to us, this land and trees are mine, the mountains, prairies and streams are mine, the deer, fish and buffalo, and even the grass that grows on the prairies and hills are mine. All are mine, from where the sun rises in the morning, to where it goes down in the night. The Black Robes say give us land so we can put up big tepees to the white men's God, then he will come and smile on our land.

"We have also come to tell In-mut-to-ya-lat-lat and his people to come with us and go on his way through our land. If the soldiers or white men shall come there to fight or bar his way, that now two hundred Pend d'Oreille warriors await the wave of Joseph's hand, to spring up and like the buffalo wolf, tear the white men and soldiers down and drive them from our land, on and to In-ola-a and into the Salish land, not a white man's tepee will stand. The white men's and soldiers' tepees at In-ola-a we will burn down and nothing of them will be left to tell where they stood, except the burned spots where no grass can grow. The Pend d'Oreille and Sapah-tan warriors with a chief like Joseph to lead them in battle, then sorry the white men shall be, who try to take our land away from us."

Then Joseph said to them, "What do your brothers the Salish say to this?" Then they answered, "Are not the Salish our brothers and your friends, and will only be too glad to help us in the end. For has not the Salish chief said to White Bird that his people could come through our land and that the Salish warriors would help them on their way? This must be so or how would we know it this way?"

Then Joseph said to them, "Then the Pend d'Oreille warriors do not know, alas, that this is so, and Joseph and people are sad to say now to their friends the Pend d'Oreilles that their dream about their Salish brothers will soon fade away like the summer snow, for now the Salish chief and his warriors, their faces and tongues are like a day in the early spring—sometimes the sun shines warm, but soon changes to gales of wind and snow. Yes, Pend d'Oreille warriors, you will soon know, that the Salish chief and his people now say that the white men are their good friends, and that they are the white men's friends. That not far from here in the white men's camp, the Salish warriors stand in their war paint and war bonnets on and their guns in their hands. Soon it will be dark. Then we will go up on the hill not far from camp. There the Pend d'Oreille warriors can see, in the light of the white men's campfires, the Salish warriors now dance their war dance, as a warning to In-mut-to-ya-lat-lat and his warriors, not to harm or wrong their friends the white men."

Then one of the Pend d'Oreille warriors said, "The Sapah-tan chief and his people in this must be wrong, for the Salish chief always was a good man to us and to his people, and never would do wrong to the white men, or to his friends the Nez Perce. If it is the way that Joseph says, then it must have been the white men's tricks and evil words of lies, for they can lie better than they can tell the truth, and must have fooled the Salish chief's good heart, or it would not be this way."

Looking Glass said, "Yes, Pend d'Oreille warriors, the Salish chief and people, their hearts and tongues are now crooked and bad, since they now think they are white men, and now have to be liars like them, though they still say the E-qui-lix's (Black Robe's) words all night, to keep them from going to sleep, so they can steal and run off the Bannocks' horses at daylight."

Then the Pend d'Oreille war chief said, "If the Salish chief and people are the friends of the soldiers and white men, then all the more wise Joseph and his people will be, if they heed my voice and come with us when we lead and show White Bird and his people the sure and safe way to our land."

But Joseph said to him, "In-mut-to-ya-lat-lat now bows his head in sorrow to say this, for where will he find friends like the Pend d'Oreilles to his people—and what they offer and would do for them? And for that friendship In-mut-to-ya-lat-lat now says that it cannot be, that now White Bird or him and their people will not go through the land of the Pend d'Oreilles and Skal-a-says [Kootenai], and cross over the big hills into King George's land, to where the buffalo stay. Joseph says this for he well knows that, if him or his people go that way, that like in the end, for him and his people, it will be an evil day for his friends the Pend d'Oreilles, for it will only mean more white men's blood spilled in this land and on the prairies in the land of the Pend d'Oreilles. Joseph and his warriors are tired of spilling white men's blood to avenge their wrongs and fight for their land. They have made the white men's blood run down the hills of our lands in streams, and seen the white men die and fall like the

grass in a storm of wind and hail—and when they fell like
this, it was only to see ten more come in the place of every
one who fell, till in the end Joseph's warriors had to run.
And now when it is too late, In-mut-to-ya-lat-lat and his
people know that the Injun cannot fight the white men on
to the end. Now all we want is to go in peace to the buffalo
lands, and do not want to fight no more white men, unless
we have to. Then Joseph's warriors will fight and die like
men. Yes, Pend d'Oreille warriors, go back to your people
and tell the warriors the words of In-mut-to-ya-lat-lat, their
friend, to them. Heed not the voices of evil that tell them to
go to war with the white men for their wrongs, for the white
man he is mighty and he is strong, and no matter if he is
right or wrong, it is for the Injun his death song, that it will
be better for them in the end to take the white men's wrongs
and not fight them. Then they will not be like Joseph and his
people today, hunted like wild wolves, without a home or
land to go to."

Many of the warriors went up on the hill with the Pend
d'Oreille warriors to watch the Salish warriors dance their
war dance in the light of the white men's campfires, where
they could see them well. And when they came back to camp,
all the warriors are mad at the Salish. The renegades and evil
warriors are whispering among themselves evil words and
say among themselves that they will fight the Salish and white
men in the morning, even if the chiefs do not want trouble,
and it will be an evil day for the Salish and white men.

Long before the light of day came, all in camp were up
and as the sun rose up, all was ready to move down to the
valley into the Salish land. Some of the scouts came back
from watching the white camp all night. They say that the
Salish warriors and white men still are asleep in their camp.
The people and chiefs were glad to hear this, as they now
think the soldiers and white men will not fight them, for if
they would, they would not be sleeping.

Then the warriors and chiefs wished their friends the
Pend d'Oreille warriors well, who now left to go back to their

land, sorry that our people would not go that way with them. Then Looking Glass, the war chief, tells the warriors to listen to his words and for the evil warriors who are whispering bad words among themselves to mind them well: that there is going to be no fighting with the soldiers, white men or Salish warriors, unless they start it, and to keep out of trouble with the white men in their camp, and so the evil ones could not make trouble for their people. His warriors would lead the way on the trail to not far from the white men's camp, then they would go up a ridge and go around and not go by the white men's camp, and let them alone so they could sleep all day if they wanted to, and the warrior who tried to make trouble on the way, he would shoot him down like a coyote.

But the bad warriors now made much trouble for the chiefs and say, "We go by the trail through the white men's camp. You are not going to let the soldiers, white men and Salish warriors say that us, the Chute-pa-lu Sapah-tan warriors, who have whipped the soldiers and white men many times in the Nez Perce land, were afraid of them and like sneaking coyotes took to the hills and were afraid of them. No, this shall not be. If the soldiers and white men with the Salish want to fight, they shall have it."

But Looking Glass, as he stood among those bad warriors, who were like mad wolves around him, was not afraid of them and with his whip cut some of them, and soon had them quiet except one renegade Walla Walla warrior, who when Looking Glass cut him with his whip tries to stab him with his knife, but the other warriors knocked him down, and Looking Glass took his gun to kill him, and would have done so only that Joseph took it out of is hands, saying, "Enough of this, maybe we will have all the fighting we want, without fighting among ourselves, and the warrior who makes trouble like this again dies."

Then the warriors of Looking Glass rode on ahead down the trail, till they came to the ridge near the white men's camp. Then Looking Glass stopped here on the trail with some warriors, their guns ready to kill any bad warriors that would try to go down the trail through the white men's camp. While the others of his warriors went up the ridge with the rest of the camp following them, a long string with the women and horses in the middle, with many warriors still coming along behind them. Soon we were on top of the ridge and on our way to the Salish land, and we could see the soldiers and white men's camp below us,* who have in no way yet tried to fight our people. The women and good warriors are glad at this; some of the bad warriors are mad yet. They shot their guns at the white men's camp though it was too far off for their guns. In this way we went, and soon came down on the trail again. The scouts ahead say there are no more white men or soldiers to bar the trail and our people went their way and soon came to the Salish land (Bitterroot Valley) near the river, and went up the river not far and went into camp.

We were not here long, when many white men with guns came our way and were soon in our camp. Joseph said to them, "Why come the white men this way? Do they not know that In-mut-to-ya-lat-lat and people are not here in the Salish land to harm or wrong no women, children or white men, nor their horses or cattle or what they have got. Go on your way in peace to your tepees, and believe not the evil tongues of the soldiers or bad white men, for now Joseph holds up his hand to the sun, and offers his other hand to his white brothers in the Salish land. And may the Great Spirit wither it on him, when he breaks his word to them, Joseph who has never broken his word yet." The white men were glad that this was so, and they all shook hands with the warriors, and smoked the pipe of peace with them. And the white men said on the blood of their women and children's heads, not to fight or bother Joseph or his people, and would be brothers to them, and would not help or be soldiers against them. As long as Joseph and people did not harm them, they could go through the Salish land in peace on their way. And for this Joseph, his warriors and people said they would be

*This armed camp became known among the settlers as Fort Fizzle.

brothers to the white men, their women and children, and them who hurt them would hurt Joseph's people and rue the day they done so. Then the white men went off to their squaws and teepees, but they sent two white men to the soldier chief and white men at In-ola-a to tell them to stay there and not to come this way with their guns to make trouble or fight Joseph's warriors in the Salish land, for they had made powwow with them, and they now are our brothers.

Our people stayed here three days and are now good friends with the white men in the Salish land, and swapped for many of the white men's things. And them who lost their tepees to the soldiers in Idaho got white men's cloth and made new ones, so to be ready to go by the Salish trail to the land of the buffalo. No soldiers came this way in the Salish land, nor did the Salish come to bother our people, though we could see them go by the camp every day. White men came every day with wagons, and brought to us many white men's things to swap for white men's gold. And our people are now glad that this is so and the chiefs Joseph and Looking Glass said to White Bird, "Did we not tell you that the white men in the Salish land would not want to fight or bother our people, or help the soldiers after they found out that we meant them no harm or wrong? It will be this way as we go on our way, to the land of the buffalo by the Salish trail." But White Bird and Cul-cul-shensah, the medicine man, said to them, "The coyote knows better and helps his brother the buffalo wolf to eat at a carcass only after he has got his belly full. Some of our white friends whisper in our ears that the reason the white men are so good to us now is that the soldiers who know better would not help the white men to shoot us down, when we first came to where we had the powwows with them."

Here some more Injuns came to our people, their chief was called Noo-stoo (Poker Joe). There were many tepees of them. They say that they want to go with our people to the land of the buffalo.

A half Bannock and Salish warrior, that lived with the Salish, came in the night to camp, with the Nez Perce half-

breed who lived in the land of the Salish. He said that his
father's people, the Bannocks, sent word to him that four
Bannock warriors will come here through the Salish land in
the night, so that no Salish or white men will see them or
know that they are here to powwow with the Nez Perce
chiefs and people. That they are bringing good words to the
Sapah-tan warriors from the Bannock warriors.

The Bannock warriors came and stayed all day in camp
and powwow with the chiefs, then went on their way that
night to their land. Next morning the chiefs say: it will now be
better for our people not to go by the Salish trail to the land
of the buffalo, but that we will go up the river in the Salish
land and cross over the big hills there; then go from there to
the land of the buffalo on the Bannock trail; the Bannock warriors say they are having much trouble with bad white men in
their land and are now fighting them, but it was no use for
them; they only lost their warriors, and still the white men
came all the more to their land; their chief was no good for
them who wanted to fight the white men to the end; he liked
the white men better than them; that if our people would
come by their land, there were many warriors of them who
would meet us on the way, and go with us to the land of the
buffalo; our warriors with them would be too strong and too
many for the soldiers or white men to fight or bother them,
any place they wanted to go to in the land of the buffalo.

Leaving this camp going up the valley and the river in the
Salish land on our way to the Bannocks' land, we did not go
far that day, and made camp and some Salish warriors rode
into camp who were drunk. They said much evil words to
our people and warriors, "That if the white men were afraid
of our warriors, the Salish warriors were not. That our people had better go on their way quick. That if they did not,
the Salish warriors would go to In-ola-a and bring the white
men and soldiers and help them to make the Sapah-tan warriors rue the day they came to their land."

Our warriors though mad, only laughed at them, saying,
"The white men's firewater makes the Salish warriors brave

today. The white men should have given their firewater to
the Salish warriors the other day, when them with the soldiers and white men barred the trail on our way. Then the
Nez Perce warriors would now all be dead, and not here
today, for the coyote only howls his best on the prairie when
he knows that the cougar stays far back in the hills, and cannot hear him. That the Sapah-tan warriors were in no hurry
to go on their way, for they liked to stay in the Salish land."

When Looking Glass came back to camp and heard what
the Salish warriors say, he is now more mad than ever, and
with the warriors said, "Now there is no need for our people
to hurry on their way." This way our people did not go far
when they moved, and still swapped for many of the white
men's things, and sometimes bad white men swapped
whiskey to the warriors and they made much trouble in
camp. Then Joseph told the white men that if the bad warriors done bad to the white men when they were drunk,
then the white men would be to blame, if they did not stop
their evil people from selling whiskey to the warriors.

Soon White Bird and the old warriors say, "Why do we
stay so long on our way in the Salish land? Let us go quickly
away from here and meet our friends the Bannocks in their
land, and go on our way to the land of the buffalo. We do
not know but that much evil will come to us here any day,
and that many white men and soldiers will come this way, to
fight us and bar our trail."

But Looking Glass and warriors say, "The white chief and
his soldiers from Idaho are still far away, and we care not for
the white chief and his soldiers in In-ola-a, who will have to
run after us on their feet. Besides, they know better than to
come this way and are afraid of us, for why did they not
come when they had the white men and Salish all there with
them?—To fight us when we first came to the Salish land?
No, we care not for them, or what the Salish warriors say or
do, for the white men in the Salish land made a powwow
with us, and are our friends and not theirs. No evil or danger now lies in our way."

But Cul-cul-shensah, our medicine man, warns our people and tells Looking Glass and warriors to quickly leave the Salish land and go on our way or our people would in the end rue the day they did not heed his warning to them.

As our people went up through the Salish land, still they did not go far each day, for the white chief and his soldiers from the land of the Nez Perce still does not come this way. And Joseph and Looking Glass with the most of the warriors are still saying that there is no more danger for our people, that our people have made a powwow with the white men of the Salish land. They had said they would not help the soldiers if they came this way after our warriors, that they would keep their word to our people, for our people had kept their word to them, and had done them no harm or wrong. If our people had been bad, they could have taken what they wanted and killed them all, and the white men knew it. Our people still would not heed the voices of our chief White Bird, Cul-cul-shensah, and some old warriors who knew the white men's tricks and lies to the Injuns, and did not believe their words to them. But Joseph and Looking Glass always went together against the good words of our chief White Bird since our people left Kamai. Some of our warriors would be mad at this and say to White Bird, "Why do you let them do this, when you are a greater chief and warrior than them, for was it not White Bird and his warriors that done the bravest fighting in Idaho and killed more white men than all the others, who fought the white men till they fell like grass in rain and hail, and died like men, and when the soldiers and white men got too many for them? They said they would stay like Nez Perce warriors and fight and die with their chief White Bird, till the last one of them fell dead, even if the others did run off and leave them there."

But White Bird talked good to his warriors and people, saying, "Maybe Joseph and Looking Glass and their warriors are right, for the voices of many warriors are better than one. Besides, they are our brothers and it is only cowards who will leave their brothers. It will be much better for us

when we come to the Bannocks' land, since we are not going
by the Salish trail to the land of the buffalo."

Our people now left the Salish land, and went up in the
big hills and crossed over them where on the other side lay
the Bannocks' land. Before they came down to the bottom
of the big hills, they camped for one day in a forest of lodge
poles, so the women could cut plenty tepee poles, to take
with us to the land of the buffalo where none grows. As
there was no feed for the horses here, we moved camp next
day down to the foot of the big hills on a big creek on the
edge of a large prairie.* The chiefs say we stay here a few
days, till the tepee poles can dry, and they can wait and see
if the Bannock warriors will come and do as they say.

Long before night came, more than twenty Bannock warriors rode into camp. Joseph said to them, "Why do the
Bannock warriors come here this way alone, like they are on
the war trail, without their squaws or people to go on their
way with us, as their warriors told us in the Salish land that
our Bannock friends would do, if we came this way? In-mut-
to-ya-lat-lat and his people do not want to harm or wrong
no one, and do not want to fight the white men, they only
want to go on their way in peace to the buffalo land, and will
make powwows with them like we did in the Salish land."

The Bannock warriors said, "The great Nez Perce chief
does us, the Bannock warriors, harm and wrong, when he
thinks that we come here for the Nez Perce warriors to do
evil for us. We come here to tell In-mut-to-ya-lat-lat and his
people that our fathers and their people, more than twenty-
three lodges of them, will wait to meet the great Nez Perce
chief and his people two suns on the trail down the river
from here, in the Bannocks' land where runs their trail to
the land of the buffalo, in the land of the Blackfeet and
Piegans, and that we will lead and bring them there."

It soon now got dark and the heavy frosts and mists
would soon begin to fall; In-who-lise said she would now

---

* In this camp the Nez Perce were surprised by army attack and fought the
Battle of the Big Hole.

have to quit telling her story, but would tell the rest of it some other time. Old Gabriel and the breeds said they would make another feast in a few days or so, for they must now hear all her story. Then everyone filled up with buffalo meat; then went off grunting to their rawhide mansion with a full belly.

CHAPTER TWENTY-SIX
Nez Perce Story Continued

I will not keep you waiting for the next installment of In-who-lise's story, but will continue as I remember it. At the time of the Big Hole fight, In-who-lise was about seventeen years old as near as she could tell. Tom-up-tsi U-pok-pok, (Gray Eagle) her father, a warrior of White Bird's band, had been in all the fights the Nez Perce had with the whites in Idaho. She had a sister two years younger named Lucy. Her mother was dead. Her stepmother Mary was still with them.

It is the break of day, August 9, 1877. Soldiers and white men volunteers from the Bitterroot Valley, 197 strong with the usual number of civilian scouts, had arrived under the command of Colonel John Gibbon. They have been waiting and watching since not long after midnight from the hillside that overlooked the sleeping and unsuspecting Nez Perce camp, which lay in a bend of the North Fork of the Big Hole about 150 to 200 yards directly across from them.

Between them and the Nez Perce camp was a narrow flat covered with scattered clumps of willows among which grew long, coarse grass. Running through this flat was a small slough. Both sides of North Fork were heavily fringed with large willow clumps. The Nez Perce camp of ninety-four tepees and wickiups was three tepees wide at the upper end, with room enough between to drive in their pack horses. The rows of tepees gradually narrowed as the village went dowstream, till it came to a point of one tepee at the lower end. The upper end of the camp was mostly of White Bird's people, the center Joseph's and the lower end Looking Glass's people.

At break of day, the hour had come. The order was given for the two skirmish lines to go forward, Bradley with the volunteers on the extreme left. Soldiers and volunteers silently make their way across the slough, through the long grass and clumps of willows. On they come toward the slumbering Nez Perce camp. As the daylight increases the troops advance out of the yet hazy morning's light. A solitary Indian from the Nez Perce camp, on his way to the horse herd on the hill, suddenly appears riding directly toward Bradley's men. So silent had the advance been, he did not hear or see them until he rode up in front of them. Three or four shots are fired and the Indian is dead. The order had been given, when the first shot is fired, fire three volleys and charge the camp. Most eagerly was this order obeyed. From in the willows on and near the creek banks, three volleys were fired in quick succession into the tepees. To the ringing word "Charge," plunging through the swift creek, some places almost armpit deep, with a yell of triumph the whole line swept into the slumbering camp. The surprise was complete. Standing among the tepees, the terror-stricken warriors were taken unawares, together with screaming squaws and children. The whites now fire their guns at them point-blank, so close that many of them who fell here had their faces and clothes burned from the powder. In a short time the whites have possession and have driven the Nez Perce out and away from their camp. And the crowning glory (though their triumph was to be short-lived) is forty-two women and children with the twenty-six Nez Perce men who fell here, some of the men with no gun in their hands.

The bullets came through Gray Eagle's lodge like hail and rain, and hit one of Hoot Owl's women in the head, killing her dead, and another bullet hit one of Hoot Owl's sons in the breast, so that he fell down and lay there. With this rain of bullets coming through the tepee and the noise of the soldiers' guns, with the warriors and white men's yells, added to this the screams and shrieks of the squaws and children, In-who-lise did not know much of what happened and only remembered hearing her father say, "It is them white dogs, the soldiers. Try and run across the creek and hide in the willows." Then they all tried to get out of the tepee at once, trying to crawl over each other, but the soldiers were there, shooting near the tepee flap which faced the river. Hoot Owl and his other woman and two of the small children were shot dead, and her father shot in the belly. All that she could remember was that her sister Lucy, who is trying to run ahead of her, now fell dead with a bullet through her head. Then something hit In-who-lise in the right shoulder and she fell down near the creek bank and lay there. How long she lay there she did not know. When she tried to get up, she must have grabbed by the leg, with her good arm, a soldier who was standing over her, shooting.

The soldier jumped back a little and quickly hit her with his gun on her good arm, then jabbed and pushed her back down on the ground with the butt of his gun. It hit her on the mouth and cut her lips and hurt her teeth bad. The soldier went away, but there was still much shooting around the tepees. Later a woman came to her and said, "The white dogs are gone from here across the creek in the willows. Come, you must not stay here, I will help you across the creek and hide in the willows." Then this woman helped her to get up but her blood ran from her shoulder and her face was all swelled up, and she did not want to stand up. When this woman pulled her down the riverbank, she cried, for she could see her sister Lucy and Hoot Owl's people lay there dead, and all along the river bank and at the tepees plenty dead people were lying there.

They had just got down the bank and near the water's edge when they seen the soldiers across the creek coming back from out of the willows, and she was now so sick that she was glad to lie down with the other woman like they were dead. The white men came back across the creek and made the tepees burn, and some of them that would not burn they pulled down and some they cut with their knives.

The white men and warriors now run, yell, fight and shoot in the willows. Sometimes some white men come by here. Some of them were good to us and some of them were bad, though the women who could talk English talked good to them as they went by here. Some warriors come here and say for the women, children and wounded warriors that can, to lie down close to the river banks, so the white dogs' bullets will not hit them. They were going to drive the white dogs out of the willows and get them in a bunch on the prairie, then they can all get around them and kill them all together. Plenty women and children, some of them who were shot, with some of the wounded warriors that had crawled here for water, now lay down close to the river banks, and by the edge of the water. The women who were not hurt would put cold mud on the sores of them who were hurt to stop their blood coming bad.

My stepmother Mary who was not hurt in the fight now came here and helped me up the bank. When now my father Gray Eagle, who was shot in the belly but thinks it not bad, with Hoot Owl's youngest boy came here. They had tried to sneak out of the willows. Each of them had only a rock in his hand, when a soldier ran on to them and quickly fired his gun at Gray Eagle, but close as the soldier was, he missed them. When he was putting a cartridge in his gun, they both sprang on him and hit him on the head. Then Hoot Owl's boy took the soldier's gun and shot him dead. Gray Eagle took the soldier's things and tore the soldier's shirt off him. Hoot Owl's boy took the soldier's cartridge belt and gun. Then they went in the thick willows where Gray Eagle fixed the bullet hole in his belly with the soldier's shirt. They found a soldier lying down and a white man sitting up, who were badly shot but not dead. The white man shot at them, but was too sick to shoot good. Then Hoot Owl's boy killed the both of them.

Then some of the warriors who had fought the white men away from here and onto the hill came back here to join some of the warriors and old men that had stayed to pack in the wounded. They said, "See our women, children and friends all lying around here and in the willows wounded and dead. What is the use of fighting? Many of us have no cartridges for our guns; the soldiers have stronger guns than us and plenty ammunition. They will kill us all before we can get to them. Then who is going to take care of our women and children that are now living when we are all dead? Let the warriors who are still fighting the white men on the hill come back here and let the evil white dogs stay there if they want to. Then we can quickly pull down our tepees and take away from here our wounded men, women and children, when we have got the chance, then some of us can stay here and bury our dead, after they go from here."

Our chief White Bird who now came here said to them, "Will you cowards let the Sioux who are men say that the Nez Perce warriors are squaws who covered up their heads with their blankets and let the soldiers and white men kill their women, children and friends as they slept. How are you going to meet your friends in the land of the dead if you sneak away from here like a coyote and leave their wrongs unavenged? There on the hill are the soldiers and white men from the Salish land (Bitterroot), them who took our hand and made powwow with us, and said that if we done them no harm or wrong that we could come through the Salish land. Then after us keeping our word to them, when we could have easily killed them all, they come with the soldiers like the crawling snakes they are and as we slept they shot into the tepees, and when we came out they shot our men, women and children down like dogs. On to the hill with you all I say. All of you are not needed here to bring in the wounded. So again I say, up on the hill with you all, where our brothers are fighting the white men and kill them all or die like men."

Then the warriors that stayed here gave their cartridges to the warriors who went back with our chief White Bird. When the white men on the hill seen the women taking down the tepees, they shot many of their bullets among the women and horses. Their bullets came so many, that the women could not take the lodges down, and the chiefs had to send plenty warriors from fighting the white men on the hill to help pull down the lodges. Even then the warriors could not go at the outside row of lodges, where the white men could see them better. They killed everyone who went there, and those lodges the warriors had to leave there.

My father Gray Eagle now came with a horse, saddle and blanket, and as he was tying my sore arm to my breast, said that the most of our things and the tepee was burned up, and that all of Hoot Owl's people are dead except the boy. Then my father and Hoot Owl's boy put me in the saddle and told my stepmother Mary to go with me and the other women and children, and the wounded that can hold onto a horse to where the camp will be up the valley. He said that he must stay here and help with the wounded, though the bullet hole in his belly is sore and then help Hoot Owl's boy to bury his dead people and my sister Lucy. Then we left and went on our way to the next camp. Most of them left what little possessions they had, and 159 of their people lay dead, not counting some who drowned in the creek.

As the sorrowing Nez Perce went on their way, in the third camp after leaving the Big Hole battlefield, Gray Eagle died in bad pain. The gun wound in his belly had swelled up and turned black in the last two days, and he was buried in a side gulch not far from camp, with another young warrior named Red Heart. Then her stepmother Mary, who always did hate her, left her and went with her own people, leaving In-who-lise to take care of herself the best she could. And in the days to come on that dreary trail, that was now to be lined with graves as the Nez Perce go on their way, In-who-lise and many other wounded women silently sat in their saddles in fevered pain and saw their wounded people and friends die tied in the saddle, and tied down on travois, on the rough mountain trail the Nez Perce made with their large herd of horses, as they go higher up in the hills to keep out of the reach of Howard and his wagon train, now only two or three days behind them.

On and on they went in and through the hell-holes of Yellowstone National Park, over and across through the rough hills and then down the Clark's Fork River.

At Canyon Creek (September 13),* they were driving their large herd of ponies on the run; many were packed and some of them dragged travois, as the squaws lash them with fury. Some of the squaws had their papoose strapped on their back, with another Injun kid holding on to her behind. It is nip and tuck in this mad race with Sturgis's troopers to the mouth of the canyon some distance away. If they cannot make it, they will be cut off and captured. But this was not to be, for into the canyon they went through a rain of bullets from Sturgis's troopers. The Nez Perce warriors fired from the bluffs, holding Sturgis's troopers at bay, and the battle of Canyon Creek was on. The Nez Perce held Sturgis in check till their women were safely on the trail.

After they left Canyon Creek, the Nez Perce had better luck than they had been having for some time. On their way they caught two wagon trains. Again at Cow Island, where they crossed the Missouri River, they found and captured plenty merchandise of all kinds that the government and others had unloaded there, as the river was too low for boats to make it to Fort Benton. After destroying and burning what they did not want, the Nez Perce headed for the Bear Paws with all their pack horses and squaw ponies loaded down to the gunnels with the plunder they had obtained without much fighting.

Early on the morning before the Bear Paw fight started, In-who-lise, who is not very well yet, was made to go with some other women with pack horses to skin and bring in meat for part of the camp. Some men had already left camp to hunt. The day was cold and stormy for that time of the year, with some snow falling, as they rode out of camp. They had not been gone very long when they came on two buffalo the hunters had killed and they could see the hunters not far away from them, trying to ride close to a small bunch of buffalo to kill one or two more.

The women stayed here and started to skin the buffalo, when soon they heard plenty shooting at camp. Though they

*Date given by other Garcia manuscript and by Merrill D. Beal in *I Will Fight No More Forever*, University of Washington Press; 1963.

could not see the camp, they knew from all the shooting there that it was another fight with soldiers. The men hunters now rode quickly up to them saying it is surely another fight, but where could the white dogs have come from. Then they all rode up on a small ridge and they could see that many soldiers on horses were shooting and trying to go to the camp. The men say for the women to go back and finish skinning one of the buffalo while they go and see if they can get back into camp and help fight. The men were gone for a long time. When they came back, they say, "No way can we get back to camp, for the white dogs with horses and afoot are all over, and shoot our brothers and with them are plenty bad Injuns." For five days those women and men had to stay out in the cold and storms. Every day Miles's Injun scouts came through the hills looking for Nez Perce people, and they had an awful time to keep out of their way. They did catch one of the men who was out scouting for them, and took him a prisoner to the white man's camp. Another of the men whose women and children were in Joseph's camp tried to sneak back, but Miles's Cheyenne Injun scouts caught him too. The rest did not know what to do, to give themselves up to the soldiers or try to go on to Canada.

The night before Miles was to start back to Fort Keough with Joseph and his people as prisoners, the man who Miles's Injun scouts first captured escaped with some more men, women and children. He found them and told them how it was. Looking Glass and plenty warriors are dead and White Bird is mad at Joseph and his friends for surrendering to the white chief without first asking him. He said the white chief lied to Joseph to get him to do this. For this reason White Bird with as many of his warriors who were not wounded, with their women and children, had escaped two days ago and were now on their way to Canada, and that in the morning Joseph and his people would be taken away by the soldiers as prisoners to someplace they did not know in the Yellowstone country. Then they could go to camp after they left and find some guns and plenty things that the people had hid on the soldiers before giving up their guns.

Early next morning as they watched from a hill, In-who-lise and the other women, their eyes in tears, saw the soldiers drive off Joseph and their friends. They had an awful time dodging Miles's scouts who were combing the hills for Nez Perce people. By the time they had escaped the troopers and scouts for good, they were miles away from the Bear Paw battlefield and the wrong way for going to Canada. They were very tired and did not know this part of the country well enough to try to travel at night. They camped here all night, with only raw buffalo meat to eat. Early in the morning they left here, and by doubling up on the horses most of them could ride. They were afraid to go back to the battlefield for guns and things the people had hid there. They had to go slowly and send scouts ahead on foot as they went on their way. In-who-lise was so sick that the woman who rode with her had to hold her to keep her from falling out of the saddle. Near night they came on an Assiniboine camp. The Assiniboines were good to them and gave them a good lodge to camp in and their squaws brought them broiled buffalo meat to eat. But when it got dark, a Gros Ventre woman who had an Assiniboine man sneaked in their tepee and in sign language told them, "The Assiniboines are only snakes and dogs for the white men. I am a Gros Ventre and hate the white men and am sorry for you. At daylight you must leave here and be on your way to Canada, two suns' ride from here. The reason that the Assiniboines in camp are so good to you is that they want you to stay here until they can get the three blankets that the big white chief says that he will give to the Assiniboines for every Nez Perce warrior they will find for the soldiers."

At break of day, though the treacherous Assiniboines coaxed them to stay, In-who-lise's people left for Canada. They left her horse so that she might find them if she got well. Early in the afternoon when the Assiniboine warriors returned to camp with some troopers and two breed scouts, they were mad because the Nez Perce were gone. Two

Beavers, chief of the hunt, wanted the lieutenant of the troopers to give him three blankets for catching In-who-lise, but the lieutenant told him that it was only the Nez Perce bucks they wanted. Two Beavers wanted the soldiers to take her away with them, but they rode off leaving her there. One of the breed scouts and one of the troopers, who were sorry to see her lying there so sick and without even a blanket, each gave her a blanket. There is no doubt that In-who-lise would have died if it had not been for this Gros Ventre woman who took her in her lodge and did the best she could for her.

Two days later a cold storm drove the buffalo south to the Missouri River, with this Assiniboine camp following them up. The Gros Ventre woman had to haul In-who-lise on her travois, as she was still sick. She stayed with those Assiniboines all winter in the Musselshell country where the buffalo had drifted. In the spring, they met up with a band of lower Pend d'Oreilles. She now left the Assiniboines who took her horse in return for keeping her all winter. And it was in this Pend d'Oreille buffalo camp that I met the wife of my youth.

CHAPTER TWENTY-SEVEN
The Devil Shining in Her Eyes

The morning the Siwash barbecue, Mexican Pete and José with their better halfs, Isidora and Buena Ventura, hit the trail to visit their aboriginal Piegan relatives in the Pend d'Oreille Injun camp. Nothing happened to relieve the monotony of camp, except the usual delegations of buck Injuns and frisky squaws going and coming.

Near noon old Gabriel came over and tries to rope me into going along with them, as the whole caboodle of them (except the kids), bucks, squaws and not forgetting the soulful-eyes Cree breeds of camp, were all going to the Pend d'Oreille Injun camp. He said that this was the day of all days, and the Pend d'Oreille squaws had bear grease rubbed in their hair braids, so if they got in a fight with the other squaws, they would be too greasy and slippery for them to pull on. There was going to be great horse races with the Assiniboine, Gros Ventres and Piegans all against the Pend d'Oreilles; there was liable to be fur flying before the wind-up. That since I was going to be tied up to In-who-lise, it was my patriotic duty to come along with them and bet and fight for my own people and relations, the Pend d'Oreilles. That I could leave In-who-lise to watch the kids, papooses and camp. I told him that I would go along, but when they were ready to pull out, I seen that Kat-a-lee and Sow-set had sneaked off and were not among the crowd that was going. I knew better than to ask old Gabriel where they were. I told him that I would not go now. I knew that if I went away, it would be the last of In-who-lise on earth. Old Gabriel went off mad at me for not going with the bunch. It turned out as I expected, because it was not long till I seen Kat-a-lee and Sow-set ride out of the brush. When they saw me in camp with In-who-lise, they did not stop but rode on to the Injun camp after the others, leaving her and I alone there.

Along toward evening as we sat by the fire wondering why old Gabriel and the bunch did not come back home, I thought that something was the matter. I rounded up all the horses and drove them up on the hillside where there was good feed, and had just got back to camp when into camp afoot staggers Sow-set. With her was Squis-squis, the same Squis-squis I have told you so much about, and whom I have not seen for some time. At first I did not know what was the matter with them, but I was not long in doubt, for it did not take a sleuth to tell that both of them were gory-eyed and drunk as boiled owls. And to fill the Squaw Kid's cup of woe to overflowing, instead of going into old Gabriel's tepee where they belonged, they came staggering up to us by the fire, where they insulted In-who-lise with much low-down dirty Injun oratory. Then both of them, with maudlin giggles, now turn up their skirts above the limits of the laws of gravity and brought forth and proudly showed me, each one of them, a large square gin bottle of whiskey.

Sow-set is saying, "Come, sweet An-ta-lee, and take a drink with your sweethearts. Who do you like the best, Squis-squis or me? I know it is me. Hear me Sapah-tan broken tooth (In-who-lise)—yes, it is me your man An-ta-lee likes the best of all, and you surely will not say that this is not so. That An-ta-lee who you say is going to put a ring on your finger and make you his squaw by the E-qui-lix (Black Robe) is a liar. No, no, sweet An-ta-lee is no liar and cares for you not. This Sow-set surely knows. Yes, as sure as the winds on the prairies that hurls and blows the snow. For did he not tell Sow-set that her eyes they were like the bright stars in the night, when the moonbeams are gleaming and the sky clear and bright? That her smile was as sweet and like a purple sunset, its wild beauty and color, he would never forget, as it beams up there in the fading blue sky, with the light of the day, to fade and to die."

Though I tried every way that I knew to coax them to go over to old Gabriel's tepee and sleep off their jag, it was no use, for this was their night to howl. They made no bones about it, that this was so. Those two drunken squaws were sitting there with me, sometime laughing and coaxing, but more times weeping, because I would not take a drink with them. The rest of the time they wanted to make love like a house on fire. This would not have been so bad, but In-who-lise, the sweet little squaw that I am going to marry, was squatting there beside the fire, taking it all in with the devil shining in her eyes.

I was wondering where they got the whiskey. I knew that, with the exception of the little I had in the shack, there was none here for many miles, to Bozeman one way and to Benton and Carrol the other way, and no white men here to go and get it for them. I soon found out from them, drunk as they were, that not only them were drunk, but old Gabriel and the bunch from our camp, with the whole Injun camp, bucks and squaws, were all drunk as Irish lords. It was a mystery no longer when they said that six white men came and were camped near the Injun camp, with a four-horse team and wagon. Two of them rode on the wagon and four of them rode saddle horses; that all of them had plenty guns on them. They said to the Injuns that they were traders and had come to swap. When the Injuns asked them if they had any whiskey, they told them they had plenty, and would swap for horses or anything else the Injuns had.

Never was a healthful and life-giving rainstorm in the deserts received with greater joy and acclaim, or licked up quicker by the parched burning sands of Arabia than when that bunch of Injuns found out they could get all the whiskey they wanted. An Injun will go to hell twice every day and three times in the night, for or to get whiskey. Those slippery vultures were soon swamped and doing a land-office business. They said they had whiskey in bottles or kegs and would give their red brothers a quart bottle for a good broke saddle horse, but not for a bronco or scrub, and that they would swap for buckskin, moccasins or buffalo robes, or anything else they could sell.

Sow-set and Squis-squis had left the Injun camp early; then on their way back to camp, met two of those white men riding by. In the end they traded their two saddle horses to them for two bottles of whiskey, and hid their saddles in the brush by the creek and started back for camp afoot, sampling the whiskey as they went. As they were not used to drinking, it was a wonder they made camp the way they did.

By the time it got dark, Sow-set and Squis-squis, stupid drunk, lay sprawled out on my robes and blankets on the ground, a thing I did not want, especially if old Gabriel should come back drunk, and find his lovely destroying angels asleep in my bed on the ground. I tried to coax In-who-lise to help me to pack them over home to old Gabriel's tepee and, would you believe it, that ungenerous squaw of mine refuses point-blank to do so. With flashing eyes and snorting like a mad buffalo bull she said, "Does An-ta-lee think I would put my hands on his drunken hussies? No, I would rather stick my knife in them." Then I tried to coax her to go and get her blankets in old Gabriel's tepee and to sleep here by the fire. Then neither old Gabriel nor her could say anything was wrong. But In-who-lise was mad at me. "Yes, let them lie and die there for all I care." And, with her head proudly up in the air, she walked to old Gabriel's tepee, leaving the Squaw Kid there with Squis-squis snoring her jag off, and Sow-set crouched half dazed, but with still enough hatred left in her, as In-who-lise was leaving, to stagger to her feet and shriek at her, "A-oe-sh-huch Chenness-mipe-sa In-oute-a-noops!" Then in a few minutes she fell over sound asleep and dead to the world.

I put some wood on the fire and the kids of Petol and Samwell came up to the fire, saying, "None has come back yet, An-ta-lee, and we are hungry." I got them something to eat and told them to eat it in the tepee, and then to go to sleep, that everything was all right, and that their people would come back in the morning. After a while I searched

Sow-set and Squis-squis; it was easy to find them two whiskey bottles in the large pocket inside their squaw skirts. Still nearly half full, I promptly smashed them in the fire and they burned like benzene.

I sat by the fire for some time, looking at Sow-set and Squis-squis, sprawled out on my bed on the ground in their drunken sleep. It kind of made me shiver as I thought that maybe it was as In-who-lise said, that they would be better dead. And the evil in me said, "Yes, this is so, they have brought you a lot of trouble tonight, and will bring you plenty more." But as the night got colder and I could feel the frosty damp air, I began to feel sorry for them and the good in me said, "Squaw Kid, cover your women up. This may not be so before God or man, but they are surely yours before the devil, and you are more evil than them." Then I got up and pulled a blanket and robe from under them, then rolled my two dusky affinities together and covered them up. I had to admit to myself, yes, this was so, that I was worse and more bad than them, for if I had left them alone in the beginning and had not hunted for their smiles, and had stayed a white man, then those wild squaws would never have come near me, and while they might be drunk some other place tonight, still they would not be now lying drunk in my bed, and done what they did before In-who-lise tonight.

And as the fire burned down in the night, the Squaw Kid sat there preaching to himself, like all them who are hypocrites and liars, about the frailties and faults of others. I started to give old Gabriel and bunch hell for getting drunk and leaving me alone to take care of the camp. Then, giving up all hopes and glad that old Gabriel and bunch were not coming back, I went in the shack and got me a couple of buffalo robes and crawled in the wagon to sleep. I was not going to take any chances (when In-who-lise with her sharp Injun eyes might be watching me in old Gabriel's tepee a few feet away) on Sow-set or Squis-squis waking up and then applying their powers of persuasion, against which I had always been a total failure.

The morning sun broke bright and clear, and all nature smiles, but appearances are most times deceitful, for smiling nature can be the damnedest liar you ever seen. The one who wrote unhappy is the head who wears a plug hat, did not know what this sorrow business is. He never woke up with two squaw affinities squatting there by the fire with murder in their eyes, and another squaw there who he is going to marry disrupting his happy home and reading the riot act to them. In-who-lise now stood there, the sunshine on her raven hair, and great was her righteous ire. Her gentle eyes were flashing fire. She was stripped for action, against the invaders of her sacred domain. Sow-set and Squis-squis, now strictly sober, but with sore heads and feeling as mean as a bear with a sore foot, were disputing her right to this, and were saying they will leave when they feel like it. That if the broken-toothed Sapah-tan she coyote wants her guts ripped out, that they were in good humor to do it for her.

Still none of the old Gabriel bunch returned from the Injun camp. This left it for me to go and round up the homes and bring them into camp, and see that none were missing. I dared not go after them and leave In-who-lise alone in camp with Sow-set and Squis-squis, so I had to take her along with me. When we got back with the horses, Mexican José and Pete with their families drove into camp, and their squaws start putting up their tepee. I said to them, "Your visit to the Injun camp was a short one."

They said, "It would have been shorter than this, if we knew yesterday what was going to turn up there, for every buck and squaw with all the breeds there is drunk, except our women Isidora and Buena Ventura, and the reason they were not drunk with the rest, they knew better, and that we would kick their bellies in for them if they did, for whiskey is now as plenty as water in the Injun camp. The squaws have got the most of the guns hid on the bucks as some of them are crazy drunk. You ought to have seen that damn old hypocrite of a friend of yours old Gabriel clean them up yesterday. That old breed is sure mean and a high roller from hell when he is drunk. They howled and yelled all last night, and it is going to be worse still today, and tonight—so we left, and will pull out tomorrow on our way back to where we came from."

Then they told me how those six white men had about cleaned up the Injuns' camp of everything they had, robes and other stuff, besides had got over forty head of horses, the best the Injuns had. That they were a tough bunch at the best and that they told them when passing their camp, that they were pulling out when the going was good, before the Injuns started to sober up. They thought they would come by this way and give me as consolation the information, that I might as well pack up and pull out of here with them. This bunch would either return or tell other whiskey traders, who would come and clean the Injuns out with whiskey, whether I liked it or not. Then the Injuns would have nothing to trade most of the time.

Soon old Gabriel's bunch of squaws and the breed women came back to camp, and look much the worse for wear. Some of them were half shot and as jolly as a lark. They said that the men still stayed in the Injun camp and that they did not care or know when they would come back to camp. It was not long after this when I seen a four-horse wagon, with a band of horses driven along behind it, coming this way. When they got opposite the camp, about a hundred yards away, the wagon came on to camp alone, while the four white men riders held the horses there.

Mexican Pete said, "I wonder what them whiskey-trading sons of bitches want to come here for. I bet they come to raise some kind of hell with you. But don't take any of their dirt and don't palabra a damn word with them, just cut loose at them, and we will only be too glad to help you fill them full of lead."

The wagon drove on into camp, when one of the men said, "Heigh you there, hallo." I said, "Hello yourself and see how you will like it." He said, "See here, no one told you to get too damned flip." Then he got out of the wagon.

He was large and rawboned, as dark as they ever make a white man, with a bushy coal-black whiskers and long hair that looked as though it had never been combed since he started to let it grow. But his face was his greatest beauty, and was a face that would have had him hung in any other place but out here, in good old Montana. He had on him two belts of cartridges, one of 45-120's for a Sharps buffalo gun, with a knife sheath holding a sticking and skinning knife, with a sharpening steel like all buffalo hunters carried. The other belt was full of forty-five Colt cartridges, and from which hung in a holster a forty-five Frontier six shooter, which, all told, was a load for a burro to pack.

The other man who still sat in the wagon was a good counterpart of the other one, only he was of a sandy color and a poker face that no one but the devil could tell whether it was good or bad. Like the other one, he carried the same kind of a layout of ammunition, knives and gun. The one on the ground said nothing more, but walks over and starts looking my prairie schooner over, then said, "I want that wagon and will give you a ten-gallon keg of whiskey to boot with our wagon, as the tires are beginning to get loose on ours. You ought to be tickled to death at this good bargain, for you are damn lucky that I am offering you that, and do not spank you and take the wagon away from you whether you like it or not."

This kind of knocked me speechless and before I could say anything, Mexican José said, "He cannot now swap that wagon to you. He promised it to us if we haul it loaded with buffalo robes for him to Bozeman in the spring."

With a snarl he said, "See here, you greaser son of a bitch, who told you to put your nose in this? For less than a two-bit piece I would fill you full of holes, and by Gawd I will do it anyway." He reached for his gun.

I said to him, "Don't do it, mister, you hairy-faced whore's bastard, just try and pull your gun, and I will put a chunk of lead in your guts that will make you cough up blood all the rest of your dirty life," for I had him covered with my gun.

Then I told him to get out of here as quick as hell would let him, his partner and their whiskey. That they could not have that wagon, that I would chop it up for firewood before I would let a low-down whiskey trader have it.

Then he said to his partner in the wagon, "What the hell, Jim, are you doing all this time, why did you not shoot them up?" His partner said, "I guess not, when that other sawed-off squaw man had his gun on me. Besides I told you to cut out this wild and woolly bad man stuff. It's about time you take a tumble that no one is afraid of you. Say, boys, do not take this too hard; this is not the first time that big stiff has had to back down and take to the water. Put up your guns, boys, for none of us want any trouble with anyone, except that big coffee-cooling snoozer. Then he expects us to get him out of it. We are only a bunch of honest buffalo hunters, putting in the time till the hunting starts, peddling our red brothers firewater. The more robes and horses we take away from them, the less liable they are to go on the warpath and raise the white men's hair. Yes sir, we are the advance guard of civilization, and are doing a humane act, for the sooner we rob the Injun of his horses and robes and kill off the buffalo, the sooner will he go to work and make Montana safe for democracy. Yes, boys, put up your guns and bury your hate, though Bill is as mean and ornery as a pole cat, when you know him right, he is harmless and just likes to hear himself talk."

When now Sow-set and Squis-squis came to me, and Sow-set said to me, "Sweet An-ta-lee, do make them bad white men give us back our saddle horses. Do you not hear my Cha-qee (sorrel) whinnering in their band over there, to come back to our horses? Evil surely was the day I ever saw them bad white men and took their whiskey for him." I told her, "You ought to have thought of that yesterday. Then you would have had him yet, and not got drunk and made all the trouble you did for me last night and this morning. Them white men will not give you back your horse, no matter what I say to them." But both of them kept at me, pleading to get them their horses back, and in the end began to snicker and wanted to know why I did not like them any more, when they loved me so well.

Dog Face said, "What the hell are you chewing the rag with them squaws so much for?" I said, "They say that you got them to swap their saddle horses to you for whiskey and want them back." He said, "Oh, I see, your sweeties made you tell that to me, and I don't blame you for trying to get them horses back in your family. Yes, that is the first thing I will do, the hell I will." I got mad and said, "Do you know, I did not think that there was a white man low-down enough to rob a squaw with whiskey out of their saddle horse, then see them go off afoot, till I seen you people. You had better give their horses back to them, or I will make the whole damn bunch of you good and sorry. For if you don't, then sure as God I will go and find the troopers and help them to trail and run you fellows down."

He said, "Soldiers, to hell with you and them, when there is not a soldier on this side of Ellis or Benton, for we took good care to find out before we came here." Then I said, "If this is so, then I surely know where there is a bunch of Blackfeet not far from here, who will be only too glad to burn up the grass to catch up with you fellows to cut your throats and take what you have got." He said, "Wrong again there, partner. If there were any Blackfeet as close as you say, why are none of them in that Injun camp with all them other kinds of Injuns?" I said, "Just because the Pend d'Oreilles and them are enemies."

His partner, who had been silently taking it in, said, "I have heard enough of this, now close your flytrap, Bill. What the hell is two bottles of whiskey to us anyway, when we can make a fifty-four-gallon barrel of good Injun whiskey with five gallons of rot-gut whiskey, one pound of bluestone, three pounds of star chewing tobacco, half a peck of stone lime, two pounds of cayenne pepper and fifty-five gallons of water? We want no trouble with this man or no other man. I will tell the boys to cut them two ponies out and they will

come over to your bunch themselves. Sorry you don't want
to swap us your wagon. Get in, Bill. We hit the trail when the
trailing is good." Then he gathered up the lines and drove
over to where the bunch of horses were held, and in a few
minutes Sow-set's and Squis-squis's saddle horses came
back on the lope, while those high binders trailed off
towards the Musselshell River.

When they seen their horses coming back to them, Sow-
set and Squis-squis (who did not understand what the white
men had been saying to me) now consider me a hero. Sow-
set, since old Gabriel is not here, don't seem to care a whoop
what she does, now with Squis-squis and before the eyes of
the cruel world, with shining eyes they start to pay their debt
of gratitude to me the cheapest way a squaw knows how—
with delightful hugs of love and affection, to which I very
weakly protested. But In-who-lise does not take this kind of
stuff as a joke no more, and blames me as much as them.

CHAPTER TWENTY-EIGHT
Old Gabriel Tries to Shoot Me

I then went over to Mexican José and kind of hinted of all the trouble I was having in my matrimonial tangle, but I got little consolation from this sagebrush philosopher, who solemnly now tells me not to get down in the mouth, that the worst was still to come. That he knew for some time that I was a damn fool, when I told him I was going to marry a slim single-footer of a squaw like In-who-lise, but now he was more than sure of it, when he seen today that I had two more high steppers whinnering after me. That when a fellow came to try and run a string of that many squaws, he would find himself landing in the hot soup, as it was only hell at the best with one of them.

I was not left long to enjoy this flattering conversation, which now came to an abrupt end. For there came through the air fierce yells and war whoops that made me shiver, and no wonder, for there, coming on the dead lope toward camp, were fifteen or sixteen buck Injuns, barebacked and in only their breechclouts and as Mexican Pete with a groan exclaimed, "Drunk as hell, mean as cat dung and twice as nasty."

I started to get my rifle, when he said, "What are you going to do?" I said, "Get my rifle and do the best I can and kill all them red devils I can before they kill us all." He said, "Don't be a damn fool and try that, for I can now see that they are only young Assiniboines and Gros Ventres. They don't seem to have any guns with them, and maybe are only out to do a little mischief and deviltry. If you shoot one of them, the old bucks of their people in the Injun camp, drunk like they are now, will be only too glad to come here and kill us all. We have got to do the best we can with rocks and clubs, to keep them from wrecking the camp and abusing the women."

Then like a cyclone they struck the breed part of the camp, and as there were only women there, they wrecked two tepees there, and when the breed woman and squaws went at them with tepee poles, and rocks, with whoops and yells they came on the lope for our part of the camp, where every squaw and us were ready with rocks and clubs, to try and turn them back and to keep them from wrecking the tepees. But we might as well have tried to stop the Missouri River from running, for we were soon all running around the tepees and camp, trying to keep their horses from running over us, and so far I had only managed to hit one of them a good lick with a rock on the head. They kept it up this way with whoop and yell, which with the shrill screams of the squaws could be heard a long ways off. They did not have their guns, but they had their warrior whips with them, the butt of which could be used as a war club and knock an enemy's brains out. They had already cut two or three of the squaws badly with the lash end of it. They rode through Samwell's tepee in which were Injun kids and pulled it down, and now the only safe place in camp where they could not get at us with their horses, was in my shack and in the wagon bed and under it. Again I wanted Mexican José and Pete to take our guns and shoot the red devils down like the dogs they were, but they still said, "No, it will be better to let them wreck the whole damn camp then to give the old bucks an excuse to come and kill us all. We were damn lucky that we did not have a bunch of them here now with their guns to shoot the hell out of us."

Next, four of them charged their tepee, which was a little to one side by itself. It was only put up weakly, as they intended to pull out in the morning. They managed to get a hold of it on the run and pulled it down on top of them two she warriors and their raft of kids. Isidora and Buena Ventura had stayed inside during the fight, but Isidora was now equal to the occasion and must have come from a race of fighting warriors. With a shriek of rage, she grabbed up a tepee pole and hurled her 250 pounds of feminine beauty and grace into the fray. A young buck accepted her challenge with a whoop and yell and wildly charged at her with his horse, but Isidora, like a valorous knight of old, braced her feet and stood firmly there and met the charge with the sharp point of the tepee pole, catching the buck in the breast and then landing him up in the air off his horse to fall flat on his back on the ground. Then Isidora brought the tepee pole down on him with all her strength, and put one buck Injun out of business for the time being. But before she could get another swing at him, another buck came up on the lope, grabbing the pole in his hand, thinking he would pull it away from her, but forgot to figure out Isidora's weight. When the buck started off with her, she grimly held on the other end of the tepee pole and the buck, who was riding bareback and his horse on the run, now found himself pulled off his horse on the ground, when Isidora with a whoop pulled the tepee pole out of his hand, and was starting to flatten him out like the other buck. Then two more bucks raced at her, one of them going on each side of her, getting her between their horses. Then they grabbed her and start off with her between their horses. Then they caught the bottom of her squaw skirt and pulled it up and over her head, then dropped her there as naked as she was born. Then with whoops and yells of scorn to us, they rode off on the dead lope, the two bucks on the ground leaping up behind another buck, with one of them waving Isidora's squaw skirt in the air as a banner of victory.

It was a good time for them to leave us, for now coming to camp was old Gabriel and bunch with the breeds. They seem to understand what has happened in camp. With whoops and yells, they took after the marauders on the lope, shooting at them on the run, but they circled around them and out of their way and went off to the Injun camp in a cloud of dust. The camp was a sight to see, with tepees torn down and things scattered around, when old Gabriel and his

bunch, with the Crees and breeds rode into camp; and they
were in no better shape than the camp. Some were drunk
and the rest of them better than half shot, and instead of
being friendly to Mexican José and Pete and myself, when I
spoke to them, they snapped at me like a mad wolf in a trap.
José said to me, "It is only the Injun devil and whiskey that
is in them and is working strong; keep away from them; they
are bad this way."

I did not take his advice, but went up and spoke to old
Gabriel, who was taking his saddle off. With his eyes shining
like a maniac, he said, "Get, and don't say anything to me." I
told him, "All right, if you want it that way." Then I went to
my camp, thinking that being drunk, he did not know what
he was saying.

The squaws were going around putting up tepees and
trying to get the wrecked camp in shape, when José and Pete
came over. We were squatted around the fire when they start
an argument in regard to the bravery of their respective
squaws. José is saying to Pete that it is up to him to buy the
calico from me to make Isidora a new skirt, because it was
she who had so bravely saved the life of his cowardly Buena
Ventura, and who had put to rout that bunch of redskin
barbarians and saved all of our lives.

Then a terrible racket starts at old Gabriel's tepee, and we
soon seen old Gabriel going after Kat-a-lee, Sow-set and
Squis-squis around the tepees with a warrior's whip. Every
time he struck one of them, they screamed with the pain.
Then in his frenzy he struck Kat-a-lee with the butt and sent
her staggering down on the ground. José said, "This looks to
me as though that crazy breed son of a ——— intends to
kill them." I said, "If he does that some more, I am going
over and kill him." Then In-who-lise said in terror, "No, no,
don't go there; get a horse and leave quick, for I think someone has told old Gabriel all." Then I was in a crazy fury. I
grabbed her arm and wrenched it till she screamed with the
pain, saying, "Yes, and it was you the Nez Perce bitch who
told him. If he kills them, I will kill you." Then In-who-lise

said, "An-ta-lee can kill me now, but I did not do this. See, old Gabriel now comes this way."

There came old Gabriel, prodding Kat-a-lee, Sow-set and Squis-squis ahead of him with his gun, their faces bloody and them cut up with whip marks. Again, In-who-lise said, "Run, run. Don't you see he has his gun?" But I said to her, "Run, hell."

Old Gabriel came up to me with them and his face was awful to see in his drunken anger; he must have been drinking some more since he got back. He pointed his gun at me, saying, "You stand. So this is the way I find you are the dirty kind, that rips your best friend down the back, the dirtiest way a man can. I know this is so now, or why do you hold down your head like a whipped dog? Better for me if you never came here. Then I would not have to do what I am going to do now, and I would not have to hear what that drunken bitch of a mother of Squis-squis and some more are now saying in the Injun camp, that Kata-lee and Sow-set are now only hand-blowing sluts, who got and coaxed Squis-squis to go off with them, lay in the brush with them and you. That she had now left the Injun camp with Sow-set and that her people could do nothing with her no more, that now I could keep her with my own two whores and get more presents of guns and blankets from that sly snake An-ta-lee, who made bad squaws of their girls, and was the cause of all this."

In-who-lise said, "They lie in the Injun camp, and you shall not kill An-ta-lee, my man. You kill them three hussies there who are the bad ones. An-ta-lee tried to be a good man to me, and he would be a better man to me, only your two strumpets with Squis-squis and two more in the Injun camp come and coax him off from me. I have wanted to tell you this many times, that them three hussies there have made me cover up my head and cry many times, and they still say they will make me cry plenty more, and that I will never see the Black Robe to make me his squaw, as long as they have soft arms and sweet lips to steal him away from me. And it was for this that Kat-a-lee tried to kill me that day I stabbed her in the belly. You leave him go now and he will do no more harm here. White Feather will take him away in the morning. She will go off with him far away from here and her eyes shall shine with joy again, when she leaves this place of evil for her forever."

But to all In-who-lise's pleading, old Gabriel only shook his head, saying, "Then if this is as you say, all the better will it be, that them evil squaws and bad white man shall die." But he changed his mind, saying, "I will do this for In-who-lise who is a good squaw, but if I was her, I would not trust that sly liar An-ta-lee, who can lie better than he can tell the truth." He said to me, "Don't move or I will plug you. What do you say to this? Now tell the truth for once in your life. Will you do as she says and go with her to where she came from in Idaho and marry her on the way the first town you come to, even if those evil squaws shall die here right now?"

I said, "What good will it do you to kill them now and let me go who is as bad as them? You let them go. I will go away with In-who-lise, just as soon as I can pack up tomorrow and will never bother them or you no more."

To this old Gabriel would only say, "No, they were told before this what they would get. This is not the first time they have shamed me and brought sorrow on my gray head. They are not going to get the chance to do this again. The place for a bad squaw is under the ground."

Then I said, "If you are a crazy enough devil to kill your own flesh and blood, you might as well cut loose at me and have it done with. The next time you do a thing like this, don't use the gun that you got as a present from the one you kill. Besides, you have no right to kill Squis-squis, and will pay dearly when the white men find out. Go ahead, you crazy drunken buck Injun, for I would rather be dead with them than to live a life in hell all my life, knowing that I would be as much to blame for their deaths as you are." I have no doubt that I could have talked old Gabriel from doing this, but Kat-a-lee and Sow-set now had to go and spoil it. With the fury of a panther, they sprang and took old

Gabriel by surprise. Kat-a-lee grabbed the gun in his hands, and they done their best to take it away from him, saying to me, "Run now, An-ta-lee. He is crazy drunk and does not know what he does." Then, saying to him, "You must not kill An-ta-lee for this, for it is us who are the bad ones."

This act did not take as long to occur as it takes to write it, and before I got over my surprise, old Gabriel, again in a crazy frenzy, easily jerked the gun from Kat-a-lee's hands, knocking her down on the ground with it, and gave Sow-set a push that sent her reeling backward on her back, several feet away, and at the same time he howled at me, "Yes, just you run you sneaking white-faced dog, for I would rather kill you on the run when I know that you have no gun." Quick as a flash, as the screams of In-who-lise and the other three rang through the camp, he leveled his carbine on me and pulled the trigger. This must have been the Squaw Kid's lucky day, for the hammer came down in silence and no sound came from his gun. He then throwed the lever down and flipped out an empty shell, then pulled the lever in place, aimed at me again and pulled the trigger. But the hammer only fell on an empty gun, for old Gabriel had emptied his gun at them young bucks who had wrecked the camp and forgot in his drunken state to load it again. This seemed to puzzle him for a second. Then he said, champing the few teeth he had left like a peccary boar in his age, "I must have forgot to load it, but I will do it right this time," quickly reaching for cartridges in his belt.

Then Mexican José said with his forty-five leveled at old Gabriel, "You try to load that gun and as sure as God, Jesus and the Madonna live in heaven, I will kill you like the crazy drunken Injun dog you are. You had your two chances to kill that damn fool but a higher one than you or I said it is not to be. You give me that gun or I will beat what little brains you have got left with the butt of my gun, as you are not worth a bullet out of my gun." Then he reached over and snatched the gun out of old Gabriel's hands, saying, "You lousy half-white Injun, if you don't listen to reason and try to make more trouble, Pedro and I will shoot up you and your lousy bunch and throw in the Crees and breeds for luck, and wipe you all off from the face of the earth, and if your friends the Pend d'Oreilles in the Injun camp feel sore at this and want anything to do with us, we can rustle up enough of our drunken friends there, the Assiniboines, Gros Ventres and Piegans, who will be only too glad to help us to push them all off along with you. You keep them damn hookers of yours at home at work tanning robes and not let them run wild through the trees and brush in the creek bottoms. Then you will not have to kill them, or the fool you find with them. You do not have to kill them for this, if you don't want them here with you any more, give them the run to some other Injun camp."

At first old Gabriel was awful in his anger when José took his gun away from him. This seemed to hurt his dignity worse than anything. But as José read the riot act to him, and let him see that he was not afraid of no breed or Injun, old Gabriel quieted down and readily agreed with him, saying, "It will be as you say. The worst thing that I can do to that white-faced sneak is to give them to him." Then he said to me, "You hear this, I leave them with you. You wanted them; now you got them and they are now yours. You and them leave here tomorrow at sunrise. If you and them are here after that, then all of you shall die, as sure as the sun shines in the sky. What does An-ta-lee say?" I said, "It will be as Gabriel says. I will go off with them and take them away from here, for this will be better than for us to stay here and die."

Gabriel went off to his tepee, taking In-who-lise, the good truthful squaw, the hope and joy of the Squaw Kid with him, leaving me there with José, Pete and my newly acquired family. Then José, the oracle of the bunch, starts in on me, saying, "Well, what do you know about that? Thought yourself smart, did you, when them copper-colored charmers let you tangle up your fingers in their hair? This is nothing to what is going to happen to you, Mr. Three Squaws, when them three bobcats of yours get to fighting among themselves about who is the boss of your tepee. Then you will wish that old Gabriel's gun was loaded, and that I had let him kill you today. I told you to keep away from them single-footers and high steppers; a thing like this would have never happened if you had liked them fat like my Isidora."

I told him to shut up and for them to figure out how I was going to get away from here tomorrow and move all the stuff I had. I told them squaws would take care of themselves. After much talk they said the only way is for us to leave our families here with Pete. He would watch them and my stuff. José would load everything that my prairie schooner would hold and haul it to friends—a Piegan camp, two days' drive from here. They would not care if I came there with one or twenty squaws. There was a small stockade there, with a large cabin inside. I could use the cabin to keep my stuff in as this place was not claimed by anyone. The hunters and trappers who had built it a few years ago had been murdered by a band of Gros Ventres, whom those men were foolish enough to let in the stockade. The Gros Ventres had turned on them and killed them all. I could use my pack train of ten horses, and put them squaws of mine to good use helping me to pack up what the pack train could take, and come along with him. He would come back with the wagon and get the robes and whatever stuff was left. I said that I did not want anything to do with that hoodoo stockade where men had been murdered, that my luck was bad enough without moving in there. I would get him to haul my stuff over to White Grass's Blackfeet camp, two days' drive from here. I thought this would be the best place for me to go to, as they were my friends.

José said, "If this is so, then the deal is off. I will see you in hell before I will haul you there to your cutthroat friends, and be murdered by them on my way back."

When Sow-set and the others heard this, they all voted against me going there, and went on a strike with the Mexicans, saying, "No Pend d'Oreille warrior or squaw goes to a Blackfeet camp. We know better than this, for it would only be a few days till them Blackfeet hussies would make An-ta-lee drive us, his women, away, then where would we stay?"

This left me nothing to do but go to the Piegan camp as they wanted. Old White Grass had not showed up yet to get what was coming to him for them four bundles of robes his warriors had left with me that night they had sneaked into camp. I was now in a bad fix about this, and did not want to leave without giving him what was coming to him. Still I had to keep my mouth shut about this to José, Pete or Sow-set and the other two, about those Blackfeet coming to me in camp in the night. I thought I might be able to send him word where I was going, by some of the Piegans. Then he would know where to come and get what was his.

It was early in the night and a quietness hangs over the camp, which after the doings of today gave it a funeral aspect. I sat there alone by the fire at my usual nightly occupation, profound meditation. Kat-a-lee, Sow-set and Squis-squis I had put in the wagon box to sleep for tonight (a rare novelty for a wild squaw to enjoy), and now was wondering how all this is going to turn out. José had said that it was hell with one squaw at the best, any way you took it. Then if that was so, it is going to be worse then that, for the Squaw Kid with three of them. I now got sarcastic with myself, saying, "Yes, Squaw Kid, you thought it smart and funny to christen old Bulleau 'Three Squaws.' Well, the joke is on you now good and plenty, and you ought to like your own medicine and have no kick coming, for you have certainly done well, in the short time you have been here, for the Kid who not so long ago went down on his knees in old Isaleta on the Rio Grande, to God Jesus and the Madonna in heaven. Surely it has not taken as deep as your good old mother did prophesy, that you would be a pillar of the church, and no less than a Bishop someday, or you would not be the hypocrite and liar that you are today, buried so deep in the snow slides of hell that all the preachers there will never be able to dig you out. And if you can only keep up your luck, you ought to soon be able to ask Uncle Sam for a reservation of your own."

It was in the fall of 1878 before the Priest came to the Cree buffalo camp on the Musselshell River, nearly one day's ride from the Pend d'Oreille camp. The Priest was a very good man, and while a whole lot more tough and rough looking than the priests and preachers of today, he was probably closer to God than some. He was called the Black Robe of the North, and his name was Father Landre. He followed the Cree buffalo camps in Canada and lived in the tepees with them like an Injun, wherever there was a camp in Montana, and said Mass and preached to them in the Cree language. His church was a large one, the vaults of heaven and generally on a creek bank under a tree. His altar stood there, the tail end of a Red River cart. It was some sight to see, on the banks of the Musselshell, in that Injun camp, on that day when In-who-lise and I were married.

There were many tepees of different tribes, most of them ready to cut each other's throats, and all of them ready to steal and run off the horses of each other. But here today in hypocritical brotherly love, Assiniboines, Crees, Bloods, Blackfeet, Gros Ventre Piegans and Pend d'Oreilles met together to hear the wise words of the white man's God. More truthfully, they are here to race horses and gamble for horses at the Injun game of playing hands. And it was certainly a wild and savage scene to see those warriors and some of the bewhiskered long-haired white men with squaws, and plenty half-breeds and their women. All of us knelt down on the ground in the hot sun during Mass, when Father Landre preached to the Crees in their language, and at the same time in the sign language telling everyone who did not understand Cree, with his hands and fingers. He made the prairie ring with his eloquence. All the Injuns in those days professed some Christianity, though it did not take any too deep with all of them, as they only used what little suited them and threw the rest of it away.

Old Gabriel and a large bunch of the Pend d'Oreille warriors had come over with us from their camp to hear the Black Robe and lend their dignity to the happy bridegroom, Squaw Kid, because Injun etiquette requires the bridegroom to feed the whole bunch and give them all a two- or three-day feast, when he will arrive with his bride back at camp and his rawhide mansion. Many of the squaws had come along to see In-who-lise married to a white man, the same as a white squaw, by the Black Robe with a ring on her finger. And all of them thought it would be heap good medicine for a squaw to have a ring like that, and to have the Black Robe put Colon Suten's (God's) words in it. I was greatly surprised when I asked Father Landre, who did not understand Pend d'Oreille or Nez Perce, if I would have to get an interpreter to make In-who-lise understand what he was saying to her. He said, "I have talked with her and she can speak English as well as either you or I can, and has been to the mission school at Lapwai." I could not get her to say a word in English as long as she lived. When we were married, In-who-lise thought she was nineteen years old and I was twenty-three years old.

The Injuns, after going to church to hear the Black Robe's holy words till noon, made the air hum all the rest of the afternoon as they chanted their Injun songs, gambling for horses at their game of playing hands. Toward night, many campfires lit up this scene of happy bucks and squaws gorging themselves on large chunks of broiled buffalo meat. After two days of this, the camp had a rude awakening. Some squaw men who had been to Carrol on the Missouri River now came back with whiskey. And those low-down, drunken white rascals filled some of their Blackfeet women's relations up to the neck with whiskey. The Blackfeet were ten to one against the Pend d'Oreilles in camp here. Then the drunken Blackfeet warriors got their guns and lances and get on their war ponies ki-yi-ing and yelling as they lope and run their horses through camp, and are saying to the Pend d'Oreilles in our camp to come out on the prairie and fight. And in vain did their war chiefs try to quiet them and get them to go to their own camp. Here was surely one bunch of Blackfeet who were out for trouble and to raise hell in general. Father Landre, hearing all this racket, now came here and, without saying anything to them, snatched a warrior's whip out of one of the war chief's hand and then went at those Blackfeet bucks, who were more afraid of him than of all the guns in camp. Drunk as they were, they now got as meek as lambs. After he got a few good swinging cuts of his whip on some of them, they faded away to their camp. If them squaw men had brought enough whiskey to camp with them for all the other Injuns in camp to get drunk on, there would sure have been hell a popping. This was a busy day for the good Father, who had now got his dander up, and goes on the warpath, whip in hand, after the scalps of those squaw men who had brought the whiskey and starts in single-handed to run them out of camp. They met this demand with drunken oaths. The good Father, though a small man, is no coward and smashes this blackguard a couple of good ones with his whip. They finally said they would leave camp as soon as their women got their lodges packed up. They told Father Landre as they left that they would get square with him for this, that they were only leaving camp to go to Carrol for enough whiskey to make all his Injun Catholics good Baptists.

Injuns have many strange ways that a white man living with them had better learn quickly and heed, or he will soon come out on the small end of the horn. The Injuns have what they call their E-sa-lat (friend), and when two Injuns make friends with each other this way it means that what one has got, the other one has got.

It was but a short while after those squaw men left camp for Carrol on the Missouri River, when I went in the Pend d'Oreille lodge where I stayed with In-who-lise in camp, and was surprised to see my new bride in tears. Not without good reason, for squatted there was this Gros Ventre woman who had been so good to In-who-lise in the Assiniboine camp. I had seen her several times here in camp, for the Two Beavers outfit and several more Assiniboine lodges were here. At first I thought it might be some kind of a squaw's pagan festival or seance, where no men are wanted, for this Gros Ventre woman was stripped to her bare pelt, without even a G-string. Before her in a small pile was her buckskin skirt with her leggins and moccasins, all a squaw is supposed to wear. While a short distance across the tepee from her was In-who-lise in tears, with everything that we had brought to camp. Before her were namely three good new blankets and a few other things, while around the tepee squatted four Pend d'Oreille women silently watching this act. The Gros Ventre woman was bitterly haranguing In-who-lise in Assiniboine and did not pay any attention to me.

I said to In-who-lise, "What is the matter with her that she is this way, and what are you doing with them blankets and the other stuff before you?" In-who-lise said, "She is my E-sa-lat [friend], and is saying what she has got, I have got and what I have got, she has got, and now says that because she is my E-sa-lat she now gives me all that she has got; her swoop-a-whop-a-can, leggins and moccasins there at her feet. For that, I must strip and swap with her, my good friend, who was good to me in the Assiniboine camp. My pretty squaw skirt, leggins and shawl of white man's cloth, with my ring. I have said to her to do anything else but this, for you had already given her blankets and other good things for being good to me in the Assiniboine buffalo camp. Now she can have those blankets and other things here, but not must strip me of the clothes I was married in, and that I will not give her my ring even if she is my friend. But she is now mad at me and says she is now sorry that she did not let me die in the Assiniboine camp, then she would not today have a false Sapah-tan slut for her E-sa-lat."

I then told her with my hands that she was not going to get the ring or anything else from In-who-lise now or after this and to get back to her lodge, till she forgot this E-sa-lat business. I then told In-who-lise to put the blankets and other stuff back where she got them, and if I ever caught her giving away her or my stuff in this Injun friendship business, I would whale the camas out of her.

Early next morning after promising the good Father Landre to say my prayers regular three times a day, to be a model husband and a whole lot of other promises that I did not intend to keep, we buck Injuns of the Pend d'Oreille camp bid the good Father good-bye, when the going was good, and started back to camp, a little better than a half day's ride from here. Nothing occurred to relieve the monotony on the way, except that two old buffalo bulls, who had retired or had been driven out of business in their old age, took a liking to the brilliant red in In-who-lise's shawl and came at us on the run, bellowing and pawing up the dust as they chased us a long way. The squaws in the outfit were laughing and saying to In-who-lise that this was a good omen for her, when even the buffalo bulls on the prairies went crazy about her beauty.

On our arrival back to camp, the Pend d'Oreilles turn out to welcome the newlyweds, and say that the happy bridegroom who marries a beautiful Injun maid, he also marries all her people, relations and the whole tribe with her, and that it was now up to him as a new beginner to feast them all no less than two or three days, though a week would be better. When I said the feast will start tomorrow, then the Pend d'Oreille buffalo camp was happy. But when they heard that one of the Cree half-breeds was going to bring two young buffalo cows for the feast, those sassy red-skins turned up their noses and said that they must have Sa-whack-wa (flour) and Tish (sugar) cooked with this, with plenty tea with sugar in it to drink, as they are tired of straight buffalo meat at home. This now left me nothing else but to get a couple of Pend d'Oreille squaws to help In-who-lise to be chief cooks and bottle washers for the feast.

It was early in June, 1879, before we could travel through the country on our way to Lapwai, Idaho, streams being too high till now. We joined another squaw man named Clark, who had two Shoshone squaws and several breed kids. He said that only one of the women was his; that the other woman was his woman's sister, whose husband was a white man that the Utes had killed near Green River.

In-who-lise only laughed about this, saying, "Them Shoshone women of that white man say to us that they are both his women and that he was the father of their children."

This man Clark was a happy-go-lucky fellow and straight as a string in his word and dealings. He had traded with the Injuns in different parts of the Musselshell country all winter and had done well, having in his wagon around 350 good buffalo robes, besides many wolf pelts and quite a lot of beaver and small furs. He was well hooked up with a good outfit, and was now on his way back to Fort Hall near where he lived. He drove one four-horse team on a loaded wagon while one of his women drove the other wagon that carried their camp plunder and surplus kids. The other woman, with a good-sized kid, trailed behind, driving a good-sized bunch of loose horses.

He said he was going to haul the robes from Fort Hall down into Utah and trade them off to the Saints for horses and cattle.

Clark said that he had been in the Big Hole country and knew it well, and would show us if we went along with him the best place to leave the Bozeman on the Corinne (Utah) stage road, to go into the Big Hole Valley and on to the Big Hole battlefield.

In-who-lise said if she could get back to the Big Hole battlefield, she could easily find her way back to the third Nez Perce camp, after the battlefield, where her father had been buried. She said I must take her there on our way to Lapwai. From the Big Hole battlefield she knew the trail back to her old home in Idaho.

Mexican Pete showed up as he agreed, to come and haul my robes and furs to Bozeman in return for the Shuttler prairie schooner that I had got from Webber and Harris last summer. Besides this wagonload of furs and robes, I had ten pack-horse loads of choice robes, made up in bundles of five, two bundles to a pack, which made a light but bulky pack. With those ten pack horses there were two more to pack our camp outfit and another pack horse to pack our tepee, together with our saddle horses and six loose horses, the two of us had our hands full to handle this outfit.

Now that we are ready to pull out, it is with feelings of sorrow and regret, and I hated to leave here, where I had so much happiness and hell all rolled up together. And as the warriors and women in camp stand around us, their swarthy faces show their regret, and they all say they are sorry to see me leave them and hope we will soon meet again.

The only one happy here is In-who-lise, for the hour for her triumph has come at last. She is now all smiles to be on her way back to her people, but more especially to get me out and far away from the influences that dwell in this Pend d'Oreille buffalo camp.

We pulled out with Mexican Pete driving the prairie schooner with a four-horse team on the lead, and headed across the country for the Yellowstone River. Clark with his outfit was in the lead, while In-who-lise and I with the pack outfit and loose horses brought up the rear. Before long we found out that two of the four work horses hauling the prairie schooner, that were supposed to be gentle and well broke and pullers from hell, were not much better than wild broncos, and done their best to smash up everything, twice taking to the hills, scattering those bundles of robes and furs along in their wake. If Clark had not given us two gentle work horses out of his loose bunch, we would never have made it through to the Yellowstone.

After four days of a rough and tumble trip for the wagons, we came out on the Bozeman trail on the Yellowstone River. Following the Bozeman trail up the Yellowstone River, I saw some changes since coming by a year ago. There were two or three new ranches above the mouth of the Big

Timber on the Yellowstone River, and we met two parties
from the Gallatin Valley looking around for a good range to
run cattle. It was too early in the season for the arrival of
emigrants from the East on the Bozeman trail, so we saw
none. Going by Hunter's Hot Springs, seeing no one
around, we kept on going. We had the good luck to be over-
taken at Shields River by a Mr. Cochrane, a robe and fur
buyer, who says he is coming back from a trip among the
Mountain Crows and the trappers and traders down to Fort
Keough. He had left at Miles City quite a cargo of buffalo
robes, hides and fur pelts, waiting for the first boat up the
Yellowstone, and that, as furs and buffalo robes were in good
demand this season, he was on his way to Bozeman to see
what he could pick up from the traders and dealers there.
Clark told him his robes and furs were not for sale, but that
wagonload of mine was. I said I would like to sell to him but
I owed three hundred fifty dollars on them to Mr. Cooper at
Bozeman. He was good enough to trust me, so it is no more
than right he gets the first crack at them.

Mr. Cochrane said I was foolish even if I was honest, to
let slip a chance like this, when he bought most of the furs
and robes when they had any from the traders and dealers
in Bozeman. What was the use in letting Mr. Cooper skin
me and make a good profit on him besides? Both of us could
whack up the difference. Saying to my excuses that Cooper
would never know the difference if I kept my mouth shut
about it, Cochrane said he would look the robes and furs
over and, if I liked his price, he would give me his check on
the First National Bank of Bozeman and would see that I got
it cashed for gold when we came there. It would be better for
both of us this way. I would not have to haul them on to
Bozeman and he would not have to haul them back. All I
had to do when I came to Bozeman was to pay Cooper that
three hundred fifty dollars I owed him, that is if I felt like it.
Or I could slip around Bozeman after I got the check cashed
into gold, with my pack train and forget Cooper. But, I flatly
stuck to it, that I was not going to do such a thing to Mr.

Cooper, after him being so good to me. Them robes and furs were going to be his till someone offered me more than him for them.

Mr. Cochrane not any too graceful said, "Then let it be so," and went over to his own camp. Clark kept telling me that I was foolish to make an enemy out of Cochrane when he was willing to give me traders' prices. If I did turn him down like this without a chance to make me an offer, Cochrane would probably ride on ahead in time to fix it up with Cooper and others in town to give me the gaff. I only had to give Cooper his money and was bound to him no other way. Clark said, "You tell Cochrane that I will overhaul and list your cargo of robes and furs with him. Then, if you like his price they are his. If not, you haul them on to Bozeman and take your chances there." I said, "All right, but it is only to see and find out."

I then went and told Cochrane that I had changed my mind. Cochrane said, "Now you are sensible. I am willing to pay a square price, but why don't you sell the pack-train load of robes along with the rest of the cargo?" I told him that was a family affair, that my woman did not want me to sell them.

Instead of pulling out next morning as we first intended, we stayed over at Shields River, and it kept Mexican Pete and I busy for some time unloading, untying and spreading out the different bundles of robes and furs, so that Clark and Cochrane could get at them. Both of them listed and graded each robe and pelt by itself, according to their own idea, and it was as I had thought, Cochrane now sings a different song. For he is a fur buyer up to his old tricks. He whines and complains that he cannot pay the prices he told us when there was not a robe or fur pelt in the whole damn wag-onload that would grade A-No. 1 prime, and that the few best in the bunch only graded good to fair at the best, and runs down every robe and pelt in the whole bunch.

Clark just as insistent as him swears that Cochrane knows he is a liar and that he is only doing this to hear himself talk, when he knew this was the best bunch of robes and furs he had seen for some time, and if Cochrane thought we were buck Injuns and he was going to get this wagonload of choice robes and furs at that kind of grading, he was going to get left. But Cochrane had robbed Injuns and trappers too long to be insulted at this. They went through my cargo and had a couple hours more of heated wrangling between them. Twice Clark told me to tie them bundles up and load them on the wagon, that the deal was off. Each time Cochrane made a substantial raise above his former price, but the third time Cochrane told me I could take his last offer or leave it. He was done with me.

Shortly after this I found myself in possession of a check from Cochrane on the First National Bank of Bozeman for the sum of two thousand one hundred eighty dollars. Clark told me I had better take that price, as he was certain he had worked Cochrane out of every drop of sweat that was in him. He would not pay any more and was giving me now a much better price than any of the dealers in Bozeman would give me.

I had no kick coming, as this was more money that I ever had in my life before. Besides, I had still left them ten pack loads of choice robes as Injun money to swap for cattle when I got to Idaho. The only thing now bothering me was whether this piece of paper would turn out in the Bozeman bank as good as he said.

Early next morning we pulled out from Shields River, Cochrane's outfit with us, leaving Mexican Pete and one of Cochrane's men still there getting ready to go down to the Countryman place at Stillwater with the load of robes and furs. We followed the Yellowstone River on the Bozeman trail and on by Benson's Landing till the trail left the river for Bozeman. We went into camp that night early at the foot of the divide.

Next morning, crossing over the divide, we stopped a while at Fort Ellis to have a talk with the boys. Big changes had occurred there since I left a year ago. Old Fort Ellis, now having no Injun troubles to take care of, had become a one-horse post compared to what it used to be. Most of the civilians and troops that I knew had gone to the new posts of Custer and Keough.

Arriving at Bozeman around noon, we went into camp about half a mile from town. It was the fourth day on the trail from Sweet Grass. Leaving Clark's outfit and In-who-lise in camp, I rode along with the Cochrane outfit to town to get his check cashed into gold. Cochrane, good to his word, tells the cashier in the bank it is his check and that I am the right party and to cash the check into gold for me, that I was on my way to Lapwai, Idaho, and wanted the gold to take along with me.

At this the cashier stood speechless then said, "But Mr. Cochrane, did I hear you right? Surely this man is not foolish enough to want to carry that two thousand one hundred and eighty dollars in gold along with him through a wild country where most of the way no one lives. I would not sleep all night if I had to keep that amount on me right here in town." It did not take Cochrane and the cashier long to convince me that this bank was right, and that I was foolish to want to pack that amount in gold, when I could leave it here in the bank with safety. Why take chances of being held up or maybe murdered on the way? I could send after it when I wanted it.

I drew out of the bank enough to pay Mr. Cooper besides fifty dollars in gold for myself. Mr. Cochrane asked me on the side as I was leaving the bank if I really intended to pay Mr. Cooper the money I drew out of the bank. I told him I surely did. What did he take me for, a damn bilk, just because I was now a fur trader like himself?

On going over to pay Mr. Cooper what I owed him, I found out from some of the citizens I met on the way that Mr. Cooper had for some time lost all hope of ever seeing me or getting his money back, thinking that I had either been killed by the Injuns, or, like most of them did, I had skedaddled to greener pastures. He did not blame me for selling them robes and furs to Cochrane, when I had got a better price than he could afford to give me. Now he wants me to go in with him trading to the trappers and Injuns in the Musselshell and Yellowstone country. Something had to be done because Bozeman was no more the town it used to be. Instead of the trappers and Injuns of the Yellowstone coming here to trade off their robes and furs, they were going to the new towns of Coulson and Miles City right at their own door. Even Cochrane the fur buyer was coming from there and bought whatever robes and furs the merchants and traders in town had.

I told Mr. Cooper that I was sorry and did not want any more trading with the Injuns in the buffalo camps or any other place. I had reformed, and was on my way and leaving Montana with my woman to some place called Lapwai.

He now said, "So then it is as they are saying around town, that you had the gall to bring back with you an Indian woman." Knowing that I had a white girl in town, at first he did not believe I would do a foolish thing like that, and said that I would soon be sorry. And, if I would take his advice, the first thing for me to do in the morning would be to give that squaw a horse and some grub and send her alone on her way to her people at Lapwai, or back to the Injun buffalo camps in the Musselshell where I had found her. That he would put in a good word and smooth things over for me with my girl's people, and help me out of this mess I had got myself into. Maybe, as no one could tell what a fool woman would do, my girl, when she understood things right, would forgive me and marry me yet.

I told him, "So this is you the good Christian, a church deacon, who rants and prays to God every Sunday, yet you tell me to do this to her, who is my wife, just because she is an Injun. Just the same, I know her better than you do. She is as good a woman as your own, and the only true friend I have got left. I told the priest the day I married her that I would stay with her till hell froze over. I meant it then and still mean it today."

When Mr. Cooper heard that I was married to In-who-lise by a priest, he apologized. He said he had thought I was like most other white men, who had Indian women and who did not believe in going to the bother of marrying them, as they only intended to throw them away when they could find a white one that would suit them better. That I was not to think that he was evil enough to advise me to leave my wife. That I had made my bed on a rock pile and could only kick myself good and plenty when I found it rocky and hard. That the only thing left for me to do was to pull out with her in the morning for Lapwai as I had intended. In this way I left the genial Mr. Cooper, wishing me well. I had good reasons to want to shake the dust off my feet, and lose no time in getting out of the town of Bozeman.

As I went on my way to the hitching rack, where I had left my saddle horse, I had to pass by several persons who had always been friendly to me. I could not fail to notice the black looks they now gave me. Instead of a friendly greeting, they went by me in silence. I knew the cause of this when I heard one fellow say to another sneeringly, as they went by me, "Squaw man."

PART FOUR
The Trail Home to Lapwai

CHAPTER THIRTY
Graves and Grief

Leaving Silver Star, we struck out across a long range of hills, following a trail that brought us to the Big Hole River. When we came to a fork in the trail, In-who-lise said, "While I have never been here before, the one to the right must follow the creek that comes from In-sah-kum-sah-nay [Big Hole battlefield]. A-O [yes], I am sure of this now. I can see the hills and divide between this valley and Ket-la-met-a-lee [Bitterroot Valley]." Then she began to wail and cry for her dead people.

We left the Big Hole River and tried to follow the creek, but the country became too swampy and we had to take higher ground without any trail. After some hit or miss rambling, we arrived at the battlefield in the middle of the afternoon on the third day after leaving Silver Star.

I had wanted to see the Big Hole battlefield, and now that I had my wish, I hope to God never to see another sight like it again!

We tried to find the grave of In-who-lise's sister, Lucy, but our search was in vain. The sight was awful to see. Human bones were scattered through the long grass and among the willows across the creek, and on this side of the creek human bones and leering skulls were scattered around as though they had never been buried. Still, it looked as if the soldiers had been buried where they fell and their graves were in fair condition.

Some of the tepee poles of this once large Injun camp still lay scattered around. The peeled ones were as good as they were two years ago on the day when some unfortunate squaw hauled and set them up here, her lips breathing with song and laughter, not knowing that tomorrow would bring their death song.

This ghastly display of Indian dead made me doubtful for the first time in my life if there is a Jesus or a God. And to make matters worse, my wife, since the time when we came to this cursed place, has been crying and calling to her dead sister's spirit in Nez Perce Injun. There is nothing so weird or mournful in heaven, earth or hell as a wild squaw wailing for her dead. You can hear it a long way, and it haunts you for days. As her piercing wails came and went, far and near through this beautiful still valley of death, they would come echoing back in a way that made me shiver, as though in answer to her sad appeals.

This was what In-who-lise had been telling me in the Musselshell and on our way here—that if the bad Injuns and white scouts with the one-armed chief had found her father's grave, they would dig him up and scalp him and leave him lying there, like they done to those at the Big Hole battlefield, and to the dead Nez Perce whenever they could find them on their way to the Yellowstone Park. Nez Perce scouts, waiting behind to see what the white men were going to do, saw this happen. They saw them dig up the dead Nez Perce warriors and scalp them and leave them to rot in the sun. It was the worst thing that could happen to an Indian, because it affected his future spiritual life, making him an evil spirit in the dark forever. In-who-lise told me it was after this that the bad Nez Perce warriors said that they are going to kill every white man they can find and burn his tepee.

As I stood there in horror, listening to my woman's cries of grief, I thought, no matter what she says, we would leave this hell-hole of sorrow at sunrise tomorrow morning. I had enough of this place. In time In-who-lise quiets down and her wails were at an end. We went on our way back to camp, a little way up the creek from where the upper end of the Nez Perce camp had been.

In-who-lise said, "In the morning we will start back on my people's trail from here to where my father is buried. After what I see here, I am afraid that some of the bad Injuns and white men from Idaho with the one-arm chief have dug him up and scalped him. E-clew-shay [yes; surely], your woman knows it now, and can tell that this is so. Or why does her father's spirit call and whisper in sorrow to his child from the land of the dead?"

But I had enough of dead people now, and of her crying and wailing. I tried to coax her out of going. I said, "There is no use in going back out of our way. Your father is all right. It is nearly two years since then; maybe you cannot find the place where the warriors hid his grave." With tears in her eyes, she reminds me that I had promised her in the Musselshell country that I would help search for her father's grave, and see that it was left in good condition. Still not bound to go, I argued, "We have all those pack horses loaded with buffalo robes; they will be too much bother for us to pack up only to drive them there and back here again." She said we could cache the bundles of robes and other stuff we did not need, and just take the horses with us loose.

I pointed out to her that there were plenty Injun signs around here. The Big Hole was Bannock country; some of the Bannocks might find the cache. But In-who-lise was too deter-mined to have me discourage her this way. She still pleads with me, saying, "Oh, my man, surely it is not with you as the old Pend d'Oreille women in the buffalo camp said—that white men are liars, evil and bad, and that I was going to be sorry for believing An-ta-lee, with his sweet crooked tongue, that can only say sweet lies to the foolish young women in camp, and make them bad and evil like himself. A-O [yes] and that I had better watch you or I would be soon sorry that I married you. I told them they were liars; it was not so. It was their own girls that were the bad ones. I did not want to believe them." With this none too flattering send-off from my better half, what could I do but say, "All right, since you will have it so, we will go, but we cannot start tomorrow, for we must pack all those robes and other things two or three miles away from here and find a good safe place to cache them in the timber."

The next day, after we cached our store in the timber, we came back to camp. Having plenty of time, I asked In-who-lise where the soldiers and white men from the Bitterroot had made their holes in the ground that prevented the Nez Perce warriors from killing them all. She pointed to the first gulch up and across the creek, and not far from our tepee, saying with bitterness, "It is over there, where the white dogs stayed and made their holes in that gulch." I wanted her to come with me and see what was there, but In-who-lise, shivering and in terror at this request, said I must not go there; that there was now only graves and evil spirits. She said I must not go over there and leave her alone when she is afraid and her heart sad.

We started on our quest early the following morning and came to the first Nez Perce camp about twelve miles from the battlefield. It was up the valley close to the main range on a good-sized creek that emptied into Ruby Creek. It was a harder job to find the way than In-who-lise had anticipated, because she was wounded and in terror when she traveled here before.

At the first two camps we found that the pursuing troops had bivouacked. There were no signs of the graves of those who were badly wounded in the battle and had died here. Although some Nez Perce had been buried near those two camps, all signs of their graves had disappeared. The country and trail seemed changed to her since she passed over it nearly two years ago.

But in a day and a half travel, we came to where the third Nez Perce camp had been pitched. Then a new difficulty confronted us. I learned for the first time, after coming this far, that In-who-lise had not witnessed the burial at all. She had to ride on with the camp when the warriors were burying her father. She had only the directions given her by the burial party, after its return to the moving camp. Riding all day long with the rest of the wounded and others in the outfit, with a rifle shot through her shoulder, her face and lips still swollen, she had all she could endure without the additional ordeal of attending her father's funeral.

At first when I heard this, I could not help being mad at her lying and bringing me back in those hills on a wild goose chase. But she insisted that she knew how to find the place. She said her father's friends had told her the place where they buried him and Red Heart was in the first side gulch across the creek and up the trail from where the old camp lay. Her father's grave would be back of the second thicket of pines on the left side of the gulch going up where the hill reached down to the bottom of the gulch at this thicket. Pine saplings had been cut and planted on and around the grave, as if they were a part of the thicket. At the third thicket further up and across the gulch would be found another grave, that of Quiel-Spo (Red Heart). We decided to keep on going till we came to the mouth of that gulch and then camp, and hunt for the grave from there. We went across the creek and up the main trail on our way, soon coming to a side gulch, that opened up to the right, we pitched our camp at its mouth. After arranging camp and having something to eat, we started up this gulch afoot, as In-who-lise said it would not be far.

That afternoon we hunted that gulch, which was about one and a half miles long. We went up and down both sides, but found nothing. There were no thickets as had been described, nothing resembling the landmarks as pictured. It could not be the place.

It was then when Kot-kot-hi-hih (White Feather), her who the Pend d'Oreilles in the buffalo camp in the Musselshell country called In-who-lise (Broken Tooth), but better known to me as Susie, my Nez Perce wife, with her sad, patient face and dark pleading eyes, realizing that we had come all this distance for nothing, just sat down in her grief, speechless.

I could see the mute despair, the growing fear in her eyes, for she had been so confident, so sure it would be so. I knew she was seeing again the lost grave of her father, torn and desecrated by ghoulish hands, while she, after coming from afar, could do nothing to perform a sacred duty and restore her father's remains to Mother Earth, in accordance with the ancient rites of her people.

For several moments she sat in silent despair, then her pent-up feelings gave away to a flood of tears. Again as at the Big Hole battlefield, her wails of sorrow rang out up and down through this silent gulch, but this time to come back to us reverberating from the towering hills, as though a thousand voices of evil and malice, the friends of hell were laughing and mocking her grief. Standing by her side, helpless, I felt that it would not take much more to cause me to join in the mourning. Finally, I lifted her to her feet and, as we stood there among those hills, I felt that I wanted to find the grave of Gray Eagle as badly as she did. I said, "Don't cry, we will find him yet; we now must go back to camp and tomorrow we will have better luck; it must be in some other gulch." She replied, "There is no use coming up here again; this is not the place and I was so sure it was."

Our walk back to camp seemed a continuous funeral for us. We said nothing to each other. After I had chased the horses up the trail so they wouldn't take the back trail in the night, keeping one of them on picket in camp, I told Susie if she had given up hope of finding her father's grave, I had not. We would look around in some of the other gulches up the trail tomorrow. She replied rather hopelessly, "Where are you going to look now in all this big country?"

Early next morning I started out to round up the horses, and following up the trail, I came to another side gulch into which the horses had gone. I followed their trail up this gulch a short way, and soon began to wonder if this was not the gulch in question. I saw that this gulch answered the description even to the thickets and was convinced that it was the right one, but I did not look for the graves. Riding on up to the low summit of the hill, I found the horses. Hastily rounding them up, I struck back for camp. I sent the horses back on the run and soon arrived there. Susie must have observed something out of the ordinary in the expression of my face, as she immediately said, "I know you have found the right place. Hurry. Eat and we will go." I told her not to be too sure of that. I merely had found what I thought was the right gulch, but not the grave of her father. While I was eating, she saddled up her horse and in her eagerness to be off would not take time for breakfast. We were soon on our way. We rode up the trail to this gulch and soon came to the second thicket of pines. Dismounting, we tied our horses.

We had no trouble in finding the grave. It had been opened, and not by bears or wolves. The half-bleached skeleton of Gray Eagle was lying alongside the shallow pit. The pine saplings had been pulled out, and were piled at one side, with most of the needles dropped off under them, showing, only too plainly, the saplings had been removed while green.

Susie saw all this, and her wailing death cry again echoed through the silent gulch and hills, saying in her grief, "Yaw, Yaw, I know now why my father's spirit came back from the land of the dead and would not let me sleep in the night. It was the one-armed white chief's bad Injun and white men Scouts, them sons of evil from Idaho who done this, they pulled him out and scalped him."

I examined the shallow pit to see if any of the trinkets or objects buried with him could be found. I scooped in the dirt with my hands, but the vandals had made a clean sweep. Nothing remained but Gray Eagle's half-bleached skeleton with a few wisps of long hair. I could not tell if he had been scalped, but In-who-lise was sure that he had, or why had they dug him up? Also, why was the most of his hair gone? He had been sewed in a blanket In-who-lise said and with him had been placed several articles, among them an old cap and ball navy six shooter, and there were copper wire bracelets of three or four coils on his wrists.

I now proposed that we look for the grave of Red Heart and then return to camp for the ax, as I would have to make some kind of a shovel. After she got over her wailing, I succeeded in getting her started for the next thicket, about seventy-five yards above and on the opposite side of the gulch from where Gray Eagle had been buried. Arriving there, we found that Red Heart also had been disinterred. It looked as though the ones who had done this had pulled him out of the loose dirt covering him, leaving the legs partly in the grave, the shoulders leaning above on the rim of the pit, and leaving the hole still full of dirt. It was an awful sight to see. No pine saplings had been stuck up on this grave and Susie did not know what objects had been buried with him. Anyway, there was nothing left in sight.

Getting our saddle horses, we returned to camp. We got there just in the nick of time. A large silver-tip bear, as much surprised as we were, came bounding out of the tepee. On seeing us, he greets us with a roar of welcome, then tore off down the trail toward the old Nez Perce camp, with our dogs who had been with us up the gulch right at his heels and making the valley resound with their wolfish howls. We found that his "Royal Nibs" had been more than busy. A saddle of venison that In-who-lise had hung on the limb of a tree had been pulled down by the bear and only the bones remained. This gent, after satisfying his appetite on venison, had been satisfying his morbid curiosity. On going into the tepee, we found the bear had made a roughhouse out of it. Our dried meat was scattered all over, with the ground and everything else white from our sack of flour. Lucky for us, the bear had dumped most of it on the blankets.

Leaving In-who-lise to pick up the dried meat and save what flour she could, I cut down a small tree and fashioned a crude shovel. We made our dinner on some of the dried meat the bear had left. During this time In-who-lise is very quiet. We were soon ready to start back, leaving our dogs this time to watch the camp.

Going back to Red Heart's grave, I scooped out all the dirt wash, but found nothing that might have been interred with him. Unlike the remains of Gray Eagle, no particle of hair was in evidence, indicating that scalping had been done, and that most effectively. I replaced the skeleton the best I could. In-who-lise would not touch anything about the graves. I filled in the earth and, knowing that nothing would disturb the remains, I dug a small pine tree and planted it at the head. Thus we left the brave Red Heart. Going back to the other grave, I cleaned it out and laid the remains of Gray Eagle therein. Kneeling by the grave, I joined In-who-lise, fervently saying all the prayers she knew in Injun. As I filled it in, In-who-lise cried pitifully and there was a welling in my own breast and a dimness came to my eyes. Mounding the earth above all that was mortal of the once stalwart Gray Eagle, I prepared to leave that hauntingly silent gulch. Susie and I stood by the low mound for a time, and after some coaxing I persuaded her to return with me to camp, leaving those two lonely graves with their bones now returned to Mother Earth, In-who-lise softly and reverently said, "In peace at last, now roam happy spirits in the land of the dead."

Going back to camp, we found everything there all right. The bear had not returned, but we still were not feeling any too good with the large grizzly in the vicinity. An hour or so before sundown, I started to round up the horses and drive them up the trail for the night. I told In-who-lise after I drove the horses away, I was going to ride on ahead further up the valley hunting for deer, as the bear had eaten up all our fresh meat. In-who-lise told me not to stay away too long, as she is now afraid to stay alone in camp with that big Sim-a-hi hanging around. She knows he is a bad one and that we have not seen the last of him.

After trying to quiet her fears, I drove the horses up to the mouth of the gulch. The grass was better than in the valley, and I would be sure to find them here in the morning. After turning the horses into the gulch, I rode on ahead still following the old trail the Nez Perce had made in the valley for a mile or more. There were plenty of deer signs, but no deer. I only seen two woodchucks. The air was sultry, not a breath of a breeze could be felt. The heat was oppressive; all is quiet and still as death. Suddenly the sky is overcast with a mighty shadow and I could see far away on the horizon and back in the towering hills, misty black clouds are obscuring the setting sun. When now there came a vivid

flash of lightning out of those black clouds accompanied by
a distant rumble of thunder, which warned me that a rainstorm was on the way. Disgusted at my hunting luck, I
turned my horse around and started back the way I came.
Passing the mouth of the gulch, I could see the horses about
a hundred yards away, grazing with their heads turned up
the gulch and good for all night.

It is a curious though well-known fact that the deer family, including antelope, elk and moose, like the company of
horses or cattle, and will come out of their haunts to mingle
with them in a friendly way. It was an easy matter for a
mounted hunter to ride up close to them. Among the horses
I could see three blacktail deer, two large does with young
fawns, besides a young doe, a fawn of last year. Sitting as still
as a statue in the saddle, I let my horse graze his way till close
to the horses. I plugged the young doe in the neck, and the
report of my rifle rang out through the gulch. The other two
does, with their fawns at their heels, took off up the gulch in
wild leaps and bounds. Not waiting to remove the entrails, I
threw the young doe up on my saddle horse, and rode into
camp holding it in the saddle in front of me.

I was surprised to see that, during my absence, In-who-
lise had been working like a good fellow rustling wood, and
had enough gathered inside the tepee and outside to last a
good week. We were only going to stay for the night, but In-
who-lise was thinking that silver-tip is going to pay us
another visit before morning. When she saw the young doe
I brought back to camp, she said, "When that grizzly scents
that venison in camp, nothing will stop him except a bullet,
after he got away with our other venison so easy." She was
going to keep a fire burning in the tepee.

I was glad in one way to see the fear of the grizzly hanging around our camp. It made In-who-lise forget, for the
time being, all about her father, Gray Eagle. I had been hearing nothing but crying and wailing for her dead people,
besides attending Injun funerals every day since we came to
the Big Hole battlefield, so that I was now wrought up and

nearly as locoed as her. I thought, bad as this is, it will be a change for the better, that is if the grizzly does not claw us up.

In-who-lise prepared her bonfire, all ready to touch off. Since it began to drizzle, she covered the wood pile with saddle blankets. While she was doing this, I cleaned and skinned the deer, giving our dogs their share, and a good-sized chunk to In-who-lise to broil over the coals for our supper. I threw a lariat over a high limb of a tree and hauled the remaining venison up to the limb, thinking if that bear wants that venison, this time he is going to have to climb for it, and grizzlies are too big to climb. It was now dusk and still drizzling. I wrapped the entrails, liver and head in the deer hide, and went up the trail a hundred yards. I bent down a good-sized sapling and fastened the whole works to it as a peace offering to the grizzly. When the sapling sprung up straight, the bundle hung too high for our dogs to reach. Still, it would be easy for the bear to bend down the sapling and get it. I could not decide what to do with my saddle horse. First, I was going to picket him close enough to the tepee. I could cut the lariat and let him go in case of trouble, but I thought that the horse picketed in camp would only be in the way of the dogs and more liable to get shot up than the bear. I did not think the grizzly would tackle the horse on picket outside of camp, so I took him a good seventy-five yards and picketed him extra good so that he couldn't pull the picket pin if he smells that bear.

By the time I got back to the tepee it was dark and heavy rain was beginning to fall; it became a continual downpour, with fierce gusts of wind coming and going. Vicious flashes of lightning cut across the sky and lit up the night like day. The closeness of the terrific thunder claps told us only too well that the lightning had struck nearby. This, with the heavy beating of the rain against the tepee, made us think at least we were lucky not to be out in that storm and had a good stout tepee to keep us warm and dry.

I was hungry and tired, after being on the go since daylight this morning. Susie had finished broiling the venison

for our supper and along with it had made coffee and frying-pan bread. The bread contained considerable fine gravel
and sand that Susie had raked up with the flour, but I was
now used to squaw cooking and it tasted good.

I cleaned both of my rifles, and loaded them and laid
them down where I could get them quick and handy. The
patter of the rain together with the warmth from the fire in
the tepee soon makes one drowsy. Though Susie was nod-
ding from the want of sleep, she is still squatting squaw fashion on the blankets and robes on the bed at my feet, and says
she ain't going to bed with that grizzly around and take a
chance on the fire dying out. I dropped off to sleep and must
have been asleep for some time, when she nudged me. I
awoke to find the rain and storm had ceased as quickly as it
came. Except for the low half whines and growls coming
from our dogs outside, all is quiet. Susie is whispering,
"Wake up. Don't you hear the dogs? Like us, they are afraid.
They are telling us that Sim-a-hi is coming. Yaw-yaw, we
should have camped some other place. Now the dogs will
make him mad and he will kill both of us." In-who-lise rakes
the coals and puts wood on the fire and soon had the tepee
lit up as bright as day. Grabbing the carbine, I lifted the
tepee flap to look outside. A streak of light from the fire
gleams past me into the dark, but all else is darkness. I could
see nothing, not even the tree where the venison was hanging; I could see nothing wrong outside. I went back and sat
down on the foot of the bed with In-who-lise, and it was not
long till either the heat of the fire or the suspense had the
sweat rolling off both of us. Then, through the night air
come snorts of terror from my saddle horse, followed by the
piercing whistling noise a wild horse makes to warn and call
the others for help. And we could hear him plainly as he
would stamp the ground with a forefoot, then would dash
madly around in a circle the length of the lariat, trying to
pull the picket pin and get away. Susie was nagging me to go
outside and start the bonfire near the tepee door. I kept saying maybe the bear won't come; to wait till he did. It would

be plenty of time then. Time slowly went by, and the horse on picket was quiet again, but the dogs kept up their low moaning growls, some distance from the tepee, but no bear had showed up.

I began to get brave, and said to In-who-lise that all our scare over that bear was for nothing. I was going back to bed. If the grizzly was going to show up, he would not have taken all this time since the dogs first started to growl; he would have been here long before this. In-who-lise disputes this, saying I can go to bed if I want to, but it won't be for long. That grizzly will come yet. He has been all this time eating the guts I had hung up on the sapling. After he is through, he will want the venison hanging in camp; a big bear like him eats plenty.

Then, as though to make her words come true, we heard the fierce wolfish snarls and yelps from our dogs. We got the surpise of our lives when three of our younger dogs came bounding through the loose tepee flap as though they had been fired out of a catapult. They were in terror with their tails between their legs, the hair along their backs standing up like porcupine quills as they growl and snarl, looking back the way they came. The sudden appearance of the three young dogs, the way they came bounding into the tepee did not improve my courage any. It sent my heart up in my mouth, and brought the sweat beads of despair out on my temples and forehead. I grasped the loaded carbine, my teeth beginning to chatter, like I was getting the swamp ague. I carefully and cautiously peeked outside, but like before in the pitchy darkness I could see nothing. I whispered to In-who-lise to get me a good live firebrand out of the fire. Still holding the rifle, I crawled outside and pulled the saddle blankets off the pile of wood. I swung the firebrand around till it burst in flames, and stuck it down in the dry leaves and twigs under the pile and quickly dodged back into the tepee. I crouched out of sight, looking out through the tepee flap, carbine in hand, with the buffalo gun lying close to my knees. Everything being wet around the pile of

wood, it seemed ages before the kindlings took fire. At first
from the pile there only came dense clouds of smoke that
hugged the damp ground and rose up to hide even the light
that gleamed for a ways outside the tepee fire. But soon
there were small flames, and it was with some relief when I
seen the whole pile was a crackling burst of flames. As they
rose up higher, they lit up the pitchy darkness in a circle of
bright light for some distance around.

My joy was short-lived when I could see the tree where
the venison was hanging. What I saw under that tree was not
encouraging. It must have surprised that bear as much as it
did me. Anyway, the grizzly stood under the tree, large as life
and twice as natural, and any fool could tell he doesn't like
this a little bit. He stood his ground, all humped up ready to
scrap, with the hair on his back standing up. He stood gazing
and sniffing toward the bonfire, then would utter fierce
growls. As In-who-lise and I crouch inside, watching all this,
our terror soon changed to sighs of relief, when, as though he
despised us, and as though we were not worthy of his notice
any longer, he calmly and deliberately squats his huge bulk
down on his haunches. He still faced the bonfire and once in
a while would lift up his head and sniff up at the venison
hanging on the limb. We could see him plainly, not over seventy-five feet away, and it would have been easy to plug him
with the buffalo gun. The only thing that is bothering me
now was whether I could lay him out for good the first shot.
I did not want to wound him, when in five or six bounds, fire
or no fire, we would have a mad grizzly on top of us. I
decided to shoot him in the head, but as I started to raise up
the gun, In-who-lise pushed the gun down. The grizzly was
still sitting contented on his haunches under the tree.

We ought to have known that everything was coming
along too good to be true. Suddenly I saw a flash of gray
come out of the darkness behind the grizzly. It was so quick
I knew it was Spe-lee, the treacherous and vicious wolf-dog,
mean and large as any wolf. Spe-lee in her sneaking way
fears nothing that has its back turned to her. She had given

the grizzly a snapping nip on his rump. The grizzly roared with rage, and at the same time half turning sends his mighty paw with its long claws swishing through the air at her, but is too late as Spe-lee was not there. This was now a busy time for the grizzly. Another wolfish form came springing at him out of the darkness. It is Callo-o-too (Short Tail), another of our Injun dogs with all the sneaking propensities of his wolfish ancestors. Quick as a flash he nips the grizzly on the other side and disappears into the darkness quicker than he came. Spe-lee and him are resenting in their own way the grizzly running them out of camp. With surprising agility, the grizzly springs into action, crunching his teeth in rage. With an active springy motion that was surprising for one so clumsy looking, he hurled himself off into the darkness. It developed into a running fight between our dogs and the grizzly. The grizzly chased the whole bunch around near the tepee; one of the dogs would come dashing in between the bonfire and the tepee and would try to get inside with us. I quickly prodded him, yelping back outside, with my gun barrel. It went this way for some time; we were badly scared. In-who-lise has the carbine and I the buffalo gun, with one of us crouching on each side of the flap, the sweat pouring off us from the heat of the bonfire. To make it worse, we could plainly hear above the howls and snarls of our dogs, the roars of anger from the grizzly every time a dog would nip him. Then would come the crashing and tearing as he chases after the dogs through the willows and brush on each side of the small creek behind our camp. Around and around they went, with us terror-stricken and every minute expecting the dogs and the grizzly to come crashing through the back of the tepee on top of us. We were not sorry when we seen our seven dogs go flying by in a scattered bunch in retreat and take off up the trail toward the old Nez Perce camp, with the grizzly bounding along a few yards behind them in hot pursuit, all disappearing in the darkness.

I whispered to In-who-lise that we are lucky them dogs for once in their lives done what was right, when they did not try to run inside the tepee with us, and that I hoped the Sim-a-hi would chase them as far as the Big Hole battlefield. I ought to have known that praising the dogs and grizzly would only bring us bad luck again. My face must have turned a sickly white as I heard yelping draw nearer and nearer, leaving no doubt that the grizzly was after one of the dogs and coming back this way. In-who-lise starts to say something, but the words never left her lips. Now out of the darkness into the circle of murky light leaps one of our young dogs, howling as he came on the dead run, and thirty feet behind him came the grizzly. The dog made a beeline for the bonfire, and with an acrobatic leap clears the bonfire and lands straight as an arrow almost in the tepee door, with one of his sides bleeding badly. Howling in pain and terror, he bounded into the tepee, striking In-who-lise square in the breast, knocking her over on the flat of her back, with her head almost in the fire, her legs going up in the air. In-who-lise, as she was going over, must have pulled the trigger of the carbine. The gun went off with a loud bang, filling the tepee with powder smoke, and worse than that, the bullet came near getting me, singing by close to the back of my neck. The hot powder smoke singed a part of my hair and blackened my cheek. The dog goes by the fire and stands whining and cringing on the bed and robes, with the blood dripping down from his side where the bear had ripped him. All I can say was that hell sure broke loose in our house! At the report of the gun, like a clap of thunder close to my face, first I thought I was shot forgetting all about the grizzly outside and letting the gun drop out of my hand, with a howl of terror that put the dog to shame, wildly I clapped my hand up to my tingling ear and cheek to feel if there was blood. By this time In-who-lise had got up on her knees and is furious. She dealt the dog a smashing blow across the ribs with the butt of the carbine that made him howl worse than the raking he had got from the grizzly. The dog came crawling up behind me. This only took an instant. Feeling my ear and cheek, I knew that I was not hit. What little nerve I had before this was now gone. A glance outside across the bonfire was enough and brought the slobbers of fear running out of both corners of my mouth. I sure had to be thankful to In-who-lise for rustling all that wood, and thinking about building that campfire outside. If that fire was not there, the grizzly would have made sausage meat out of us by now.

I could see him better now; he was not over twenty feet away. He must have weighed nine hundred pounds. He stands there, the incarnation of all that is powerful and terrible, his vicious eyes red, glaring with hatred and venom at us across the fire. The short, pointed ears are flattened back on his broad head. His powerful jaws open and shut, uttering vicious snarls, exposing his long yellow fangs that he crunches and snaps in his furious anger. He throws up his head, sending terrific roars of rage reverberating through the night. His unwieldy-looking body is now animated; it quivers and sways with seething life, making him terrible to behold, a monarch of the brute world in all his mighty strength. He works and braces his hind legs in unison with his powerful front legs as though he is about to spring; his front paws open and shut in their fury, tearing up the grass and ground under them, with his long sharp claws.

The loaded buffalo gun is forgotten, though still on the ground at my knee. I was petrified, as though in some horrible nightmare, unable to resist or help myself. The grizzly's eyes are on mine, gleaming like two vivid coals of fire—compelling, penetrating. Some irresistible force in them draws and holds mine on them. There is a weird uncontrollable fascination for me in them gleaming bloodshot eyes and red-gaping, frothy mouth, with its bared fangs.

The thousand thoughts and acts of a lifetime flashed through my mind in a furious jumble. I do not believe the man lives who could express all of this swift drama of horror. The terror I felt is not to be conveyed by pen or words. I can only say that in those few seconds that seemed ages, I paid with compound interest for all the deviltry that I had ever done.

Time and again I made frantic efforts to lift up the buffalo gun; but my arms shook and my trembling hands are powerless. The gun refuses to budge and seems fastened to the ground. The grizzly has me mesmerized. My lips are now dry and feverish; my tongue refuses to move and is stuck to the roof of my mouth.

In desperation, like a drowning person that clutches at a straw, I thought of In-who-lise. I had forgotten about her, but any fool could see that In-who-lise is a badly scared squaw, as she crouches near my side with the carbine still clutched in her trembling hands. She was now only a woman, scared speechless, with beads of sweat dripping like rain from her nose and temples. Her teeth chatter through her trembling lips. Her eyes are pleading to me to save her.

As before, I failed to lift the gun off the ground. I tried to hide my shame from her accusing eyes, but she sees the terror in my face. For an instant a look of pity swept across her face. Then her breast heaved; her lips curled in contempt as her eyes flash me a look of withering scorn.

This was the hardest blow of all. My woman, now at death's door, despises me—the only one who before this had faith and believed in me. Her accusing eyes bore through me and brought me to my senses. I quickly push the set trigger ahead and cock the hammer.

Slowly but surely I raise the gun up to my shoulder. This time my nerves are iron; the gun does not wobble or tremble while I try to catch the grizzly between the eyes. But the flickering campfire light made the front sight dance. The grizzly, in the moments that seemed a thousand years, is still uttering his roars of rage that seemed to shake the tepee and awake the valley. He kept wagging his head from side to side, still tearing up the ground with his claws. His head was too hard a shot to take a chance on. I lowered the muzzle until the top of the burnished copper front sight gleamed like a small star through the rear sight, catching the grizzly at the base of his neck. Bracing myself and pulling the gun tight against my shoulder, a slight touch on the trigger sent Betsy

Jane off with the kick of a mule and a roar that filled the tepee with smoke.

The grizzly staggered backward with a moan that seemed almost human, then rears up on his hind legs, clawing at his bleeding breast for an instant. He plunged forward, then toppled over, falling in a huddled heap, with his nose close to the campfire. His bulky form lies quiet and still across the fire from us.

Slipping in another shell, I cocked Betsy Jane and waited. Except for my heart now beating like a triphammer, everything is still as death, as I gaze exultantly at our fallen enemy. In-who-lise gets impatient; she touches me and whispers to give the grizzly a bullet in the head to make sure he was dead.

Then a slight tremor ran through the grizzly's huddled form, and In-who-lise wrings her hands in terror, screaming, "See, the Sim-a-hi is not dead! Shoot him again!" The grizzly was now moaning and gasping in pain. Slowly at first he feebly struggles, then tries to raise up his huge body off the ground, each time to roll back helpless, only to try it again. Now with a mighty effort, an awful sight to behold, groaning in pain, with the blood spurting out of the gaping bullet hole in his breast, using his front legs, slowly raises part way up on his haunches, swaying as in a drunken stupor, with his hind legs sticking out sideways paralyzed and helpless, as he feebly braces his front legs to keep from falling over. His bulky form now half sits up on his haunches, with his head lying helpless on his breast. Time and again he struggles and tries to raise his head, only for it to fall back on his breast again.

I watched the grizzly with the gun cocked and ready. I could see plainly the death haze beginning to cover his bloodshot eyes, and hear the death rattle in his throat. His fevered breath like steam came wheezing, panting, thick and fast as he gasps and utters low piteous moans of pain, and every time he coughed, a tremor shook his body, with the blood still squirting out of the gaping bullet hole, leaving his breast a crimson red, to come trickling down his front legs and dripping on the ground. The grizzly was a very sick bear.

I slowly raised the buffalo gun until the top of the front sight caught the dying grizzly between the eyes; it was with a feeling more of pity than of triumph. Pressing the trigger, Betsy Jane again went off with a roar. Without a moan, the grizzly rolled over—blood trickling out of a round hole in his forehead. A convulsive tremor ran through his body and legs as he opens and shuts his murderous claws. Then with a long sigh he stretched out in death.

A few minutes after this we stood outside viewing the bulky form. I told In-who-lise, "Here is one grizzly who will never scare the daylights out of us again." Calling the dogs to see if the grizzly had killed any of them, it was some time before they would show up. When they came, I could see that Spe-lee is limping with one side of her face bleeding; besides Callo-o-too and Ku-ton-a-can (Big Head) have more than one long bleeding slash along their sides. None of the dogs would come up to us at the campfire, on account of the dead grizzly lying there. They sat on their haunches at the edge of the light made by the fire, uttering fierce growls and sniffing over toward the dead bear.

We could now see by the grayness of the sky it would soon be daybreak. There was no use in trying to get any sleep. I put more wood on the campfire and went back in the tepee. In-who-lise, after pounding coffee berries in a rag with a rock, starts in to make coffee. She also pounded some of the dried buffalo meat that the grizzly had mauled around in the afternoon. It was as hard and tough as sole leather, but it was good stuff after it had been softened between two rocks. When the coffee was boiling, In-who-lise tries to wash the black burn off my face, but with poor success. The gun had put it in to stay till I wear it off. As she was doing this, her midnight eyes are aflame with love. Her face is wreathed in smiles of pride as she says that now I am an Injun hero. As soon as it is daylight and I go after the horses, she says she is going to cut off the grizzly's front claws so that she can make a hero's necklace out of them for me to wear. When the Injuns see them and she tells them how bravely I killed that grizzly, the Injuns will hold a pow-wow and christen me Sim-a-hi-chen (Grizzly Bear). Then the men will envy me and the women will be jealous of her, that she has a man who killed a grizzly, a great honor. I had plenty doubts about my being in any hero class, still I did not dispute her. Let her have her sweet dream.

We had a sumptuous repast of dried buffalo meat and straight coffee. It sure tasted good to us, who were young, had good teeth and didn't know any better.

When it got light enough to see for a short distance, I went to my saddle horse. I could see by the circle he cut in the ground during the night that he had run several miles at the end of the lariat, trying to pull the picket pin to get away. Coming into camp with him, he had a whiff of the dead grizzly lying in front of the tepee. With a snort of terror, he rears up and wheels around, taking me along with him. I held on with both hands. Being close to the horse gave him the best of it on his end of the lariat. I was swept off my feet, with the horse dragging me along like a wooden toggle, through the grass and brush at a stagecoach clip, headed for the hills. If I let the lariat run through my bare hands, it will burn my hands to the bone. If I let the lariat go, I'll lose the horse. My chance came as the horse tries to make it around a clump of willows. Being unable to pull me around the willow clump, he finds himself hung up. Still holding onto the lariat, I soon had him snubbed fast to the butt of the willow clump.

In-who-lise, hearing the racket I made cussing the horse, came running over. Both of us, after plenty more trouble, got him snubbed up to a small cottonwood tree about a hundred feet away from camp, and while this horse was otherwise gentle enough, and thought nothing of leaping over a dead buffalo, and used to running among dead buffalo in the Injun buffalo hunts; still he would not stand for a bear and, though we tried our damnedest, this was as close as we could get him into camp.

After the dragging I got, I was some sight to see. I had to pack my saddle from camp over to my horse, who is still snorting and rearing up on the short end of the lariat. After plenty more trouble, I got the saddle on him and had him cinched up.

I was now in bad humor and out to fight someone—having no one else to fight, I lit into In-who-lise, telling her them dead Injun relations of hers up in the gulch were bad medicine. That both of them, her father Gray Eagle's and Red Heart's spirits had it in for me and were out to get me, because I was a white man. I blamed them to her for all our troubles here and even accused them of putting the devil in that grizzly's head. In-who-lise only stood there and bore it all with downcast eyes and in silence. This hurt me worse than a tongue-lashing would have done.

I told her to cover the dead grizzly with saddle blankets and to burn some venison in the fire. We would never get the horses back to camp if they got a whiff of the bear. Then I rode up the trail. Giving my saddle horse the rein, he lights out at a furious lope, which just suited my humor.

As I have said, I was born down on the Rio Grande in southwest Texas and near the New Mexico line, being of Spanish-American extraction and of a people whom even at that time still clung to the manners, customs and superstitious beliefs of the Dark Ages. As a kid at home, I had been taught as the gospel truth to believe in ghosts, haunts and to dread the evil powers of witches in league with the devil, which could only be warded off by charms.

I had been living for the last ten months in a Pend d'Oreille buffalo camp, talking nothing but Pend d'Oreille and eating, sleeping and out hunting buffalo with Injuns their superstitious talks about their evil spirits of the river of death and of Indian devils that haunted certain spots, lying in wait (both day and night) for the unwary to do them evil. At night I would have to listen to some old bucks' chants to the good spirits of the air for them to bring good luck on tomorrow's hunt, while in another tepee another buck would be chanting to them to keep the evil spirits away and prevent them from scaring the buffalo away.

After a couple of days of bad luck in the hunt, then Cha-qua-lu, the Clay-quiel-ish (medicine man) would get busy and start making medicine to offset the bad luck. First he would heat the rawhide face of his Po-men-ten (drum) over the medicine fire, with the heat making it draw up as tight as a fiddle string. Then his incantations to the good spirits would start. With him soon to be joined in by the ki-yis of several other bucks. While the rest of the bucks in camp stripped down to their breechclouts, with paint and feathers on their heads, livened up this savage scene. As they furiously danced around Cha-qua-lu and the medicine fire far into the night, making enough noise to scare out of the country all the wolves, buffalo and Indian devils. Though some may laugh at this, I had imbibed some of their savage superstitions along with my own superstitious beliefs.

Now I was left alone with my thoughts, far away from the haunts of white men, amid those towering hills that rose up to the skies on all sides of me, with only the cayuses for company. I rode along, driving them ahead of me down the gulch, headed for camp.

Now that I had the time to think things over, my superstitious mind was fully aroused. I could not help thinking about the sinister way things had come to pass for me ever since yesterday morning, and that ever since then this place had been a hoodoo to Susie and I. Ever since I had returned the skeletons of Gray Eagle and Red Heart to Mother Earth, my well-intended acts must have done their spirits more harm than good. It seemed I was the intended victim of premeditated sinister acts of bad luck that were designed against me by evil forces. I dolefully soliloquized, there is surely something to this Indian talk and belief that a dead scalped warrior became forever an evil spirit in the dark. Even Susie had refused to touch the skeleton of Gray Eagle, her own father. This ought to have been warning enough for me. She need not deny that the scalped spirits of Gray Eagle

and Red Heart were now evil spirits, in cahoots with the
devil to do us up, and that all the preachers and praying
from here to hell could not do them any good now. The
more I pondered over this, the more firmly I became convinced that this gulch was haunted and the abiding place of
evil spirits. And worse still, they were out to get me! Anyone
could tell by the way that grizzly acted last night that it was
possessed of the devil. I would have been dead long before
now, but, fortunately for Susie and I, I wore tied to my neck
in a small buckskin sack a potent talisman that I had got
from Cha-qua-lu in the buffalo camp, making me immune
particularly against the machinations of any evil spirits or
Injun devils that might beset my way. Though they could
torment me, still yet they could not destroy me. To afford
me greater security, as those evil spirits and Injun haunts
were hard to see and harder still to hit with a bullet, I had a
charm of weasel skin and raven feathers tied to the trigger-
guard of my carbine. Cha-qua-lu fully guaranteed I could
hit anything I aimed at.

As I approached with the cayuses closer to the graves, all
reverence for Gray Eagle and Red Heart vanished, to be
replaced by a superstitious dread that bordered on panic.
What other kind of eviltry had they in store for me? Would
Cha-qua-lu's powerful charms save me next time or would
they get out of this accursed gulch? As though to add to my
torture, the horses in the lead, as they came up to the small
pine thicket where lay Red Heart's grave, seeing the fresh
dirt mound, came to a halt. With their suspicions aroused,
they refused to go past Red Heart's grave and stood there
sniffing and snorting, ready to wheel around and stampede
back up the gulch. Again I sweat some, and I was not any too
sorry to see them continue in the right direction. The rest of
the bunch behind, with a whistling snort and shying bolt,
wildly sprang by Red Heart's grave, bucking and squealing
and following the leaders. As soon as the last cayuse shied by
Red Heart's grave, I gave my saddle horse the quirt, and in a
bound or two I sent him flying, with me wildly riding up to

the rear ones, furiously slashing at them with my quirt. I kept them on the run. Leaping, snorting and shying, they went past Gray Eagle's grave, and I kept them on the dead run until they came out of the gulch and onto the main trail in the valley. None too sorry that I was leaving behind this hoodoo gulch forever, casting glances behind me, as though the devil was still after me, I sent the cayuses flying down the trail until I came near camp. Susie was safe and anxiously awaiting my return. This was one time that my little squaw sure looked good to me. She helped me to turn in and rope the cayuses in the little corral that she had made by tying and stretching the lash ropes from one tree to another.

Susie was now as willing to leave here as I was, for she had everything packed up for our immediate departure. So after our meager breakfast it did not take us long to saddle up the cayuses and pack up. Leaving the dead grizzly lying there, I headed my cayuse down the trail, followed by the pack cayuses in single file. As I was starting off, I watched Susie out of the corner of my eye, to see what she would do, now that we are leaving here. When after a glance or two in the direction of the gulch in which all that was once mortal of her father lay, she swung her saddle pony around and came on behind, driving the bunch.

CHAPTER THIRTY-ONE
The Only Way Out is to Fly

The second day after we returned to the battlefield after burying Susie's father and Red Heart, we were prowling through the willows and found a lance that some Indian must have used in the fight. The long handle was broken off, about a foot of the handle remaining with the lance head. I did not care for it then—maybe I was superstitious. Anyway, my wife was, and she said, "No, you shall not take away that what is of some dead warrior of my people. He may want it yet, he may come back from the land of the dead for it, and then, if it is gone, he will do evil things to us." "All right," I told her, "we will hide it in this clump of willows for him, or some white man surely will find it," and we hid it there. Many times since I have thought of my good, little squaw and wondered if anyone ever found that lance head. When I started to write this book about her, I knew that I ought to go to the Big Hole, but kept putting it off, as I thought, "What is the use in going there—it will only make me more sorry for her." But, in the fall of 1930, I finally found I would have to go there to refresh my memory.

I went down to the Indian camp place and knew right away where I was. At the monument I asked if I could look over the field. I was told, "You are right in it." I said, "This is only a part of the battlefield, where the white men dug in after the Nez Perces licked the hell out of them. I want to go down in the creek bottom where Gibbon's bunch shot up the bucks and murdered the squaws and papooses. I used to have a squaw that was in this battle. I came here with her in 1879, and I know this place and where I want to go."

"I will go along with you," he said, and he did. He came along to try to learn something about those places. I went back there on the sly in a few days and did my work in peace, though I felt like crying when doing it. I hunted for the lance head, and without much trouble located it in that clump of willows. The lance was rusted badly and I had a hard time getting it out of the willows, as the blade was two feet long and as the old willows had died, the young shoots had grown up and wedged it in. The men at the monument did not try to take the lance away from me. I brought it home.

In-who-lise and I left the Big Hole battlefield in June, 1879, on our way to the Bitterroot Valley, and I was glad to leave this charnel house of sorrow. When we came to a fork in the trail, I started to take the left, or white men's trail. In-who-lise, driving the pack horse behind, said, "No, not that way. Turn right and take the Injun trail, the way my people came over here."

I told her the two white men* at the battlefield had told me not to take the Injun trail, that it was full of fallen trees. Susie flies in a rage at this, and starts crying, "Yes, it is now always white men with you, when you know I hate them— them evil white men who helped to kill my people. E-ah, they would have killed you this morning if it were not for your woman's sharp eyes and the gun in her hands. After all of their evil, you are still listening to them, and no more heed the voice of your woman."

Without saying a word, I swung my horse around and headed up the old Injun trail. At first the trail was not bad, as this part of the country was fairly open and flat. Making good time, it was not long till we came to the camp in the pines where the Nez Perce women cut tepee poles to bring with them to the buffalo country nearly two years before this.

In-who-lise, penitent for the tongue-lashing she had given me, wants to make up. Failing at this, she starts in at her old trade, wailing for her people, and said that we must camp here. But I was still mad at her for making me take the Injun trail. Knowing that if we camp here, it will only be for

---

* A lengthy account of this meeting has been omitted. The names of the white men were Seymore and Heltd.

me to attend another Injun funeral, I said, "I am the man, and no woman tells the man where to camp. It is a long day yet; we keep on going."

The trail still was not bad, but I was soon to find out that a good beginning means a bad end. The closer to the summit we came, the thicker the lodge poles grew, until they were as thick as the hair on a dog's back. Tall and majestic, they stood so thick that the sun never shone on the ground. It was a continual jumping of fallen trees across the trail.

Our horses were prairie horses, and not used to dodging through the thick timber with bulky packs. They would rub the lash rope off the corners of the *aparejos,* and get hung up between the trees. I had been on trails in timber, but had never been in anything like this. We came to logs across the trail that my saddle horse refused to jump. I gave Susie the dickens for getting us into a jackpot like this.

In-who-lise said scornfully that this was a good Injun trail and that I did not know much if I could not get my horse through a good trail like this. I told her that it was up to her to get us through. She could lead, and I would drive behind, till we came out in God's country again.

Before this I had heard the story of the American who rode his horse till he was exhausted and fell down on the trail, and, do as he would, the American could not get him up to go any further. Leaving him there, he went on his way. It was only a few minutes later when along comes an Injun. The Injun, in some brutal way known only to Injuns, gets the weary and played-out horse up on his feet, mounts and rides ten miles further, when again the horse fell down exhausted. Do as the Injun would, he could not get the horse up again. Failing in this, in disgust he went on his way. Before the Injun got out of sight, along the trail comes a Mexican, who on seeing the almost dead horse lying by the trail, said to himself, "*Gracias a Dios,* but this is good. Never yet did a Mexican walk when there was a good horse like this lying by the trail for him to ride." The Mexican now like the Injun, and by other brutal means known only to Mexicans, gets this nearly dead horse up on his feet, mounts and goes on his way with him, making ten miles and was congratulating himself on what a good horse he had when the horse, much to the disgust of the Mexican, fell dead on the trail.

Just why this slur was put on the Mexican is hard to say. While the Mexican is a hard rider, there are few people except the Arabs who have a greater love and affection for Allah's pride the horse than the Mexican. I was to find out today, and many times after that the Injun has no affection, gratitude or pity for the horse. Many times after this, I was thankful that, of all things on this earth, I was not born an Injun's horse.

In-who-lise, being now in the lead, needs no second bidding to make her words good. Cutting herself a pine sapling the size of a fish pole, she came up behind my saddle horse who had refused to leap over this fallen tree up to his breast across the trail. One crack from the sapling by In-who-lise was enough. With a snort of terror as the blow landed on his rump, he rears up and like a steeplechaser cleared the fallen tree. As each one of the pack horses came up to the fallen tree she could come down on him with her pole, and over the high log he went.

As we went along, sometimes the fallen trees across the trail would be higher, and the pack horses could not make it the first time, an extra crack or two from In-who-lise, then the poor brutes who could not turn around to get away would rear up, getting their front feet over and scramble over on their bellies. It was not long till all of our horses were bruised and skinned up, besides having long welts on them, where In-who-lise hit them with her pole.

The trail kept getting worse. I told her that I had had enough of this brutality. Telling her to get behind where women rightly belonged, I said that I could do better than her, without having to bruise and smash our horses up.

With Susie sulking behind, we came to a place where I could see that, by cutting a couple of the fallen trees out of the way, we could get out of this eternal windfall into what looked like open timber. I thought we could make it this way and thought I was doing fine.

Soon Susie said, "You are going the wrong way already, and soon we will be turned around and lost among all those trees that look alike."

I told her that I was doing this, and that she should drive them cayuses along faster, so that we could get back on the trail.

I kept on going making good time. Whenever the trees got too thick and blocked me, I could swing off and find another opening that led another way, still thinking that I would find another opening in the thick trees where I could swing back in the right direction.

Susie is still nagging me to turn back to the Injun trail before it is too late. The third time she rode ahead to me, she said that I was lost even if I thought that I was not.

Finally she said, "If An-ta-lee my man will not heed my voice, when I know I am right in this, he can go on his own trail, and I go on mine. Your woman goes no further with you this way. I am going back to the Injun trail and leave you here."

Instead of this threat making peace between us it got worse, and in the end it wound up with me telling her to get back to the Injun trail if she wanted so bad to leave me here, that I would be well rid of her and glad to see her go.

At first In-who-lise did not believe I meant this. But when I offered to whack up everything we had, she refused, saying, "Then if An-ta-lee my man wants me no more, I want nothing from him." With her head bowed down to hide the tears, turning her horse around, she silently rode off, leaving me in this dark timber, to get out the best way I could, with eleven horses packed and six loose besides my saddle horse. Though I would not admit this to her, I knew now that I was lost.

Putting all the blame on her for this, I thought I was well rid of her, as I bitterly thought, "Just let me get out of here. Then it's back to the Injun buffalo camps, in the Musselshell and Milk River country, no more of this tall timber country for me."

I had been told by the wise ones that there was nothing to it when lost in the woods. "Don't get excited," they said, "sit down and compose yourself." In this way I sat down talking to myself, anathematizing the squaws in general, telling my audience, our seven Injun dogs who are wagging their tails around me, that they are the only friends I now had left, and for them to take a warning from this—to beware of the she stuff.

But as the time went by and the shadows of the approaching night deepened, I missed something, and kept looking back the way In-who-lise had gone, as though expecting to see her coming back like she always did in the end. But no In-who-lise showed up when I needed her bad. Still darker deepened this silent forest of lodge pole pines. It was then that grave doubts began to assail me from all sides; they are whispering what struck terror in my heart, saying with an evil leer, "She is never coming back to you. This is the time you drove her off once too often."

Then I realized the trouble I was in with all this stock to drive, in this forest of trees that all look alike, and, worse still, seems to have no end. The more I thought of this, the worse my terror got. I would go now before it got too late to overtake her and beg her to come back.

Leaving our dogs there, with some of the horses tied, taking my carbine along, I start off afoot, and had only gone a little way when I noticed for the first time, that even with all the horses we had along with us, they left no sign of a trail on the pine needles under the trees.

I ran back to the horses and, discarding my rifle for an ax, I was quickly on my way again, putting a blaze on the trees here and there to keep from getting lost from the horses. I just had to find In-who-lise to pull me out of this. If I could just get my eyes on her once more, never would I be mean to her again. I would be her humble slave all my life.

Climbing over and crawling under the fallen trees, I surely was lost, but suddenly, much to my joy, I heard a horse snuffle. Crawling to where the sound came from, coming out of the windfall, I nearly ran into In-who-lise. She was squatting beside her horse near a fallen tree, a picture of woe with her head bowed down on her knees. Sometimes she would raise her head, and I could see that she was silently crying. Crawling back out of her sight, I lay there watching her. At first I wanted to go and give her a grizzly-bear hug, and my conscience is telling me, "Squaw Kid, you are a damned brute when you do this to the only true friend you have."

But the spirit of evil said, "Don't listen to them foolish thoughts. That fool woman is going to come back to you like she always did. No use in spoiling her. If you coax her, then she will do this she thing every chance she gets, just to make you run after her."

I listened to the voice of evil as usual, saying, "Me humble myself to her? Not on your life. I will see all the squaws in hell first. I will teach her to pull off any more stunts like this."

Hand in hand with the devil, I had no trouble following the blazes, going quickly to arrive at the horses before Susie got back, and found them and the dogs all right. As I expected, In-who-lise soon rode up, and is all sheepish smiles.

She got off her horse and, coming up to me, I could see the sorrow in her eyes. She said, "No, I did not come back to stay. I came back to see if you are sorry like I am. Do you still like me, or do you want me to go away?"

Then I knew my deviltry had gone far enough. In-who-lise had come back to make up. Standing there watching me with sad despair, I could tell that she had made up her mind that this was the end, one way or the other. Her face is now expressionless, her dark eyes now stern and inscrutable.

Once more the spirit of good won out. I swore to God, like I had done many times before, only this time I meant it, that there was no other woman like her to me. The black clouds have cleared away. Hope and love are again beaming in her midnight eyes, as she said never again will she forget her words to Colon Suten and the E-qui-lix, that she would follow her man on his way till the end of the trail.

We camped there, since it was not too dark to travel. The horses were tied to the trees with nothing to eat, and, worse still, without a drink since we left the last Nez Perce camp. Taking the packs off, unrolling our robes and blankets, we ate some dried buffalo meat, and went to sleep without a fire. Susie said it was too dangerous for fires with the thick pine needles under the trees and no water. The horses, hungry and dry as they were, were restless and pawed the ground all night.

At the break of day we were packing up, and soon on our way. I said to In-who-lise that it was up to her to lead the way and pull us out of this. She declined that honor, saying that she was turned around and lost herself, that any way was as good as another now.

On we went through this seeming endless forest of lodge pole pines. Sometimes they were tall, large and majestic, and for a way looked as though they had been planted in rows a certain distance apart by the hand of man. Again we came to thickets of them where they grew tall and slim and so thick and close together, it would have bothered a man afoot to work his way through them. On we went only to run into windfalls, making us swing in another direction. On we went over ridges, and across gulches in this eternal shade. Not a sign of wild life had we seen, no grass or water had we found and only pine needles that in some places carpeted the ground nearly a foot deep. On we went, to tell you the truth, I don't know where. This way and that with only one wish, that will show us an opening between the trees, how to get out of this lodge pole forest that seems to have no end, to where we can find water and grass for the horses and a drink for ourselves.

It must have been near the middle of the day. Yes, God is good, when through a kind of an opening we could see some distance above us bare rocky hills with scattering trees here and there. If we could make it and get up there on the hill, we might be able to tell where we were. We came out of it at last. Taking what looked to be the easiest way, we started sidling to make it to the top, so that we could see over the timber. On our way we found a small rivulet made by snow water, where the horses and us got a drink, the first since before noon yesterday. We came to small patches of buck brush and bear grass, and would let the horses stop to eat. The buck brush was not so bad, but bear grass is too tough and wiry and sour for stock to eat if they can get anything else. Still our hungry horses went at it; it was so tough they sometimes pulled a mouthful out by the roots, and thought it good.

Up we went sidling along this long range of hills, and soon we began to see over a part of the tops of the trees of this forest we had been lost in. It took us some time the way we went, with the horses eating here and there before we reached the top.

Coming to the top nothing entered my mind, except a bitter curse. Where to find a place to get down and back out of here, without having to go through that lodge pole forest again! Every way we could see on both sides of this ridge below us for miles stood out this belt of green trees, between the Big Hole and Ross's Hole on the Bitterroot side. From here not an opening could we see.

Squaw men have been accused of about all the crimes there are, except of being poetical and dreamers, but I must tell you that it was some sight to see and was probably never duplicated before or after this, superb in its gigantic splendor, the mighty mountain peaks in all directions as far as the eye can see, and the bullheaded An-ta-lee and the ornery In-who-lise away up there sometimes almost in the clouds. The scenery was grand even if you can't eat it, as they went on their way, riding along on the Continental Divide, the backbone of the Rocky Mountains, driving a pack train and their several loose horses, all their worldly wealth, including seven Injun dogs.

In this way sometimes the going was good, other times bad, as on we went, sometimes up, more times down, again it would be across and over rock slides to wind up on a rocky sideling where a false step of your horse would send you and him rolling and crashing to land down on some rocky canyon a quarter of a mile below, getting by this only to go skirting over loose rock slides around the base of some rocky peak that towered above us, its crests gleaming white with snow, winding our way around this only to run into something far worse and hair-raising.

Time and again we crossed over the ridge from the Big Hole side to the Ross's Hole side, looking down for a way to get down from here and find an opening through the timber below. There was none that we could see, and the only way to get down from here now without going back the way we got up here is to fly. And I should have known that no woman would keep her word of honor, when it comes to keeping her mouth shut, for In-who-lise has broken her word to me, and now again bewails our sad lot. She wants to know where I am headed for, saying it will be better for us to turn back the way we came and try to make it back to the Big Hole Valley through the lodge pole forest, then take the white men's trail this time. Sometimes as she drives the pack and loose horses along, In-who-lise to relieve her feelings is crooning an Injun funeral dirge, but was soon smiling and happy again, when we came on a long stretch of country that was good going. Then our luck changed for the worse again. We came to a divide where this ridge was broken in two, while maybe more than three hundred feet below us lay quite a flat that connected the ridge we were on with the ridge on the other side. Down in this dismal hole were several scrubby pines, bear grass and buck brush.

We had a hell-roaring time, getting down into this hole. It was swift going as long as it lasted. We found ourselves standing on a large slide of gravel, shell rock and sand, at the base of a bluff that rose up and frowned down on us more than a hundred feet high. It stood there almost straight up and down, with its thousands of tons of gravel, shell rock and sand honeycombed into many fantastic shapes. All of them standing there and looking as though a person had only to blow his breath on some of those towering structures of wash to make them topple over and come tumbling down.

Below was the accumulation of many years' cave-ins of them bluffs. We came upon the head of the slide, and, seeing this was the only way to get down, we did not stay long.

I told In-who-lise to say quickly all the prayers she knows in Injun, and for her to watch her saddle horse's step, and not let him get sideways with her, if the slide started to run.

Starting down the slide on the lead, with the horses following down in a long string, we were going at a good fast clip, the horses with their rumps high above their heads, with their front feet braced ahead of them, with the wash up to their bellies, each horse pushing waves of loose gravel, shell rock and sand ahead of it. Down the plunging horses went toward the bottom, accompanied by waves of rattling gravel and shell rock, the sand in it making clouds of dust, that hid what was before or behind. The horses on the lead finally struggled out of the wash onto the flat.

But on looking up the slide, through the rifts in the floating dust, it is with horror I can see that In-who-lise is still not halfway down the slide and that there are several horses still strung out ahead of her. And not far behind her came a large wave of wash that came swishing down from them tottering bluffs and now caught up with her terrified saddle horse. In-who-lise was bravely holding him from getting sideways when the terror-stricken brute rears up and plunges down the slide with her, landing sideways in the fast-moving slide with her still in the saddle, and was quickly swept off his feet and covered over with running wash. In-who-lise leaps out of the saddle on the up hillside, as her horse rolled over. Coming down this way to the bottom, her horse quickly struggled to his feet, and lost no time in rejoining the rest of the horses that were already rambling over the flat, looking for grass or brush to fill up on.

In-who-lise did not have as good luck coming down as her horse did. Springing wildly into the running wash at the bottom, I tried my best to make it up a ways, to try to meet and help her, but for every step I tried to make in the cursed stuff I lost two, and was pushed back out on the flat. Finally, the oncoming wash spreading out more as it reached the bottom, I was lucky enough to be able to grab In-who-lise by the arm as she was coming by. I got her up on her feet, but it was only for an instant, it seemed, when another wave of wash came swishing down into us, and taking us along with it, as we struggled and clung to each other to keep from falling down. We were shoved and pushed along with the wash, a good fifty feet further out on the flat, among some of the scrubby pine trees, and, lucky for us, to where we were able to scramble to safety. All covered with dust, her hair, eyes and ears full of sand, In-who-lise was some sight to see, but, lucky for us, had only a few scratches here and there.

She wished now that she had let me take the white men's trail, from the Big Hole battlefield to the Bitterroot Valley.

I told her not to be down in the mouth for a little thing like this. If we lived through a few more days in this awe-inspiring country, it was going to make a mountain man out of me yet. Besides it was root-hog-or-die with us now, for no horse was ever made that could climb up that slide and back up on the ridge.

Finding a good spring of water and plenty of wood, with some buck brush and a tough sour grass for the tired horses, we went into camp for the night. The packs and *aparejos* were off for the first time in two days. In-who-lise crooned a plaintive ditty, squatting cooking by a roaring fire, with a motherly look on her scratched face. Our campfire sent its beams in a friendly way far out in the night, adding a home-like appearance to this weird scene.

Nearly all night long, as though misery likes company, gusts of wind came passing over us, from someplace on their way across this divide, sighing and moaning, as though a delegation of lost souls were passing by on their way to hell. In the intervals we could hear a large hoot owl using profane language. The moon and stars gleaming on the white snow on the surrounding peaks lit up the night almost like day.

At the break of day the ground was gray with frost. In-who-lise was cooking breakfast, as I moved shivering with the biting cold, putting the *aparejos* on the huddled and shivering pack horses. After investigating both sides of this divide, the only way that was left to us was the main ridge east out of this hole. We soon found ourselves back up, as it looked, a stone throw from the clouds, and looking back we could tell that ever since we started yesterday we had been going higher up in altitude. The mountain peaks we had dodged yesterday were only the babies of the peaks that loomed in front of us. Sidling along steep rocky hillsides, with slopes that looked a good quarter of a mile to the bottom of them, the horses loosened good-sized boulders that rolled down the steep slope. As the boulders increased their speed, they would leave the slope and go flying through the air, to land crashing far away below us.

Again it would be over and across steep and deep rocky gulches, and, though it is the latter part of June, above us they are still full of snow. Suddenly this ridge we had been trying to follow swung abruptly to the north, with high bluffs staring us in the face, hiding all views before us. Plainly we had come to the end of our rope. We could go no further this way up here. In-who-lise wildly protesting that a mountain goat could not get down from here, that ourselves and all the horses were going to be killed, I told her that anything is better than the way we were now.

The outfit in a long string, the horses with their rumps high above their heads, in a half slide and half crawl as they carefully brace one forefoot ahead of the other, down-down and sidling from one rocky ledge to another on we went, trying to follow the base at the side of those bluffs. Climbing along and over ledges of rock that overhang deep rocky canyons far below, we went sidling on our way.

After many ups and down, we came out on another ridge or spur. Losing no time, we started following down this spur, which, though it is far below the ridge we had been on, was no little foothill. On down we went and, while the going was not any too good, still it was a paradise compared to what we had already gone through. It did not take very long to reach the bottom of the divide among a scattering of pine trees. There before our eyes lay what was either an elk or a seldom used Injun trail.

Tired and weary and covered with dust, we had now been on the go through the long June day since a little after sunrise. It was now about an hour to sundown and this was no place to camp, as there was no feed of any kind for the horses.

We went into camp for the night just as the sun went down behind the hills. The dusky shade of the approaching night was now filling up this narrow gulchlike valley, with its towering hills on both sides of us. Turning the horses loose and driving them further down the trail, so they won't come back too soon, I went back to camp through the half-dark, to eat supper.

CHAPTER THIRTY-TWO
Too Good a Joke

Leaving here early next morning, we followed on our way down this strange trail that led us into the dark unknown. The going was not bad. Sometimes there were fallen trees across the trail, but we easily got around them, and this trail that at first we thought might only be a large elk trail, to our joy we soon seen that it was an Injun trail that was used for hunting. We ran onto plenty Injun signs, and the standing tepee poles of three lodges, that were made last fall. In-who-lise says she knows them signs and camp was made by Salish (Bitterroot) Injuns, that came here to hunt elk, as there were a number of elk toes left by the squaws hanging in bunches from the limbs of the trees. The Injuns, being superstitious, say that if they waste any of the meat of any of the deer tribe, they will know this and be mad at them, and will not let them kill them, and the Injuns will have to go hungry. In the summer months they kill only for their immediate use, and in their fall hunts enough to dry, to bring them through the winter. The women leave only the hair of the hides they tan on the ground, and carefully tie all the hoofs of the deer tribe in small bundles and hang them up on the limbs of trees, for the deer to see that they have used everything except their hair on the ground and their feet and horns in the trees.

Sometimes the trail left the small creek in the bottom, to avoid some high-walled canyon of huge boulders and fallen timber. Injun style it went up steep climbs to the benches above, only for us to have to come down slipping and sliding the best way we could into the bottom again.

On we went all day through this hunters' paradise, seeing all kinds of elk and black-tail deer. I killed a small spikehorn buck, and lashed it across a pack. We camped early as we had found fairly good feed for the horses. It looked like rain so I helped Susie cut the tepee poles and put up our tepee.

It rained heavily through the night. We pulled out early next morning, and as the brush and everything was wet along the trail we were soon soaking wet. On, on we went with the country sometimes looking as though it was going to open up, only to close up on us again tight as a closed-up jackknife.

Finally this narrow gulchlike country seems to be widening out. For some time we had been seeing large grassy spots up on the ridges among the trees. In-who-lise, on seeing those alluring signs, starts in ki-yi-ing an Injun melody of doubtful harmony. We came out on a beaver meadow with scattering willow clumps and good enough grass. There were plenty of beaver signs. We went into camp at the upper end of meadow much earlier than we had been doing lately.

Leaving In-who-lise busy fixing up camp for the night, I drove the horses to feed among the willow clumps at lower end of meadow. A bunch of moose were standing around among the scattered clumps of willows across the slough from us, eying us and our horses with doubt and suspicion. There were six or seven cows with their calves, and two bulls. Their large spreading bladelike antlers were in the velvet.

The older bull starts in lowering and raising his head at us, taking a step or two toward us and stamping a front foot on the ground. We quickly left them and stayed close to camp.

We left early next morning, as the sun was coming up over the hilltops a crimson ball of glory, which proclaimed the coming of a fine day. Our horses were puffed up with a good night's rest and feed, and all is now happiness as we follow down the large creek, not caring if school keeps or not. The country widens out, and rolling foothills with grass began to appear on our right. I was ki-yi-ing and giving all the different tribes' war whoops, but fell down when I tackled the Kootenais' (Scal-a-says'). In-who-lise, with the light of love beaming in her dark midnight eyes, told me not to grieve at this one failure, for she had heard the old Pend d'Oreille warriors say with scorn that the Scal-a-says stunk and were lousy.

In this way as we went along, we laughed, howled and sang. All this hilarity was due to the fact that, on coming around a bend in the hills and creek, we found that we had come at last out of the mountains, or at least a part of them. At last God's country did greet our weary eyes.

Stretching away far away between another range of hills to the right of us was a wide stretch of low rolling foothills covered with waving grass, with here and there small patches of timber on them, while on the left still lay the great range of hills between us and our goal, the Bitterroot Valley, with a towering bald mountain peak looking down at us.

After a day of travel, we say that there might be a storm in the night; we went into camp. I helped Susie put up the tepee and stake the edges down good, rustled her up some wood, then drove the horses up on the small ridge to the left of us, riding back to camp and putting my saddle horses on picket in good grass close to camp. As the sun went down behind a black cloud that night fifty-four years ago, telling of the approaching storm, how were we, who were never here before, to know then that we were on Rock Creek and that the morrow would bring us bitter sorrow?

The storm arrived early. Lightning flashes accompanied by crashing peals of thunder soon brought on a steady downpour of rain with fierce gusts of wind through the greater part of the night. That made us glad that we had staked down our rawhide mansion good and well. It withstood the storm and we were warm and dry.

In the morning I was up at sunrise to go and round up our horses. On going out of the lodge, I was surprised to find that in the storm my horse had pulled the picket pin and had taken French leave, going off to join the others, dragging the picket rope along with him. Also gone was another horse that generally came back to camp after he got filled up. Hanging around the tepee, that horse just loved to have human company. But for once he had stampeded off to join the others, leaving us high and dry on the lone prairie afoot. I told In-who-lise to cook breakfast quick so I could be on my way after them. There was no way of telling how far they ran in that storm.

After breakfast, taking my carbine along and a lariat, I struck out for the ridge where I ran the bunch last night. Not a hoof-sign of them could I find, which showed they had left here in the first part of the storm and the rains washed out their trail. After going about a quarter of a mile, I ran on their trail, fresh after the rain. Following their trail a short ways down along the ridge, I stood there in surprise, having run into a kind of a wagon road. This road came up from the creek and went straight up the ridge. I thought I might as well follow it to the top of the ridge not far away, and see where it went on the other side.

Soon gaining the top of the ridge, I was looking down from the wagon trail into a small narrow valley or a large gulch, and I could see two cabins about a quarter of a mile away down in this gulch. The large cabin stood about a hundred yards above the smaller cabin. Forgetting about the horses, I thought this is good, just what I want. I will go down and see if anyone lives there. I wanted to find out if there was a trail back across the mountains to the Bitterroot Valley. Following the slight wagon trail which ran to the large cabin, with the extreme Injun caution of a sneaking coyote, my moccasined feet made no sound. Silently dodging from tree to tree, I wanted to see who were in the cabin first before they seen me. Satisfying myself that no one was outside watching my actions, I reached the cabin. There being no window, I put my ear against the chinks, listening intently. All inside was quiet as death. Stealing around to the door, I saw it was tied on the outside with a string. I knew it was empty.

I could see on the trail from the door fresh tracks made by two men that had just left this cabin. Taking care not to

leave any sign of my moccasined feet around here, I followed this trail dodging from tree to tree. Soon I could see
an open cut ahead and could hear a whirring murmur as
though made by falling water. At last I found a safe place on
the top of the bank, where I could look down in the cut.

It was a mystery no longer. I seen two white men about a
hundred feet away in the bottom of the cut. They were
placer mining. I could now see up and down this gulch the
worked-over bars of wash or tailings, and knew that this was
a placer mining camp. Both men stood to one side at a
spring of clear water, one of them was washing a pan of dirt,
as the other stood looking on waiting to see the prospect the
other got. They had a full head of water running through
ground sluice and string of sluice boxes. There was a line of
galvanized hydraulic pipe that came from a penstock on a
small ridge higher up than their diggins and across the cut
and diggins from me. Attached to this hydraulic pipe ran a
heavy six-inch canvas hose, on the end of hose was attached
with an iron strap a large gauntlet nozzle, the hose resting
on a tripod. The pipe head was running and turned on, bor-
ing into the face of the drift or cut.

Like all bonafide squaw men of that time, I usually wore
buckskin clothes from toes to chin. But after this heavy rain,
to keep my pants from getting wet in the long grass and
brush, as wet buckskin gets heavy and uncomfortable
besides being hard to dry out, I had wrapped an Injun blanket of rainbow colors around me, fastening it around my
waist with my cartridge belt.

Silently crawling on the bank of the cut, I lay there like a
savage with deadly hatred gleaming in my eyes, as I look at
those two white men. Now like the bad Injun bucks and old
squaws in the buffalo camps did whenever they seen a white
man, I hissed to myself, "Souie-app-e [white men] A-O
[yes]. In-who-lise says they are all bad. She hates them.
There is only one good white man and that is I, all the rest
are evil and bad." Coming to my senses, I remember it was
not so long ago when I was a white man myself. Then I

yearn to hear the voices of them men, to talk with them. I would go and talk with them and laugh with them. In-who-lise in the tepee over the ridge on the creek, who will only talk to me in Injun, will never know. But first I would fool them. What was the use in me practicing to be a buck Injun for eleven months, if I could not put my art to some use. I would let them see how well I could do this. Then I would go to them and have the laugh on them white men.

Like the fool I was, just to show off, I stepped out on the edge of the bank above them, where they could see me well and not fifty feet away from them. I raised the Injun blanket up over my shoulders, and up over the lower part of my face. Assuming a dramatic pose, straight as a ramrod with my broad-brimmed hat pulled down so they could not see the rest of my face, I stood erect as a statue, gazing sternly down at them, with my rifle resting in the hollow of my arm.

The one who was washing the pan of wash on his knees at the spring now stands up to show the other the prospect he had in the gold pan. Now he gets a good sight of me. He stands looking at me an instant or two, as though petrified, letting the gold pan drop out of his hand to come rattling down at his feet. Now he finds his voice and yells to the other, "Get, Bill, Injuns, Injuns." His partner fairly leaped. Both were off across the old tailings and across the gulch like startled deer. At first I could not help but roar with laughter, seeing them legging it for their lives in their heavy hip gum boots. It was not long when I saw what a cussed fool I had been. My joke might yet cost me dear, if them white men get away out of my sight. For all I knew this might be a bad Injun country, full of hostiles, and where might it all end?

I threw down my blanket and rifle to let them see I meant them no harm, and took after them, calling that I was a white man, that I was no Injun. But the more I yelled, the faster they went. I was young and some sprinter myself, but they got in the lodge pole thickets in spite of me, and I had to give up the chase.

On my way back I found where they had kicked off their large gum boots, leaving them and large-sized rags, called California socks, scattered along their trail, and I knew that they were legging it for their lives in their bare feet to find help—and that I had better get to hell out of here quicker than I came in. If them white men get their eyes on me and my Injun rig, there is going to be bad trouble for the Squaw Kid.

Recovering my blanket and gun, and giving the large cabin a wide berth, like a skulking coyote, I went sneaking and crawling down through the beds of wash. Carefully making my way through the scrubby willows nearly opposite the lower cabin, I nearly ran into another diggins, but heard the ringing of a pick in time. The willows grew up to the edge of the cut on my side, but there were none on the cabin side which looked like worked-over ground for some distance on that side up and down the gulch.

Knowing I had better make myself scarce when the going was good, I still wanted to take just one peep and see what was going on there. Easily crawling to where I could look down over the edge of the cut, which was seven or eight feet deep, and after being sure that no one could see me carefully parting the willows, I could see that it was another placer claim, worked on a similar plan as the one above.

The water came from the upper claim to make the sluice head. There was also a small hydraulic pipe line, but no pipe head was running. Standing at work picking in the face of the drift, where the sluice head came and poured over the bank, I saw a light bewhiskered, tall rawboned man, with a forty-five Colt in holster and cartridge belt strapped on him, warning me all too well. And something made me shiver as I saw a Winchester rifle standing handy against the tripod that held up the hose nozzle a few feet away from him.

I thought, "It is lucky for you that it was not here you came to pull off that Injun stunt." He was picking alone on the face of the drift, making a course for the head of water to strike and undermine the bank, so that it could cave and fall in the ground sluice, the sluice head carrying off most of the dirt and small wash down through the sluice boxes, leaving only the rock and heavy gravel there.

As I lay there watching this man at work, I was not aware that some of White Bird's people had come through here on their way from Canada to Idaho and that they killed three miners. How could I know then that I was in this very spot!

As I watched this man from the brush at work in the diggins, how could I then know that this man I watched, with a forty-five Colt strapped on him, was none other than the man called Nez Perce Jones, the one miner who had escaped, and that in those same diggins and close to me where he was working, a brutal murder had been committed the year before, almost at this same time of the year, while in that cabin across the diggins from me was Art Hays, brother of the murdered miner John Hays, who now means anything but good to all buck Injuns in general.

Getting a hunch that I had been here long enough for my own good, like a skulking redskin I lost no time in making it over to the Ross's Fork side of the ridge where I soon ran on the horse trail. I found the horses down this ridge, near where it comes in a sharp point into Rock Creek and almost at the mouth of Ross's Fork.

CHAPTER THIRTY-THREE
Half-Breed Renegade

Catching the trailing lariat of my saddle horse, it took only an instant to mount him. Wrapped in my blanket, rifle in hand, I rode and drove the other horses along this ridge of long waving bunch grass. On this the last day of June, 1879, on the way back to In-who-lise in camp on Ross's Fork, to relieve the monotony on the way, I will tell you this story. As I ride along I will tell you about a few things that no other white man has ever heard before in this sad affair, the brutal murder of the miner, John Hays.

It was then early in the forenoon of the day July 11, 1878. They came up from Willow Creek, by the rocky Injun trail that runs up Rock Creek, through this narrow canyon between lofty hills, and where this trail emerges out of this canyon, and where the West Fork of Rock Creek comes into Rock Creek.

A band of Injuns rode out, sixteen heavily armed warriors they were, one of them a half-breed, together with their women and children, making three lodges. Their women were driving along a considerable band of horses, and the usual number of Injun dogs trailing along.

Coming out of the canyon, this wild and savage band sat silently on their war ponies. Most of the men have a sinister look on their swarthy and battle-scarred faces that even their Injun stoic cannot hide, proclaiming them bad Injuns, not to be trusted under any circumstances.

While the women and children with their dark inscrutable eyes, impassive as Sphinxes as they sat in silence on their ponies, grouped up behind among the pack and loose horses. The men slightly ahead of them are pointing and talking among themselves in low guttural whispers, as though they are afraid the trees and hills will tell what they are saying. They glance about them in all directions. Nothing escapes their scrutiny, as though they expected dangers from every quarter, and are taking no chance on being seen first.

Still do not blame them, for there is good reason for their guilty sneaking actions. They are a part of that band of Injuns who went through with Joseph and escaped to Canada from the Bear Paw Mountain. After wintering there, this band of renegades with a few Nez Perce warriors are now on their way to their old home in Idaho. With murder and robbery their specialty, they have left a trail of fire and blood in their wake, from Sun River Crossing by Cadott's Pass, and down the Big Blackfoot. Only four days before this they murdered and robbed two miners near old Beartown, putting in some of the remaining time stealing some of the Flint Creek ranchers' horses.

A tall middle-aged warrior who seemed out of place among those renegade cutthroats is saying to the breed and renegade warriors, "E-ha, evil ones, here at last is the place we told our brothers we would wait for them till they got back from In-ola-a [Missoula] with cartridges. Yes, here is the Salish buffalo trail that runs on its way from Ket-la-met-a-lee [Bitterroot Valley] to faraway Cha-kel-tish [from where we have come], the land of the buffalo, Blackfeet and Piegans. Well do I know this place, for many times have I gone by here with our fathers and people on our way to hunt the buffalo in far-off Cha-kel-tish. Alas, that it is as now, they will never come here no more. For now is gone In-mut-to-yah-lat-lat [Joseph], and our people lie scattered and dead along strange trails, no more to hear the joyful voices of our warriors' songs. The Wallowa, our dead fathers' land near the setting sun, is now the white man's and knows our people no more."

As the warriors hear this, sitting on their war ponies with scowling faces, the Breed, their leader, says, "Then let it be near here, away from white men's and Salish warriors' prying eyes we shall camp and wait."

The old warrior said, "No, not yet, this is not wise. No Sapah-tan warrior tells the women to make camp till he reads the trail where he is first."

The Breed said, "The old are wise and know best. When we all know that much danger might lurk here for us from them plenty white men in their strong tepees over the hills and not a half a sun's ride from here [Philipsburg]. Evil for us shall it be if some Salish warrior would see us, and whisper to them white men that we are here. Let the women with the horses stay here with some of us, we shall see what the Salish trail says first."

At this two warriors ride off scouting up the West Fork, while the Breed with three warriors crossed over the West Fork and ride up the Salish trail along Rock Creek.

Suddenly they detected a sound they all knew well, the sound being of fording horses, crossing Rock Creek toward them. They quickly wheeled their horses, riding out of sight, behind a thicket on the hillside, silently sitting on their war horses with their rifles ready.

The Breed holds up two fingers to the others, meaning that two horses were fording Rock Creek, coming their way. They had not long to wait before they saw a large white man with a rifle across his saddle, leading a loaded packhorse out of the ford.

The Breed and three warriors behind the thicket sit in their saddles still as death, and when they seen the lone white man their eyes gleam with hate. As in one breath, the Breed and warriors hiss to one another, "Souie-app-o [white man]," while fingering their rifles with hellish joy. The Breed, with hell written all over his swarthy wolfish face, draws a forefinger across his throat. This white man, instead of following the trail running toward the West Fork, turns off and leaves this trail going on his way up a slightly used trail into McKay's Gulch. This lone rider was John Hays, who had left Philipsburg that morning with his pack horse loaded with provisions after celebrating the Fourth of July.

When the Breed with the three warriors seen the white man slip through their fingers, as it were, by riding off the opposite way from them, one of the warriors brandished his rifle, digging his heels in his pony's sides, as though he was going to ride after and overtake the white man.

But a sign from the Breed made him fiercely pull his pony back on its haunches. At this breach of his authority the Breed snarled, "Son of a woods Cree, would you do this, when that white man has a stronger gun in his hands than any of us, and will see you from afar and in time to kill you, coming up that gulch without trees to hide you?"

This was not the first time this warrior disputed his authority as leader. At the thought of this a vicious gleam comes in the Breed's eyes that the two renegades fear and know well.

He said, "Brothers, we will see first why and where that white man goes by that trail. It will be time for us then. Fear not, your brother is wise to white man's ways."

The Breed with a few words to them, with a wave of his hand, sends the two renegade warriors to trail the white man.

The two renegades, on gaining the top of the ridge, could now plainly see the white man riding some ways ahead of them on the trail in the bottom of the gulch.

They mutter low guttural exclamations of approval to one another, saying, "Yes, our chief the Breed is more wise than that Nez Perce warrior."

They could now see in the bottom of the gulch a small cabin, while maybe a hundred yards further up the gulch stood a larger cabin. They see the white man ride up to the small cabin and dismount, taking the pack off, carrying it into the cabin, coming outside and picketing his saddle horse. Soon smoke was coming out of the fireplace chimney.

As soon as the two renegade warriors left on their way to trail the miner, John Hays, the Breed sent the other warrior to scout on the trail for a ways toward Philipsburg. Then he rode back to the waiting band. He tells them nothing about seeing a white man riding by.

He says, "We camp not far from here, let us be on our way," and whirls his horse around to start back the way he had come. An old warrior and two youngish Nez Perce warriors rode up before the Breed. The old warrior said, "Evil one of fire and blood, to what evil wouldst thou lead thy mother's people to do now? If it is not to do evil, why lead us back the wrong way, when our right trail leads from here up this creek toward the Salish land [Bitterroot Valley] on our trail back to the land of our fathers? Near here on this creek we shall wait for the evil warriors to come from Missoula."

The Breed, denying this, said that it was only a short distance back on this trail where they will camp, where there was plenty good feed for their horses, and no one going by on this trail would know that they were camped there, while here it was only a narrow rocky canyon with no place to hide and no feed for their horses. He told the good Nez Perce warriors that them and their women could pull out on their way alone if they wanted, that the camp would be well rid of them.

After a powwow of bitter intensity, the good Nez Perce people in this outfit, who only wanted to go back to Idaho without harming anyone, were again, as always, overruled by the majority, by the Breed and renegade warriors, together with three or four bad revengeful Nez Perce warriors under the Breed's evil influence. They were afraid to leave the band.

The Breed, saying no more, starts off leading the way back on the trail to Ross's Fork, the warriors following, with the women and children driving the horse herd in the rear. Going up Ross's Fork till well out of sight of Rock Creek, with a wave of his hand, he says, "Here we camp." He tells the women to put up the lodges and get them something to eat. The warriors take off their saddles and put their horses on lariat. The women take off the packs, turning their saddle ponies loose with the herd to graze. Soon the women had fires going and the lodges up.

The two renegade warriors who had been scouting up McKay's Gulch came riding into camp. Those two well-trained cutthroats, their evil faces unfathomable as the Sphinx, had no words as to where they had been. Nevertheless, in sign language, whenever they got the chance, told the Breed and renegade warriors, with the few bad Nez Perce warriors in camp, what they had found up in McKay's Gulch.

The bad Nez Perce warrior who had the trouble with the Breed at Rock Creek Ford, returning to camp, reports to the Breed, saying that there was no other sign of white men on the trail except the trail of the white man they had seen.

The Breed tells this warrior to say nothing about their trouble at the ford, nor nothing else, to the other Nez Perce warriors in camp—that their friends the two renegade warriors had found two cabins, and that white man did stay in one of them; that he could have the white man's strong gun as his own when they killed him tonight. They were going to see, after they ate, if there was any more cabins where white men lived further up in that gulch. They would see first— then evil for the white dogs would be this day and night.

The Nez Perce warrior, not to be placated by the Breed's generous offer of peace between them, with a scowl on his face at the Breed, tells him that he would not tell the other Nez Perce warriors what was done, but after this, he heeded not the Breed's evil voice, nor followed his trail of fire and blood no more. Leaving the Breed, he rides over to the lodge where he stayed.

After eating their frugal meal, the Breed with the two renegades who had gone scouting, accompanied by another renegade, got their saddle horses. They told those left in camp they were going to hunt meat for the camp, and pulled out.

But all of the Breed's secrecy and caution was in vain, when a woman put her finger in the game. One of the renegades had told his woman where they were going. As all of the women in camp were Nez Perce, it was soon known to all left in camp that the white dog would be robbed and killed tonight.

It did not take the Breed and renegades long to find out all they wanted to know. The narrow gulch was, even then in 1878, nearly worked out, and its bottom from rim to rim was a jumbled mass of placer tailings. In the edge of timber near the diggins they found three cabins. The first, though deserted, had been recently used, as all of someone's belongings were still there. A little further down was another cabin, and further down near the mouth of the gulch stood another. Both cabins were deserted with their doors wide open, showing that they had not been used for some time.

The Breed tells the two renegades to go scouting up the main gulch from here to see what they can find up that way, that he would scout around here and see if anyone lived in the large cabin across from him. After that, he was going to see what the white man in the small cabin was doing. When they found out what was further up the gulch, to strike back through timber for the horses. He would meet them there, so that they could go back to camp together with the same hard luck story about their deer hunt.

The two renegades, like two bloodhounds, silently fade away in the lodge pole pines. Their moccasined feet make not the slightest sound as they glide along from tree to tree. Wary and cunning are they at this, going on their evil way.

The Breed crosses over to east side of the gulch and soon found out to his satisfaction that, while the large cabin was only recently occupied, it was now empty. Crossing back across the gulch the same way he came over here, crawling and dodging through willows and brush down the gulch on left side going down, he parts the willows and is looking down into John Hays's placer diggins. His cruel face is gloating with hellish joy, as standing there not many feet away from him is John Hays with a forty-five Colt strapped on him, and holding the hose nozzle piping in the face of drift.

The Breed's eyes take in every detail, even to the deadly strong shooting rifle standing conveniently near the white man. And while the Breed could have shot and killed John Hays from where he was, still that was not his way. He would know first what the two renegades found further up the gulch.

He went back up the gulch, and as he was telling the renegade what he had seen, the other two renegades appear silently out of the timber, their savage faces aglow with a murderous light at what they had found further up the gulch.

They found only one more cabin up there, not far. In this cabin lived three white men. They knew this, for they had seen them working in the ground for white man's gold. The white men had no guns on them; they had none in their cabin. Yes, they knew this, for as two of them watched the white men at their work, the other went in their tepee.

They mounted their ponies, going back down along the ridge the way they had come, and as they ride along, they are talking in low guttural tones, each one with a plan of his own, the best way to kill them white men. The Breed says, "Yes—the white man, his gun will not save him tonight. The white men up the gulch will not hear the white man's gun, for there must be no guns fired tonight when we kill the white dog first. It is not time yet; we shall see."

Before the Breed and renegades reached camp, a renegade from the camp intercepted them, with the news that there was going to be more trouble for them from some of the Nez Perce warriors in camp. One of the renegade's women had told it all to a woman friend of hers, so that now the whole camp knew that there was going to be robbery and murder.

The Breed told the renegade to fear not what Scar Face and others said in camp. He was the chief and did not care what his troublemaking friends said or done, themselves all liars who talked like the Black Robes, saying for all the rest in camp to be good and not to kill white men. Yet, themselves rode on stolen white men's horses, and would kill a white man as quick as them, only they were afraid of getting caught.

The renegade riding off another way, the Breed and three renegades rode into camp with haughty unconcern, knowing well the storm will blow over soon, as it always did. They rode by Scar Face and his friends as though they did not see them. Squatting in a circle outside their lodge, holding a powwow among themselves, the Breed rides by them in silence on his way to another lodge, where several of his renegade confederates are anxiously waiting to hear if they have found any more cabins and white men up in the gulch.

Not long after this, the women brought them large chunks of broiled venison from the fire nearby, laying it before them. The Breed with the renegades, making a wild and savage-looking scene, as they squat around on the ground grouped together, as they talk in low guarded voices, planning among themselves the best way to kill them three white men after they kill John Hays.

While this was going on, the bad Nez Perce warrior, the one the Breed had the trouble with at Rock Creek Ford, has been holding himself aloof from all the others. Sulking and nursing his wrath against the Breed, this Nez Perce warrior is a bad one, who before this had been the most desperate and fearless of all the Breed's bloodthirsty cutthroats.

The Breed on getting through eating, seeing this warrior still squatting alone under a tree nearby, tries to make friends with him again. He goes over to this Nez Perce warrior and playfully touches him with the toe of his moccasin, telling him they missed him this afternoon, when they had found another cabin further up the gulch with plenty white men's things in it. That three white men lived there with no guns on them or in their tepee. That he must come with them. Maybe before sundown the first white dog would be dead. As he told him before, the white man's strong shooting gun would be his, and besides the gun he could have the white man's saddle horse and saddle.

The Nez Perce warrior, who knew the Breed's previous promises only too well, said nothing to this. Springing to his feet, his eyes and face gleaming with hate and fury, he made

head, who, though wounded and bleeding on the side, is still sitting there unconcerned.

The Breed said, "So this is you, the snapping coyote who only bites and never howls. Yes, you would have done this, kill your chief when you thought you could. Then die for this, traitor, whose hands are redder than mine with white men's blood."

As the Breed stands gloating over his enemy, his gun still held close to the warrior's head, fierce murmurs of dissent are heard from the Nez Perce warriors, and from most of the renegades, all who had a savage liking for their Nez Perce brother in bloodshed and crime, and do not want the Breed to kill him.

Not to be balked out of his prey, as the angry warriors threateningly began to crowd around him, with a wolfish snarl, pulling his other gun, the Breed waves them back from him, saying that he was their chief and would kill them who tried to stop him. "Yes, this treacherous warrior shall die for this. No more will he disobey me when he is dead."

Seeing and hearing all this, a sister of the Nez Perce warrior who had a renegade warrior for her man is telling him not to let the Breed do this, that if he lets the Breed kill her brother she would leave him. Yes, she would put her knife in his side when he slept, and kill the Breed the first chance she got.

The renegade warrior, knowing this is no idle threat of hers, said to the Breed with encouragement from the others that if he killed his friend, his woman's brother, that he would not be long chief, when he would be dead with the Nez Perce warrior, for him to put down his guns and let his woman's brother go. Did he forget it was time for them to be on their way to kill them white men up the gulch?

At first the Breed only laughed at this threat, but then he could see that, as the report of his gun rang out, the rest of the warriors in camp would shoot him to pieces. Losing his bluster and bravo, he backs down from this brutal act, saying, "The heart of your chief is now good again, and will forget that the evil and treacherous Sapah-tan tried to kill me.

Then let this be so. Yes, it is time to be on our way up the gulch. Them white dogs up there die."

But some of the good warriors would not have this. Together as one with Old Scar Face, they saw the Breed's evil influence was now for the first time broken. Old Scar Face now waxes eloquent, saying to them the time had come at last. Yes, his heart was glad, when he knew they would heed no more the evil voice of the Breed. If they killed them white men up the gulch, evil for them all would it then be. Was it not already evil enough for them all in camp when the Breed, their evil chief, and six bad warriors on their evil way had found and killed two white men, after they had taken their things away from them, four days before they came here. Yes, this was so, or why was them dead men's horses' saddles, guns and things in their tepee now? He now wants his evil warriors here in camp to kill them white men up the gulch, when the white men could talk like the evil spirits far through the day and night on their click clack. The white men far away would know and the soldiers would come from In-ola-a to catch them on their way to the Lolo trail. Then what were they all going to say to the chief of the soldiers when he knew they had done this. Yes, evil would be that day.

The lives of those white men up in McKay's Gulch would have been spared a cruel death, had not one of the women disliked the effect of Scar Face's eloquence in camp.

This warlike virago works herself into a frenzy as she hurls taunts and insults at the warriors, saying, "Are you warriors, are you men, that heed the evil voices of them traitors and liars? No, you are Cree squaws, afraid to kill a white man, just because you like them." Again, pleading and moaning, shrieking, "Kill! Kill them all, the evil white dogs! Like they did us at In-sah-kum-sah-nay! Did the white men and soldiers spare them and the warriors with no guns in their hands when they held up their hands to soldiers and white men? Did they spare the women and children when they cried and pleaded to them? No, the white dogs shot and killed the women and children, like they killed the men. E-clew-shay [yes, it is]." She remembered they did not. She had lost, A-O [yes], killed, her man, her baby, a brother and mother, left dead there, and with her dead people lay the dead of many others. "Yes, those squaw warriors know this is no lie, when they were there and seen this themselves. Yes, kill the white dogs when all white men are vile and bad!" In her blind fury she snatches a rifle out of a warrior's hand, wildly brandishing it over her head, saying that since they were not men no more here, she would go, yes, herself along, and kill them white men. At this fierce display of squaw bravery three other women joined her ranks, and when they got through with their unholy oratory, the little hope to spare them white men's lives was now dead, so well did those frantic women do their deadly work of hate.

Most of the warriors in camp, their eyes agleam, their faces distorted with deadly hate for all the white race, say all together, much to the satisfaction of the Breed and renegade cutthroats, "Yes, it shall be so, no more will our women have to call us squaws for this. Our good chief knows this is so. All white men are liars, evil and bad to Injuns. Them white men up the gulch shall die for their evil white brothers' wrongs to us. Yes, this is good. Them white men shall die by our hands. Then the white women will cry and wail for their dead, like the white men made our women cry and wail for their dead warriors, children and friends. The white men and soldiers killed our people for nothing as they slept at In-sah-kum-sah-nay and again along the trail to the land of the buffalo. Yes, for that! The white women, like ours, their cries shall reach up to the sky to the white man's God, who will not help them or them white men up the gulch from our vengeance tonight!"

Still, after all hope for them white men's lives was gone, old Scar Face and one or two others tried to get them only to take the white men's things, guns and horses, but not to kill them. But they might as well have pleaded to the wind and hills of rock as to those red hellions, now thoroughly aroused.

Old Scar Face said, "Sons of evil who are better off dead, then let it be so, so that again the white men and soldiers will come after us, like they did after our evil brothers in Idaho, and will make your evil women wail for you all." He strides off to his lodge in disgust and scorn, followed by four good Nez Perce warriors.

The Breed was highly elated at his hard-earned success, and once more the undisputed chief of his cutthroat band. Like silent evil spirits they depart from camp on their evil mission of robbery and death. In the bunch are eight renegades and one bad Nez Perce warrior, which, with the Breed, made ten of the most treacherous and murderous rascals to be found on this side of hell. That left in camp, not counting the women, five Nez Perce warriors and one renegade warrior who all say they will not do this.

They rode up the right-hand ridge going up the gulch, soon coming opposite to John Hays's cabin in the gulch below. Gazing, well concealed from the ridge, they can see no one was now at work in the claim. The whole bunch, riding together this time, went down the side gulch through the timber to where this gulch comes out in the main gulch and nearly opposite the large cabin.

Leaving their horses, they silently, like evil shadows, go their way as directed by the Breed, crawling and dodging through the brush and willows, as silent as a snake in water, to lie hidden at John Hays's claim down the main gulch not far below here.

CHAPTER THIRTY-FOUR
Murder of John Hays

The miner John Hays had been warned that morning, before leaving Philipsburg, to be careful and to be on the look out for bad Injuns, as the ones who had robbed and murdered the two miners near old Beartown were supposed to be returning Nez Perce warriors, revengeful and bad. They were now thought to be on their way, going up Rock Creek to strike the Salish Indian buffalo trail, after having stolen horses on their way through the Flint Creek country.

John Hays said in Philipsburg that morning, not to fear for him, that he savvied an Injun, and would like to see the color of the Injun's hair who could get near him when he had his old stand-by, his 45-70 Winchester Betsy Jane to fall back on.

No one was ever to know why it was, after quitting his work at the usual time, probably to cook his supper, in the long July daylight and some time yet to sundown, that he left his cabin to go back to the diggins. With his forty-five Colt hanging at his hip, his faithful Winchester on his shoulder, glancing cautiously up and down the gulch, he went on his way to the diggins close by, and saw no danger in this peaceful little valley. And as he goes down the low bank into the diggins, how could he know that a few yards away from him, fierce savage faces, their eyes gleaming with hate, are peering at him? The sluice and pipe head had been shut off for the night to save the water. And only a light head of clear seepage water ran through the ground sluice and sluice boxes.

Leaning his rifle on a rock near him, John Hays starts in cleaning bed rock, shoveling the bedrock dirt into the ground sluice. As the sun sunk lower back in the big hills in the distance, some presentiment must have whispered to him a timely warning that danger lurked here. Twice since coming here John Hays quits his work, as though to go back to his cabin. Taking his rifle, he goes up on the bank of the cut and gazes anxiously up and down the gulch. Seeing no danger each time, he returns to his work.

A few minutes after going up on the bank to look the second time, what his thoughts were only God knows, for sitting on their war ponies like statues between him and the cabin were what appears to be three Injuns with their rifles in their hands. Seeing this, John Hays grabs up his rifle. Quickly stepping behind a pile of boulders, he stands holding his rifle in both hands, ready to shoot if he has to.

The Injuns, seeing this, lay their guns across their saddles in front of them, holding up both their arms in the air, to let him know they are friendly to him. The middle Injun, with his arms still held up, steps his horse a step or two closer to the diggins, making signs that they only want to talk.

John Hays waves his rifle at him, making signs at him to go back, not to come nearer to him, and for them to go away, he does not want them there.

Instead of leaving, as Hays told them, the Injuns got off their horses. They laid their rifles down on the ground beside their horses, and one of the Injuns, our friend the Breed, takes off a cartridge belt with two forty-fives in holsters, laying them down on the ground with the rifles. Showing Hays they have no more guns of any kind on them, the three go some ways off to one side of them.

The Breed then, with his hands held up, goes a short way toward the diggins, to where Hays can well hear what he says. He says in good English for the white man not to be afraid of them, that he is a Bitterroot half-breed, and this his two friends are Salish (Flathead) Injuns who live at Stevensville. That they all belong to a large party of Salish who were camped for the night near the mouth of Ross's Fork, on their way back to the Bitterroot Valley from hunting buffalo all last winter across the Big Hills in the land of the Piegans. Yes, for him not to be afraid that they were bad Injuns when they were his friends, who only came here to tell him they had been told by a white man from Philipsburg on their way today, that there were plenty bad Nez Perce warriors robbing and killing white men on their way through here on the Salish trail, for him to look out for them as they would kill him if they found him here alone. Besides he wanted to see how it was the white man washed for gold. He (the Breed) was sure he knew where there was plenty. If he only knew what way the white men did to get it, he would try himself.

John Hays lowered his rifle, knowing well the Salish were always good Injuns and good friends that never yet harmed a white man, many of them camping around here in their fall hunts. After thanking the Breed for warning him, he invited the Breed and two renegades into the diggins.

He told the Breed he would show them all he knowed about washing gold. The Breed and two renegades gladly accepted the invitation, and this trio of hellions lost no time in joining John Hays in his placer diggings.

Still cautious, rifle in hand, the obliging miner shows them the ground sluice and sluice boxes, and tells the highly interested Breed that it was simple as falling off a log to learn, and only required considerable strong-arm labor to loosen up the dirt and gravel.

The Breed asks Hays if he finds plenty gold here. The cautious and wary miner replies, "Alas, no. There is not much to be found here."

Getting more confidential all the time, the Breed brings forth a well-filled buckskin sack, spilling out of it, to the astonished miner's gaze, nuggets and coarse gold, all that the scooped palm of his hand would hold, saying to the white man, as guileless as a child, "Is this gold? If it is, I know where I could find plenty more, where I picked up this sack nearly full among the rocks and gravel with just my hands."

He sees the nuggets and coarse gold in the Breed's hand at first with envy, then with the inherited greed and avarice

of the white man beaming in his face and eyes. Forgetting all
caution, he leans his rifle down on a boulder. Eagerly holding out his trembling hand, as the obliging Breed puts the
nuggets and coarse gold in his outstretched hand. The gold
in his hand sends waves of ecstasy sweeping through him
like a prairie fire. He stands entranced, and lovingly as a tenderhearted sweetheart, caresses the nuggets with his other
hand. His eyes cannot hide their joy and envy. He tells the
Breed in a whisper, "Yes, this is gold. Gold. Gold." Gold,
gold, gleaming gold that the white man, since the beginning,
has braved death, cold and hunger for, even selling his soul
to hell. Wading through rivers of blood to obtain, its cursed
lure like the songs of the sirens of old.

As John Hays stands enraptured, the two renegades show
no interest in what was going on. The Breed waxes more and
more eloquent about what he has already seen in the diggins, but what he would like to see was how the white men
washed for gold with a gold pan.

At this the miner John Hays, coming out of his dreams
with a sigh of regret, holds out his hand to give the Breed the
nuggets and gold dust back. The Breed tells Hays he may
keep the largest nugget for himself. Yes, he would give him
the big one.

John Hays thanks the Breed for his offered gift, telling
him he did not have to give him the nugget for showing him
how to use a gold pan, when he would do it for nothing.

The Breed, not to be outdone at this generosity, gently
pushes Hays's outstretched hand away, saying that for his
friend's heart being so good to him, to show him how to use
a gold pan, his good friend must take all the gold in his
hand.

The good-hearted miner said that he did not want to do
this when the Breed might soon need it himself.

The Breed said not to fear for that; did not his good
friend hear him say that he knew where there were plenty
more? He would come back soon and bring his friend with
him. There would be plenty gold for both of them.

John Hays objected no more, and took a small buckskin
sack out of his pocket. After putting nuggets and gold dust
back in it, he returns the sack to his pocket. As he done this,
could he only have known that the Breed's gift was a part of
the bloodstained gold dust and nuggets of the two murdered miners near old Beartown?

John Hays was now more than willing to reward the
Breed's generosity. Leaving his rifle still leaning on the boulder pile nearby, he picked up a gold pan and put a shovel full
of rich bedrock dirt in the gold pan. He went to the ground
sluice, accompanied by the enthusiastic Breed, the two renegades trailing behind. Their moccasin feet tread the ground
as silent as a stalking panther. John Hays kneels down on
one knee beside the ground sluice, saying to the Breed, "See,
it is just this way." He dips the gold pan in the clear ground
sluice water till nearly full and whirls the water and gravel
around in the gold pan.

The Breed's beady eyes gleam with interest, his burly
form silently crouched down by the white man. The trust-
ing John Hays, unconscious of his peril, with professional
pride whirls the water and gravel around in the gold pan.
Time and again, dipping the gold pan with a swinging side-
motion in the ground sluice water, sending small riffles of
water washing the top gravel out of the gold pan. When
nearly all of the gravel was washed out, several grains of
gold, like little stars, gleam in the black sand in the bottom.
All this time the two renegades stand like two statues behind
John Hays and the Breed. Not a sign on their faces betrays
their hellish thoughts.

The Breed now flashes them a look of understanding. He
crouches closer to the white man. The hour and the minute
had come. One of the renegades steps in between John Hays
and his rifle. The Breed's arm moves with the rapidity of a
striking rattler's darting head. His hand grabs the protrud-
ing gun butt hanging on John Hays's belt. With a quick twist
and a wrench, the forty-five Colt is in his hand. The Breed
springs to his feet, flourishing the gun, and gives John Hays

a kick in the back that sent him sprawling face downward in the ground sluice. The renegade picks up Hays's rifle as the other renegade hurls a rock striking him between the shoulders. The half-stunned white man had not fully realized what had happened, as seven more red devils came leaping out of the brush and down the bank into the diggins, throwing down their blankets, stripped for action in leggins and breechclout, they picked up rocks as they came.

What John Hays's thoughts were only God knows, as he sprung to his feet, dripping wet, to find himself surrounded by a living wall of savages. He thought they only meant robbery, because they could have shot him dead without going to all this bother to get his rifle and pistol away from him.

With a look of blind fury at the Breed, he tells this limb of Satan just what he thinks of him, saying, since when was it that the Flathead Injuns had become thieves and liars to do a dirty trick like this to a good friend who had always used them well? He told them to take what they wanted and that he would know better next time than to trust a breed or Injun of any kind.

The Breed, with a crafty look, meets this with stoic silence. Then he tells the others in Nez Perce that this was good. The white man still thought they were Flatheads. He had not thought of this before.

The Breed, with Hays's rifle in his hand, stands to one side, encouraging them on. Like a band of hungry wolves, the nine warriors needed no second bidding and hurl themselves at the defenseless white man as though they would tear him to pieces.

John Hays was a large and powerful man and his desperation and fury added strength to his burly form. With a sweep of his powerful arms, he hurls them aside like ninepins. He made a spring toward one renegade and grabbed him by the arm. There was a swift twist and wrench upward, with the cracking of bone. He swung the terrified Injun off his feet, one limp and broken arm hanging at his side. The other warriors in their fury to get at the white man

were always in each other's way. Some of them drew their
knives, but soon put them back in their sheaths when one of
them, making a slash at the white man, cut another warrior
instead. Hays took off his heavy-loaded cartridge belt and
met the milling and oncoming renegades, swinging the
heavy cartridge belt full of cartridges with telling effect. One
crack was enough for the renegade that came within its
reach. Charging after them with this improvised weapon, he
soon had the astonished redskins on the run, and dodging
in and out around him, firing rocks at him whenever they
got the chance.

Hays had not much trouble in breaking away from them,
and starts off on the run away from them down through the
diggins, the surprised warriors running after him. Rather
than see him escape, the Breed raises the rifle, but could not
shoot Hays without hitting some of the renegades.

John Hays's mad dash for his life and liberty was short-
lived. Hampered as he was with his heavy hip gum boots, he
was no match for his fleet-footed enemies. Running through
the loose wash in the digging, he stumbles in a hole, sprawling on the slippery gravel. Before he could rise, the first of
his pursuers came up and, with a whoop of triumph, sprang
at him, pulling the cartridge belt out of his hand. Hays
ducked a blow in springing to his feet, only to find himself
again surrounded by his tormentors, all of them panting
and out of breath.

The Breed coming up, gun in hand, is furious at the warriors for letting the white man get away from them. He said
they were worse than squaws, who would have killed the
white man before this. Since they were only snapping coyotes, afraid to face a white man, only being able to bite him
in the back, they should spread out in a circle and he would
help them to kill the white dog with rocks. Putting the rifle
down, he joined them.

In this circle of death, going up through the diggins amid
flying rocks, many of which found their mark, John Hays,
now bruised from head to foot, still done his best and

fought them back with rocks, but in this unequal struggle there could be but one end. No matter what way he turns and charges them, others would slip around behind him. Smaller and closer to him grew the death circle of determined fiends. Twice whizzing rocks struck him on the head and brought him down on his knees, only for him to spring up on his feet again, but he was getting weaker and weaker, realizing that the end will soon come. John Hays, with superhuman effort born of despair, leaps through a volley of flying rocks, and clutches one of the surprised warriors. In a deadly embrace, as the warrior vainly struggles to release himself, both fell to the ground, the white man on top with a death clutch on the Injun's throat. The Breed and renegades for an instant seem stupefied at the white man's desperate bravery. Hays, with his other hand, reached and grabbed a rock, and smashed in the gurgling warrior's brains. Almost at the same instant one of the renegades leaps at the white man, swinging his rock slingshot, striking Hays with terrible force on the back of his head.

Without a moan or struggle, the powerful arms and clutch on the dead Injun's throat relaxed their grip in death. John Hays's bruised body lay silent in the death embrace of the dead warrior still underneath him.

CHAPTER THIRTY-FIVE
Nez Perce Jones and Big Pete

The sun went down behind the big hills in a fiery ball of red, God's sun, which for some unknown reason shines on the good and bad alike. John Hays lay with his face in the seepage water where the Breed and renegades had thrown him, after taking what they wanted off him. They left the dead Injun near him, together with torn pieces of blanket, leggins and breechclouts scattered around through the diggins.

The Breed and two renegades were ransacking the cabin, trying to locate Hays's gold-dust cache, with Hays's dog disputing their right to do this. The other renegades were prowling in and out of the cabin as Hays's earthly possessions are brought out of the cabin and hastily bundled up by two of the renegades' women who had ridden up the gulch bringing three pack horses with them.

Two of the renegades go with a pack horse into the diggins and put the dead Nez Perce on the pack horse. The women drove the saddle horses back to camp, including Hays's saddle horse and pack horse loaded with plunder, the women driving them on their way down the gulch, going down the gulch with the broken-arm renegade and dead Nez Perce in the pack string.

As they left, the Breed told the women to tell two or three of the women in camp to start at sunrise with some pack horses to get the white men's things from their cabin up the gulch.

Making a large fire from Hays's woodpile, the Breed and seven renegades prepare to camp here for the night. The renegades were all the worse for wear from the rough handling they got from the miner, as they squat around the fire eating the dead miner's grub. Their gleaming fire sends its friendly beams afar into the darkness of night. All of them were more determined than ever that the three white men further up the gulch shall die at sunrise. Each one of them satisfied his husky appetite, and having no conscience to bother their dreams, with an Injun grunt of content, they rolled up by the fire in their blankets.

At dawn, without stopping to eat, they put on their cartridge belts and each one now has a six shooter in holster, one of those pistols being Hays's forty-five Colt. Silently they trail along in the cold morning, with their blankets tightly drawn around them, their rifles resting in the hollow of their left arm, making their way on the narrow trail up the gulch through the scattering lodge pole pines.

When they could see the cabin, they stood back out of sight, and the Breed and renegades hold a whispered confab. Then the Breed sneaks up to the cabin, telling them, "It is good. The white men are still asleep." In a few whispered words he told his plan to kill the white men.

The Breed, with his two renegade lieutenants, went up boldly and stood outside the cabin doorway. With his arm he makes a half circle to the other five renegades, as he points to them with an expressive glance, for them to hide themselves in the pines nearby. Then with his hands in the sign language, with a villainous grin, he draws his forefinger across his throat. Then the Breed knocks with his rifle butt on the door.

Getting no answer to his first summons, the Breed knocks again. Soon come the words, "Who is there?" The Breed says, "It is me, Injuns. Get up, white men, it is getting late." The voice from inside wants to know if they are Nez Perce or Flatheads.

The Breed says not to be afraid; they were good Injuns. "Yes, Flatheads from the Bitterroot Valley."

The door slowly opens and the Breed fills the open doorway, standing there smiling at the white men. In good English he tells them not to be afraid; that they were Flatheads from the Bitterroot Valley.

The spokesman for the white men, who at first acted suspicious, invites the Breed and two renegades to come in the cabin. The Breed and renegades stand their rifles outside against the cabin wall, a little to one side of the door, and let the top of their blankets fall down over their cartridge belts before they entered.

The white men were dressed, and one of them asked the Breed if they were hungry. The Breed saying yes, one of the white men (Elliott), pointing to stools, tells the Breed for them to sit down. They can eat with them as soon as they can cook breakfast. One of the white men (Jones) is chopping kindling and starts a fire. The other white man (Elliott) washes his hands and face, and quickly starts mixing dough to make bread.

The Breed and renegades paid no attention to the invitation to sit down. One renegade stands guard near the door, while the Breed asks the white men all kinds of questions while he and the other renegade continue to prowl around the cabin, their beady eyes taking in everything the white men have got.

As the Breed and two white men talk on, the crafty Breed starts the white men talking about the Nez Perce war, and wants to know if they were with the white men from the Bitterroot who helped the soldiers to fight the Nez Perce at the Big Hole.

The white man (Elliott) said they were not there, though they would have been glad to have been there to help kill some more of them red bastards, that they had started to go, but had turned back when they heard they were too late.

Meanwhile since the Breed and renegades have been in the cabin, the third white man (Jory) has been sitting on the side of his bunk, saying nothing to his partners or to the Injuns, and he eyes the Breed and renegades with suspicion. Hearing this Nez Perce war talk from the Breed, he gets still more suspicious that the Breed and two Injuns with him are Nez Perce. He fills and lights his pipe. Getting up off the bunk, going up to the Breed, he offers him the pipe to smoke with him.

The Breed refuses the pipe.

The white man then offers the pipe to the renegades. Both of them refuse to smoke.

At this, seeing the other two white men are beginning to get suspicious, the Breed laughs this off, saying, "We don't like white man's pipe. Too strong for Injuns."

Jory goes to his bunk, cutting off a large piece of smoking tobacco from a plug and offers it to the Breed and two renegades, only to be refused by them all, and this time in stony silence.

What the white man (Jory) intended to do, no one knows. As he walks to the open door, the renegade steps out of his way. Then the white man stepped outside the cabin. His feet hardly leave the doorsill when two rifle shots rang out almost as one from the small lodge pole pines in front of the door. And the white man pitched forward, dead before he hit the ground.

The white man (Elliott) standing at the table, hearing the shots, turns around, and can see through the open doorway. Two other Injuns, guns in hand, are standing over the dead body. He says to Jones, "My God, Jim, they have shot Bill." The words were hardly out of his mouth when the Breed and two renegades whip out their pistols, the Breed saying, "Yes, you son of a bitch, he is dead. Take that." He fires his pistol point-blank at Elliott's head, the bullet going through the side of his head, and bedding itself in the cabin wall.

As the Breed fires his pistol, almost instantaneous with him, one of the renegades also fires his pistol, sending a bullet crashing into Elliott's body. Elliott falls dead at the Breed's feet on the dirt floor.

As the words of Elliott rang out to him, the terrified Jones was stooped down at the fire, and as the shots that killed Elliott rang out like a cannon, filling the cabin with powder smoke, the second renegade was not idle. Springing fiercely at Jones, he cocks his pistol and points it close to the terrified Jones's head and pulled the trigger. Twice he did this and twice his gun only snapped. With great presence of mind, as the Injun in fury was trying to fire his gun at him again, Jones sprang up at the Injun throwing his arm up just in time as the Injun's pistol went off this time with a loud bang. The bullet went up through the roof of the cabin.

Jones, in a frenzy, attacks the Injun with his fists, and hurls him backward, the Injun tripping in the smoke-filled room, landing on his back across the dead body of Elliott lying on the floor.

Leaving the surprised Breed and two renegades in the cabin, and bounding out through the open door, not seeing on his way the three rifles that are still leaning outside against the cabin wall, the desperate and terrified white man in his haste nearly fell over the three Injuns who are kneeling down snarling among themselves, as they strip what takes their fancy from the dead body of Jory.

Not giving the three Injuns time to get over their surprise, Jones dashes around the cabin and out of their sight. On rounding the corner of the cabin he ran into two more Injuns who had been behind the cabin investigating what was in the small root-house. Strange as this may appear, though both Injuns had their rifles in their hands, and could easily have killed the white man, neither offered to shoot.

Leaping down the steep banks, Jones quickly ran across the diggins, and starts climbing up the hillside on the right side of the gulch.

The Breed and the renegades, furious at the escape of the white man, now more than a hundred yards away from them, cut loose at Jones with their rifles, sending their bullets thick and fast around the fleeing white man. One of their bullets hits the white man in the arm near the shoulder.

The Breed and renegades, seeing the white man stagger, think that they have got him. With fiendish yells of triumph, they start after him, but they saw him redouble his efforts through the scattering pines to make it up to the top of the ridge.

After escaping many bullets on a long and harrowing chase, Jones left them a hard trail to follow up through bars

of gravel among the willows. The white man after going
some distance, making his way silently and quickly up the
gulch, stands for a few seconds resting behind a large clump
of willows, panting from his hard run. He is beginning to
congratulate himself that he has left them Injuns behind for
good, but, on glancing around behind him at a slight
rustling sound, again the cold chills of terror ran down his
spine. Standing there a few feet away was an Injun with his
pistol at full cock and leveled at him ready to shoot.

It was Big Pete, the Walla Walla renegade, the tallest and
biggest Injun of all the men who had gone through with
Joseph the year before.

Jones sees at a glance that all hope for him is gone.
Standing there with a rock in each hand, he pleads with the
Injun not to kill him, to go back to the cabin and take every-
thing there, it will all be his.

At the sound of the white man's voice, there comes in the
Injun's face an unconcealed look of admiration for the white
man who had come through volleys of bullets, and made
such a brave race against eight of them for his life. This soon
changed to looks of pity for the white man, and the Injun
lowers his pistol down to his side.

For it was then that Big Pete remembered when, two
years before this, he was well known in the Walla Walla
country as a good-hearted and harmless Injun. Everyone
said there was no harm in Big Pete.

As this story goes, one day Big Pete and his brothers had
each taken up what was called an Injun homestead, most of
it being good meadow land. Big Pete was not much on work,
and most of the time was away with the other Injuns, fishing for salmon or hunting. When they came back from one
of their long hunting jaunts, they found that a white man
had jumped their claims and had taken possession of their
land, and had put up a house that was nearly finished and a
new fence all around their meadow. The white man and his
brother-in-law stood there with their rifles, telling Big Pete
and his brother there was going to be two dead Injuns if they

break the fence and try to go inside to their cabins. Big Pete and his brother went to the white men and their laws for justice, but were to find out in the end that an Injun has no rights even in the land where he was born.

Big Pete's brother, telling the other Injuns in camp that he was going to ride over to that white man's house, to try to talk to him good, not to do this evil to him, that he would give him most of his horses and all of his cattle if the white man would go away from his land. The Injuns in camp told him to keep away from them white men. Did he not already find out that they were bad ones?

And so it came about in this way. Big Pete's brother went riding unarmed over to the white man's house, to try and talk good to him. The white man, seeing the Injun riding toward the house, climbs up with his rifle above the door on the loose boards, lying inside on the beams of the still yet unfinished house. The Injun raps on the door, the door opens and, as the Injun enters the house, the white man fires his rifle from above, the bullet hitting the Injun in the top of the head, killing him instantly.

Hastily dragging the dead Injun outside the door, and putting an old loaded rifle at his side, the brother-in-law mounts his saddle horse and lopes furiously to tell the limb of the law to come over to the ranch, that they had to kill that buck Injun, Big Pete's brother, who had rode over to the ranch with blood in his eyes, and drunk as a boiled owl, to kill both men with his gun, and trying to assault the woman.

The brother-in-law arrived back at the ranch with the deputy sheriff, followed by whites and Injuns of the surrounding countryside. That worthy defender of the peace told the white man that he knew just how it is, that that Injun was a bad one, but even though he was willing to swear on a stack of Bibles that this was a dead open and shut case of justifiable homicide, still the majesty of the law must be respected. It was his sacred duty to ride over to the justice of the peace, old Judge Hug-em-both at his ranch fifteen miles away, and there to lay this matter before the judge.

Soon after the deputy left, white men and Injuns came and viewed the dead Injun, still lying on the ground outside the door. There was the usual hullabaloo, most of the whites being of the opinion that the Injun only got what was coming to him, still there were some who did not approve of the way this white man had tricked and bluffed Big Pete and his brother out of their land.

Those white men, with the Injuns, saw the bullet hole in the top of his head, and the old loaded rifle lying beside him. The Injuns told those white men that the gun was not the dead Injun's, that his gun was left by him in camp; he had no gun and was not drunk when he left camp.

Four days after the white man killed Big Pete's brother, the Injuns having buried the dead buck and given him a magnificent send-off, according to the ancient rites and ceremonies of their race, Big Pete's dead brother's woman and children having gone back to their people, the whites noticed that Big Pete had disappeared with his stock and family. To the whites' inquiry as to where he went, the Injuns said to them with sullen looks, "Me no savvy."

It went this way for nearly two weeks when one day, early in the morning, the white man who had killed Big Pete's brother, along with his brother-in-law, went out to feed their teams from a haystack in their corral, when the Injun, Big Pete, steps out, rifle in hand, from behind the haystack, and before the surprised white man could pull his gun, Big Pete shot him dead in his tracks. The brother-in-law, having no gun, took out on the run for the house close by. Again Big Pete's rifle barked and the brother-in-law crumpled up in a heap on the ground. Getting his cayuse from behind the haystack, Big Pete calmly rides up to another white man's ranch, more than a mile away, and tells this man and his horror-stricken family that he had killed the white man and also this white man's brother-in-law. He had left him over there dead. He said to ride over to the deputy's ranch and tell him that Big Pete had killed them two white men, and wants to talk with him. He would wait for him till they came back.

The white man rides off for the deputy's ranch and was soon back on the lope with this worthy. This deputy, who had a deadly hatred for Injuns, and was the cause of much of Big Pete's troubles, was armed to the teeth as he furiously spurred his horse along the trail. With his carbine in hand, as their panting horses come up out of a coulee, they almost ran into Big Pete waiting on the trail. As the deputy fiercely pulled his horse back on its haunches, there were two rifle shots that rang out as one. The deputy lurches out of the saddle, falling in a huddled heap on the trail, his rifle lying at his side. Big Pete's horse trembled as it staggered a step or two, falling dead on the trail, shot through the head and sprawled out in death from the deputy's bullet.

Leaping out of the saddle as his dead horse hits the ground, Big Pete rushes up and grabs the reins of the deputy's snorting horse. He took off the cartridge belt and forty-five of the deputy, picked up the deputy's rifle and mounts the deputy's horse. Telling the terror-stricken rancher to be on his way, Big Pete turns the horse around and rides off, leaving his dead horse and the deputy lying slumped across the trail.

Big Pete, now an outlaw with a price on his head, was well on his way through the sagebrush country, headed for Snake River in Idaho. He was another bad Injun and desperate renegade on his way to swell the ranks with the Nez Perce, the only place where they were safe from the white man's laws. Under Joseph, fighting the white men and soldiers, many were the bloody acts they committed.

As the renegade Big Pete lowers his pistol to his side, whatever thoughts he had about Jones, he changed his mind, when another renegade glided up from out the willows, asking Big Pete why he did not shoot the white man. He kneels down on one knee to aim his gun at the white man. Jones, seeing that the Injun is ready to pull the trigger, lets fly with a rock, causing the Injun to miss. Jones also pasted Big Pete with a rock, causing him, close as he was, to miss too. And before the surprised Injuns could fire again, the elusive white man was off on the run up the gulch through the willows, with both of the Injuns after him. Their guns barked at him whenever they got a glimpse of him on another long chase until an Injun with his pistol leveled at him said in good English, "You son of a bitch, I have got you now," and fires at him and misses him. Furious at this, the Injun, laying his pistol across a willow branch to steady his aim, said, "You son of a bitch, I'll get you yet." As the Injun said that, the white man hurls the rock in his hand, which landed with smashing force on the Injun's hand and knocked the pistol out of his hands. Jones goes on his way tearing through the willows, with the Injun blazing away at him with his pistol.

The Injun, coming out of the willows into the open, with his pistol empty, sees the white man well above him, making it up the steep slope of the divide. As he stands there loading his pistol, the Breed and other renegades come out of the willows to his side, only in time to deliver a farewell volley as the white man disappears over the top of the divide, with the Breed and renegades scrambling up the slope of the divide after him. Although they could sometimes hear him running through the thick timber, the Injuns never got another sight of him.

Taking no chances on them finding him again, Jones was soon climbing up the ridge. Going six or seven miles further, staggering up through the brush and rocks in the hot sun, he finds himself on the steep rocky peak of Baldy, a wild and rugged peak that towers far up above all the other mountain peaks of the surrounding country, and a good thirty-five miles from Philipsburg, the closest place of safety.

Hungry and wounded he plodded along and made his way back to Philipsburg some time around midnight, having been on the go since sunrise, and having had nothing to eat since the day before.

Jim Jones, unarmed, time and again escaping out of the clutches of those eight relentless savages, made a spectacular run, untouched except once by their closely fired volleys of bullets, and fought for his life in a way that is very seldom duplicated in real life, and only found in the wildest kind of fiction. And what makes this border even more on the miraculous is that I can assure you that the Breed and those seven renegades were not just common wild Injuns. Instead, all of them were case-hardened ruffians and dead shots with pistol and rifle. They held their own and the lives of others cheap. They had come through with Joseph and his Nez Perce warriors, had fought the white men and soldiers of Idaho and Montana to a standstill.

The white man, Jim Jones, hereafter known as Nez Perce Jones, lived an honest and industrious life at Philipsburg to the ripe old age of eighty-five years, dying a respectable citizen on April fourth in the year of 1926. He was buried on April sixth in Missoula, Montana.

After failing to find the trail of the white man, the furious Breed and the disgusted renegades gave up the chase and went back to the murdered miners' cabin. Three of their women had come with pack horses and brought their saddle horses for them. They had already stripped the cabin of everything that was of any use to them. They had ripped open the straw ticks of the beds, scattering the straw and covering the body of Elliott.

The Breed told the women that one of the white men had got away from them, and they would have to pack up quickly. The women soon packed up the lodges, along with their stolen plunder (mostly horses), and all went on their way up the Ross's Fork, reinforced with the six warriors who finally caught up with them. They crossed over the divide going down Sleeping Child Creek, headed for the Bitterroot Valley, and did some more shooting and depredations at Sleeping Child Hot Springs. They made their way down the Bitterroot Valley to the Lolo trail, and followed this trail back to their old home in Idaho. The name of the Breed and most of the other Injun cutthroats, who had left a trail of fire and blood behind him on their way from the Musselshell to the Bitterroot Valley, were reasonably well known to the authorities of Montana Territory, still no determined effort was made to bring them to the bars of justice, most of them living to a ripe old age.

CHAPTER THIRTY-SIX
Prank Backfires

I was driving the horses along the grassy ridge back to our camp, that day in 1878, having taken time out for Nez Perce Jones's story. On crossing over the wagon trail, I was surprised to see that twelve shod horses had come up this ridge and were headed at a lively clip for McKay's Gulch. Their brisk gait plainly told me they were twelve saddle horses.

I was wondering if the men who rode them horses were just visitors, or did they live over in that gulch where I had given them two white men the scare of their lives? As I seen those horse tracks on the trail, it set me to thinking, knowing that if they had forded this creek they could not help but see our tepee.

Not feeling any too good at this, some sort of a presentiment kept warning me to go quickly back to camp and pull out and take In-who-lise away. Coming to camp with the horses, just a while before the sun was in the middle of the sky, Susie came out of the lodge and wants to know why I have been gone so long.

Forgetting to tell her what I had done to scare the two white men, I told her this was one time I knew that she would be glad, when I told her that I had found two cabins where white men lived near here. It was too late to move today; besides I wanted to find out from them where we could find a trail. Also I would go out and kill a deer. Tomorrow morning we would pull out.

At the mention of white men Susie cocks up her ears and wants to know if I had seen the white men. I truthfully told her I had seen three of them. Then she wants to know why I had not spoken to them when I was there. Again I straddled the truth, telling her, "I did try to talk to two of them, but they must have been in a hurry, they would not stop to listen to me, even when I yelled at them. Besides I was in such a hurry to find our horses so that I could get back to you."

Now, like all the squaws, she doubts the sincerity of my honied words to her, saying, "I know why you have been gone so long, and you never thought of me here alone. It was to them evil white men who you like better than me that you went, and not after the horses. It was them sons of evil who kept you away from me all this time. Yes, your woman knows more than you think." I said, "Susie, if you know so much, why don't you keep your mouth shut?"

In-who-lise said, "Keep my mouth shut, son of evil, I will do no such thing. It was not much long after you left camp, to trail the horses, when I heard our dogs growling and snarling like they always do when they smell white men from afar. I went out of the tepee and hid in the brush, and could see the white sons of evil with their rifles across their saddles shining in the sun. They were fording down the creek not far from here. I could see and count them as they rode up on the bank. They were as many and two more as there is fingers on my hands; they rode fast out of the ford and on their way of evil up and over the ridge. An-ta-lee, did you see them, tell your woman did you talk with them? I would know that."

I said I did not, that I had only seen the trail they made. I told her to quit her foolishness of being jealous of and hating every white man, when the white men were not bothering us. I then told her to get some dinner.

Not long after this Susie was again smiling and happy as she cooks by the fire. I was lying there on the robes, thinking that as soon as we eat our dinner I would change my Injun rig and innocently, as though I had never been there before, would ride over the ridge and ask them about the trail.

But this was not to be. Hearing a snarling and howling commotion among our dogs, I sprung to my feet. Susie was already peeping out under the tepee and whispers to me, "Yaw. E-S white Souie-app-o. What deviltry have you done to them that they now come here with their guns in their hands?"

Then the flap was thrown violently back, and I was surprised to find myself looking into the rifle muzzles of several half-drunken white men. They say, "Come out of there, you and them buck Injuns, and be sure you don't try any monkey work."

When I came out alone, two of them stuck their rifles and heads inside the tepee, saying, "Hell, Mack, there is no Injuns in here. There is only this fellow's squaw in here."

Mad as hell, I asked, "What's this stick-up for? You drunken stiffs have surely got your gall if you think you are going to get away with this."

"We will damn soon show you, dirty renegade. Where are them Injuns that are along with you?"

I said, "There are no Injuns here that I know of except my wife."

With awful oaths they prodded me with their rifles and called me a liar.

Their leader tells them to stand back, levels his rifle at my head, saying, "Don't try to put that over on us, when just over this ridge in McKay's Gulch early this morning Red Jim and Bill Uquhart were chased out of their diggins by a large band of Injuns, the red devils howling and shooting at them and done their best to kill them."

They said they knew a way to find them Injuns, and unless I did tell them where they were, they were going to string me up till I did tell them. Another of the bunch, prodding me in the ribs with his cocked rifle, said, "What do you say to that, are you going to talk or would you rather stretch good rope on that cottonwood tree?"

This surely set me to thinking. Two or three of them who seem drunker than the others made the air blue with their profanity, adding the word squaw to every vile word they could call me.

I told them it was myself alone who was the Injun they had seen and that scairt them. I was now sorry that I had done this and did not know they would scare so easy. They could string me up, but it would not do them or myself any good. I could not tell them where to find them Injuns, when there were none here.

One said, "Hey you there, Bill Uquhart and Red Jim, did you hear that? It was only this long-haired squaw jigger that gave you fellows the run of your lives. Haw, haw, this is rich. What about that large bunch of twenty Injuns that tried to get you?"

Every eye turned on them, when the one called Bill Uquhart with a sheepish grin, spoke up. "I did not say how many Injuns there were. I never looked back to count them. It was Jim who said that he could see more than twenty Injuns dodging through the brush. Maybe what that fellow with the squaw says is true. You boys can let him go as far as I am concerned."

I surely felt grateful to the rough miner when I see the changed looks for the better come over the faces of several of them. But whatever hope I had now went a-glimmering, for that worthy Red Jim had a different idea. Red Jim was tall and lanky with a thick mop of red hair, and a long flowing beard of fiery intensity that covered his face and adorned his bosom and belly in both summer and winter, and was demonstrating what a few shots of booze can do. He was giving me the bad eye, saying, "You lousy son of a bitch, you would do it, would you!" Armed to the teeth and with a lariat coiled around him over his shoulder and under his arm, Red Jim made an impressive appearance that I did not like. Something told me I made a bad break this morning, when I played Injun to Red Jim, sending him running for his life and upsetting his dignity.

After more abuse, he said, "Boys, as sure as hell and, may Gawd rike me dead, there were and I see'd twenty or more as I sed, of them lousy Siwash after they chased us across the gulch into the timber, and I kin lick that chicken-hearted, pizened face Bill Uquhart with one arm tied, if he says again there ain't no twenty Injuns in this deal."

Standing there calling each other a liar, it was only after considerable snarling and wrangling, most of it being pro-fanity that could not be made to stick on paper, that Red Jim reluctantly admitted, that while there might not be exactly twenty Injuns in the bunch who chased them, there were a whole lot of them Injuns, and that he could lick the both together, them damn liars, Bill Uquhart and I, if we said again that it was not so.

Though the bunch still kept their eyes on me, they had lowred their rifles. With the exception of Red Jim and Art Hays, they were getting more friendly to me all the time. They were getting more sober, and did not seem so anxious to string me up, but Susie had to come out and spoil it all.

She was out of the lodge before I seen her. I clucked to her like a sage hen, warning her to go back into the lodge, but I was late. As she started back into the lodge, a white man stepped between her and the door, saying, "Not so fast, my Injun beauty. We don't like the looks in your dusky eyes." All eyes are turned on her.

Her eyes flashed fire at them, as she came up to me. She whispered to me, "I have your pistol in holster strapped on one leg above my knee and my knife strapped on the other where them white men can't see them under my skirt. I have cut a hole in each side of it so that you can get your pistol and I my knife quick. What do you want me to do?"

I told her, "Maybe they will do me no harm. Now watch them two who packed ropes with them—they were the bad ones. We will have to wait and see."

The white men soon got suspicious. "Hey you, we ain't going to stand no more of this Injun blabber. You tell that woman of yourn to talk United States or shut up her mouth."

I said, "How can she talk English when she can't under-stand a word of it?" Another said, "Are you sure of that?" I said yes.

"Is that woman of yourn a Flathead?" one asked.

"No, Nez Perce," I replied. "Joseph's band?" asked someone.

Like a damn fool, I answered, "Yes."

Before this they had not mentioned their dislike of any particular kind of Injun, and I was still wondering why it was they all had such a deadly hatred for Injuns in general. I was now to know that this was not so, and that I had put my foot in it worse than ever.

This word, Nez Perce, was met with howls of rage, and hell gleamed in every face, as they again threaten me with vile words and crowd around with their rifles at full cock. They snarl all together, "We know you now. You are that damn white renegade that went through with Joseph's bunch in 1877, and got away at the Bear Paw fight, and came through from Canada with them murdering Nez Perce last summer. We have got you dead to rights."

"This is not so," I replied. "It is as I told you all before— I am a stranger here. Never was in these parts before. I know none of the people who got away at the Bear Paw except my wife. What did the Nez Perce do to you people to make you hate them so bad, and why do you call me such names when you all know well that you have never seen me before?"

"We will soon show you," said Art Hays, "you damn renegade that travels with Nez Perce Injuns who kill and rob innocent white men, like they did my brother and two other white men, over this ridge in the next gulch from here."

Another accuses me of coming back here with that Nez Perce squaw of mine to lift the gold cache of the murdered miner, John Hays.

As I heard this I did not believe there ever was such a renegade with them Injuns, but afterward was informed by some—who seemed to know more about this than they should, that there was such a white man with this bunch of Injuns and Breed. At first in fact, there was two of them, two white horse thieves and all-around bad men who had their hangout before this around White Sulphur Springs.

In denying anything, I was only wasting my breath and helping out this gent whose only ambition in life at the present time is to put a rope around my neck. Then one of them starts in about In-who-lise being a Nez Perce woman of White Bird's people, saying, "She got away with them at the Bear Paw, didn't she?"

I answered, "Yes." He said, sneeringly, "She got away, didn't she? And so did you with her. So did that bunch of Injuns that done the killing around here. They were White Bird's bucks that got away at the Bear Paw with her into Canada. I'll bet you an ounce of gold dust against nothing that she knows every one of them that done the killing around here."

I said, "That is a lie. You leave my woman out of this."

He said threateningly, "Do you mean to say that I am a liar?"

I said, "No. You are worse and lower down than that. Liar is too good a name for you."

Mack said, "Just say that to me once again and I'll save the boys here from wasting good rope on your lousy carcass."

I said, "Oh, ain't we brave when the gang is all here? Say, mister, just whisper it, where do you bury your dead anyway?"

Mack was now interrupted by one in the bunch who said, "How long are you going to chew the rag with that squaw feller? It is about time you and him stopped that gab, when we are all getting dry. When we left the Burg this morning we were only coming here to fish, and to have a time licking up that two gallons of licker we brought with us. Come to think of it, what is the matter with us? We kin take this feller and his woman over with us to the Gulch and put them in Jim Jones's root-house. They will be as safe in there as in New York City jail. Then we kin take 'em back with us to the Burg tomorrow and send for the sheriff at Deer Lodge. The way it looks to me now it is a job for him and not for us."

But Red Jim vigorously protested. "You fellers make me sick, if you think you are going to hold them two badgers hogtied in that root-house. That woman's teeth are as sharp as a razor, and she will chaw through them ropes tying him quicker than a mad dawg can bite the seat out of your pants. With the both of them loose in there, nothing but solid walls of rock kin keep that mangy groundhog and his Injun she badger from digging their way out."

Red Jim and Mack were furious at the way things were turning out, and Art Hays, with a malevolent look, said, "It is as plain as the nose on my face, this squaw feller is the same and only son of a bitch, it's him and no other that was seen trailing along with that Nez Perce Breed and Injuns that killed my brother. Hanging is too good for his kind. He ought to be burned alive. If the rest of you want to go back to the Gulch just to swill up your guts with licker, then take the squaw and get to hell out of here with her, the quicker the better, but you are not going to take that squaw feller with you."

At this In-who-lise wants to know why after her bringing my pistol to me, I let them three white men threaten to hang me and maybe her, and why don't I quickly put my hand in through the slit in her skirt and get my pistol and kill them three lying white men? They were not watching us any more with their rifles.

I whispered, telling her it will be all right in the end. "Don't let them white men catch you talking and making them signs to me. The longer I can keep them talking, the better for us with the others. Them other white men don't want to string me up, or they would have done it before this."

Twice I caught her stealing her hand toward the slit in her skirt where my pistol was, saying in a low whisper to me, "You are not going to let them evil white men do that to me before you will kill some of them with the pistol?"

I tried to quiet her fears, saying that the other white men were not low-down enough to do that. Still if they did try to take her away with them, that would then be the time for me to get the pistol.

CHAPTER THIRTY-SEVEN
Return of a Favor

In-who-lise entered the harangue, speaking English in spite of my warnings. The crowd from the Burg warned Art Hays, time and again, not to blackguard that woman even if she was only an Injun squaw. Art Hays paid no attention to them, and lost no chance to poke smutty jibes at her and at everything she said.

Protesting, I objected to this, saying, "How much longer is this going to last? I might be a low-down squaw man, but I had enough of that white man's blackguarding talk to my woman."

This only brought on a tongue-lashing tirade in which both of us went out of our way to tell the other in a manner that left no doubt, of the low-down contemptible opinion we had for each other.

Art Hays said to me, "You keep your damn face out of this now. You wanted her to talk English to save your damn neck, and talk she is going to, whether you and her like it or not."

Standing close to her with his rifle in one hand, putting his other hand almost in her face, Art Hays, like all braggarts do, starts in to haul In-who-lise over the coals. But on calling In-who-lise a lying Injun bitch, she sprung at him with the fury of a wounded panther. In-who-lise grabs his extended arm, then with her other hand gave him a swinging back-hander across his face that brought the claret dripping from his nose, then pushed him away from her with such force as to send him reeling backward. And he would have fell on his back on the ground, had he not fell against one in the crowd from the Burg who caught him. In-who-lise in her anger almost shrieking at him and the astonished crowd, "Yes, call me Injun, call me a squaw, that's all right; I am that. Evil white dog that you are, who can only fight a squaw, just call me an Injun bitch again, and I'll kill you this time where you stand."

Deaf to the jeers at him from the crowd, Art Hays stands glaring at her, at first as though stupefied. Wiping the dripping blood from his nose with the back of his hand, on seeing the blood on the back of his hand, he seems to realize what has happened, and that the crowd are laughing at him. At first with a snarl like a cornered wolf at In-who-lise, then uttering a bloodcurdling oath, he quickly cocks and starts to raise up his rifle, as though he was going to fire point-blank at her.

But before he could get his rifle up to his shoulder, to make his intentions good, a burly one called Porter, standing close to his side, gave Art Hays a staggering blow with his fist on the side of his face that sent that gent reeling sideways, his rifle going off and the bullet going into the ground, throwing up the dirt around Red Jim's feet, much to that worthy's discomfort.

The loud report of Art Hays's rifle went echoing down the valley and had barely ended when hell now broke loose among the whole crowd of them. For a few minutes Art Hays had a kind of a squally time, several with their rifles pointed at him, and telling him they mean business. If he makes any more breaks like this again, they will fill him full of lead.

With the excitement going on, both of us could have easily got away into the tepee where, with rifles and pistols, we could have made it highly interesting for them all, as long as we lasted. But I told In-who-lise, who is still on the fight and wants me to kill Art Hays, now that I had the chance I told her point-blank that I would not do it, that we had all the trouble we wanted without doing that. Then In-who-lise gets mad as hell at me.

Then, blind with fury, Art Hays sprung to his feet, picks up his rifle and stands trembling like a leaf, looking wildly around for someone that he is not afraid to abuse. His vicious gaze lights on Porter who had struck him. His anger rising to a shriek, "So it was you who hit me for that damn squaw! Well, you did not surprise me any—I always knew you were a two-faced son of a bitch. Yes, Sam Porter, help that squaw man and his Injun bilk, the both of them who helped murder my brother. Sure as God made little apples, I am going to blow your damn onery head off for this, and I would do it now if I thought I could get away with it."

Porter turns purple in the face, quickly whirls around with his rifle raised and stood facing Art Hays with the drop on him, saying, "The man don't live that can say that to me and get away with it. Blow my damn head off, did you say, well I guess not this time, when I got you dead to rights, and I am going to blow your rattle-brained head off right now, to see how you like it." And there was no doubt about it, this Porter's intentions to do as he said were good, but two in the crowd stepped between them and a kind of a cat and dog peace was restored.

For the brutal murder of his brother and the other two defenseless white men, Art Hays could not very well be blamed at first for the bitterness and venom he displayed against us. He had a good reason to be suspicious of us. As Mack, Red Jim and himself said that myself and Injun wife were along with them Injuns, and knew more about the killing of them white men around here than either of us were willing to admit. But now that we had proved, to the satisfaction of everyone else here, that we had nothing to do with this horrible affair, nor knew who the perpetrators of those crimes were, Art Hays still would do us further evil if he can, and he curses the crowd from the Burg, saying that this was the end of it. He was going to get that squaw man and his squaw on general principles. And make us all the trouble he could. Even if the bunch from the Burg said we were innocent, he didn't believe a damn word of it. He was going to ride over to the Burg and sic the law on us, and would swear out warrants against the both of us. Then we would find out that we had to lie better than we did here, and that squaw of mine was going to have a harder job in bamboozling the deputy sheriff and judge into believing that cock and bull story of ours than she did with this bunch of suckers here. When the county of Deer Lodge together with the Territory of Montana each offered a reward of five hundred dollars for the apprehension of them murderers, this would put the kibosh on us good and plenty. Everyone said that the deputy sheriff and justice of the peace would go to hell for a two-bit piece any time.

I had been looking at two men that were with the crowd. One of them was a little man with a reddish mustache; the other man husky built, with black whiskers. Both of them took very little part in what was going on. I knew I had seen them someplace, but where, I could not tell. Now, hearing another fellow in the crowd calling the little man Sim, it came to me like a flash.

I said, "Hey, there you, mister, is not your name Sim Shively? And your friend beside you, Jack McDonald?" At this the crowd stood gaping, and there was some whispering among them. It was some time before anyone said anything to me. Any fool could tell both of those gents are not over-anxious nor overjoyed to acknowledge my claim to their acquaintance. Then the one I had called Sim Shively growled kind of surlily. "Well, what if it is, when we sure as hell don't know you? How do you know our names?"

I said, "Mr. Shively, don't you remember me, the one the troopers at Fort Ellis called the kid, when you and that man there with several more prospectors had in 1876 went overland from Montana to the Black Hills gold excitement, and were returning from there in 1877, when you went into camp at Benson's Landing on the Yellowstone River, and the Crow Injuns stole every saddle horse and pack mule you fellows had, and set you afoot. And when you fellows came to the Fort for help to get back your stock, it was then Lieutenant Doane sent a corporal with five troopers and I along with them to track your stock. After finding this stock cached on

Boulder Creek and bringing it back to you fellows, when you and that man said to me, when you and the others were leaving Ellis, that your name was Sim Shively, and that man said his name was Jack McDonald from Philipsburg, and for me to remember, if I ever came around them diggins, to hunt you fellows up, and you would be glad to see me and make this right. Well, you fellows have got a good chance now to make it good, without costing you any money."

Sim Shively said, "You that kid, well I'll be damned. You have changed a lot since then. I suppose that and having that Injun woman with you is why I failed to recoguize you. Why did you not tell me this in the first place? It would have saved you and your woman all this bad trouble."

I said, "How could I do that, when I only recognized you a few minutes ago, and had plenty bother the way it was to get you to remember me?"

Sim Shively said to the crowd, "Boys, this feller is all right. Jack and I know him. He could not have had anything to do with them killings around here last summer."

So it was with feelings of more than relief that I heard those words from Sim Shively. And now the crowd stand around in good humor, telling me that I can be thankful that it turned out the way it did, and to take their advice, and after this not to try and pull off any more of my Injun stunts, as this kind of shenanigan was not popular with the people in this part of the country, and if I did, I might not be as lucky as I was today, when the joke came damn near being on me.

It would be no use in writing down what Art Hays said to Sim Shively and Jack McDonald for sticking their damn faces in none of their business, as the rest of his dialogue would only have Uncle Sam arrest the publisher and I. His last words to me, being hopeful and assuring, that he was going to get me and that damned squaw of mine proper this time, that if I pulled out of that, then this earth was going to be too small a place to hold the both of us. While most men would have plugged him for saying that, I took the advice of

Porter and others, who said not to pay any attention to him, when he was only a half-cracked nut at best, who when he got a drink was plumb loco for a week. Otherwise he was not such a bad fellow, and the poor devil could not very well be blamed for taking it so hard after the killing of his brother by them Injuns.

They told me not to feel sore at them. After the way them Injuns had murdered their friends they could not be blamed for coming over here like they did. After the brutal murders around here last summer, the Nez Perce warriors were hated and feared more than all other Injuns put together. The whole country was still aroused and in terror. Men were afraid to go out in the hills alone, and there was still small bands of returning Nez Perce, sometimes accompanied by cutthroat white men, passing through the country. And while no more white men had been killed so far as they knew, still those outfits made up the difference by stealing horses and killing cattle.

To make it all the worse, there were also large bands of Injuns passing on their way through the country on the Salish trail, on their way to and from the buffalo range, on the east side of the Rockies. Sometimes white men with their Injun women and half-breed offsprings came along with them. No one could tell if they were good or bad. Those men, once free trappers, had roamed the prairies and hills, free and untrammeled, most of them fierce and savage as the Injuns they ran with, the good and bad of them having no respect for laws except their own, an eye for an eye and a tooth for a tooth, with the quickest man on the draw getting the favorable verdict.

Those men read the writing on the wall, and knew by the way the settlers were pouring into the country, even the buffalo would soon be gone. They bitterly resented the encroachments of the settlers on what they claimed with the Injun as their own boundless prairies. They hated the settler, as bad if not worse than their aboriginal brothers-in-law, the Injuns, and lost no chance to instigate their red brethren to devil the settlers all they could. There was no doubt that some of the crimes laid at the Nez Perce warriors' door were committed by other Injuns, at the instigation of those gentry.

I thought I had better pull out of this man's land where women are so scarce. If I did not get out soon, I was going to be shy of my woman. This nutty bunch of stags from the Burg fell good and heavy for In-who-lise, and went plumb loco over her, making no bones about leaving me out in the cold, and giving her all the credit and praise for saving my neck today, and for the way she tackled and struck Art Hays. And no wonder. She was an Injun squaw, but just the same, In-who-lise was a pretty woman and hard to beat. One old bellwether from the Burg, one of them silly old boys says that woman of mine was some scrapper. Yes, a regular ring-tailed snorter with four white feet, that I ought to feel proud of her—when he would rather tackle barehanded a sack full of wild cats than her. He wants to know how she got that broken tooth and scar on her upper lip, not that it spoiled her beauty any, only that it gave her a suspicious military and warlike appearance that would make a feller think twice not to stay away all night with the boys, or to come back soused in the early morn.

I quickly changed the subject, by asking them if there was any way to get out of this country into the Bitterroot Valley.

They told me, yes, down the creek from here, about a mile and a half you will come to the Salish buffalo trail, that this trail crossed Rock Creek near the mouth of Ross's Fork. After it left Rock Creek, it followed up the West Fork to the divide, then crossed over to the Skalkaho and followed down this creek into the main Bitterroot Valley.

On my inquiry if the trail was good or bad, and how many days it took a pack outfit to make it over to the Bitterroot Valley, they said that none of them were over it, but from what they heard it was a hell-roarer and only fit for an Injun. Few if any white men used it. There was plenty fallen timber and windfalls, and as the Injuns never cut a log out of their way, how they made it through, only themselves and the devil knew. Across the divide on the west side going down the Skalkaho, it was steep and a long hard drag up or down to the bottom, in fact it was worse than trying to ride down a sixty-degree house roof, the trail following down the Skalkaho straight as a gun barrel, without a twist or a turn through a rough broken up country of rock slides and through large granite boulders.

The Salish Injuns had another way, going up the Burnt Fork of the Bitterroot from Stevensville, then cutting across the country, but as only the Salish Injuns knew this country no other Injuns came that way.

They did not know how many days it would take us from here. That would be up to us. They wanted to know when we intended to pull out from here.

I said, "We will pull out from here at sunrise tomorrow morning and take the Skalkaho trail, even if it is a rough one."

They done some kicking at this, saying, "Why leave here so soon after we went to all this trouble to get acquainted? Better move over to the Gulch tomorrow, and visit a few days." They wanted to buy some of them buffalo robes from me. They would each take one or two maybe, if I was not too steep with the price. And they were sure if I went to the Burg for the Fourth of July with them, I could sell the people all kinds of robes for good gold money.

I said, "No sir, the Burg is one place I don't go to, much as I would like to. I don't intend to stay here and let the grass grow under my feet, just to visit or sell robes." I and the woman was sure much obliged to them for their kindness to the both of us here today, and would like to stay a few days with them, but thought it better to light out when the going was good.

In the end I agreed to stay a day or two and move over to McKay's Gulch in the morning.

Leaving only Sim Shively here with us, this good-hearted crowd left and went back to spend the night with their friends over across the ridge in McKay's Gulch. With peace and tranquility once more restored, even if it was funny to see Bill Uquhart and Red Jim run through the loose wash, I firmly resolved never to play Injun in this part of the country to a white man again.

At first I had thought that Sim Shively belonged to the bunch from the Burg, but I found out from him, that him and Jack McDonald are partners in a placer claim over in McKay's Gulch, and that they had bought out Jim Jones, together with the rights of the dead miners Elliott and Jory, and that Jack McDonald and him were now working the claim and living in the same cabin where the Injuns had murdered Elliott and Jory.

This man Shively, who I was so lucky to meet and recognize here, was an old-timer in Montana. Born in Pennsylvania in 1830, he came to Montana Territory in 1866; occupation, miner. He died in Philipsburg, February 24, 1908. He was well and favorably known around Philipsburg, and especially in the Flint Creek country, as a man of sterling qualities.

CHAPTER THIRTY-EIGHT
Blackfeet Deal the End

Leaving Rock Creek, we went to Stevensville and Fort Owens, and encountered some trouble at each place, on account of my wife being a Nez Perce. Wherever we went, the whites seemed to think that I was a renegade trying to work my way back from that long pursuit that ended near the Canadian border. We continued traveling and landed at Mr. Conlon's ranch near the Lolo trail. He told me that when the Nez Perces came through there on their retreat, his neighbor, Mr. McClay, and family left home and sought safety in a fort erected by the settlers. The Indians entered the McClay house and took some provisions, but left in exchange a few horses, which they put in McClay's corral and branded with his own iron. This stock, Mr. Conlon said, more than paid for the articles taken. He told me this, although he did not have any liking for the Nez Perces. In fact, he was only too willing to express his low regard for both them and the squaw man camped there with his Nez Perce wife. We had some argument on this score and finally Mr. Conlon admitted he was in the wrong and sorry for what he had said. The Nez Perces had not molested him, he said, nor done him injury of any kind. He was an honest, truthful man, as I afterward came to know him.

We left the Conlon ranch and went on up the Lolo trail toward Lapwai. I still had several horse loads of tanned buffalo robes, which In-who-lise said we could swap for horses or cattle with either the Indians or whites when we got to Lapwai. We thought we would stay there and take a ranch. Before we had traveled half a day, we met four Nez Perce men and several women from Lapwai on their way to the Jocko in Montana. We all camped, and I remember that one of the men was George Johns, who could speak very good English. I understood little Nez Perce, although In-who-lise had tried to teach me that language. She now had quite a powwow with these Nez Perce. When through, she told me in Pend d'Oreille that we could not go on to the Lapwai or the Wallowa, adding, "These people tell me that the agent will catch me and maybe send me back where Joseph and the others are. Some of the men got back but they have to keep quiet and out of sight, and the whites will make trouble for you because you are married to one of Joseph's band."

"Where can we go?" I asked her.

"Any place you want," she answered. "I have no more home in the Wallowa. My people are far away and I will never see them again."

"Are these people here of your tribe?" I asked.

"They are of the upper Nez Perce and belong to Lapwai. They have talked to me bad. They tell me that Chief Joseph and his band made trouble for them by killing those white men in Idaho."

I then had a talk with the man, George, who told me that I had better not go on through to Lapwai, for I only would have trouble with the white men over there. The white people were very mad at Joseph and his bunch for killing whites on the Salmon River, George said.

I could see that these Nez Perce were not friendly to us, as they did not ask us to go along with them, and when I suggested that she ask them if we might not join them, she said something sharply in Nez Perce. She was both angry and unhappy and sorely wounded in spirit. She was an outcast from her native country. I, too, felt the loneliness of our situation, and all the more because of our honesty of purpose.

We let the others start first next morning, thinking perhaps we could find our way to the Kalispell Valley, the home country of the Pend d'Oreilles. We succeeded in getting there, and soon we started again with our adopted tribesmen for the buffalo range.

While on our way to the hunting grounds, like a fool, I agreed to join with some of the young men in a horse-stealing raid against the Blackfeet, in whose country we then were. The old men told us not to go, as we had women in our camp, but we did not listen to their advice. We moved the camp three days ahead and then about fifteen of us started back to strike a Blackfoot camp and run off some horses. After a time, we cut a Blackfoot trail. We followed it a considerable distance, until we discovered that it was swinging in the direction of our own camp. We turned and rode like the wind, but the Blackfeet got there first. They struck our camp just before we arrived, and we rode right into them. There was a hell of a mix-up in the very midst of the tepees. We got seven of them and lost two men, one of whom was mortally wounded. One woman was killed and my wife was wounded mortally. A Blackfoot warrior struck her on the side of the face with his coup stick with such force as to bulge the eye from its socket, leaving it completely exposed on her cheek.

After the enemy had been driven off, we packed camp, put the wounded on horses and pulled out, knowing full well that the Blackfeet would return in greater numbers if they had any help near. Our wounded could not stand the hard pace we were riding, but the others refused to stop on their account. Their indifference was due to the fact that neither the man, a renegade Spokane married to a Pend d'Oreille woman, nor my wife belonged to their tribe.

The wife of the wounded warrior and I decided to take a chance on the Blackfeet, so we pulled away from the trail at a favorable place and made camp. The next morning the wounded Spokane, Tiam-ah-hichen, thought that he could stand to ride, and I had to go, with Susie so badly off that I had to tie her on her horse. Within a few hours she was dead—she died in the saddle. The warrior grew so distressed that we made camp again off the trail. He died at sundown. His widow, Sapell, and I buried them both the next morning, close together in a rock slide about a half mile from camp. We had nothing with which to dig graves, and besides, we could hide them better from the Blackfeet by burying them in the slide.

By hard riding and long hours in the saddle, the woman and I overtook the band at the end of the third day. They had all my horses and robes with them, with the exception of the two saddle horses and one pack horse I had with me. I returned with them to the Kalispell Valley, where most of them belonged.

It has been more than half a century since I laid my beloved Susie, my In-who-lise, to rest among the blizzard-swept crags of the wild Marias Mountains, where the summer skies often are darkened by swirling snowstorms. All of my associates of those rough and ready years have crossed the Great Divide, and the Squaw Kid wanderer awaits the final journey.